Donated by
Joseph and Diane Bast
to The Heartland Institute
2015

When We Are Free

*Lawrence W. Reed and
Dale M. Haywood
editors and co-authors*

With a Foreword by Leonard E. Read

NORTHWOOD INSTITUTE PRESS
Midland, Michigan 48640

FIRST EDITION
© 1981 by Northwood Institute Press

All rights reserved. Inquiries and requests for permission to reprint should be addressed to the editors, Northwood Institute Press, Midland, Michigan 48640.

LCN 81-83459   ISBN 0-87359-026-0

Printed in the United States of America

TO

THE STUDENTS OF NORTHWOOD INSTITUTE

AND

STUDENTS OF LIBERTY EVERYWHERE

Table of Contents

Preface vii
Foreword *by Leonard E. Read* ix
Introduction: The Northwood Idea *by V. Orval Watts* xi

UNIT I: THE NATURE OF MAN AND PROPERTY
   1. The Only Kind of People There Are — *Roger J. Williams* ... 3
   2. Blessings of Discrimination — *F. A. Harper* 7
   3. Importance of the Premise — *Leonard E. Read* 15
   4. Nature's Laws and Man's Laws — *William H. Peterson* 23
   5. Source of Rights — *Frank Chodorov* 27
   6. Property Rights and Human Rights — *Paul L. Poirot* 33

UNIT II: WHAT ABOUT GOVERNMENT?
   7. Government: An Ideal Concept — *Leonard E. Read* 43
   8. A Human Action Taxonomy — *Dale M. Haywood* 49
   9. The State — *Frederic Bastiat* 53
 10. What's A Seat Worth? — *H. L. Richardson* 61
 11. Restitution, Regulation, and Redistribution —
     H. L. Richardson 69
 12. The Individual in Society — *Ludwig von Mises* 79

UNIT III: SYSTEMS OF ECONOMIC ORGANIZATION
 13. A Look at the Systems — *Lawrence W. Reed* 89
 14. The Case for Economic Freedom — *Benjamin A. Rogge* 93
 15. Legislated Security Is Bondage — *Samuel Gompers* 103
 16. Liberty and Property: One and Inseparable —
     William Henry Chamberlin 107
 17. The Man Who Defied Castro — *David Reed* 113
 18. Getting Rid of Communism — *Leonard E. Read* 119

UNIT IV: THE RISE AND FALL OF CIVILIZATIONS
 19. In Defense of Insecurity — *Lois A. Sargent* 127
 20. Impotent Abstractions — Potent Individuals —
     Dale M. Haywood 131
 21. The Fall of Rome and Modern Parallels — *Lawrence W. Reed* 137
 22. The Demonetization of Money — *Lawrence W. Reed* 145
 23. Why I Left Sweden — *Eric Brodin* 149
 24. The Last Candle — *Jack Schreiber* 153

UNIT V: THE AMERICAN EXPERIMENT
 25. The Thanksgiving Story — *Charles Hull Wolfe* 159
 26. The American Experiment — *Robert LeFevre* 163
 27. Against All Enemies — *Robert Bearce* 165
 28. NOT in the Constitution — *George W. Nilsson* 173
 29. Not Yours to Give — *Edward S. Ellis* 183
 30. We the People — *Ralph Bradford* 191

UNIT VI: THE ROLE OF THE MARKETPLACE
31. I, Pencil — *Leonard E. Read* 201
32. The Success of Failure — *Thomas W. Hazlett* 207
33. A Matter of Taste — *Lawrence Ingrassia* 215
34. Procter & Gamble: A Good Listener — *John A. Prestbo* 221
35. The Liberation of Women — *Bettina Bien Greaves* 227
36. The Parable of the Parking Lots — *Henry Manne* 233

UNIT VII: ENTREPRENEURSHIP
37. If Men Were Free to Try — *John C. Sparks* 241
38. Self-Interest at Work — *Dale M. Haywood* 243
39. The Entrepreneur as Hero — *Dick Bjornseth* 249
40. Food From Thought — *Charles W. Williams* 257
41. A Story of Apples and Entrepreneurship — *Lawrence W. Reed* 263
42. A College That Became the Partner of Business —
    David E. Fry 269

UNIT VIII: MYTHS ABOUT FREE MARKETS
43. Capitalism and Its Industrial Revolution —
    Camille P. Castorina 275
44. Witch-Hunting for Robber Barons: The Standard Oil Story —
    Lawrence W. Reed 281
45. In Defense of Profits — *Timothy G. Nash* 293
46. Who Conserves Our Resources? — *Ruth Shallcross Maynard* 299
47. The Economics and Politics of Discrimination —
    George C. Leef 307
48. Am I My Brother's Keeper? — *William Henry Chamberlin* .. 313

UNIT IX: SOLVING PROBLEMS IN FREEDOM
49. Open the Doors! — *Donald H. Carpenter* 321
50. Pages from U.S. Energy History — *Peter Beckman* 327
51. What to do about the Post Office — *Scott W. Bixler* 341
52. Medicine and the State — *John C. Goodman* 347
53. Regulation — Political or Market? — *Dale M. Haywood* 353
54. A Free Market Foreign Policy — *Ron Paul* 359

UNIT X: HOW TO ADVANCE LIBERTY
55. A Thought Starter — *Dean Russell* 369
56. Liberty and the Power of Ideas — *Lawrence W. Reed* 373
57. You Cannot Get Even — *Hans F. Sennholz* 379
58. Isaiah's Job — *Albert Jay Nock* 383
59. The Essence of a Free Society — *William Simon* 391
60. Voices in the Wilderness — *Leonard E. Read* 397

About The Editors 403

Preface

This is a book about *freedom* — what it is, what it means to be free, and what happens when men *are* free. It is an unapologetic endorsement of freedom and all of its corollaries: individualism, responsibility, private property, limited government, moral law, free markets, and business enterprise. We think it entirely appropriate to refer to these noble principles as the very ideals upon which America was founded. They have made America very special in the long history of nations.

It is our purpose in assembling this collection of works to help restore lost freedoms and preserve those which, as Americans, we still enjoy. This book is meant to be an additional weapon in the intellectual arsenal of the freedom philosophy. Battles, we believe, are never won by troops who have no ammunition, no knowledge of the enemy, and no sense of purpose on the battlefield.

The editors wish to acknowledge the efforts of many people who contributed time and talent to this project. Our first acknowledgment goes to Dr. V. Orval Watts.

Dr. Watts, more than any other person, was our inspiration. A tireless fighter for freedom for more than six decades, he has radiated that special light which attracts others to a cause. The philosophy of Northwood Institute — what has become known as "The Northwood Idea" — has no more able representative. His guidance, his wisdom, and his example, have been indispensable to our work. We feel a special sense of gratitude and admiration for his being so much a part of our lives and those of countless students of liberty over the years.

This volume contains the works of forty-six authors, living and dead. What value this collection has, needless to say, is due mainly to these individuals. We wish to express our appreciation for the many years of toil and scholarship their contributions represent.

Invaluable assistance was graciously provided on many occasions by the staff of the Foundation for Economic Education: Leonard E. Read, Bettina Bien Greaves, Robert Anderson, Paul Poirot, Edmund Opitz, Roger Ream, and Brian Summers. A substantial share of the articles reprinted here appeared originally in *The Freeman,* the monthly publication on liberty assembled by them. Their resources, advice, moral support, and inspiration were important to us. We deeply appreciate their help.

Others were also generous in granting permission to reprint articles or chapters: Caroline House Books, American Economic Foundation, The Caxton Printers, Ltd., *Reader's Digest, The Wall*

Street Journal, Policy Review, and *New Guard.* The articles taken from these sources are the copyrighted properties of the original publishers and may not be reprinted, in whole or in part, without the written permission of these publishers.

We also wish to express our gratitude to colleagues at Northwood Institute who helped in one way or another: Dana A. Peringer, John M. Pafford, Robert W. Serum, Edgar A. Madden, and David E. Fry. Finally, we would be remiss not to mention Arthur E. Turner and R. Gary Stauffer, the co-founders of Northwood Institute who made the dream of a college committed to freedom a marvelous reality.

It is our hope that freedom will forever be America's standard. To that end, we contribute this anthology.

Lawrence W. Reed
Dale M. Haywood

June 1981
Northwood Institute
Midland, Michigan 48640

Foreword

No social movement in history has ever succeeded without a literature: good books are the fountainhead of good movements; bad books set evil forces in motion. It is easy to see why this must be so. Books release the ideas from which people structure their beliefs. It is in accord with human nature for men and women to act out their basic beliefs, for as we think, so we do. Sound ideas about facts and values result in good actions; evil actions may be traced back to a warped ideology.

A great man writes a seminal book, and readers of *The Wealth of Nations* — their minds made receptive by the body of literature from many pens from Locke to Smith — carried its ideas into marketplace and forum. A new mentality came into being. New beliefs and opinions supplanted the old. Appropriate action followed and the face of society was transformed. The great and good social movement labeled Liberalism and Capitalism in the nineteenth century limited political power and freed people to act productively and creatively. Citizens of western nations prospered in every department of life; they were fed and housed better, they had better and more education, they were healthier and had better medical care, philanthropy flourished.

But then a warped mind of considerable energy produced *Das Kapital* and other evil books. The springs of intellectual life were poisoned. Malignant ideas inflamed cunning minds, activating the dark forces of human nature, releasing destructive energies. The collectivist movements of our time — communism, nazism and fascism — have spawned a literature which provides a specious rationale for tyranny, terror, predation, and "wars of liberation." But the armed might of collectivist nations, their seeming power, depends on their collectivist ideology. Debunk the ideology successfully and the hands that hold the weapons falter. Expel the false ideas of Marx, straighten twisted minds by the attractive presentation of a coherent body of truth, and collectivism crumbles.

There is only one way to do this, and that is by teaching. Teaching may occur in a classroom, it may come from a book, or a pamphlet, or a conversation. The educational process is a mysterious thing; it is not something one person can do for another. A good teacher may warn off a would-be student from pursuing dead-ends and he may be able to offer the student some materials for self-instruction. In the end, all education is self-education.

And so we stress the critical importance of a body of literature. How else is any teacher created in the first place, except by contact with the printed word, enlivened by the personality of earlier teachers?

And so I commend this book of readings most heartily. It is the work of many minds at work on a common theme, the philosophy of freedom. If one author's approach does not strike deep into a student's mind, another will. The literature of liberty has here a worthy reinforcement.

— Leonard E. Read

Irvington-on-Hudson, New York
June 1981

Introduction: The Northwood Idea
By V. Orval Watts

The Northwood Idea — the thought that went into the founding of Northwood Institute — is as *conservative* as The Ten Commandments or The Golden Rule.

It is as *liberal* and *progressive* as the gains that come to humans as they learn to live by these principles.

Yet this does not make The Northwood Idea new or different. "Education," we hear again and again, is the one way to solve our problems of crime, poverty, prejudice, racism, and war. Particularly in these United States, schooling in regard for one another's welfare and in the skills necessary for making ourselves useful in a peaceful society are what every parent and teacher want for our huge investments in the world's greatest educational effort.

This schooling, we all agree, should teach the ways of peace, goodwill and mutual aid.

Yet crime — especially juvenile crime — is higher than ever and is increasing faster in our cities and states where these expenditures of time and resources are greatest. Levels of literacy and self-discipline actually rose faster in the days *before* these great investments in compulsory and universal schooling.

The menace of terrorism, war, economic breakdown and famine is greater despite advances in technology which make peaceful cooperation more fruitful than ever before in human history. They offer the opportunity to abolish hunger, famine and pestilence forever.

Clearly something is wrong or lacking in our systems of schooling. At least, the founders of Northwood Institute thought so. Therefore, they ventured and risked greatly to offer something different from the general run of college schooling. My work and contacts with these men and women, and with their helpers and supporters, almost from the beginning of this institution, make me think of their aims — The Northwood Idea — in these terms:

First, the philosophy of Northwood's founders springs from certain oft-forgotten aspects of the Judeo-Christian Ethic, or culture. In particular, it implies firm belief in the fact of personal, individual responsibility.

Second, the founders and supporters of Northwood Institute have shown by their lives and dedicated efforts that they look on work not merely as the means for obtaining the material necessaries and comforts of life but also as the way to what some call "mental health." Strenuous and continuing effort in the hope of achieving a better life for oneself and others they see as essential for spiritual (psychological, emotional, mental) well-being.

Finally, they recognize that human progress depends on freedom for business enterprise. This requires private property. It means freedom to buy and sell, freedom to advertise and dicker, freedom to lend and borrow, and freedom to save and invest for profit.

This free-enterprise business, they believe, has been essential in the rise of great civilizations. It arises with acceptance of individual responsibility, the work ethic, and the self-discipline necessary for freedom.

I. THE JUDEO-CHRISTIAN ETHIC

As to the Judeo-Christian Ethic, I've been tempted to use instead the phrase "Bourgeois Ethic," meaning the ethic of the tradesman, but Karl Marx and others have given that phrase so nasty a connotation that I know I would have two strikes against me at the outset if I called our moral code the "Bourgeois Ethic." Yet, whatever we call it, the moral basis for our Northwood philosophy is the ethic which is necessary for a good life as a trader or financier.

The Idea of Individual Responsibility

This ethic begins with the idea of *individual responsibility*. That concept is basic for the Judeo-Christian Ethic.*

The Ten Commandments and the moral injunctions of both the Old and the New Testaments were always directed to the individual: *"Thou* shalt have no other gods before me"; *"Thou* shalt not make unto thee any graven image"; "Honor *thy* father and *thy* mother: that *thy* days may be long upon the land which the Lord *thy* God giveth *thee."*

Note that "thou," "thy" and "thee" are singular pronouns, not plural as is "you" or "your." Therefore, these ancient commandments were directed to one person, the individual, who is thereby charged with responsibility for what he chooses to do. They take it for granted that humans can choose. Our actions are not determined by instinct.

---

*The Islamic faith, we should note, stems from the Judeo-Christian ethic and theology.

In fact, humans *must* choose. That is what individual responsibility and self-determination mean. Ideas and acquired values determine our specific actions, and they may prompt us to ignore various influences in the outside environment. We can direct our own actions to prolong and enrich our lives, or we can choose suicidal paths as people choose to smoke when they have abundant evidence that it shortens life. We can choose to jump off cliffs, we can choose to play Russian roulette; or we can choose to follow ways of life, ways of health and well-being.

The Idea of Moral Law

Of equal importance in the Judeo-Christian Ethic is recognition of the enduring nature of Moral Law. The essence of this moral law is summed up in the "Golden Rule," and it derives from the fact that *humans need one another.*

Without other human beings, we cannot be born, cannot be reared, cannot prosper; and to have the cooperation of other humans — to avoid the conflicts which would be suicidal for humans — we must follow the "Golden Rule." When we apply that rule in practice, we find it is the unifying principle of these commandments that refer to the relations between the individual and his fellows: "Thou shalt not steal," "Thou shalt not kill," and "Thou shalt not bear false witness."

Now, it should be clear that obedience to Moral Law means voluntary cooperation and freedom. If we don't steal, we leave other persons free to use their talents in peaceful and cooperative ways to produce goods for their own use, for exchange, or for gifts to others, such as gifts to one's family or heirs.

Therefore, we have a state of individual freedom if we live by the "Ten Commandments." We have private property and numberless associations for voluntary cooperation. Humans develop as humans and make progress only in this condition of individual freedom and voluntary association established by adherence to these moral principles. Therefore, these moral principles are antecedent to and take precedence over all man-made laws and customs.

Respect for Property

In other words, these enduring moral principles require of us respect for the property rights of other people — that is, respect for their rights to control their own persons and for their rights to control those things which they obtain in voluntary cooperation, whether by gift, by voluntary exchange, or by the productive use of these things. Living by these principles requires that we fulfill our contracts, that we speak the truth, and that we revere the laws of Life and Nature. The first four of The Ten Commandments tell us of this need for reverence: a Higher Authority enforces laws vastly more enduring and exacting than the statutes of kings and parliaments.

We should note, incidentally, that this voluntary cooperation and exchange is doubly productive of benefits in contrast to the one-sided gain that anyone may get by coercion, as for example, by burglary, by slavery, or by taxation. In voluntary cooperation, all participants must benefit if the cooperation is to continue, for if it is voluntary, anyone may withdraw when he feels he is not benefiting, when he feels that the gains are distributed unjustly or going entirely to one person or group at the expense of the time and energy of others.

We should note also that living by the Golden Rule involves respect for privacy — the right to be left alone and the right to choose one's associates. Coercion — the attempt to compel people to associate with others — leads to conflict rather than to the attitudes and actions which are mutually beneficial. Freedom established by the Moral Law of the Golden Rule and the Ten Commandments includes the moral right to withdraw from an unwelcome contact with other persons, as well as the right to cooperate freely in mutually beneficial ways.

As Paul wrote in his "Second Letter to the Corinthians" two thousand years ago, "Be ye not unequally yoked with unbelievers; for what fellowship hath righteousness with unrighteousness and what communion hath light with darkness? . . . Wherefore come out from among them and be ye separate saith the Lord . . . and I will receive you." (II Cor. 6:14-17)

II. EMPHASIS ON WORK AND THRIFT

Next, I wish to call attention to Northwood's emphasis on work and thrift as marks and means of human progress. It is fashionable in some circles nowadays to disparage both of these values. But, work is merely persistent, purposeful effort. It is investment of human time and energy for long-range, indirect benefits.

Long-range benefits are those that occur in the future. Indirect benefits are those that may first benefit another person, but bring a return benefit of some sort to us later.

Such planned, purposeful effort for a long-range or indirect benefit is surely necessary for human survival and progress; and the traits of character and personality developed by such effort we regard as virtues.

Thrift is the postponement of present consumption in order to obtain greater satisfactions in the future. Like work, it requires the highest human qualities of understanding and imagination to foresee the future and to hold it in mind in order to gain the necessary self-restraint.

In short, work and thrift require understanding, self-control. They are means, not only of self-development, but of service to others.

We'd Still Live In Caves

Where would we be today had it not been for the thrift and work involved in the creation of our buildings, and the production of the myriad tools, or capital goods, that we use? The answer is we would still be living in caves, scratching out a short-lived, hand-to-mouth existence derived from the roots and grubs we could dig up, the small animals we could catch in our hands, and the berries we could get in season.

Everything that we call the material aspects of civilization, and the moral and spiritual ones as well, our understanding that enables us to live longer, to live better and to cooperate — all of this comes from thrift and work, the accumulations of thousands of years of human effort, inventiveness, planning, thrift and self-discipline.

This Puritan Ethic — this system of values, this way of life — is essential to progress. It is essential not only for economic progress but also for developing the qualities that are most distinctively human, the qualities that make us humans. It is mental, moral and spiritual "therapy," to use a modern cliche.

III. THE IMPORTANCE OF BUSINESS

Finally, if we are to have cooperation, we must exchange services; and as the cooperation gets more and more complicated, we need specialists to work out the terms and procedures of the multitudinous exchanges. Therefore, we must use money and credit; and we must have traders and financiers, advertisers, brokers and salesmen, accountants and collection agencies to complete the exchanges, including those exchanges which are made over a period of time and which therefore require credit and finance.

Finance is the monetary aspect of credit. Credit is merely a delayed exchange, an incomplete exchange. In every civilized society, most exchanges take time to complete because they are indirect, three-cornered or four-cornered exchanges, taking place over a distance and involving roundabout capital-using methods of production. In all such time-consuming transactions, we must have credit (trust and waiting). Therefore, money, credit and financial experts are as necessary for civilized life and progress as are tools and machines, mechanics, and engineers.

Business, then, means those aspects of voluntary cooperation which we call commerce and finance, and the function of the businessman is to promote, inspire, and guide cooperation. He organizes and teaches competitive cooperation — cooperation to provide better opportunities for life and for a more abundant life. These business activities — organizing, inspiring, leading and teaching cooperation — promote development of the highest qualities of mind, character and personality.

Now, from time immemorial — from the first introduction of money and the specialists who traded and promoted trades — business has been widely regarded with suspicion and looked down upon as a degrading occupation. In primitive societies, the view prevails that a merchant or moneyleader profits only at the expense of producers. This belief helps explain why such societies remain backward, or "under-developed."

Of course, this belief is an entire misjudgment as to what most of a businessman's wealth consists of and what he contributes to the value of other producers' services and incomes. Most of his wealth consists of the means for serving his customers, and he contributes some of the most essential ingredients of human progress.

Wherever this disparaging attitude toward business becomes general, we find that business is harassed, regulated, plundered and repressed. Under such persecution, the character and wisdom of businessmen tends to fall.

Where opinion-makers teach that business is a dishonest racket, then those who are willing to be racketeers or cheats will monopolize business, while achievers who value the good opinion of their fellows will choose other occupations, such as religion, politics and the military. Then we find the kind of government the Pharaohs had in ancient Egypt, or that prevailed as the Roman Republic gave way to a welfare state Empire. Under such oppressive governments, a businessman must be something of a trickster to survive.

Spreading Hostility

As hostility to businessmen grows, politicians tax them more heavily, while debasing and inflating the currency to maintain an illusion of prosperity. Then, when these policies cause rising price levels, a deluded populace demands price controls, which ambitious politicians are all too ready to impose.

The resulting shortages and "black markets" provide further excuses for more government action to combat these supposed evidences of private "greed."

This cancerous growth of government produces political "leaders" who promise peace and plenty even while they squander the fruits of industry in pauperizing the poor and waging "perpetual war for perpetual peace."

The result must be, sooner or later, a spreading decline in the quality of life despite (or because of) the increasing largess to "the poor" and the privileged, the rise of great new public works, and the display of awe-inspiring armaments.

Civilization progresses when business is widely regarded as Horatio Alger represented it in his stories seventy-five or more years ago. In those once-popular tales, work and thrift in honest business service were the high road to personal success in the broadest sense of that word. That view of business helped attract able, enterprising youths into business careers. It prevailed in this country long before Alger wrote and helps explain the astounding economic and cultural progress of the United States during the past two centuries.

On the other hand, insofar as we lose the Horatio Alger understanding and spirit, we succumb to increasing paternalism and despotism, collectivism and war, which demoralize and belittle the individual and produce a wide-spread cultural decline. This retrogression has happened time and time again in history, and if we don't learn the lesson from this history, we shall be doomed to repeat it.

Every nation has developed and flowered — with art, music, and the other ornaments and means of civilization — only on the basis of flourishing business, trade, commerce. This was true of the Phoenicians, Ancient Greece, and Ancient Egypt, the Chinese civilization, the Byzantine Empire, Venice, Florence, Spain, England, France, Germany and the United States. Go through the history of each and you'll find in its origins that period in which commerce and finance were highly regarded and relatively free in a developing civilization.

Again and again, however, these eras of progress have ended as the intelligentsia became worshipers of the Almighty State. Then these intellectuals — scribes and priests — became more and more scornful of businessmen; and business lost its vision because it lost its men of vision. Men of talent and imagination, instead, accepted the faith of the state-employed intellectuals that a well-schooled elite must make more and more choices for the general run of the population and compel the inferior masses to accept this planning and direction of their lives.

Submerging the Individual

With this elitist excuse for tyranny, governments organize militaristic and imperialistic gangs to substitute forms of slavery for the voluntary cooperation of free individuals. Then, as in Communist countries today, even the ablest of the ruling bureaucracies find that any individual is expendable — trapped and exploited or liquidated — as millions of humans are sacrificed on the altars of Planned Perfection. The Moral Law of the Golden Rule and of the Ten Commandments may be violated, but not with impunity. He who harms others, harms himself; he who deceives another, cheats himself.

This faith in Moral Law permeates the philosophy of our Northwood administration and faculty. Along with it goes insistence on the fact of individual responsibility and a broad, long-range view of personal success. A businessman's moral responsibility is no less than that of a teacher, physician, minister, artist or writer.

Essential to The Northwood Idea, then, is appreciation of the unlimited opportunities for character development in voluntary business enterprise.

Temptations correspond to the opportunities, and each occupation has its own peculiar temptations as it has its own peculiar opportunities. As few find the "strait gate" and "narrow way" of righteousness in other walks of life, likewise few businessmen will claim that they have always followed the right path in their work. Only those who look for business profits in life-supporting efforts that are mutually beneficial can achieve success in the true meaning of that word.

This objective may be the most distinctive feature of The Northwood Idea — the view that our graduates should look on business not merely as an easier way to attain ease and affluence but also as an opportunity for utilizing their highest human qualities and attaining lasting satisfaction in a life well spent.

Unit I: The Nature of Man and Property

Many pioneers of Nebraska built their homes from sod. Some Eskimos still build their homes from snow. Obviously, people build their homes with the materials available. "Building" a philosophy is much the same in the sense that a person formulates a philosophy with the "materials" available.

The overall purpose of this book is to help the reader formulate, or refine, a sound philosophy of life and business. To do this, he first has to know what "raw material" he has to work with and what its properties are. The purpose of this first unit of the book is to examine what we believe is the most basic "raw material" of philosophy, viz., individual man. (As we use "man," by the way, we mean male *and* female, *every* individual human being.) A sound philosophy of life and business rests on a thorough knowledge of the nature of man. A sound philosophy must be consistent with the way man *is* — not with the way we might wish man were.

In the first two chapters of this unit, "The Only Kind of People There Are" and "Blessings of Discrimination," Roger Williams and F. A. Harper discuss the uniqueness of every single individual and the importance of the individual's developing the ability to discriminate, respectively. Then, in "Importance of the Premise," Leonard Read, as distinctive and as discriminating an individual as we know, poses the fundamental philosophical question, "What is the purpose of man's earthly existence?" and gives us his answer to that question.

In "Nature's Laws and Man's Laws," William Peterson explains how vital it is for man to live in accord with natural laws.

The authors of the last two chapters in this unit show the very close connection between the individual and property. As Frank Chodorov puts it in "Source of Rights," "These things (e.g., food, clothing, and shelter) do not come to you because you want them;

When We Are Free

they come as the result of putting labor to raw materials. You have to give something of yourself — your brawn or your brain — to make the necessary things available . . . . But the energy you put out to make the necessary things is part of you; it *is* you." With "Property Rights and Human Rights," the final chapter in this unit, Paul Poirot blows away the clouds of confusion that befog us when we think in terms of two separate sets of rights, viz., property rights and human rights. As the last two authors show, the connection between the individual and property is so close that it is probably correct to say that in formulating a philosophy of life and business there is indeed just one fundamental "building block," i.e., individual man.

CHAPTER 1

The Only Kind of People There Are

by Roger J. Williams

If Socrates were resurrected, I suspect he would call attention again to what was written about 25 centuries ago: Know thyself; if you know a lot about other things and are ignorant of yourself, this is ridiculous.

We in this advanced and scientific age have never taken Socrates seriously on this point. I maintain that we are being ridiculous; we seek to plan and yet are not informed about ourselves for whom we plan. Of course, we know *something* about ourselves, but science has never undertaken a serious job of understanding people — a multidisciplinary undertaking. We have not tackled the job of understanding ourselves with one-tenth of the fervor we have shown in our research in outer space.

One of the most important facts about ourselves we have not grasped: All of us are basically and inevitably individuals in many important and striking ways. Our individuality is as inescapable as our humanity. If we are to plan for people, we must plan for individuals, because that's the only kind of people there are.

In what ways are we individuals? First as to our bodies. These ways are tangible and not subject to argument. Each of us has a distinctive stomach, a distinctive heart and circulatory system. Each of us has a distinctive muscular system, distinctive breathing apparatus, and an endocrine system all our own. Most surprising and significant perhaps, each of us has a distinctive set of nerve receptors, trunk nerves, and a brain that is distinctive in structure and not like other brains.

We are individuals also with respect to our minds. We do not all think with equal facility about the various things that can be thought about. Einstein was an extremely precocious student of mathematics, but on the other hand, he learned language so slowly that his parents were concerned about his learning to talk. William Lyon Phelps, the famous English professor at Yale, on the other

---

From *The Freeman,* January 1969.

hand, confessed that in mathematics he was "slow but not sure." There are at least forty facets to human minds. Each of us may be keen in some ways and stupid in others.

The importance of this individuality in minds would be hard to exaggerate. Because of it, two or more people agree with each other only *in spots*, never totally. The grandiose idea that all workers of the world can unite and speak and act as a unit is wholly untenable because of individuality in the minds of the individual workers. Nor can all capitalists unite, and for the same reason. Neither can all Negroes, all Latins, all Chinese, all Jews, all Europeans, or all English-speaking peoples.

It is often assumed that people disagree only because of self-interest and differences in their education. They also disagree because their minds do not grasp the same ideas with equal facility. Sometimes an individual has a specific idea which seems to him perfectly clear and potent. To him it seems certain that once this idea is expressed it will gain automatic acceptance. Practical trial shows, however, that it does not. To other individuals, because the patterns of their minds are different, this supposedly clear and potent idea may appear foggy, dubious, or even unsound.

Failure to recognize individuality in minds is widespread and is a revelation of the fact that we are ignorant about the people for whom we plan.

"Environmental Determinism"

I do not know that anyone else has ever expressed it this way, but on a long walk with Aldous Huxley about a year before he died, he decried to me the fact that the prevailing philosophy today may be described as "environmental determinism." Environment is assumed to be the only factor in our lives; inborn individuality in body and mind are completely neglected. According to this philosophy, every child who is placed in a slum environment becomes a delinquent and a criminal. This, from the work of the Gluecks at Harvard and others, is manifestly untrue. Neither is it true that every child who is furnished with plenty becomes for this reason an honorable and upright citizen.

Our "social studies" and "social science" teaching in all our schools and universities is permeated with environmental determinism which shows no interest in the crucial facts of individuality and quite inevitably tends to destroy all moral responsibility. A delinquent cannot help being a delinquent, we are told. Society should take all the blame. A criminal is that way because society has made him so, so society is to blame. This is blatant oversimplification in the name of social science! It disregards how human beings are built — their fundamental nature — and can by its short-sightedness lead to a breakdown of our civilization.

What I have been saying does not in any sense deny the importance of environment. Environments are what we can control, and to study how to improve them is the essence of planning. But we, the people, are not putty; we are individuals, and *we* need to be understood.

Individuality Is Crucial

To me it seems certain that the facts of individuality need to be taken into account. There are three areas, related to planning, in which I have some special knowledge. In all these areas individuality is crucial.

Take for instance the area of nutrition and health. It would be relatively easy to produce economically in factories a "man-chow" which would supposedly be the perfect food for the average man. Laboratory experiences as well as wide observations show, however, that this "man-chow" idea is completely unrealistic. It will not work. Because of biochemical individuality we do not all like the same foods nor can we thrive on the same mixture. Many human beings are so built that they derive a substantial part of the satisfaction of life out of eating. Taking variety and choices from them would be depriving them of their pursuit of happiness. The best food planning devised involves supermarkets where thousands of kinds of foods in great variety are available.

The Food and Drug Administration in Washington has, at least until very recently, done its planning on the basis of the hypothetical average man and has sought to regulate the marketing of medicinal substances, vitamins, and the like on this basis. This cannot work because of the hard facts of biochemical individuality. Real people — individuals — do not react in a uniform manner either to drugs or to nutritional factors such as amino acids, minerals, and vitamins.

No planning in the area of nutrition and health can work on a long range basis unless the facts of individuality are taken into account. If we plan for people, we must plan for individuals, because that is the only kind of people there are.

Another area of planning in which I have some special knowledge is that of education. I have recently completed my fiftieth year as a teacher. While I have in mind no pet schemes for reorganizing schools or universities, I have had for years a growing consciousness that no successful long-range planning can be done unless we recognize fully that every mind is a distinctive one and that every young person is endowed with peculiar aptitudes which need to be recognized, developed, and used. One of the worst lacks in modern education is the failure of youngsters to know themselves and to recognize their own strengths as well as weaknesses. Education for the hypothetical average child is no good. We must plan for individual children; that's the only kind there are.

Closely related to the problem of planning education is planning to curb crime, violence, racial hatred, and war. As Clement Attlee aptly pointed out years ago, the roots of war are to be found in the minds and hearts of men. The late Robert Kennedy pointed out when he was Attorney-General that peaceful relations between people cannot be enforced with guns and bayonets.

In my opinion, we will get nowhere in planning to curb violence by thinking in terms of the city of Dallas killing John F. Kennedy, the city of Memphis killing Martin Luther King, or the city of Los Angeles killing Robert Kennedy. Of course, social factors enter into violence, but there are important individual factors, too.

No informed person can think that curbing crime and violence is a simple problem. Because it is difficult, it is all the more important that we seek out — thoroughly — the root causes. I maintain that a great weakness which we exhibit in this modern scientific age is *ignorance about ourselves.*

Finally, let me say that our love of liberty and freedom is based upon this individuality. If we all had the same kinds of stomachs, the same kinds of muscles, nerves, and endocrine glands, the same kinds of brains, planning would be simple. We would all like exactly the same things. We would all be satisfied to read the same books, have the same amusements, eat the same food, and go to the same church. In short, we would all live happily in the same rut.

Planning is not that simple. We must plan for individuals — that's the only kind of people there are.

CHAPTER 2

Blessings of Discrimination

by F. A. Harper

When a child is born, his development is watched with anxious anticipation by those who wish him well. He begins to laugh and scream with pleasure and displeasure about more and more things, as his capacity for discrimination increases more and more. This is not a tragedy; it is a blessing. A child without any sense of discrimination is cursed with the threat of self-destruction.

The case of Beverly Smith, as reported by Dr. Frank R. Ford of Johns Hopkins Hospital, is interesting and significant. Due to some defect or short-circuit in Beverly's central nervous system, she has no sense of pain. When she falls down, or bumps her head, or puts her hand on a hot stove, or cuts herself with a knife, there is no pain. A blessing to Beverly? No. This censoring of Nature's important warnings may save her some initial pains, but it exposes her to the terrible consequences of ignoring the danger signals of pain from heat, broken bones, or appendicitis. All this because Beverly can not discriminate in feeling. She is a tragic care to her mother, who can protect her in some ways but who has no way of protecting her against all those dangers where Nature sends a private warning only to the threatened victim. The results would be exactly the same if a person capable of discrimination were to fail to act on its guidance.

Another child fails to develop any discrimination for sound. He is deaf and dumb, and destined to suffer all the tragedy which that implies. He is spared the alarm of startling noises, whether it be an explosion or the warning of a rattlesnake. He is protected from having to endure an off note in a symphony, but in being relieved from suffering off notes he is also prohibited from ever enjoying a harmony. In being saved the alarm of noises, he must forego the sound of warnings. He is victimized by his own inability to discriminate.

Wisdom Means Discrimination

Discrimination was said by Gautama Buddha to be the greatest essential human virtue. Truly it is a blessing — a blessing that is also in harmony with Judeo-Christian ideals. It is necessary to progress and to the advancement of civilization.

Many of the leading problems of our day, I believe, stem from a thought-disease about discrimination. It is well known that discrimination has come to be widely scorned. And politicians have teamed up with those who scorn it, to pass laws against it — as though morals can be manufactured by the pen of a legislator and the gun of a policeman.

What is this thing, this discrimination, which has become so widely dubbed as an evil?

Discrimination is the exercise of choice. It necessarily arises from knowledge and wisdom. And the greater the knowledge and wisdom, the higher the degree of discrimination. Visualize a person who can discriminate nothing. He would be as a stone! He would have no capacity for choice, no ability to guide any of his own affairs or to be in any degree his own master through self-controlled and independent acts. He would be utterly and wholly dependent, if indeed he could live. He would be as much the slave of others as is a stone the slave of the winds, the floods, and chemical changes — incapable of any selective control of his place in the universe.

Nature Demands Discrimination

Man was obviously intended to be a discriminating being. But the animals, too, have this capacity for discrimination. We know how certain animals have one or another of the senses developed to an even higher degree than *Homo sapiens.*

The outstanding thing about discrimination in man, in contrast to other forms of life as we know them, is his capacity for choice beyond the direct application of his senses to his immediate surroundings. He is sometimes called the reasoning animal because of his capacity for thinking in the abstract, or reasoning. It is this quality that makes possible all invention, all discovery, all advancement. The discovery of something new obviously means that someone has explored possibilities beyond the direct observing and sensing of what is present.

We may properly, then, take pride in the development of the power of discrimination in the child. The more the better, especially when it takes the form of reasoning and abstract thinking. Unusual powers of discrimination are the tools by which he may become a great scientist, or a creator in some other form. He is able to develop something notable only as he is capable of, and exercises, choice. He then becomes able to contribute to the advancement of human welfare, rather than merely to exist in civilization in such a manner that human welfare is no better for his having been here.

It is the power of discrimination which makes it possible for the child to exercise that blessed capacity for choice. Yet when the child grows to adulthood, because of some peculiar twist of "modern thought," he is confronted on every hand with the idea that discrimination is a sin. At its ultimate and logical conclusion, this concept flowers into governmental prohibition of choice, because government is the principal agent of force used to rob men of their right of choice. Carried to its ultimate, a controlled society removes choice from every sphere of human conduct, including religious practice, place of work, whom one will hire, with whom one will trade, and at what price. Let us now take a closer view of one or two forms of this thought-disease about discrimination.

Discrimination in Employment

The "fair employment practices" laws are of this type. According to these laws, one is prohibited from discriminating against the employment of a person because of his race, color, and the like. This type of law reveals, on closer scrutiny, the dangers inherent in the "nondiscrimination" thinking of our time.

Not everyone can work at every job. Only one person can work at each job, which means that nobody else can have it at the same time. Such is the nature of things — a natural law which no man-made law can revoke. It follows, then, that there must unavoidably be a selection of the person who is to work at any one job. There must be discrimination in this situation. The only remaining question is: Who shall have the right of decision? He must somehow choose the one for the job; he must somehow discriminate.

The method used in a free and voluntary society is to allow agreement between the two persons concerned — the employer and the employee. No one else is rightfully concerned. If A wishes B rather than anyone else to work for him, and if B wants the job, there is a meeting of minds by choice and agreement of the only two persons who merit a vote in the matter.

If it were to be said that C has a right to claim the job, it would mean that the right of decision, which properly belongs to A and to B, has now been confiscated by C. Not only that, but D and E and all the others who might want the job should, in justice, have rights equal to those of C; the result would be innumerable equal claims to the one job. This is a non-equation, subject to no solution. A decision must somehow be reached.

If there continues a denial to A and B of their rights in the matter, so that the question persists of who shall have the job, it becomes necessary to select an arbitrator. Under socialism in any of its forms and by any of its names, arbitration becomes the business of government, since government is supposed to be the unquestioned reservoir of justice. But the government has no basis for selecting the man who shall have that job, except as some one bureaucrat renders the decision arbitrarily and exercises his own personal choice or preference. Discrimination has not been eliminated; it cannot be eliminated, by the very nature of things. All that has happened has been the transfer of the rights of discrimination to a bureaucrat who has no basic concern — and no fundamental right of choice — in the matter. He now becomes the discriminator, under a scheme supposedly designed in the first place to eliminate discrimination by the employer.

The Right to Choose

The claim is made, of course, that an employer is "unfair" or "discriminatory" if his choice is on some basis that is said to be unwise. It is charged, for instance, that A hired B instead of C because he did not like C's race or color or religion or something. But the basis for A's considerations in his choice, or his motives, cannot possibly be known with certainty by any other person. How can any law like these "fair employment practices" laws, then, be fairly administered? How can a judge render a wise decision on the basis of unknowns?

And in any event, what difference does it make how A arrived at his choice? One cannot question the basis for a choice without questioning the right of choice itself. There isn't much sense to saying that I have the right, for instance, to select any kind of cheese I wish, but that I have no right to select one in preference to another because it tastes better, or has a more appealing color, or is made from the milk of better cows. The right of choice is the right of choice, and the reasons therefore become a sacred part of the right of choice itself. This same analysis should apply also to B's discriminating choice of the job offered by A.

If there were no discrimination in employment — no rights of choice — there would be no means by which persons could find their best place to work; no means by which persons could develop and use their best talents; no means by which management could be good rather than bad; no means by which accomplishment and merit could find reward.

Discrimination in Association

One of the leading areas for charges of discrimination is that of association. It would seem that if one is to be non-discriminating, he must share his company equally with every race, every shade of color, every nationality, every religion, every age, each sex, and every one of innumerable other differences which comprise the means of discrimination. One cannot help but wonder in this connection what would comprise non-discrimination, for instance, in the realm of matrimony. Monogamy would certainly disappear — unless, again, the state were to take over all matrimonial affairs, and then it would be a bureaucrat who would become the discriminator for the victims.

All friendship is founded on discrimination. Are we to conclude that friendship is an evil thing? Should attempts be made to communalize friendship? There comes to mind the story of one ne'er-do-well who was asked by another if he liked the Jews.

"No," he replied.
"Do you like the Japanese?"
"No."
"The Chinese?"
"No."
"The Italians?"
"No."
"Who, then, do you like?"
"My friends, just my friends!"

Non-Discrimination and Conflict

The prevailing attitudes about discrimination in employment, or in friendships, or in anything else, are based on the assumption that discrimination leads to conflict, and that legislation against it is necessary to keep order and the peace. On the contrary, I believe that laws against discrimination generate rather than quell disputes and conflict.

Note if you will, in the illustration about employment, the peaceful decision when A decides to hire B for a job, and B decides to take the offer. Compare it as a peaceful decision with the situation that arises when all others who might want the job are made to believe that they have a right to that job. Nor does the chaos and conflict subside when a non-discrimination law is passed to give legal backing to all these impossible claims to rights — when a bureaucrat takes over and rations the job to one of his friends, perhaps with a view to vote-getting.

Fallacy and Fact

Trouble over discrimination against Negroes seems to have become intensified in this country in recent years, under an acceleration of accusations and after passage of non-discrimination laws. We have been led to believe, for instance, that lynchings of Negroes have been on a long-time increase and that such legal measures have become necessary to keep order and the peace. The fact is, on the contrary, that there has been a long-time decline in the number of lynchings, which had all but disappeared a quarter of a century ago; this decline from its peak in the nineties applies to the lynching of whites as well as Negroes.

Promoters of the communist ideals have generated chaos and class conflict by generating this phobia about discrimination and persecution. This has led to false claims of rights. Part of the same kit of communist tools is the idea that private property is the consequence of discrimination against those who do not own it. If non-owners can be made to believe this and to help pass laws to correct it, they will fight to have it corrected by "fair ownership laws" whereby all private property is confiscated for the "ownership of all." This is the essence of communism itself, and it is already far advanced in the United States under devious and subtle devices.

Wherever personal rights to discriminate and choose are violated, either by a sweep of emotional sentiments or by law, peaceful solutions to Nature's law of limitations are replaced with chaos and conflict.

When the attempt is made to widen rights and create claims in excess of what is available to fulfill these claims, conflict becomes inevitable and persistent. Two or more claims to one job cause conflict. Two or more claims to the same land cause conflict. Two or more claims to the same husband or wife cause conflict.

The Solution

Conflict in all these areas can be curbed only by some device which will restrict rights or claims to any desired object, so that there is the necessary equality between the supply of a thing and the valid claims against it. There must be only one right to one job; only one deed to one piece of property. The function of the device of private property, in contrast to the impossible socialist-communist concept that everyone owns everything under "ownership in common," is to equate ownership with the property to be owned. The function of price in a free market, in contrast to a controlled price with rationing of an artificial shortage created by a governmental bureaucracy, is likewise to equate supply and demand for what is available.

The Judeo-Christian admonitions about the brotherhood of man and about loving one's fellow men can hardly mean that man-made laws should be allowed to interfere with these methods of peaceful adjustment to human preferences and to the scarcities of desired things. Man should be allowed to continue his self-improvement on earth through the exercise of judgment and freedom of choice according to his conscience. When this concept of rights is combined with conduct according to the familiar guides of Judeo-Christian ethics, I believe that the destiny of man will best be fulfilled and that peace will reign at its maximum.

If man is to continue his self-improvement, he must be free to exercise the powers of choice with which he has been endowed. When discrimination is not allowed according to one's wisdom and conscience, both discrimination and conscience will atrophy in the same manner as an unused muscle. Since man was given these faculties, it necessarily follows that he should use them and be personally responsible for the consequences of his choices. This means that he must be free to either enjoy or endure the consequences of each decision, because the lesson it teaches is the sole purpose of experience — the best of all teachers.

When one's fellow men interpose force and compulsions between him and the Source of his being — whether by the device of government or otherwise — it amounts to interrupting his self-improvement, in conflict with what seems to be the Divine design. Man must be left free to discriminate and to exercise his freedom of choice. This freedom is a virtue and not a vice. And freedom of choice sows the seeds of peace rather than of conflict.

When We Are Free

CHAPTER 3

Importance of the Premise

by Leonard E. Read

One of the great debates of our time concerns the role of government in human affairs — government limited to defense of life and property versus government regulation and control of every aspect of our lives. Not that this is a new problem, for the proper role of government in society has engaged the attention of the ablest minds since the time of Plato. At present, however, the debate bogs down. The more the matter is discussed nowadays, the more confused become people's beliefs and the further they seem to move from any common understanding of the problem or agreement on the answer.

Never in all history has the discussion been on such a scale as now, never such airing of views — with practically everyone seemingly bent on setting all others straight. But the more that some people contend with each other over the issues, the more is discord promoted, the less is harmony achieved. Force, rather than personal freedom of choice and action, mounts the driver's seat. Why this unhappy state of affairs?

The reason may be nearer to home than most of us suspect. Few libertarian proponents of strictly limited government are sharply conscious of why they believe as they do. Nor have most authoritarians bothered to examine the why of their positions. Much less does either pretend to know or really care what is in the other's mind, or why. Obviously, persons with no fundamental premises of their own are unlikely to have anything fundamental in common with each other. So, let us first examine the *why* of our own beliefs.

The reason we do not know why we believe and act as we do is because we are not aware of our basic premise or prime value or fundamental point of reference. With our lives anchored to nothing, we tend to believe and act aimlessly; that is, we obey emotional compulsions instead of adhering strictly to the disciplines imposed

---

From *The Freeman*, January 1962.

by some transcendental premise or value or principle personally thought out and accepted. People swayed by a variety of emotional compulsions — acting outside the realm of reason and with no knowledge of what moves them or others — can find no common ground, regardless of how much they talk or fight. They lack a *common* premise; individually, they lack a *conscious* premise.

Covetousness is an example of an emotional trait, as is fear of disapproval or desire for approbation. Suppose one person covets only political power and another only material wealth. With such diverse motivations, how could discussion lead them to agreement or even common understanding on, let us say, the TVA idea (government ownership and control of the means of production)? The former would sense an advantage; the latter would think his ambitions thwarted. And the more logically they argue from such nonreasoned premises — from their emotional compulsions — the more widely would they diverge.

Marcus Aurelius remarked, "If you would discuss with me, first define your terms." Good! But much more important and useful would be to say, "First, let us at least understand each other's premise, even though we may not agree." For it is fruitless to discuss economic, political, social, and moral subjects without first understanding our own premises as well as the premises of others. Otherwise, no party to the discussion can possibly know how to evaluate another's statements.

Man's Purpose

"What is your object in life? What is it you hope to achieve by your earthly existence? What, in your view, is your purpose here?" These would be appropriate questions to ask anyone who sees fit to argue about man's relationship to man.

Many people have never raised these questions with themselves, much less reflected on the answers. In this unthoughtful state, they do not qualify as instructors on questions of what's right and what's wrong in social, political, and economic affairs.

To arrive at a basic premise, one must ask and answer a fundamental human question: What is the goal of man's earthly striving; that is, what is life's highest value?

Is man's purpose here longevity, to extend creatural existence, stretch his life span?

Is it to accumulate wealth, pile up material possessions, get rich?

Should man aim to achieve supremacy over his fellow men, gain personal power, make others behave as he sees fit?

Importance of the Premise

Ought man to expend his life's energies in trying to remake others in his own likeness; that is, become the ultimate arbiter of humanity?

With the questions put in this stark form, most people, even without prior reflection, would acknowledge that man is made for other things than these; he should have higher values. Yet, things such as these, in infinite variation, have served as motivations for countless actions, including those of "statecraft." Lust for power, glory, fame, title, notice, adulation, pomp, riches — all for a momentary show-off before earthlings — is about as much of a life goal as many people have. Try to discuss sensibly with people thus motivated a subject such as the scope of government!

Consider, briefly, the current rash of public discussions, debates, and "interviews" — radio, TV, and grand ballroom variety — and reflect on the why of their inanity. Of course, in the first place, they are designed mostly for entertainment. As the educational director (this was his title) of a national network said to seven of us prior to going on the air, "While we prefer that you not use profanity, don't let anything stand in the way of making this a hot scrap." Second, and by the very nature of these verbal brawls, the incentive is not to shed light but rather to out-clever one's adversary. And third — by far the most important reason for the puerile nature of these insincere shows — is that no participant has the slightest notion what the other fellow's premises are, and may not know his own!

To demonstrate further the futility and the aimlessness of discussions where premises are in the dark, merely reflect on personal experiences with friends and associates. Note how often attempts to "talk it out" lead to nothing but sharpened awareness of disparity in viewpoints. Failure to understand each other's basic point of reference or prime value is more apt to yield bad feelings than harmonious conclusions.

Consider again those two persons, one whose chief aim is political power and another whose major purpose in life is the accumulation of material wealth. They decide to discuss or debate the efficacy of the TVA idea. In all probability, neither is fully aware of his own motivation, and it is almost certain that neither is conscious of the other's basic point of reference. Should each argue logically from his own major object in life, the former would have to judge the TVA idea to be consistent with his life's pattern; and the latter, seeking opportunity for private investment, would judge the idea to be inconsistent with his life's pattern. The longer they argue logically from their motivations — the further they move from agreement concerning TVA. It cannot be otherwise.

When We Are Free

How much better if each were to start by examining his own premise and explaining it to the other! The first would confess, "I have no object or life value above that of political power." The second, "I have no object beyond that of great wealth." At this point they could conclude in unison. "It is useless for us to discuss the efficacy of the TVA idea. We should, instead, confine ourselves to a discussion of our varying premises. For, unless we can find a common or near-common premise, our reasoning and argument will only lead us astray and apart."

Variable Objectives

The variation in our respective life-values is enormous. Some men want power; some riches; a few seek justice.

"Men have sought all sorts of other things — they have sought God, they have sought beauty, they have sought truth or they have sought glory, militarily or otherwise. They have sought adventure; they have even — so anthropologists tell us — sometimes believed that a large collection of dried human heads was the thing in all the world most worth having."[1]

These comments are important and relevant. First, reflect on the senselessness of two individuals, discussing social, political, economic, and moral matters, the life object of one being only dried human heads and the sole object of the other being riches. Arguing logically from such shallow premises, one would condone murder and the other would see nothing wrong in buying thousands of acres of land and having the government take money from other people to pay him for not growing wheat on it. There is no need to belabor the futility of such argument. *It is quite evident that all philosophical argument which does not proceed from a conscious premise is, perforce, a nonconscious argument — idle nonsense.*

Second, while there is no prospect of any substantial number of people thinking through and adopting a common premise, we can recognize a fairly general but vague search for such motivational background. Merely observe the attempt of people to "pigeonhole" others. Are they Republicans? Democrats? Socialists? Leftists? Rightists? Pinks? Reds? Physiocrats? Benthamites? Liberals? Reactionaries? New Dealers? Conservatives? Libertarians? These are fuzzy questions to which nothing better than fuzzy answers can be expected; nonetheless, they do demonstrate that many of us like to know what is at the root of people's actions and positions. If an

---

[1] See "Life, Liberty and the Pursuit of Welfare" by Joseph Wood Krutch in the Adventures of the Mind series, *Saturday Evening Post*, July 15, 1961.

individual's standard doesn't measure up to our own, we cross him off our list as unworthy of instructing us. Who would want advice from one bent only on collecting human heads? Or political plunder? Or coercive power over others?

Third, basic premises or life-values are on a scale of their own. They range from bad to good, from hellish to heavenly, from evil to virtuous, from senseless to sound, from immoral to amoral to moral. In short, it does matter what one's major premise is — indeed, it may matter more than anything else in this earthly experience.

A "Good Will" Guide

A most admirable premise was developed and set forth by Immanuel Kant. His premise was that *good will* is the highest good, but he did not use the phrase as the equivalent of mere good intentions or general friendliness. The exercise of *good will*, according to Kant, is an affirmation of man's moral freedom by which he participates in the world of things as they really are, and acts in terms of his own nature. He wrote:

"Everything in nature works according to laws. Only a rational being has the capacity of acting according to the conception of laws, i.e., according to principles. This capacity is will. Since reason is required for the derivation of actions from laws, will is nothing else than practical reason."[2]

Kant's *good* was measured by whether he could answer yes to the question, "Can I will that my maxim become a universal law?" No rational being could will that lying or stealing or killing should be universally practiced; therefore, lying, stealing, and killing must perforce be rejected as maxims for personal conduct. They are bad!

Kant argued that any discussion which makes no reference to fundamental principles (basic premise) produces a disgusting jumble of patched-up observations and half-reasoned principles. "Shallow-pates enjoy this, for it is very useful in everyday chit-chat."[3]

On the positive side Kant contended that a basic premise was indispensable "because morals themselves remain subject to all kinds of corruption so long as the guide and supreme norm for their correct estimation is lacking."[4] Each individual must, of course, determine his own basic premise or supreme norm, deriving as

---

[2] See *Foundations of the Metaphysics of Morals* by Immanuel Kant (New York: The Liberal Arts Press, 1959), p. 29.

[3] *Ibid.*, p. 26.

[4] *Ibid.*, p. 6.

much instruction as possible from others who have seen fit to devise and accept basic premises for themselves.[5]

The Emerging Individual

While having only admiration for Kant's system of reasoning, my own adopted premise, though not inconsistent with his, is stated quite differently — certainly less profoundly — and is set forth for such reflection as anyone may wish to give it. My supreme norm or premise or fundamental point of reference has its origin in my answer to the question, "What is the purpose of man's earthly existence?"

Admittedly, the answer to this question has to be highly personal. It will vary according to one's fundamental assumptions. To me, it is self-evident that man did not create himself, for man knows almost nothing about himself. Man is the creature of God, or, if you prefer, of Infinite Principle or Consciousness or Intelligence. And there's more to life than the five senses reveal. Thus, these assumptions can be summarized as follows:
  a. A belief in the primacy or supremacy of an Infinite Consciousness;
  b. A conviction that the individual human consciousness is expansible; and
  c. A faith in the immortality of the human spirit.

For anyone with assumptions such as these, the answer to the question, "What is the purpose of man's earthly existence?" comes clear: It is for each individual to come as near as he can to the realization of those creative powers which are peculiarly and distinctively included in his own potentialities. *Man's purpose here is to grow, to emerge, to hatch, to evolve in consciousness, partaking as much as he can of Infinite Consciousness.*

If the above is accepted as the highest purpose of earthly life, it follows that any force — psychological or sociological — which binds or retards or in any way restrains the individual human spirit in its emergency must be thought of as an immoral and evil force. Conversely, the absence of such retarding and restraining forces — *the personal practice of freedom* — is moral, good, virtuous.

---

[5] C. E. M. Joad's *Decadence,* particularly the first eight chapters, is a brilliant explanation of what follows the "dropping of the object," that is, the disastrous results of not having high principles as premises.

A Point of Reference

With this as a supreme norm or fundamental point of reference, it is easy enough to stand any and all proposals and propositions up against it and to form fairly accurate judgments as to whether they inhibit or promote a movement toward this ideal. Not only does this establish a basis for consistent action but it also permits others to judge whether one's moral, social, economic, and political positions are logical deductions from the acknowledged premise. Others may disagree with the premise, which is their privilege.[6] In this case the only discourse that makes sense must have to do with the varying premises. But, if the premise be adjudged satisfactory, then all issues can be intelligently discussed with enlightenment to the parties concerned.

Be it noted that in the above premise, as well as in Kant's, each individual is assumed to be an end in himself. Anyone who acknowledges an Infinite Consciousness cannot help respecting fellow human beings as the apertures through whom Infinite Consciousness flows and manifests itself. Can man — any of us — predict which individuals will be most graced in this respect? Indeed not! Throughout recorded history the breakthroughs have occurred in the most unlikely individuals. Thus, it is the height of egotistical arrogance to doubt that each person — regardless of status, station, education, or whatever — is an end in himself. It would seem that no premise could qualify as good or moral *or libertarian* which fails to meet this qualification. Reason clearly dictates that "we treat humanity, whether in our own person or in that of another, always as an end and never as a means only."[7]

Individual Achievement

In deciding on a supreme norm or fundamental premise for oneself it is advisable to select one that is unattainable; such, for instance, as the expansion of one's own consciousness — the more one advances, the more there is to be conscious of. It is a road of individual progress that has no end.

---

[6] "If a man does not keep pace with his companions, perhaps it is because he hears a different drummer. Let him step to the music which he hears, however measured or far away." Henry David Thoreau. *Walden*. Ch. XVIII.

[7] *Foundations of the Metaphysics of Morals*, p. 47.

Consider this: A person has his eye set on scaling the world's highest mountain. This is his life's ambition, his only goal. Repeatedly he fails, but the challenge will not down. Finally, he succeeds and triumphantly stands in the rarefied air of his accomplishment — his mission achieved! No other object lies before him.

Reflect on the planning, the physical training — the growing in strength — that accrued to him so long as the object was before him. Now, contemplate what happens in the way of fading, weakness, atrophy, when life's deed is done, when there is no further object.

People arrive in a new land confronted with a wilderness. Clearing the forests and overcoming all the obstacles nature offers is their lot. Observe their development. Now, let them succeed, become affluent — their object realized, no other goal before them. Their moral fiber becomes soft, flabby; they become sloppy thinkers.

"Nothing fails like success," Dean Inge used to say; that is, no one can set himself an attainable object and, after its achievement, continue to grow. Thus, one's object ought to be of the unattainable variety, one that calls for perpetual striving, leading the individual on an endlessly emerging road.

Reduced to the workaday world of practical affairs, a philosophy which concedes that each individual is an end in himself is a philosophy that precludes the practice of the few using the many as means. This philosophy is diametrically opposed to the socialistic scheme under which most of us unwillingly serve as means to the nefarious ends of those exercising unprincipled political power.

A high-principled premise for each rational human being is seen to be of the utmost importance. Lacking it, there can be no sensible discussion of moral questions, and without such discussion there can be no foundation for a free society. The adoption and strict observation of high-principled premises will, on the other hand, result in as straight thinking and as consistently sound action as rational individuals are capable of. How well men and women do this determines the extent of freedom in society.

Yes, freedom depends on you. The individual is both its means and its end — the only foundation of freedom, and also its crowning object.

CHAPTER 4

Nature's Laws and Man's Laws

by William H. Peterson

He that tilleth his land shall have plenty of bread: but he that followeth after vain persons shall have poverty enough.

Proverbs 28:19

The law of life works infallibly. In 8 minutes and 20 seconds a life-giving ray of the sun hurtles the 93,000,000 miles (at the fantastic speed of 186,000 miles per second) from the sun to the Iowa farm envisioned in Grant Wood's painting, *American Gothic.* The ray is one of an infinite number which have made such a trip through the eons of time, drenching and renewing the land of milk and honey in Biblical Canaan, the vineyard in Roman Gaul, the manor in medieval England, the rice paddy in present-day Burma, the farm in modern Iowa.

In all, the basic biology of life is the same: sun and water, seed and soil.

The Iowa farmer deposits a kernel of corn, one of countless, an inch or two in the soil, into the womb of Mother Earth. The elixir of life begins; sun, soil, and water break through the tough-shelled tomb of the seed; the corn seed, very much alive, explodes roots downward and a stem upward. Against relatively enormous weight, the minute stem pushes aside tiny stones, dirt, and debris, and pierces the earth's crust seeking, mysteriously, the life-sustaining rays of the sun.

On the ground a small whitish plant emerges, fragile but alive and vibrant, beautiful to the eye and delicate to the touch. Soon, breathing air, absorbing water, defying gravity, the at-first insignificant corn stalk soars majestically, a triumph of Nature's engineering and architecture, turning to the sun and bending with the wind. Then ears and tassel and the seeds with which to begin again the endless cycle of growth and regrowth, and for man the age-old process of cultivation.

Meanwhile, locked in the harvested ears of corn is the life-giving energy of the sun transmitted at a level no human eye will

---

From *The Freeman*, November 1958.

ever see, probably not even with powerful microscopes yet to be designed. This is photosynthesis: life, substance, energy, transmitted from ray to plant and, ultimately, to animals and humans; life sustaining life, in strict accord with the laws of Nature.

Do such laws regulate the affairs of men? Some 25,000 years ago, man — a crude nomadic hunter, a garnerer of nuts, a berry picker — saw the possibilities of harnessing seed and seasons into a regular pattern of cultivation and harvest, and the problem of *Homo sapien's* survival was greatly eased. The laws of Nature were recognized, understood, and applied. The Agricultural Revolution was born, and, more than that, the time and energy and anxiety spent on the eternal hunt for food were released for division of labor, for trade, for capital accumulation, and, later, for reflection on the meaning of life and, eventually, for literature, architecture, art, music, and philosophy. The Agricultural Revolution laid the basis, in short, for permanence, for civilization.

Laissez Faire

More than 24,000 years later, from the latter part of the eighteenth century until World War I, came the Industrial Revolution and, relatively speaking, laissez faire. The nineteenth century was a remarkable century. It was a century of political liberty, free trade, and the gold standard, a century in which slavery was banished almost the world over and the British corn laws repealed, a century of science, a century of choice, a century of the inherent dignity of the individual. Essentially, no government burned coffee, operated public granaries, issued fiats on permissible acreages, paid farmers not to farm, nor sold surpluses to foreigners more cheaply than to its own citizens. The farmer "was a free man, independent on his own acres, beholden to no one but his God, assured of a living if he only worked hard enough. It was a wonderful dream. It *did* happen. It *is* passing. Now it belongs to history and the poets."[1]

The tragedy of "modern" farm intervention is twofold. One tragedy stems from man's efforts, in a sense heroic, to repeal Nature's laws, to substitute bureaucratic rule for the rule of the market place, to set prices below the market price and decree, vainly, that there shall be no shortages, and to set prices above the market price and assert, again vainly, that there shall be no surpluses. So under the banner of "farm policy," and armed with legislative authority, court orders, administrative directives, and no little courage and smugness, the interventionists commandeer the market place and

---

[1] Haystead, Ladd. *The Farmer and his Customers.* Norman, Oklahoma: University of Oklahoma Press, 1957, p. 92.

"adjust" farm prices and ultimately the farm itself. Politics enter. Legislative blocs emerge (e.g., "the farm bloc"). Pressure groups pull this way and that. One intervention fails. A new one is tacked on. The jerry-built edifice wobbles anew. So still more intervention.

A generation of "farm policy" adds up to hopeless tinkering, fantastic losses, planned chaos, a lost war against Nature's laws. The battles have names: The Fordney-McCumber Tariff, the McNary-Haugen Bills, the Farm Marketing Board, the Smoot-Hawley Tariff, the AAA, Soil Conservation, the Ever-Normal Granary, the Food Stamp Plan, 90 Per Cent of Parity, the Brannan Plan, Flexible Parity, the Soil Bank, Overseas Surplus Disposal. The irony is that the farmer to be "saved" wasn't; since the New Deal, one of every three farmers has quit. The exodus from farming, in a sense a triumph of efficiency over bureaucracy, continues to this day.

The second phase of the tragedy of "modern" farm intervention is that it is but a chapter in a much longer but unfinished story; it is a part of a philosophy, a way of life, a return to mercantilism, a recall to the planned society of Imperial Rome. How will the story end?

Many farmers bemoan the loss of their economic liberty but do they bemoan the censorship of a movie in Philadelphia or a play in Boston, the lifting of mailing privileges for a radical weekly? Does the interest of a Jehovah's Witness in freedom of religion extend to an interest in the publisher's concern for the freedom of the press? Does the publisher worry over the worker's loss of civil liberty in having to join a union against his will? Does the worker lose any sleep over the scientist who is denied a passport and hence is unfree to travel abroad? Does the atomic scientist complain when the Japanese-American is put into a federal concentration camp or the Nazi is judged under ex post facto laws?

Freedom Eroded by Force

Freedom is total; as long as man exercises neither force nor the threat of force against his fellow man, freedom exists. The duty of government, then, is to preserve freedom — to use its force only to repel force; the spirit of free enterprise and liberalism will do the rest. The modern dilemma is that competition, the law of supply and demand, however worshiped in the abstract, is nowadays shot through with privileges extended by government and eagerly sought by its citizens.

The farmer is not alone. Government, as Voltaire noted, has become the art of taking from some and giving to others. The businessman looks for a tariff, the veteran for a pension, the shipper for a subsidy, the worker for a minimum wage, the periodical publisher for an artificial mailing cost, the industrialist for a defense contract, the silver producer for the monetization of silver, the labor official for immunity from the antitrust laws, the elderly for Social Security, the bureaucrat for power, the debtor for inflation, and so on and on, the State ever swelling, the individual ever shrinking.

It is an age of amorality, an age of seeking Something for Nothing, of shedding private responsibility and becoming wards of the State — the Welfare State. It happened before. Rome, for instance, had its "bread and circuses." It tried to repeal Nature's laws — for example, the law of self-reliance and the law of supply and demand. Nature was not denied then. Will she be denied now?

In the words of Ralph Waldo Emerson, more than a century ago:

> The harvest will be better preserved and go farther, laid up in private bins, in each farmer's cornbarn, and each woman's basket, than if it were kept in national granaries.
>
> In like manner, an amount of money will go farther if expended by each man and woman for their own wants, and in the feeling that this is their all, than if expended by a Great Steward, or National Commissioners of the Treasury.
>
> Take away from me the feeling that I must depend upon myself, give me the least hint that I have good friends and backers there in reserve who will gladly help me and instantly I relax my diligence.
>
> Give no bounties, make equal laws, secure life and property, and you will not need to give alms. Open the doors of opportunity to talent and virtue, and they will do themselves justice and property will not be in bad hands. In a free and just commonwealth, property rushes from the idle and imbecile to the industrious, brave, and persevering. The level of the sea is not more surely kept than is the equilibrium of value in society by demand and supply; and artifice and legislation punish themselves by reactions, gluts, and bankruptcies.

In the words of President Grover Cleveland in vetoing federal aid to the Texas drought farmers of his day: "It is the business of citizens to support the Government, not of the Government to support the citizens."

Which will triumph, Nature's laws or man's laws?

CHAPTER 5

Source of Rights

by Frank Chodorov

The axiom of what is often called "individualism" is that every person has certain inalienable rights. For example, "individualism" holds that property *as such* obviously has no rights; there is only the inherent right of a person to his honestly acquired property . . .

The axiom of socialism is that the individual has no inherent rights. The privileges and prerogatives that the individual enjoys are grants from society, acting through its management committee, the government. That is the condition the individual must accept for the benefit of being a member of society. Hence, the socialists (including many who do not so name themselves) reject the statement of rights in the Declaration of Independence, calling it a fiction of the eighteenth century.

In support of his denial of natural rights, the socialist points out that there is no positive proof in favor of that doctrine. Where is the documentary evidence? Did God hand man a signed statement endowing him with the rights he claims for himself, but denies to the birds and beasts who also inhabit the earth? If in answer to these questions you bring in the soul idea, you are right back to where you were in the beginning: How can you prove that man has a soul?

Those who accept the axiom of natural rights are backed against the wall by that kind of reasoning, until they examine the opposite axiom, that all rights are grants or loans from government. *Where did government get the rights which it dispenses?* If it is said that its fund of rights is collected from individuals, as the condition for their membership in society, the question arises, where did the individual get the rights which he gave up? He cannot give up what he never had in the first place, which is what the socialist maintains.

What is Government?

What is this thing called government, which can grant and take away rights? There are all sorts of answers to that question, but all the answers will agree on one point, that government is a social instrument enjoying a monopoly of coercion. The socialist says that the monopoly of coercion is vested in the government in order that it may bring about an ideal social and economic order; others say that the government must have a monopoly of coercion in order to prevent individuals from using coercion on one another. In short, the essential characteristic of government is power. If, then, we say that our rights stem from government, on a loan basis, we admit that whoever gets control of the power vested in government is the author of rights. And simply because he has the power to enforce his will. Thus, *the basic axiom of socialism, in all its forms, is that might is right.*

And that means that power is all there is to morality. If I am bigger and stronger than you and you have no way of defending yourself, then it is right if I thrash you; the fact that I did thrash you is proof that I had the right to do so. On the other hand, if you can intimidate me with a gun, then right returns to your side. All of which comes to mere nonsense. And a social order based on the socialistic axiom — which makes the government the final judge of all morality — is a nonsensical society. It is a society in which the highest value is the acquisition of power — as exemplified in a Hitler or a Stalin — and the fate of those who cannot acquire it is subservience as a condition of existence.

The senselessness of the socialistic axiom is shown by the fact that there would be no society, and therefore no government, if there were no individuals. The human being is the unit of all social institutions; without a man there cannot be a crowd. Hence, we are compelled to look to the individual to find an axiom on which to build a nonsocialistic moral code. What does he tell us about himself?

Desire To Live

In the first place, he tells us that above all things he wants to live. He tells us this even when he first comes into the world and lets out a yell. Because of that primordial desire, he maintains, he has a right to live. Certainly, nobody else can establish a valid claim to his life, and for that reason he traces his own title to an authority that transcends all men, to God. That title makes sense.

When the individual says he has a valid title to life, he means that all that is he, is his own: his body, his mind, his faculties. Maybe there is something else in life, such as a soul, but without going into that realm, he is willing to settle on what he knows about himself — his consciousness. All that is "I" is "mine." That implies, of course, that all that is "you" is "yours" — for, every "you" is an "I." Rights work both ways.

But, while just wanting to live gives the individual a title to life, it is an empty title unless he can acquire the things that make life liveable, beginning with food, raiment, and shelter. These things do not come to you because you want them; they come as the result of putting labor to raw materials. You have to give something of yourself — your brawn or your brain — to make the necessary things available. Even wild berries have to be picked before they can be eaten. But the energy you put out to make the necessary things is part of you; it *is* you. *Therefore, when you cause these things to exist, your title to yourself, your labor, is extended to the things. You have a right to them simply because you have a right to life.*

Source Of Government

That is the moral basis of the right of property. "I own it because I made it" is a title that proves itself. The recognition of that title is implied in the statement that "I *make* so many dollars a week." That is literally true.

But what do you mean when you say you own the thing you produced? Say it is a bushel of wheat. You produced it to satisfy your desire for bread. You can grind the wheat into flour, bake the loaf of bread, eat it, or share it with your family or a friend. Or you can give part of the wheat to the miller in payment for his labor; the part you give him, in the form of wages, is his because he gave you labor in exchange. Or you sell half the bushel of wheat for money, which you exchange for butter to go with the bread. Or you put the money in the bank so that you can have something else later on, when you want it.

In other words, your ownership entitles you to use your judgment as to what you will do with the product of your labor — consume it, give it away, sell it, save it. Freedom of disposition is the substance of property rights.

Freedom Of Disposition

Interference with this freedom of disposition is, in the final analysis, interference with your right to life. At least, that is your reaction to such interference, for you describe such interference with a word that expresses a deep emotion: You call it "robbery." What's more, if you find that this robbery persists, if you are regularly deprived of the fruits of your labor, you lose interest in laboring. The only reason you work is to satisfy your desires; and if experience shows that despite your efforts your desires go unsatisfied, you become stingy about laboring. You become a "poor" producer.

Suppose the freedom of disposition is taken away from you entirely. That is, you become a slave; you have no right of property. Whatever you produce is taken by somebody else; and though a good part of it is returned to you, in the way of sustenance, medical care, housing, you cannot under the law dispose of your output; if you try to, you become the legal "robber." Your concern in production wanes and you develop an attitude toward laboring that is called a "slave" psychology. Your interest in yourself also drops because you sense that without the right of property you are not much different from the other living things in the barn. The clergyman may tell you you are a man, with a soul; but you sense that without the right of property you are somewhat less of a man than the one who can dispose of your production as he wills. If you are a human, how human are you?

It is silly, then, to prate of human rights being superior to property rights, because the right of ownership is traceable to the right to life, which is certainly inherent in the human being. Property rights are in fact human rights.

A society built around the denial of this fact is, or must become, a slave society — although the socialists describe it differently. It is a society in which some produce and others dispose of their output. The laborer is not stimulated by the prospect of satisfying his desires but by fear of punishment. When his ownership is not interfered with, when he works for himself, he is inclined to develop his faculties of production because he has unlimited desires. He works for food, as a matter of necessity; but when he has a sufficiency of food, he begins to think of fancy dishes, a tablecloth, and music with his meals. There is no end of desires the human being can conjure up, and will work for, provided he feels reasonably sure that his labor will not be in vain. Contrariwise, when the law deprives him of the incentive of enjoyment, he will work only as necessity compels him. What use is there in putting out more effort?

Therefore, the general production of a socialistic society must decline to the point of mere subsistence.

Decline Of Society

The economic decline of a society without property rights is followed by the loss of other values. It is only when we have a sufficiency of necessaries that we give thought to nonmaterial things, to what is called culture. On the other hand, we find we can do without books, or even moving pictures, when existence is at stake. Even more than that, we who have no right to own certainly have no right to give, and charity becomes an empty word; in a socialistic order, no one need give thought to an unfortunate neighbor because it is the duty of the government, the only property owner, to take care of him; it might even become a crime to give a "bum" a dime. When the denial of the right of the individual is negated through the denial of ownership, the sense of personal pride, which distinguishes man from beast, must decay from disuse . . .

Whatever else socialism is, or is claimed to be, its first tenet is the denial of private property. All brands of socialism, and there are many, are agreed that property rights must be vested in the political establishment. None of the schemes identified with this ideology, such as the nationalization of industry, or socialized medicine, or the abolition of free choice, or the planned economy, can become operative if the individual's claim to his property is recognized by the government.

When We Are Free

CHAPTER 6

Property Rights and Human Rights

by Paul L. Poirot

Tricky phrases with favorable meanings and emotional appeal are being used today to imply a distinction between *property* rights and *human* rights.

By implication, there are two sets of rights — one belonging to human beings and the other to property. Since human beings are more important, it is natural for the unwary to react in favor of *human* rights.

Actually, there is no such distinction between property rights and human rights. The term *property* has no significance except as it applies to something owned by someone. Property itself has neither rights nor value, save only as human interests are involved. There are no rights but human rights, and what are spoken of as property rights are only the human rights of individuals to property.

Expressed more accurately, the issue is not one of property rights versus human rights, but of the human rights of one person in the community versus the human rights of another.

Those who talk about two sets of rights apparently want to discriminate between property income and labor income — with the implication that the rights to rental and investment income are inferior, as a class, to the rights to income from wages and salaries. Actually, this is an unwarranted assumption. It must be evident that all persons have rights which are entitled to respect. Safeguarding such rights is essential to the well-being of all. This is the only just principle. Thus, the problem is not to establish priorities on human rights in the community, but rather to determine what the respective rights are in the particular cases under dispute. This is the real problem in human relations, and it is one that calls for the exercise of wisdom, restraint, and true administration of justice under law.

What are "Property Rights?"

What are the property rights thus disparaged by being set apart from human rights? They are among the most ancient and basic of human rights, and among the most essential to freedom and progress. They are the privileges of private ownership, which give meaning to the right to the product of one's labor — privileges which men have always regarded instinctively as belonging to them almost as intimately and inseparably as their own bodies.

The ownership of property is the right for which, above all others, the common man has struggled in his slow ascent from serfdom. It is the right for which he struggles today in countries emerging from feudalism. The sense of this right is so deep-rooted in human nature, so essential as a stimulant of productive effort, that even totalitarian regimes have been unable to abolish it entirely.

It is a mistake to belittle the importance of property rights. Respect for these rights is basic to organized society, and the instinct of individuals to acquire property is at the root of all economic progress. Unless people can feel secure in their ability to retain the fruits of their labor, there is little incentive to save and to expand the fund of capital — the tools and equipment for production and for better living. The industrial development of this country, which has given us the highest standard of living in the world and has made possible a miracle of production in war and peace, is dependent upon the observance of property rights. Who is going to work and save if these rights are not recognized and protected?

The right to own property means the right to use it, to save it, to invest it for gain, and to transmit it to others. It means freedom from unreasonable search and seizure and from deprivation without due process of law or without just compensation. It might also be fairly taken to imply a limitation upon taxation because "the power to tax involves the power to destroy." For a like reason, it should imply assurance against governmental dilution of the money whereby the government takes property which otherwise could be claimed by wage and salary checks and other credit instruments. Further, it should insure against other measures so burdensome or restrictive as to prevent the employment of savings in legitimate productive enterprise with a reasonable prospect of gain. Violation of any of these rights can nullify, in whole or in part, the right to property.

The Bill of Rights in the United States Constitution recognizes no distinction between property rights and other human rights. The ban against unreasonable search and seizure covers "persons, houses, papers, and effects," without discrimination. No person may, without due process of law, be deprived of "life, liberty, or property"; all are equally inviolable. The right of trial by jury is assured in criminal and civil cases alike. Excessive bail, excessive fines, and cruel and unusual punishments are grouped in a single prohibition. The founding fathers realized what some present-day politicians seem to have forgotten: A man without property rights — without the right to the product of his own labor — is not a free man.

Property Rights and Human Rights

He can exist only through the generosity or forbearance of others.

These constitutional rights all have two characteristics in common. First, they apply equally to all persons. Second, they are, without exception, guarantees of freedom or immunity from governmental interference. They are not assertions of claims against others, individually or collectively. They merely say, in effect, that there are certain human liberties, including some pertaining to property, which are essential to free men and upon which the state shall not infringe.

The Class Struggle

To many people, the expression "putting property rights first and human rights second" brings to mind the oft-drawn political picture of a struggle between a few "rich plutocrats" and "soulless corporate monopolies" on the one hand and the great body of humble citizens on the other. Much of what the public reads and hears about the recurring union wage controversies conveys the same impression, with emphasis almost entirely on "the workers" versus the "big companies." John L. Lewis' blast against what he called the "rapacious and predatory" steel industry illustrates the point. In a message to Philip Murray, President of the United Steelworkers, offering a loan of $10,000,000 of coal miners' dues from the union treasury to back up the 1952 steel strike, Mr. Lewis said:

> We are conscious of the strength of the vast array of adversaries which confront you. Rarely has a union membership faced such a formidable grouping of financial and corporate interests as now oppose the steel workers of the nation in their long-standing struggle to achieve their rightful aims and objectives in the industry.

In all such talk about "big companies" and "formidable groupings of financial and corporate interests," hardly anything is said about the shareholders, little and big, who are the real owners of the business and whose money, plowed into plant and equipment, has made possible the large employment and the record output.

Who are the "Propertied Classes?"

Actually, ownership of property cuts across those imaginary lines between economic classes in the United States; and in no other country is the stake in property rights so great and so widely distributed. While we hear much about large corporations with thousands of employees and millions of dollars in assets, it is probably not generally realized that there are about 11,000,000 non-farm business enterprises in this country. Of these, the vast majority are classified by the Department of Commerce as "small business" on the basis of their number of employees or dollar volume of sales. The importance of "small business" in the economy is further shown by the fact that it accounts for about 40 per cent of the nation's total output of goods and services.

One of the largest of our "propertied classes" — the farmers — includes over 4,500,000 farm owners whose lands are valued at $696,000,000,000. Farmers work these lands with $97,000,000,000 worth of machinery. And in 1980, they had livestock valued at $64,000,000,000.

Even among large corporations, the ownership of stock is widely distributed; the 50 most widely held corporations in the United States each have over 130,000 registered shareholders. American Telephone and Telegraph has the most stockholders, 2,939,000. General Motors, with 1,237,000 shareholders, is this country's next most widely held corporation. Nearly 30,000,000 Americans own shares in one or more investor-owned corporation. Fifteen per cent of these shareholders have incomes of less than $10,000; 57 per cent of them have incomes between $10,000 and $25,000; and the remaining 28 per cent have incomes of over $25,000. On the average, each of these investors owns stock worth $4,000.

What are "Human Rights?"

Now what about the so-called human rights that are represented as superior to property rights? What about the "right" to a job, the "right" to a standard of living, the "right" to a minimum wage or a maximum workweek, the "right" to a "fair" price, the "right" to bargain collectively, the "right" to security against the adversities and hazards of life, such as old age and disability?

The framers of the Constitution would have been astonished to hear these things spoken of as rights. They are not immunities from governmental compulsion; on the contrary, they are demands for new forms of governmental compulsion. They are not claims to the product of one's own labor; they are, in some if not in most cases, claims to the products of other people's labor.

These "human rights" are indeed different from property rights, for they rest on a denial of the basic concept of property rights. They are not freedoms or immunities assured to all persons alike. They are special privileges conferred upon some persons at the expense of others. The real distinction is not between property rights and human rights, but between equality of protection from governmental compulsion on the one hand and demands for the exercise of such compulsion for the benefit of favored groups on the other.

The "Right" to a Job

To point out these characteristics of the so-called human rights is not to deny the reality nor belittle the importance of the social problems they represent. Some of these problems are real and important. They are also complex, and in this further respect they are different from the rights guaranteed by the Constitution.

There is no great difficulty nor danger in declaring that certain individual rights shall not be tampered with by the government — and in adhering to that principle. It is quite another matter to say that the government shall seize the property or curtail the freedom of some of its citizens for the benefit, or the supposed benefit, of others. To adopt this view is to cast both the government and the citizen in radically new roles, with far-reaching effects on economic behavior, political practices, and individual character.

Consider, for example, the so-called *right to a job*. This is a fine-sounding phrase that evokes an emotional response. It creates a mental image of an unemployed worker and his family suffering hardship through no fault of their own. No one would deny the reality nor the seriousness of that, especially when the unemployed worker is multiplied by millions. To find the best remedy, however, is a difficult matter, and it is not made easier by the use of such misleading catchwords as the "right" to a job. One man's "right" to a job implies an obligation on the part of someone else to give him a job. Who has any such obligation?

An economy of private enterprise functions by means of voluntary contracts entered into for the sake of mutual advantage. Jobs arise from such contracts. The obligation to fulfill his contract is the only right any person can have to a job. Both sides of the contract have to be fulfilled. The employer's job — his side of the contract — is to anticipate what the consumers will want in the market place. His capacity to offer jobs to employees depends upon how well he understands the market pattern of consumer preferences. He has no right of control over the market. There is a limit to his capacity to provide jobs. And in the final analysis, an employee's so-called *right to a job* is determined by what consumers think the product or service is worth to them.

As with the "right" to a job, so with the other so-called human rights. These are not rights in the constitutional sense of respect for privacy; they are, instead, social programs which the government has undertaken or has been asked to promote. These programs, unlike true rights, are selective, coercive, complex, and experimental. Hence, they need to be carefully considered each on its own merits with due regard to the serious threats they may involve to the real and basic human rights that have enabled free men to build a society with the highest level of material well-being ever achieved anywhere.

Triple Threats

On the economic side, the gravest threat is that productive enterprise will be so burdened and impeded by high taxes, prohibitions, red tape, and controls that industry will stagnate. Without the products of industry, social programs of any kind become empty promises. New political powers and functions increase the cost of government and drain manpower from farms and factories into administrative bureaus. The great bulk of the money for benefit payments to favored groups must be taken from those who produce by putting forth their own efforts or by investing their savings. Minimum-wage rates wipe out the entire lower range of job opportunities in the business world. Only the government, with the power to tax, can pay more for labor than it is worth. Maximum-hour laws further limit the opportunity to be productive. Artificially pegged prices and wage rates interfere with the normal market process of gearing production to the maximum satisfaction of consumer wants.

On the political side, the increase of power multiplies the opportunities for the abuse of power and the harm that can be done by such abuse. High tax rates expose taxpayers and collectors to strong temptations. The disbursement of billions of dollars in public funds opens new avenues for favoritism and corruption. This system of political distribution of the wealth of a nation encourages government by pressure groups, with the favors flowing toward the groups with the most votes. Demands for more liberal benefits on the one hand and for tax relief on the other converge upon the public treasury. Deficit financing and currency depreciation tend to become national habits which feed upon the savings of individuals and wipe out the means of production and progress.

On the human side, the individual citizen discovers that it is increasingly difficult to get ahead by enterprise and thrift — increasingly profitable to join in the scramble for governmental favors and handouts. The sense of relationship between services rendered and payment received grows weaker. Personal initiative and self-reliance give way to an attitude of: let the government do it. Free citizens tend to degenerate into wards of the state.

These are not imaginary effects, but real ones. They are visible here and now. They are the consequences of placing social programs, mislabeled "human rights," above the *real* human rights, disparagingly called "property rights," which underlie the productive strength of free men.

When We Are Free

Unit II: What About Government?

The second unit of this book is about government. It might be useful to the reader to think of this unit as having three parts.

The first three chapters make up the first of the three parts. The authors of these chapters discuss *why* we need government; *what functions* government *should* perform, ideally; and *what functions* government *should not* perform.

In "Government — An Ideal Concept," Leonard Read says, "It (government) is not, as some assert, a necessary evil. *When limited to its proper defensive scope*, it is a positive good. When exceeding its proper limitations and becoming aggressive, it is not a 'necessary' but a positive evil." (Emphasis added.) In this chapter, Mr. Read refers to Frederic Bastiat in a footnote. The author of "A Human Action Taxonomy" acknowledges his debt to Bastiat in the body of that chapter. The reader may correctly infer from these references that Frederic Bastiat is a teacher of teachers. We believe this Frenchman who lived over one hundred years ago more clearly understood and delineated the proper role of government than anyone we know who lived before or after him. The third chapter of this unit, "The State," is a sample of Bastiat's work.

The second part of this unit, "What's a Seat Worth?" and "Restitution, Regulation, and Redistribution," is probably the most entertaining part of the unit — and at the same time the most tragic. In these two chapters, the author gets down to particulars. H. L. Richardson is a California state legislator. From that position, he is well qualified to describe what Bastiat calls, in his book, *The Law*, "perversions" of government. Mr. Richardson's illustrations explicitly show how government gets out of bounds — how government becomes evil.

The third part of this unit deals with getting government back in bounds. The single chapter that makes up this third part deals, in

When We Are Free

large measure, with the market economy. We conclude this unit on government with this selection because we believe, as Ludwig von Mises writes,

> No government and no civil law can guarantee and bring about freedom otherwise than by supporting and defending the fundamental institutions of the market economy. Government means always coercion and compulsion and is by necessity the opposite of liberty. Government is a guarantor of liberty and is compatible with liberty only if its range is adequately restricted to the preservation of economic freedom. Where there is no market economy, the best-intentioned provisions of constitutions and laws remain a dead letter.

In short, even in, perhaps we should say *especially* in, this unit on government, we believe the focus should continue to be on the individual, on freedom, and on the market economy if government is to be good government.

CHAPTER 7

Government: An Ideal Concept

by Leonard E. Read

Government would not exist, nor would there be any reason for its existence, if men did not have problems with one another. Therefore, to determine why we should have government and to find out how much of it we should have, we must first form judgments on (a) what aspects of man are social, (b) what aspects are individual, and then (c) by analyzing the nature of organized force (the distinctive feature of government) decide on the extent to which force should be employed in man's relationship with man.

There can be no denying the assertion that man is a social as well as an individualistic being. Both the social and the individual aspects of our own lives are emphasized to us daily. These emphases are presented so numerously and in so many forms — indeed, so confusingly — that it is with difficulty we can tell one from the other. Some folks are so impressed with the social emphases that they see nothing individualistic about man, and others are so impressed with the individualistic emphases that they see nothing social about man. The former are likely to conclude as socialists; the latter, as anarchists — both being types of authoritarianism.

Man cannot live alone. This is meant, not as a figurative, but as a literal expression. Remove from any one of us all the rest of mankind, past and present, and no one of us could exist. We are an interdependent breed of creation. The writer of this essay, for instance, does not know how to raise the food he eats, to build the home in which he lives, to make the car he drives, to create the opportunities that are constantly presented to him, to write most of the books he reads, to get from the earth the gas that keeps him warm. Relative to the advantages that are his, he knows next to nothing. Alone he is impotent to the point of nonexistence. The same thing can reasonably be said about others.

Unanimity Requires Common Interest

Cooperation is required among members of society to perform the negative function of prohibiting obstacles to production, communication, and exchange. The cooperation ought to be as nearly unanimous as possible. Cooperation can approach unanimity only if the activities of the defensive agency be limited to those actions which have a common benefit to creative effort. Ideally, the only dissenters would be those who want to live by predation. If the agency of defense finds itself being used as an agency of plunder (aggressive force) — as in the case of our government today — cooperation will not tend toward unanimity. For in this instance, some of the members of society cooperate to benefit themselves at the expense of the other members, employing the agency to achieve their ends. The plundered members find it difficult to cooperate with the plundering members.

Mere participation in the activities of society's agency, such as unwilling military service or the unwilling payment of income to support the agency in overextended activities, does not qualify as cooperation. Cooperation in its highest form is a willing response, not the choice of the lesser of two evils. Willing response, approaching unanimity, is much to be desired. *But it is impossible except as society's agency is itself an accurate response to man's single in common social requirement: defense against those actions of man which inhibit creative energy and its exchange.* Man is a member of society in common with all other men in this respect only. His social agency, to be useful and not harmful, must limit itself to this one small but extremely important function which all men have socially in common. Then reason and justice, at least, will supply the basis for unanimous cooperation.

Limitation of Government Prescribed By Its Justification

Let the above ideas be emphasized in these terms: Any logical and just organization by society derives its existence from only one source: the common need for every man to protect himself against those who would limit his creative opportunities. Every human being is born with as much right to live his life creatively as any other man. Man, however, is incapable of protecting his life as a personal, individual project, and at the same time of realizing his human potential. That part of his inheritance which designates him as a product of society precludes this. By reason of this social circumstance, he is committed, in principle, to cooperating with his fellow men in the protective project of "one for all and all for one"; in a project that should make no distinction whatever as to persons; in a project where all ought to be regarded as equal; in a project where special privilege should be unknown.[1]

---

[1] It cannot be too much emphasized that human beings are not equal. Yet, we should all be equal before the law in the sense that we think of ourselves as equal before God.

Government: An Ideal Concept

The principle which justifies society's organization of a defensive arm — man's inheritance as an interdependent being — also prescribes the limitations on what the organization should do. In short, the law's limitation inheres in its justification.

Force is a dangerous thing. Therefore, society's organized arm is a dangerous instrument. It is not, as some assert, a necessary evil. When limited to its proper defensive scope, it is a positive good. When exceeding its proper limitations and becoming aggressive, it is not a "necessary" but a positive evil.

Two Types of Force

Force of the kind here discussed is of two types. There is repellent or defensive force. There is aggressive force. The latter is always evil. There are no exceptions. No man has any moral right to use aggressive force against any other man. Nor have any number of men, in or out of societal organizations, any moral right to use it. One of the most distressing fallacies having to do with government and liberty is the assumption that the state, an agency presumably of the people, has rights beyond those possessed by the people. For example, the state uses aggressive force against an individual, compelling him to exchange some of his income for the alleged prosperity of Tennessee Valley residents. No reasonable person would sanction such an aggressive action on the part of any single citizen. Therefore, no reasonable person can logically believe that any such control belongs to a multitude of citizens. From what source does this extracurricular "right" of the state to use aggressive force derive? It has no derivation. It is an arrogation. This arrogation is as untenable as the divine right of kings theory; indeed, it is the same thing with the divine excuse omitted.

Any person has the natural and moral right to use repellent or defensive force against any other person who would aggress against him. No person on this earth has any moral right of control over any other person superior to the defense of his own life and livelihood. Two persons banding together do not acquire moral rights of control over others superior to the rights held by each before their association. No increase in the number of individuals involved morally alters this in any way — even when the number reaches the 226,000,000 of this nation. Rights not possessed by individuals cannot properly be delegated to an agency, political or otherwise. Society's agency, then, will find the proper limits of its scope in exercising for everyone, without favor to any, the natural and moral rights inherent in its members.²

Tool of Liberty

The above concludes what is little more than a bare outline — a skeleton, so to speak — of the ideas that need to be considered in arriving at the principles and the theories of government and liberty. Government — which no doubt is what we will continue to call our organized agency of society, even though it be limited to defensive functions — is, if properly employed, an essential tool of liberty.

Government organized strictly in accord with right principle is an object more to be ardently hoped for than seriously expected. Yet, right principle must be deduced and have some measure of understanding if political expediency, controlled as it is by demagoguery and special interests, is not to rule and eventually overcome us. Political expediency feeds on the destructiveness it breeds. Every evil it evokes sets in motion other "compensating" evils. Political expediency, by its very nature, inevitably leads to a dead end.

Right principle is man's only compass. He often deviates from the course it suggests, but at least he can be aware of where he is by reference to it. Right principle is a beacon by which man can reverse himself after he has ventured into the evil ways which constantly beckon him.³

Right principle as relating to the limitation of government is deducible. Protecting the release of creative human energy and its exchange is suggested as the basis for sound deductions.

Victims of Hallucinations

There is, however, one unmistakable fact that can be gleaned from observation: Authoritarianism (aggressive force) is a fake! There is not a man nor any set of men who should ever have authoritarian power over creative energy and its exchange. Man's forceful intervention can only thwart, restrain, detain, repress, destroy. Let man intervene in the affairs of others only to restrain destructive energies; otherwise, insofar as others are concerned,

---

²An excellent development of this idea is to be found in *The Law* by Frederic Bastiat (Irvington-on-Hudson, N.Y.: Foundation for Economic Education, 1950).

³What is right will, of course, always remain debatable as between persons. The nearest anyone can come to practicing right is accurately to follow that which his conscience dictates as right. "Right principle," therefore, as I use it is obviously and necessarily right principle as I see it.

leave human energy alone! Contemplate the utter absurdity of any person's directing the energies relating to one day in the life of another! What man, then, is ever to be trusted who thinks he could direct the energy and energy exchanges of a whole nation of people? Does it seem obvious that authoritarians are the victims of hallucinations, for do they not believe that God's role is in no sense beyond their competency?

It is the riddance of authoritarianism in all its forms about which we need to concern ourselves socially. Authoritarianism is destructive, vicious energy.[4]

Man's intervention to restrain destructive action demands a society-wide organization — government. It is this defensive intervention that justifies as well as sets the limit for government. The defensive function is extremely difficult and calls for experts in the science of defense. The fact that incompetents get elected or appointed to public office, and substitute aggressive meddling in others' affairs for the defensive work which they find they cannot or will not perform, in no way lessens the need for government limited to defense.

The Purpose of Liberty

In concluding this essay, it is well to emphasize the idea that every living human being, if he would correctly interpret his own welfare, has a vested interest in the creative emergence of every other human being; that each person has a vested interest in the free, uninhibited flowing and exchange of the energies thus released; that the true interests of all, therefore, are in harmony; and that, finally, every individual has a vested interest in common with all other men in restraining all inhibitory influences to creative energy and creative energy exchanges. It is this latter common interest that constitutes the social aspect of man and warrants his organization of government within societies for defense. All else is individual, voluntary, and co-operative as individuals may choose; for all else is creative. This is the vast, indeed, the infinite, area of emergence.

Emergence — man's highest purpose — has two primary requirements. The first is an awareness of an Infinite Consciousness that man's emergence may have conscious purpose and direction.

---

[4] The use of repellent or defensive force does not qualify as destructive energy. If a person attempts to destroy me and he is destroyed by my defense, it is he who is accountable for his own destruction. He initiates the act that brings about his downfall. In effect, he commits suicide.

The second is liberty in order that emergence may be uninhibited and possible. Liberty can be defined, psychologically, as man freeing himself from his own negations and, sociologically, as man not playing God, either individually or collectively, through government or otherwise.

CHAPTER 8

A Human Action Taxonomy

by Dale M. Haywood

A taxonomy is a technique of classification. The zoologist, for example, uses the categories phylum, class, order, family, genus, and species to classify animals. This system of classification makes the zoologist's study more manageable, thus enabling him to "peg" correctly any given member in the entire animal kingdom.

The student of liberty may also find it useful to have a taxonomy, a taxonomy of human action. In his book, *The Law*, Frederic Bastiat provides just such a system for classifying human action. With knowledge of this taxonomy, the student of liberty can readily "peg" any human action and thus distinguish between actions that promote liberty from actions that erode liberty.

I have tried to extract the essence of *The Law* and put that essence in the form of a diagram — my human action taxonomy.

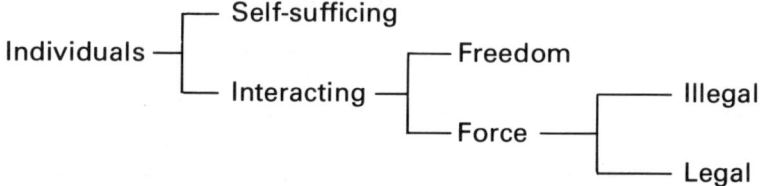

Reading the diagram from left to right, the starting point is the individual. All human action ultimately reduces to the actions of specific individuals. The individual is the most important element in society.

The individual may choose to be self-sufficient or to interact with others. At least theoretically, an individual can go it alone in life. However, at this stage in history, it is practically impossible to be self-sufficient. Realistically, we find ourselves on the "Individuals — Interacting" branch of the diagram.

There are alternative ways of interacting. We may interact with others freely, voluntarily, peacefully. Individuals interacting with others voluntarily are motivated by the prospect of profit, by the

---

From *The Freeman*, December 1978.

prospect of gain for *all* parties to the transaction. Thus, it seems logical to try to *maximize* the number of voluntary human actions.

Alternatively, we may interact with others forcefully, under coercion or the threat of coercion. When an individual interacts with others under compulsion or the threat of compulsion, not all parties gain. The predator may gain; the individual preyed upon certainly loses. Thus, it seems logical to try to *minimize* the number of human actions rooted in force.

Note that "Force" has two branches in the diagram. The upper branch is "Illegal." From time immemorial, some types of human action have been generally condemned. Actions such as theft, rape, and murder are examples of illegal, forceful interactions of individuals. Since most people are alert to such actions and since there is widespread agreement that these actions are reprehensible, these constitute a relatively small percentage of all human action. It is doubtful that the greatest perils to civilizations come from this category of human action.

We come now to perhaps the most instructive part of the diagram, the "Legal" branch of "Force." Government subsidies are examples of legal, forceful interactions of individuals. It is obvious that subsidies are legal, being duly sanctioned by law. Although the force in subsidies may not be so obvious, it is there nonetheless.

The Threat of Force

Subsidies are financed with taxes such as federal personal income taxes. I pay income taxes partly in fear of forceful reprisals if I do not. Tens of thousands of other citizens of the United States reason and act the same way I do, I surmise. So it is from the threat of force that at least some of us pay income taxes, from which subsidies are paid. Thus, it seems to me, subsidies are an example of legal, forceful interactions of individuals.

There is a feature of legal, as opposed to illegal, forceful interactions of individuals that makes this category of human action a special threat to our welfare. Since the federal government of the United States was founded, in part, to "establish justice," I suspect we may be lulled into thinking that all of the federal government's activities are consistent with this objective, i.e., that all such activities are just. Thus, legal, forceful human actions may insinuate themselves into a society of inattentive, uncritical individuals. But the fact that actions rooted in force are implemented by a government designed to "establish justice" leaves such actions still rooted in force.

Recall that in transactions rooted in force, the predators may gain but those preyed upon certainly lose. Those preyed upon are necessarily the producers in society. Surely as predators prey upon producers, the producers will become less inclined to produce. True, if the producers have accumulated output from the past and if they are currently very productive, they may endure considerable predation with no *apparent* harm to society for a while. But if the amount of predatory human action keeps growing and growing, the producers will, sooner or later, become less inclined and then disinclined to produce no matter how well off they are at the outset. With predation waxing and production waning in a society, that society is surely doomed.

It is not inevitable that this destructive process continue. By increasing the proportion of their voluntary, mutually profitable transactions, any group of individuals can invigorate, or reinvigorate, their society. Equipped with this human action taxonomy, the proponent of liberty can readily "peg" any human action and thus decide which actions he will take or support, and which actions he will reject or oppose. I trust that others may find this human action taxonomy helpful in the cause of human liberty.

When We Are Free

CHAPTER 9

The State

by Frederic Bastiat

(Editors' Note: Frederic Bastiat (1801-1850) was an economist, statesman, and author during a period when France was drifting rapidly toward socialism. His clear description of that trend and its evil consequences, written in 1849, merits serious consideration in the United States of America today.)

I wish someone would offer a prize — not of a hundred francs but of a million, with crowns, medals, and ribbons — for a good, simple, intelligible definition of the term, *The State*.

What an immense service such a definition would render to society!

The State! What is it? Where is it? What does it do? What should it do? We only know that it is a mysterious being; and, it is certainly the most petitioned, the most harassed, the most bustling, the most advised, the most reproached, the most invoked, and the most challenged of any being in the world.

I have not the honor of knowing my reader, but I would stake ten to one that sometime in the last six months you have designed Utopias, and if so, that you are looking to The State for the realization of them.

But alas! That poor unfortunate being, like Figaro, knows not which plea to hear nor where to turn. The hundred thousand mouths of the press and of the platform cry out all at once —

Organize work and the workmen.
Cover the country with railways.
Irrigate the plains.
Reforest the hills.
Establish model farms.
Colonize Algeria.
Educate the youth.
Assist the aged.
Equalize the profits of all trades.
Lend money without interest to all who wish to borrow.

From *Ideas on Liberty*, November 1955.

Emancipate Italy, Poland, and Hungary.
Encourage the arts, and train musicians and dancers for us.
Restrict commerce, and at the same time create a merchant marine.
Discover truth, and put a bit of sense into our heads. The mission of The State is to enlighten, to develop, to ennoble, to strengthen, and to sanctify the soul of the people.

"Wait, Gentlemen! A little patience," says The State beseechingly. "I will try to satisfy you, but for that I must have some resources. I have prepared plans for five or six entirely new taxes, the mildest in the world. You will see how gladly people will pay them."

But then a great hue and cry arises: "No! No! A fine thing — doing something with resources! This is hardly worthy of The State! Instead of loading us with new taxes, we call upon you to repeal the old ones. Decrease the salt tax, the liquor tax, the stamp tax, custom-house duties, monopoly license fees, and tolls."

In the midst of this tumult, the people have changed their government two or three times for failing to satisfy all their demands. To date, everything presenting itself under the name of The State is soon overthrown by the people, precisely because it fails to fulfill the somewhat contradictory features of its platform.

I fear we are, in this respect, the dupes of one of the strangest illusions which has ever taken possession of the human mind.

Work or Plunder

Man recoils from effort, from suffering. Yet, he is condemned by nature to the suffering of privation if he does not make the effort to work. He has only a choice then, between these two: privation, and work. How can he manage to avoid both? He always has and always will find, only one means: *to enjoy the labor of others;* to arrange it so that the effort and the satisfaction do not fall upon each in their natural proportion, but that some would bear all the effort while all the satisfaction would go to others. This is the origin of slavery and plunder, whatever form it takes — whether wars, impositions, violences, restrictions, frauds, etc., monstrous abuses, but in accord with the idea which has given them birth.

Slavery is subsiding, thank heaven, and our disposition to defend our property prevents direct and open plunder from being easy. However, there remains the unfortunate, primitive inclination in all men to divide the lot of life into two parts, throwing the trouble upon others and keeping the satisfaction for themselves. Let us examine a current manifestation of this sad tendency.

The State

Vehicle For Plunder

The oppressor no longer uses his own force directly upon his victim. No, our conscience has become too sensitive for that. There is still the tyrant and his victim, but between them is an intermediary which is The State — the Law itself. What could be better designed to silence our scruples and — more important — to overcome all resistance? Thus do all of us, by various claims and under one pretext or another, appeal to The State:

"I am dissatisfied with the ratio between my labor and my pleasures. In order to establish the desired balance, I should like to take part of the possessions of others. But that is a dangerous thing. Couldn't you facilitate it for me? Couldn't you give me a good post? Or restrain my competitors' business? Or perhaps lend me some interest-free capital, which you will have taken from its rightful owners? Or bring up my children at the taxpayers' expense? Or grant me a subsidy? Or assure me a pension when I reach my fiftieth year? By this means I shall achieve my goal with an easy conscience, for the law will have acted for me. Thus I shall have all the advantages of plunder, without the risk or the disgrace!"

All of us are petitioning The State in this manner, yet it has been proven that The State has no means of granting privileges to some without adding to the labor of others.

The State is the great fiction through which everybody endeavors to live at the expense of everybody.

Today, as in the past, nearly everyone would like to profit by the labor of others. No one dares admit such a feeling; he even hides it from himself. So what does he do? He imagines an intermediary; he appeals to The State, and every class in its turn comes and says to it: "You, who can do so justifiably and honestly, take from the public; and we will partake of the proceeds."

Alas! The State is only too much disposed to follow this diabolical advice; for it is composed of ministers and officials — of men, in short — who, like all other men, desire in their hearts and eagerly seize every opportunity to increase their wealth and influence. The State quickly perceives the advantages it can derive from the role entrusted to it by the public. It will be the judge, the master of the destinies of all. It will take a lot: then much will remain for itself. It will multiply the number of its agents, and increase its functions, until it finally acquires crushing proportions.

But the most remarkable thing is the astonishing blindness of the public while all this takes place. In the past, when victorious soldiers reduced the vanquished to slavery they were barbarous, but they were not foolish. Their object, like ours, was to live at the expense of others; but they succeeded, where we fail. What are we to think of a people who never seem to realize that *reciprocal plunder* is no less plunder because it is reciprocal; that it is no less criminal, because it is carried out legally and peacefully; that it adds nothing to the public good, but rather diminishes it by the amount of the cost of that expensive intermediary we call The State?

The State Personified

And this great illusion we have placed, for the edification of the people as a frontispiece to the Constitution. Here are the first words of the preamble:

"France has constituted itself a Republic to . . . raise all the citizens to an ever-increasing degree of morality, enlightenment, and well-being."

Thus it is France — an *abstraction* — which is to raise the French — or *realities* — to morality, well-being, and so on. Isn't it our blind attachment to this strange delusion that leads us to expect everything from a power not our own? Isn't it suggesting that there is, apart from the French people, a virtuous, enlightened, rich being who can and should bestow its favors upon them?

The Americans develop a different idea of the relationship of the citizens with The State, when they placed these simple words at the beginning of their Constitution:

"We, the people of the United States, in order to form a more perfect Union, establish Justice, insure domestic Tranquility, provide for the common defence, promote the general Welfare, and secure the Blessings of Liberty to ourselves and our Posterity, do ordain . . ."

Here is no shadowy creation, no *abstraction*, from which the citizens may demand everything. They expect nothing except from themselves and their own energy.

I contend that the *personification* of The State has been in the past and will be in the future, a fertile source of calamities and revolutions. There is the public on one side, The State on the other, considered as two distinct beings; the latter obligated to bestow upon the former, the former having the right to claim from the latter a flood of human benefits. What must happen?

The State has two hands, one for receiving and the other for giving — a rough hand and a smooth one. The activity of the second is necessarily subordinate to the activity of the first. Strictly speaking, The State can take and not give back. This can be seen and can be explained by the porous, absorbing nature of its hands, which always retain part and sometimes all of what it touches.

But that which is never seen, which never will be seen, and which cannot even be imagined, is that The State can return *more* to the people than it has taken from them. Therefore it is ridiculous for us to appear before The State in the humble attitude of beggars. It is utterly impossible for it to confer a specific benefit upon some of the individuals who make up the community, without inflicting a greater injury upon the community as a whole.

The State's Dilemma

Our demands, therefore, place The State in an obvious dilemma! If it refuses to grant the requested benefit, it is accused of weakness, ill-will, and incapacity. If it tries to grant their requests, it is obliged to load the people with increased taxes — to do more harm than good — and to bring upon itself general displeasure from another quarter.

So, the public has two hopes, and The State makes two promises: *many benefits and no taxes* — hopes and promises, which, being contradictory, can never be realized.

Is not this the cause of all our revolutions? For between The State, which lavishly promises the impossible, and the public, whose hopes can never be realized, there come to interpose two types of men: the ambitious and the Utopians. The circumstances give them their cue. These office seekers need only cry out to the people: "The authorities are deceiving you. If we were in their place, we would load you with benefits and exempt you from taxes."

And the people believe, and the people hope, and the people substitute a new government for the old.

No sooner are their friends in charge of things, than they are called upon to redeem their pledge. "Give us work, bread, assistance, credit, instruction, colonies," say the people, "and meanwhile deliver us, as you promised, from the clutches of the tax gatherer."

The new government is no less embarrassed than the former one, for it is easier to promise the impossible than to do it. It tries to gain time which it needs for maturing its vast projects. First it makes a few timid attempts: on one hand, it slightly expands primary education; on the other, it makes a small reduction in the liquor tax. But the contradiction always confronts the administration: if it would be philanthropic, it must attend to its treasury; if it neglects the treasury, it must give up being philanthropic.

These two promises are always and inevitably clashing with one another. To live upon credit, that is, to exhaust the future, is certainly a temporary method of reconciling them — an attempt to do a little good now, at the expense of a great deal of harm in the future. But this procedure calls forth the specter of bankruptcy, which puts an end to credit. What is to be done then? Why then, the new government defends itself boldly. It unites its forces to maintain itself: It smothers opinion, has recourse to arbitrary measures, ridicules its former slogans, declares that it is impossible to govern except at the risk of being unpopular; in short, it proclaims itself *governmental*.

And this is what other candidates for office are waiting for. They exploit the same illusion, follow the same course, obtain the same success, and are soon swallowed up in the same abyss.

Big Benefits, Little Taxes — Impossible!

The latest manifesto of the Montagnards, which they issued at the time of the presidential election, concludes with these words: — *"The State ought to give a great deal to the people, and take little from them."* It is always the same tactics, or rather, the same mistake. The State must:

Give free instruction and education to all the citizens.

Give a general and professional education, as much as possible adapted to the needs, talents, and capacities of each citizen.

Teach every citizen his duty to God, to man, and to himself; develop his perceptions, his aptitudes, and his faculties; teach him, in short, the skill of his trade; make him understand his own interests, and give him a knowledge of his rights.

Place within the reach of all literature and the arts, the heritage of thought, the treasures of the mind, and all those intellectual possessions which elevate and strengthen the soul.

Give compensation for every disaster, fire, flood, etc., experienced by a citizen. (The *et cetera* means more than it says.)

Act as mediator in the relations between capital and labor, and become the regulator of credit.

Give substantial encouragement and effectual support to agriculture.

Purchase railroads, canals, and mines — and doubtless administer them with its characteristic industrial ability!

Encourage useful experiments, promote and assist them by every means likely to make them successful. As a regulator of credit, it will have extensive control over industrial and agricultural associations in order to assure their success.

The State *must* do all this, in addition to the services to which it is already pledged! For instance, it is always to maintain a menacing attitude towards foreigners. The signers of the manifesto say

The State

that: "Bound together by this holy union, and by the precedents of the French Republic, we carry our wishes and hopes beyond the barriers which despotism has raised between nations. The rights which we desire for ourselves, we desire for all those who are oppressed by the yoke of tyranny; we desire that our glorious army should, if necessary, again be the army of liberty."

You see that the gentle hand of The State — that good hand which gives and distributes — will be very busy under the direction of these reformers. You think perhaps it will be the same with the rough hand — that hand which penetrates and takes from our pockets?

Do not deceive yourselves. The politicians would not know their trade, if they had not the art, when showing the gentle hand, to conceal the rough one. Their reign will assuredly be the jubilee of the taxpayers!

"It is luxuries, not necessaries," they say, "which ought to be taxed."

Won't it be wonderful that the treasury, in overwhelming us with favors, will content itself with curtailing our luxuries!

This is not all. This party of reformers intends that "taxation shall lose its oppressive character, and be only an act of brotherhood." Good heavens! I know it is the fashion to thrust brotherhood in everywhere, but I did not imagine it would ever be put into the proclamations of the tax gatherer.

Well, I ask the impartial reader, is this not childishness, and more than that, dangerous childishness? Is it not inevitable that we shall have revolution after revolution, if it is once decided never to stop till this contradiction is realized: "Give nothing to The State and receive much from it?"

Citizens! At all times, two political systems have been in existence, and each can justify itself with good reasons. According to one of them, The State should do a lot, but then it should take a lot. According to the other, this twofold activity ought to be limited. We have to choose between these two systems.

But the third system, which partakes of both the others, and consists in exacting everything from The State without giving it anything, is chimerical, absurd, childish, contradictory, and dangerous. Those who advocate such a system are only flattering and deceiving you, or at least are deceiving themselves.

As for us, we consider that The State is and ought to be nothing whatever but *community force* organized, not to be an instrument of oppression and mutual plunder among citizens, but, on the contrary, to guarantee to each his own, and to cause justice and security to reign.

When We Are Free

CHAPTER 10

What's A Seat Worth?

by H. L. Richardson

What is a seat in the legislature worth?

Not too long ago a special election was held for a vacated seat in the California State Senate. By the time the dust had settled, over $400,000 was spent to elect a new man to the office.

People asked, "Why was so much money spent for a job that pays only $21,000?" Answer: Because of what the job represents. A state legislator may vote on expenditures exceeding eighteen billion dollars, and often a single vote can be very important.

Eighteen billion dollars. That's a lot of money. I could give you a few staggering examples of how much a billion is, but just try to count dollars (one dollar, two dollars, etc.) as fast as you can. Go ahead, try it. If your voice and lungs could hold out, in about an hour you would be up to 9,800 dollars. In a twenty-four-hour day you would be up to 135,200; in a week, 946,400; and in a month, 4,056,000. A year would take you to a little over forty-eight million. In other words, yakking away as fast as you can, you haven't even dented a billion in a whole year. In fact, if you started counting on your first birthday, you couldn't count to eighteen billion if you lived to be 360 years old.

If that doesn't stagger you, nothing will. Yet, a billion dollars is how much the California legislature spends in less than one month and the feds do it in a single day. When a legislative body taxes and dispenses enormous amounts of capital, you can bet your bottom dollar that those who want their share are going to make a beeline to the hallowed halls of the legislature and that the legislators are going to receive a great deal of attention from both the GOTS and the WANTS.

Those who have a vested interest in maintaining the power of the legislature play an inordinate role in perpetuating their favorites in office or electing "their kind of men."

Extracted from *What Makes You Think We Read the Bills?* by H. L. Richardson and reprinted here with permission from Caroline House Publishers, Inc., P.O. Box 738, Ottawa, Illinois 61350.

"Their kind of men" usually means the kind that can be counted upon to vote the "right" way on bills relating to the industry.

Getting Political Clout

Let me offer an example of a group that has a great deal to gain from the "right" decisions by the legislature.

The CTA (California Teachers Association) represents approximately 200,000 teachers in California. Most teachers belong to this group. The teaching profession is heavily influenced by the actions of the legislature. Their tenure, sabbatical leaves, vacations, sick pay, retirement, salaries, and a host of privileges are directly influenced by the actions of the legislature.

Quite a number of years ago the teachers employed a little elementary arithmetic and discovered that it is a lot easier dealing with a handful of legislators than having to influence each school board in the state. In fact, all that need be done is to control the committees that hear education bills. In the senate, eight of the eleven members of the education committee receive substantial contributions from the California Teachers Association.

Some folks think that lobby money comes into play only after a candidate has been elected. The prevailing assumption is that every new legislator arriving in Sacramento is a political maiden waiting to be deflowered by some unscrupulous lobbyists.

Actually, pressure groups are seldom attracted to political Pollyannas. Most successful pressure groups are active in the primary campaigns, trying to get "their kind of statesman" nominated. One may be sure they will have checked out the candidate's "feelings" on certain matters.

For a flight into fancy, imagine the representatives of the California Teachers Association, the extremely powerful and well-heeled teachers' union, interviewing a candidate in the following manner:

CTA: Do you believe that teachers are underpaid?

CANDIDATE: Teachers are overpaid, by and large. If anything, some teachers' salaries should be cut while others should be raised. I believe in a merit system.

CTA: Hmm! How do you view our tenure laws?

CANDIDATE: I believe they should be abolished. Too many incompetent teachers hide behind tenure and should be dismissed.

CTA: Mercy! Do you believe in collective bargaining for teachers and the right of teachers to strike?

CANDIDATE: I do not! I believe the educators have a captive

monopoly on education and secure jobs that preempt those rights. Any teacher who strikes should be fired!

CTA: Golly jeepers! Thank you, sir, for your frank opinions. We certainly respect your right to your views, and because we believe that the legislature should be a forum for all kinds of opinions, we are going to contribute heartily to your campaign.

Quite a fairy tale, isn't it?

If you know anyone who believes that the CTA hands out campaign contributions under the above circumstances, then protect him. It won't be long before somebody sells him that bridge that stretches from Oakland to San Francisco.

When the day arrives that the CTA or a union gives money to its opposition, then Bambi will rule the forest, Alice will have returned from Wonderland, children will refuse free passes to Disneyland, and lawyers will turn down cases because of ethical considerations.

Candidates who run for political office are screened, reviewed, and, if there is a possibility of their being successful, financially helped by special-interest groups.

Pay the Piper, Call the Tune

This brings up a very important point. Most candidates usually have a certain philosophical perspective *before* they are elected, and it is often because of their "reliability" that special-interest groups such as the State Employees Association and the teachers unions support them.

The public-employee unions and other special interests then become the candidate's constituency. For all practical purposes they are willing to cast green bread upon the political waters. Money is needed to get elected and then reelected. Printers are swell guys and so are typesetters and copywriters and photographers, but each has definite mandrake capabilities. To prove my point, just ask one voluntarily to give of his time and effort to compose a campaign brochure. Watch him vanish into thin air.

Campaigns are costly and all of the gobbledygook about broad citizen participation is usually restricted to voting. Less than one percent of all registered voters contribute directly to political campaigns. People are willing to part with their opinions but not with their money. Those who do contribute gain the ear of the candidate. There are those who contribute because they like to support men who reflect their own political principles and who ask nothing but that the candidate stay faithful to his beliefs. These are usually the politically active party faithful.

Some people contribute because they are familiar with the candidate and want someone elected whom they know. I call these volunteer contributors. They are important, and if a candidate receives the bulk of his contributions from these sources, he has a greater degree of independence. But in many cases, this constituency is the minority. Soliciting this kind of contribution takes time and usually these contributions are small by comparison. The CTA drops $10,000 at a time. Most hometown contributors who donate $25 feel like philanthropists.

It's a rare day someone calls a candidate and says, "Charlie, I hear you are running for office. My $1,000 check is in the mail and if it's not enough, I'll send more."

If any candidate or officeholder says that he received the bulk of his contributions in unsolicited donations, don't leave your wallet unattended. Chances are, the truth is not his constant companion. Contributions rarely come without effort. Even churches have to solicit funds every Sunday. Ushers systematically walk up the aisles with empty receptacles waiting to be filled. If the Lord's churches have to ask, no one else is immune from passing the plate, least of all, politicians.

Most solons like being in the legislature, so the contributor who puts the biggest hunk of folding money into the platter is the one who gets to sit in the first political pew.

Government Department Lobbyists

It would not be fair if I didn't mention another kind of lobbyist who rattles around the legislative halls. They are not called lobbyists. But for all intents and purposes, that is what they are. These are the "representatives" of the many government agencies and bureaus that have so much to gain or lose by legislative action. These stalwarts of verbal evasion are supposed authorities who are sent forth to advise the legislature on matters affecting their departments.

Bureaucrats assigned to represent the different departments before the legislative committees are the most masterful practitioners of the art of omission. With unbounded authority they speak longer than most, and say less more eloquently than any other group of witnesses.

Everyone has heard of the professional lobbyists, those who are employed by industry, labor, "consumer" groups, et al., but rarely does one think of a governmental department as having lobbyists who come before committees. Nonetheless, they do exist and they do lobby for a particular point of view — that of their respective departments.

If a bill causes displeasure, one can count on the department's representative to be present and accounted for when the committee is called to order. Even if that department has no "official position" one can rest assured that it will get its two cents in one way or another. Many a governor has found that the administration he supposedly controls often sabotages his own favorite legislation. There are few politicians equal to an upper-level civil servant in the art of guile, and no greased pig at the county fair can match a civil-service public-relations man who doesn't want to answer a direct question.

After many years, it must become habit-forming. I know a representative for the State Department of Education who doesn't have *yes* or *no* in his vocabulary.

One must remember that these department representatives are paid to be professional noncommittors. All of them are chock-full of statistics, dates, surveys, and conference reports — miniunivacs in unobtrusive suits, ready to spout irrelevant information whenever needed to confuse inquiring legislators.

It's a fact: one better know the answer before the question is asked, if one wants the straight dope from a bureaucrat. Also, the departmental expert must be convinced that the legislator can find out the answer before he will respond accurately.

Legislators can be a threat to the bureaucracy, so we are always a potential problem to the sanctimonious civil servant. One may be assured that the representative assigned to feed the legislators whatever they "need" to know will be the best silver-tongued smoothy the department has to offer.

Confrontation with Lobbyist

Lobbying is only for those with the toughest hide, the smoothest smile, and the calm befitting a saint. Ruffled feathers are a no-no; anger is not cool. Those who can't handle the action soon retire.

A number of years ago a new lobbyist for the foreign-language teachers association asked for an appointment so that he could lobby me on a bill dear to the hearts of all foreign-language teachers. The bill would have required study of foreign languages in the elementary grades — a real plum for all of the unemployed foreign-language teachers.

He was a pleasant chap. I assumed a relaxed pose and we had a delightful discussion about education in general and the importance of learning for the little tots. The bill he was lobbying for proposed expanding, as he stated, "the opportunities to enrich a child's learning experience." I asked him why he thought a child needed to study Spanish, French, or German in the fifth grade. What was the value to the child?

"Senator," he replied, "language is a meaningful experience. Someday that child may find himself in a foreign land and he would be capable of communicating with people of other countries, thereby enriching his life and bringing greater understanding among people of the world." He smiled, reclined in his chair peacefully. I'm sure he thought he had given me a beautiful thought for the day. He was ill prepared for my response.

"Horse pucky," I replied. I leaned forward and glared at him from over my desk. "Our colleges are graduating boatloads of teachers who have majored in foreign languages and they can't find jobs. Your job is to get legislation passed which mandates expanded foreign-language programs so that more foreign-language teachers can be hired!" He sat there with his mouth agape, stunned. Obviously, nobody had questioned his pitch before now.

I continued. "Listen, we're barely teaching kids to read English. Few can properly structure a sentence by fifth grade, and now you want to cram a foreign language down their throats — a language that ninety-five percent will forget by the time they reach the age of fifteen. Most of them will be lucky to remember what 'adios' means." I was purposely rough on him. He was new and I wanted to see how he would react.

"Boy, you're tough!" he replied.

"Well," I shot back, "it's true, isn't it?"

"Well, er, ah, uh," he stammered. He was too honest to say I was wrong and too chicken to say yes. He mumbled a lot and beat a hasty retreat from my office. Needless to say, he didn't last long as a lobbyist. I ran into him a few years after, and he was comfortably ensconced in a job that did not require legislative contact. He seemed much happier.

Bonnie and Clyde

An effective representative for those who constantly seek governmental handouts from the taxpayer goody-wagon must have a passel of defensive clichés ready for all occasions and the ability to slip a verbal punch with the agility of a trained boxer.

A proper and accepted response to my verbal blast would have been to use the "wide-eyed and wounded" technique. First, open the eyes as wide as possible and hold them open for at least five to ten seconds. Then draw back, if seated, or step back if standing, and stagger imperceptibly to create the impression of being mortally wounded. "Senator! How *can* you say that! We are just interested in the well-being of the children. Language is an important part of the learning experience and foreign-language teachers spend years learning how to master communication. Why, if nations could speak to each other we could possibly stop wars. . ."

See what I mean? A real pro would have feigned a mortal wound and then bled all over me. I would have been an isolationist for opposing his bill, a child-hater, and, of course, a warmonger.

An effective legislative advocate learns to live the role and as the famous dramatist Chayefsky stated, "If you are going to play the part of an apple, *be* an apple." If you are going to be a legislative advocate, *believe* in that turkey legislation and dare any opponent to doubt the efficacy of your gobbler.

Lobbyists are here to stay — that is, as long as the people keep turning over their hard-earned money for legislators to dole out to whom they see fit.

Lobbyists and legislators — like Bonnie and Clyde.

CHAPTER 11

Restitution, Regulation, and Redistribution

by H. L. Richardson

People make a mistake when they pay their legislators good salaries, expect them to work full time, and then complain about all the governmental intervention in their lives. Do we get mad when a jackass brays or a pigeon decorates a statue? So, why become irate when legislators do their thing?

The nature of legislators is to legislate, and that is what they do. They work full time introducing new bills that create more agencies, bureaus, commissions, and regulatory functions of government. They believe that this is what is expected of them, and as long as the public expects legislators to make laws, they will.

One must remember that laws are not just friendly suggestions on how people should act; each carries with it the full force of the police power of the state. Refusing to adhere to the letter of the law is punishable by fines or trips to the Crowbar Motel. Just willfully break some regulation, and see how long it takes the police powers of the legislature to punish your indiscretion.

Laws can be divided into three different categories. I call them the three Rs — restitution, regulation, and redistribution.

Restitution

Restitution is the fundamental premise of both our criminal and civil laws. If the person or property of a citizen is injured or damaged, our Judeo-Christian and English common-law heritage holds that government should apprehend the offender and hold him responsible for his actions. The simple justice of this system is sometimes not readily apparent to the modern mind, conditioned as it is to such phrases as "crimes against society" and "social justice."

Although crime was indeed regarded as a sin against God, restitution was made directly to the victim. When a fine was imposed or a period of servitude required, the money did not flow into the

---

Extracted from *What Makes You Think We Read the Bills?* by H. L. Richardson and reprinted here with permission from Caroline House Publishers, Inc., P.O. Box 738, Ottawa, Illinois 61350.

coffers of the state, nor was the labor diverted to penal institutions to paint license plates. Any consideration extracted from the criminal accrued to the victim or the victim's family.

Before casting this concept aside as barbaric and outmoded, let us first consider the present state of affairs in our criminal-justice system. Current judicial thought holds the criminal responsible for a "crime against society." Society, or the state, is the victim; and, when a fine is paid, it is the state which receives the benefit. The actual victim is looked upon as nothing more than a witness. Instead of restitution for his loss, the victim instead must pay taxes to feed and clothe the criminal while he works off his "debt to society" in prison.

The older idea of restitution places an actual value on the damage or injury, and thus the punishment fits the crime in a very real sense. The current concept of crimes against "society," however, has made any genuine restitution to the actual victim virtually impossible. Since criminals are not held specifically accountable for their crimes, we have created an entire class of criminals for whom crime pays, figuratively and literally.

Before the advent of societal crime, those who refused to make restitution or those who habitually victimized their neighbors did indeed suffer punishment. But for the great mass of those committing crimes, rather than to languish in a jail cell, the opportunity was given to "make right" offenses.

By permitting the offender the opportunity to work productively to clear his record and his conscience, the system made restitution to the victim, punished the offender in proportion to his crime, and provided rehabilitative services superior to those found in our current criminal-justice system. By comparison, our current practices look like a twentieth-century version of debtors' prison.

Since our present system has had the effect of creating a class of career criminals, we accomplish little more through incarceration than fattening up our thieves and murderers for another foray into the community. Most are not rehabilitated. They suffer no remorse. And, needless to say, unless capital punishment serves as the ultimate sentence for the habitual offender and incorrigible, no system of restitution, whether it be incarceration and payment of fines to the state or payment or service to the victim, can effectively control the criminal population and maintain peace and order in the community. Instead of leaving both criminal and victim bitter, as does our current system, restitution tempers justice with mercy.

Although the abandonment of this concept of restitution has been most evident in our criminal laws, the growing judicial practice of assigning liability where there has been no fault threatens to spread the medical "malpractice" dilemma into every area of our civil law. If that occurs, then the last bastion of lawful restitution will have been sacrificed to the advocates of "social" justice.

This concept of social justice, by denying individual fault, denies individual responsibility. It should come as no surprise, then, to find that as the principles of individual liberty and restitution wane, the two other Rs — regulation and redistribution — come increasingly into play.

Regulation

Regulatory laws are founded upon the premise that government has the right, as well as the social responsibility, to prevent people from performing certain acts. You-can't-build-this-high-unless-you-build-this-wide laws. You-can't-mix-this-glop-with-this-gook laws. You-can't-ratchet-this-unless-you-remedy-that laws. You-can't-teach-this-unless-that-regulation-is-met laws. Regulatory laws are laws that deny elbowroom.

Legislative authors always have a good reason for proposing such laws and the "public" is always the beneficiary — so they think. But, inevitably, somebody is told he can't do what he was doing before, unless some agency or bureau gives him approval.

Governmental do-gooders love to regulate; they love to protect us from ourselves. Regulation appeals to the mother instinct, not to mention the egos of legislators and bureaucrats alike. Since they know what's best for us, it stands to reason they must protect their "children" from harm. They view man as a purely social animal, who has neither responsibility for his actions nor a claim to inalienable freedoms.

Regulating human behavior is very tempting to legislators. It makes us feel so noble. Legislative nobility has been responsible for laws that prohibit people from skydiving while drunk. We regulate how sweet a grape must be before it can be sold, the sizes of boxes in which all produce is shipped, and even the amount of water permissible in toilet bowls. Next we probably will regulate how many times one may flush.

Regulation Always Hurts Someone

Whenever government really gets rolling on the regulation road, someone always gets hurt; individuals suffer, often those who are incapable of fighting back. As an example, let me tell you about Carl Forsberg, chicken plucker from Auburn.

Carl Forsberg is a man in his early sixties — independent, proud and a distinct individualist. Mr. Forsberg is also a cripple, and many normal avenues of employment are therefore restricted to him. However, as it is with most Americans of his generation, ingenuity is practically a part of his character. With the help of friends he constructed on the back of his property a three-room shack. The structure was not beautiful, but it was functional enough to house the equipment Carl had bought. The machinery was chicken-plucking equipment. Carl Forsberg had gone into the chicken-plucking business.

Anyone who has ever had the experience of relieving fowl of their feathers will testify that it is an occasion not soon forgotten — a foul experience, if you will pardon the pun. I have yet to find a person who takes delight in it, but many people do things because of economic necessity. To Carl, it was a financial decision. It was either plucking chickens or becoming a ward of the public.

It wasn't long before many people in the Auburn area frequented Carl's business and several of the restaurants came to him for his services. His final product was a plucked chicken, clean and neat, placed in a cellophane bag, twenty-five cents a bird. Carl wasn't prosperous, but at least he wasn't standing in the welfare line.

Enter villain — stage left, the Division of Public Health, Department of Agriculture, protector of the people. It seems that the department, in 1968, raised its standards concerning what constituted a sanitary chicken-plucking house; and, alas, Carl's homemade establishment did not meet the new regulations. In order to comply with the suggested changes made by the department, it would have cost Mr. Forsberg thousands of dollars. There were cracks in the cement floor, his wiring was exposed in some places, the refrigeration unit was not what the department liked, etc.; so Mr. Forsberg was asked to bring his establishment up to standards or shut his doors to business.

Mr. Forsberg, in order to comply with the law, closed down. But now this rugged individual from Auburn was caught between the proverbial rock and the hard place. He still abhorred welfare. He enjoyed being his own man and friends still came to him wanting him to clean their chickens. They were not concerned about department standards because they knew he kept his place extremely clean, cracked floors and all. So Mr. Forsberg, against the restrictions of the Department of Agriculture, plucked a few chickens for friends who wanted his services. The paradox is that the regulations allowed Mr. Forsberg to pluck wild birds, pheasants, ducks, quail, and geese, but somehow or other forbade him from picking domesticated birds. The distinction may seem somewhat obscure to you and me, but not to the minds of the Department of Agriculture's Division of Public Health.

It was not long before the government found out about his undercover chicken plucking, so public-health officials hauled him before the court and he was ordered to desist. He was breaking the law, it was stated. The court gave him the proverbial slap on the wrist.

Not long afterward, and again out of the kindness of his heart, he accepted a deal from a friend. If Carl would clean some birds, in exchange for his services he could keep half of them to feed his family. He accepted the offer; no money was being exchanged. Unfortunately, Carl was caught cleaning the chickens. He was arrested. This time the judge fined him $200 or ten days in jail. Mr. Forsberg did not have the $200, so he spent ten days in the county jail. His crime? Plucking chickens for a friend. The offense? Breaking a government regulation.

Was anyone hurt by Mr. Forsberg's actions? No. Were people forced to use his services? No. In fact, they wanted Carl to clean their chickens. It is a sorry state of affairs when an American citizen can be jailed like a common criminal for performing a service others desire while harming no one in the process.

I believe the tail feathers have been plucked on that proud eagle that represents this country. Can one doubt that Americans are going to regulate themselves right out of their freedoms if the direction in which the bureaucracy is headed is not altered? Have not other nations strangled themselves to death in rules and regulations purportedly enacted to protect their citizens? The case of Carl Forsberg should be a warning to all.

Regulation to Control Competition

Lying beneath the facade of "public good" that comes from governmental regulations lurk the special interests which prosper from governmental intervention and restrictions.

Mediocre corporations and businesses find that regulating competition out of existence is sometimes far easier than competing in the marketplace. The free market has its perils and many large bureaucratic corporations, fearing competition from smaller, more efficient competitors, seek regulations and standards to which they alone can adhere.

Some businessmen find it "convenient" for government to regulate facets of their industry for the advantage of some within their profession. Standardization is the watchword. Businessmen naively believe they can control the governmental commissions they help create, but inevitably, the regulatory agency grows and grows until it is questionable who controls whom. The question is ultimately answered to the dissatisfaction of all, save the government bureaucracy.

Many businesses recognize that regulations are convenient tools for controlling competition. Here's a classic case of regulating competitors.

Many years ago, some segments of California agriculture asked the legislature to control the size of *all* containers used to ship fruits and vegetables, right down to the slat size on the boxes. Standardization was the reason given. If a grower wanted to ship cantaloupes to market in a bigger crate, for instance, he would have to get a bill passed allowing him to do so.

One poor soul had the misfortune to be inventive. He successfully experimented and developed a larger cauliflower. It was a superior product. He came to the Department of Agriculture to request permission to ship his product to the eastern markets in a larger box. The standard box was too small for three heads across and too big for two heads. A temporary permit was granted. His product was a smashing success! The next year he had his local senator introduce a bill to allow him to continue using the larger crate. His bill was defeated.

Why? you ask. Simple. His competitors couldn't grow a cauliflower as large as his, and since there were more of them than there was of him, they implored their legislators to defeat the bill — which they did. The consumer will never have the opportunity to buy this cauliflower because the inventive farmer went back to growing the standard sizes. The housewife, to this day, doesn't know she was denied a better product because of regulations.

Regulatory laws have been used to control competition from time immemorial. Associations, unions, businessmen, pressure groups, do-gooders — all love the regulatory laws of government. They can restrict and modify behavior to fit their norms. Americans have become so accustomed to accepting the regulatory function of government that they hardly question the rightness of regulatory laws or the legitimacy of government's "right to regulate."

The more I see of government intervention, the surer I am that America would be better off if we abolished *all* regulatory laws, took our chances with a few who would take advantage of the lack of regulation, and then stiffened our laws on fraud and bunko. In other words, sock it to the merchant or worker who deceives, cheats, and defrauds, but leave the vast number of citizens alone from the stifling impact of governmental regulations. I'm sure that the consumer would be better off in the long and short run. True competition and free entry into the labor market soon would bring prices down for the consumer — not to mention the vast saving in taxes paid to run the governmental agencies that oversee all the regulatory laws.

Redistribution

The third type of law is the worst — redistribution of the wealth. These laws are the ones that attract most of the special-interest groups to the legislative halls — organizations, special lobbying groups, governmental beneficiaries — to make sure they get their share of the loot, or, conversely, to make sure they do not pick up the tab.

Redistributive laws take from one group and (as the legislators see fit) give to some other group. They are properly called nest-feathering laws. Somebody's nest gets the feathers from some plucked taxpayer; or put another way, one group gets the nest and the other gets the bird.

People shouldn't confuse redistributive laws with taxes imposed for direct services received by the public.

Nobody complains too loudly about taxes when they are the direct beneficiaries, as in the case of fire and police protection, a municipal sewage system, or water district. Taxes are usually proportionate to the use, and the taxpayer can see the direct benefit to himself and his family.

The major tax inequities are inevitably in areas where there is no measurable direct benefit to the taxed — welfare, food stamps, education, foreign aid, and a myriad of other social programs designed to redistribute wealth from the haves to the have-nots — to the plucker from the pluckee. Redistributive laws are responsible for over two-thirds of all governmental taxation.

The vast number of today's politicians see themselves as the arbitrators overseeing who gets what from whom and who keeps how much of what's left. Unfortunately, the public has grown to accept the socialist premise that redistributing the wealth *is* the function of representative government; and if the elected government takes from one to give to another, then it is moral. Somehow, the process of passing a law makes that which was immoral, moral. Somehow, when a majority of those elected vote affirmatively to allow one group to plunder another, legitimacy is conferred upon an act once deemed thievery. Redistributive government is an alien concept to those who profess freedom of individual rights, and such government is repugnant once it is understood.

Suppose I asked someone to set aside money for his medical benefits and he refused, and then suppose I pulled a weapon and forced him to contribute, I would, quite properly, be regarded as a thief, a blackguard, a tyrant, a robber, and a brute. But — and here's the fascinating part — if I were an elected official and did the same thing, I would be regarded as a socially responsible humanitarian.

In both cases the principle is the same; one is just more personal than the other. Both use force, both have an unwilling contributor, both have the same goal.

When government plunders, it does so on such a grand scale that the expropriated feel comfort that they haven't been the only ones singled out. Also, when one's own government plunders, one tends to justify the forcible act as a "necessary" use of police power. Although the dollar amount may be the same in both areas, the government establishes a system of thievery that is semipainless (withholding) so the theft is never completely understood or observed. The plunder is then wrapped in the swaddling clothes of humanitarianism, and the exploited are cast in the role of being against security or health if they object too loudly.

What is involved is a fundamental concept of justice. Let me ask you, the reader, three simple questions.

1. Do you believe someone has a right to improve his own lot at your expense? Put another way, do you believe someone has a right to feather his nest with your feathers?

If you answered no, then you are to be applauded. No one has a "right" to that which belongs to you. Conversely, you have no right to that which someone else has earned through his peaceful endeavors.

2. Do you believe someone has a right to feather another's nest at your expense?

If you answered no, you are right again. Just because a third party is the beneficiary of that which has been taken from you doesn't remove the taker from the role of a plunderer.

Put it in a more contemporary light: Does an Australian aborigine have a right to anything an American lawfully owns? Does a Canadian Indian have a right to any wealth legitimately accumulated by an Israeli Jew? The answer is obvious. No. Then, why should an affluent American black be forced to support an unproductive southern white? Or why should anyone be forced to support another? *There is no moral right for me to benefit at the expense of others.*

Let's understand one thing. Every person has a personal, moral obligation to help those less fortunate, but the ultimate decision to do so resides with the one who is the owner of the disposable commodity.

3. Do you believe that might makes right? That strength constitutes righteousness? If you replied no, then bravo again. Might has never been a guarantee of righteousness. That a man has greater strength than a woman gives him no right to impose his will upon her. Likewise, that there are more of us than of you, doesn't make us right. Might, whether strength of arms or sheer numerical superiority, does not by itself constitute right.

So, let's put them together. Does a majority vote make right the actions of the legislature to take from one and give to another?

If you think so, perhaps you should take another look at your premises. Because if you believe that the majority has that right, you should not be surprised when all that you possess (including your life) falls subject to the arbitrary power of the men the majority elects.

When We Are Free

CHAPTER 12

The Individual in Society

by Ludwig von Mises

The words freedom and liberty signified for the most eminent representatives of mankind one of the most precious and desirable goods. Today it is fashionable to sneer at them. They are, trumpets the modern sage, "slippery" notions and "bourgeois" prejudices.

Freedom and liberty are not to be found in nature. In nature there is no phenomenon to which these terms could be meaningfully applied. Whatever man does, he can never free himself from the restraints which nature imposes upon him. If he wants to succeed in acting, he must submit unconditionally to the laws of nature.

Freedom and liberty always refer to interhuman relations. A man is free as far as he can live and get on without being at the mercy of arbitrary decisions on the part of other people. In the frame of society everybody depends upon his fellow citizens. Social man cannot become independent without forsaking all the advantages of social cooperation.

The fundamental social phenomenon is the division of labor and its counterpart — human cooperation.

Experience teaches man that cooperative action is more efficient and productive than isolated action of self-sufficient individuals. The natural conditions determining man's life and effort are such that the division of labor increases output per unit of labor expended. These natural facts are: (1) the innate inequality of men with regard to their ability to perform various kinds of labor; and (2) the unequal distribution of the nature-given, nonhuman opportunities of production on the surface of the earth. One may as well consider these two facts as one and the same fact, namely, the manifoldness of nature which makes the universe a complex of infinite varieties.

From *The Freeman*, June 1971.

Innate Inequality

The division of labor is the outcome of man's conscious reaction to the multiplicity of natural conditions. On the other hand, it is itself a factor bringing about differentiation. It assigns to the various geographic areas specific functions in the complex of the processes of production. It makes some areas urban, others rural; it locates the various branches of manufacturing, mining, and agriculture in different places. Still more important, however, is the fact that it intensifies the innate inequality of men. Exercise and practice of specific tasks adjust individuals better to the requirements of their performance; men develop some of their inborn faculties and stunt the development of others. Vocational types emerge, people become specialists.

The division of labor splits the various processes of production into minute tasks, many of which can be performed by mechanical devices. It is this fact that made the use of machinery possible and brought about the amazing improvements in technical methods of production. Mechanization is the fruit of the division of labor, its most beneficial achievement, not its motive and fountain spring. Power-driven specialized machinery could be employed only in a social environment under the division of labor. Every step forward on the road toward the use of more specialized, more refined, and more productive machines requires a further specialization of tasks.

Within Society

Seen from the point of view of the individual, society is the great means for the attainment of all his ends. The preservation of society is an essential condition of any plans an individual may want to realize by any action whatever. Even the refractory delinquent who fails to adjust his conduct to the requirements of life within the societal system of cooperation does not want to miss any of the advantages derived from the division of labor. He does not consciously aim at the destruction of society. He wants to lay his hands on a greater portion of the jointly produced wealth than the social order assigns to him. He would feel miserable if antisocial behavior were to become universal and its inevitable outcome, the return to primitive indigence, resulted.

Liberty and freedom are the conditions of man within a contractual society. Social cooperation under a system of private ownership of the means of production means that within the range of the market the individual is not bound to obey and to serve an overlord. As far as he gives and serves other people, he does so of

The Individual in Society

his own accord in order to be rewarded and served by the receivers. He exchanges goods and services, he does not do compulsory labor and does not pay tribute. He is certainly not independent. He depends on the other members of society. But this dependence is mutual. The buyer depends on the seller and the seller on the buyer.

Self-Interest

The main concern of many writers of the nineteenth and twentieth centuries was to misrepresent and to distort this obvious state of affairs. The workers, they said, are at the mercy of their employers. Now, it is true that the employer has the right to fire the employee. But if he makes use of this right in order to indulge in his whims, he hurts his own interests. It is to his own disadvantage if he discharges a better man in order to hire a less efficient one. The market does not directly prevent anybody from arbitrarily inflicting harm on his fellow citizens; it only puts a penalty upon such conduct. The shopkeeper is free to be rude to his customers provided he is ready to bear the consequences. The consumers are free to boycott a purveyor provided they are ready to pay the costs. What impels every man to the utmost exertion in the service of his fellow men and curbs innate tendencies toward arbitrariness and malice is, in the market, not compulsion and coercion on the part of gendarmes, hangmen, and penal courts; it is self-interest. The member of a contractual society is free because he serves others only in serving himself. What restrains him is only the inevitable natural phenomenon of scarcity. For the rest he is free in the range of the market.

In the market economy the individual is free to act within the orbit of private property and the market. His choices are final. For his fellow men his actions are data which they must take into account in their own acting. The coordination of the autonomous actions of all individuals is accomplished by the operation of the market. Society does not tell a man what to do and what not to do. There is no need to enforce cooperation by special orders or prohibitions. Non-cooperation penalizes itself. Adjustment to the requirements of society's productive effort and the pursuit of the individual's own concerns are not in conflict. Consequently no agency is required to settle such conflicts. The system can work and accomplish its tasks without the interference of an authority issuing special orders and prohibitions and punishing those who do not comply.

Compulsion and Coercion

Beyond the sphere of private property and the market lies the sphere of compulsion and coercion; here are the dams which organized society has built for the protection of private property and the market against violence, malice, and fraud. This is the realm of constraint as distinguished from the realm of freedom. Here are rules discriminating between what is legal and what is illegal, what is permitted and what is prohibited. And here is a grim machine of arms, prisons, and gallows and the men operating it, ready to crush those who dare to disobey.

It is important to remember that government interference always means either violent action or the threat of such action. Government is in the last resort the employment of armed men, of policemen, gendarmes, soldiers, prison guards, and hangmen. The essential feature of government is the enforcement of its decrees by beating, killing, and imprisoning. Those who are asking for more government interference are asking ultimately for more compulsion and less freedom.

Liberty and freedom are terms employed for the description of the social conditions of the individual members of a market society in which the power of the indispensable hegemonic bond, the state, is curbed lest the operation of the market be endangered. In a totalitarian system there is nothing to which the attribute "free" could be attached but the unlimited arbitrariness of the dictator.

There would be no need to dwell upon this obvious fact if the champions of the abolition of liberty had not purposely brought about a semantic confusion. They realized that it was hopeless for them to fight openly and sincerely for restraint and servitude. The notions liberty and freedom had such prestige that no propaganda could shake their popularity. Since time immemorial in the realm of Western civilization liberty has been considered as the most precious good. What gave to the West its eminence was precisely its concern about liberty, a social ideal foreign to the oriental peoples. The social philosophy of the Occident is essentially a philosophy of freedom. The main content of the history of Europe and the communities founded by European emigrants and their descendants in other parts of the world was the struggle for liberty. "Rugged" individualism is the signature of our civilization. No open attack upon the freedom of the individual had any prospect of success.

New Definitions

Thus the advocates of totalitarianism chose other tactics. They reversed the meaning of words. They call true or genuine liberty the condition of the individuals under a system in which they have no right other than to obey orders. They call themselves true *liberals* because they strive after such a social order. They call democracy the Russian methods of dictatorial government. They call the labor union methods of violence and coercion "industrial democracy." They call freedom of the press a state of affairs in which only the government is free to publish books and newspapers. They define liberty as the opportunity to do the "right" things, and, of course, they arrogate to themselves the determination of what is right and what is not. In their eyes government omnipotence means full liberty. To free the police power from all restraints is the true meaning of their struggle for freedom.

The market economy, say these self-styled liberals, grants liberty only to a parasitic class of exploiters, the bourgeoisie; that these scoundrels enjoy the freedom to enslave the masses; that the wage earner is not free; that he must toil for the sole benefit of his masters, the employers; that the capitalists appropriate to themselves what according to the inalienable rights of man should belong to the worker; that under socialism the worker will enjoy freedom and human dignity because he will no longer have to slave for a capitalist; that socialism means the emancipation of the common man, means freedom for all; that it means, moreover, riches for all.

These doctrines have been able to triumph because they did not encounter effective rational criticism. It is useless to stand upon an alleged "natural" right of individuals to own property if other people assert that the foremost "natural" right is that of income equality. Such disputes can never be settled. It is beside the point to criticize nonessential, attendant features of the socialist program. One does not refute socialism by attacking the socialists' stand on religion, marriage, birth control, and art.

A New Subterfuge

In spite of these serious shortcomings of the defenders of economic freedom it was impossible to fool all the people all the time about the essential features of socialism. The most fanatical planners were forced to admit that their projects involve the abolition of many freedoms people enjoy under capitalism and "plutodemocracy." Pressed hard, they resorted to a new subterfuge. The freedom to be abolished, they emphasize, is merely the spurious "economic" freedom of the capitalists that harms the common man; that outside the "economic sphere" freedom will not only be fully preserved, but considerably expanded. "Planning for Freedom" has lately become the most popular slogan of the champions of totalitarian government and the Russification of all nations.

The fallacy of this argument stems from the spurious distinction between two realms of human life and action, the "economic" sphere and the "noneconomic" sphere. Strictly speaking, people do not long for tangible goods as such, but for the services which these goods are fitted to render them. They want to attain the increment in well-being which these services are able to convey. It is a fact that people, in dealing on the market, are motivated not only by the desire to get food, shelter, and sexual enjoyment, but also by manifold "ideal" urges. Acting man is always concerned both with "material" and "ideal" things. He chooses between various alternatives, no matter whether they are to be classified as material or ideal. In the actual scales of value, material and ideal things are jumbled together.

Preserving the Market

Freedom, as people enjoyed it in the democratic countries of Western civilization in the years of the old liberalism's triumph, was not a product of constitutions, bills of rights, laws, and statutes. Those documents aimed only at safeguarding liberty and freedom, firmly established by the operation of the market economy, against encroachments on the part of officeholders. No government and no civil law can guarantee and bring about freedom otherwise than by supporting and defending the fundamental institutions of the market economy. Government means always coercion and compulsion and is by necessity the opposite of liberty. Government is a guarantor of liberty and is compatible with liberty only if its range is adequately restricted to the preservation of economic freedom. Where there is no market economy, the best-intentioned provisions of constitutions and laws remain a dead letter.

Competition

The freedom of man under capitalism is an effect of competition. The worker does not depend on the good graces of an employer. If his employer discharges him, he finds another employer. The consumer is not at the mercy of the shopkeeper. He is free to patronize another shop if he likes. Nobody must kiss other people's hands or fear their disfavor. Interpersonal relations are businesslike. The exchange of goods and services is mutual; it is not a favor to sell or to buy, it is a transaction dictated by selfishness on either side.

It is true that in his capacity as a producer every man depends either directly, as does the entrepreneur, or indirectly, as does the hired worker, on the demands of the consumers. However, this dependence upon the supremacy of the consumers is not unlimited. If a man has a weighty reason for defying the sovereignty of the consumers, he can try it. There is in the range of the market a very substantial and effective right to resist oppression. Nobody is forced to go into the liquor industry or into a gun factory if his conscience objects. He may have to pay a price for his conviction; there are in this world no ends the attainment of which is gratuitous. But it is left to a man's own decision to choose between a material advantage and the call of what he believes to be his duty. In the market economy the individual alone is the supreme arbiter in matters of his satisfaction.

Consumers Choose

Capitalist society has no means of compelling a man to change his occupation or his place of work other than to reward those complying with the wants of the consumers by higher pay. It is precisely this kind of pressure which many people consider as unbearable and hope to see abolished under socialism. They are too dull to realize that the only alternative is to convey to the authorities full power to determine in what branch and at what place a man should work.

In his capacity as a consumer man is no less free. He alone decides what is more and what is less important for him. He chooses how to spend his money according to his own will.

The substitution of economic planning for the market economy removes all freedom and leaves to the individual merely the right to obey. The authority directing all economic matters controls all aspects of a man's life and activities. It is the only employer. All labor becomes compulsory labor because the employee must accept what the chief deigns to offer him. The economic tsar determines what and how much of each the consumer may consume. There is no sector of human life in which a decision is left to the individual's value judgments. The authority assigns a definite task to him, trains him for this job, and employs him at the place and in the manner it deems expedient.

The "Planned" Life is Not Free

As soon as the economic freedom which the market economy grants to its members is removed, all political liberties and bills of rights become humbug. Habeas corpus and trial by jury are a sham if, under the pretext of economic expediency, the authority has full power to relegate every citizen it dislikes to the arctic or to a desert and to assign him "hard labor" for life. Freedom of the press is a mere blind if the authority controls all printing offices and paper plants. And so are all the other rights of men.

A man has freedom as far as he shapes his life according to his own plans. A man whose fate is determined by the plans of a superior authority, in which the exclusive power to plan is vested, is not free in the sense in which the term "free" was used and understood by all people until the semantic revolution of our day brought about a confusion of tongues.

Unit III: Systems of Economic Organization

Since time immemorial, men have endured the punishing demoralization of slavery. It has taken many forms and been referred to by various names, but slavery has been our lot for most of recorded history.

The first chapter of this unit attempts to clarify and categorize systems of economic organization in the world today. A major theme of the chapter is that *either man is free or he is not,* that slavery and freedom are really the only two distinct choices we have, with all other "systems" being mere unstable mixtures of the two.

Professor Benjamin Rogge is so convinced of the moral underpinnings of the free society that he unequivocally declares that he would prefer freedom "even if it were demonstrably less efficient than alternative systems, even if it were to produce a *slower* rate of economic growth than systems of central direction and control." He presents a most persuasive argument in "The Case for Economic Freedom."

Samuel Gompers was one of America's early labor leaders, having been president of the American Federation of Labor from 1886 to 1924. Many freedom believers have bones to pick with the tactics and proposals of labor unions today, but they will find no quarrel with Gompers' observation that where the features of "compulsory benevolence" have been established in the world, "you will find the initiative taken from the hearts of the people."

That view is supported eloquently by William Henry Chamberlin in "Liberty and Property: One and Inseparable." He notes "the overwhelming testimony of experience that anyone who wishes to eat as much as he wishes and as wide a variety of foods as he wishes should stay away from communist and socialist lands."

When We Are Free

Cuba is just such a land. David Reed's article from *Reader's Digest* is a chilling tale of torture and inhumanity in this place where all power is wielded by government. It is a story which sadly is being played out in many other unfree countries of the world as well.

And finally, "Getting Rid of Communism" by Leonard Read is a fitting conclusion to this unit. Here Read lays bare the philosophical essence of communism and prescribes the only effective way of meeting its global challenge.

CHAPTER 13

A Look at the Systems

by Lawrence W. Reed

In any introduction to the social sciences, particularly economics and political science, the student is deluged with "isms" — those polysyllabic concoctions which defy both pronunciation and memory. The following cogent descriptions by an unknown author make a few of the economic isms a lot easier to grasp:

Socialism: You have two cows but the *government* orders you to give one to your lazy neighbor.

Communism: You have two cows but the *government* takes both and gives you ¼ of the milk.

Fascism: You have two cows but the *government* takes both and sells you the milk.

Nazism: You have two cows but the *government* takes both and shoots you.

Capitalism: You have two cows but *you* sell one and buy a bull.

The first four "systems of economic organization" have a great deal in common. They are, in fact, "peas of the same pod." Each of them, as the descriptions suggest, keep the individual in subjection to *government*. Only under "capitalism" is the individual encouraged to grow and develop on his own and in voluntary association with others — to be the master of his own destiny.

In theory, only two distinct systems of economic organization exist — capitalism and socialism. Either man is free or he is not. It's as simple as that. Any attempt to combine features of these two systems does not create a new one. Let's examine these systems one at a time.

Capitalism

Perhaps the most outstanding characteristic of capitalism is *private property in the tools of production.* Even in the Soviet Union, where this concept is condemned, the State endeavors to protect a citizen from a thief who would steal his bread. Only in a capitalist country, however, is the citizen permitted to own and control the factory where the bread is made.

Under capitalism, the factories, the offices, the businesses, the farms, and the land are owned by private individuals. This ownership implies the ability to use and dispose of this property as the owner — not the State — deems appropriate, so long as the legitimate rights of others are not abridged.

Among those friendly to it, capitalism sometimes goes by other names, each of which describes some feature of the system:

1. *Free enterprise:* Anyone with an idea and necessary funds (borrowed or saved) can start his or her own business. The hope of profit and the avoidance of loss become the fuel which generates production for the masses.

2. *Competitive order:* Individual businesses do not operate in a vacuum and no one firm's success is guaranteed. The drive to survive gives rise to competition, which rewards excellence and penalizes sloppiness.

3. *Free market:* All economic exchange under capitalism is undertaken voluntarily; there is no forced redistribution of income. The consumer is "king," and his decision to buy or not to buy will determine the fate of the largest corporation. Prices in the market reflect conditions of supply and demand, not the whims of power-hungry politicians.

4. *Laissez faire:* Roughly translated from the French, this means "leave people alone." Government is confined to protecting life and property, not plundering or even directing them. It acts as a nightwatchman or referee, and not Santa Claus, Robin Hood, or Bonnie and Clyde.

The system of limited government, free markets, and personal responsibility, i.e., capitalism, is what America's Founding Fathers had in mind when they produced the Constitution in 1787. Having thrown off the yoke of British tyranny, they clearly wanted government to stay off the people's backs, out of their pockets, and out of their way. They had faith in the freedom of the individual and what it could accomplish.

Socialism

Now let's take a look at the system known as socialism. With a very long history behind it, socialism ought to conjure up a testimony of repeated oppression and failure. It is the system of government domination, orchestrated by the few and powerful whose commands all others must carry out.

Under one variant of socialism, the government owns (holds legal title) to the tools of production. The factories, the farms, the businesses, the newspapers, and all but the simplest of things are the property of government; it is illegal for anyone outside the government to compete. There is one employer, one producer, one "master." The communist countries, such as the Soviet Union and Red China, most closely approximate this form.

Another variant is seemingly less radical. Government dominance, though overwhelming, does not take the form of outright ownership in most cases. Legal title to the tools of production is left in private hands (private citizens may own a steel mill through holdings of stock, for instance) but the managers of enterprise *take their orders from government officials.*

Nazi Germany and Fascist Italy of the 1930s practiced this latter variant of socialism. In these countries, private ownership (at least on paper) was left largely intact, but lieutenants of Hitler and Mussolini told owners what to do, when to do it, and what to charge for it. And of course, the State always reserved the right to simply eliminate anyone who would not fit into the "scheme" of things.

It is a crude imitation of this second form of socialism, under the guise of a "Welfare State," which has been busily taking root in the United States since the turn of the century. The federal government has not gone the route of confiscation and nationalization of industry, but it has steadily extended its authority nonetheless. As this is being written (January 1981), signs are appearing that a new administration may slow down this socialization. Whether decades of accumulating power in Washington will really be substantially reversed remains the paramount question of our time.

My political and economic beliefs were in their formative stage during my high school years in the late '60s and early '70s. As a member of Young Americans for Freedom, I read a great deal of literature which was pro-capitalist and anti-socialist. One piece which impressed me very much was an article by Richard S. Wheeler entitled "The Fascist Threat to America." The following passage from that article indicates how far socialism in its "fascist" form has advanced in this country:

> The federal government sets minimum wages and establishes practical limits on personal income through taxation. Its purchasing policies influence wage levels. It fixes prices in a number of ways, ranging from agricultural marketing agreements to the vast regulatory activities of the Justice Department, Labor Department, the Federal Trade Commission, the Interstate Commerce Commission, the Civil Aeronautics Board, and a slew of other agencies. It's "labor guidelines" heavily influence both the cost of labor and the price of products. It establishes employment conditions through the Na-

tional Labor Relations Board, the civil rights law, and legislation governing the length of working days. It prohibits new economic activity through its agricultural controls, licensing, and monopoly regulation. It hatches new businesses through its depressed areas legislation, the Small Business Administration, and defense contracting. It operates a number of socialized enterprises, ranging from power companies to fertilizer plants and shipyards. It subsidizes agriculture, the airlines, the merchant marine, and other enterprises. It has partially nationalized banking and credit, transportation, and electrical power. In short, the liberal American state exerts almost as much economic control as the fascist states.

The essay from which this excerpt is taken was written in the mid-1960s. It was even later, in the decade of the 1970s, that we witnessed the greatest growth of federal agencies, regulations, and spending in American history!

Those who champion socialism because it supposedly represents progress should understand that humans are social beings who progress if they cooperate with one another. Cooperation implies a climate of freedom for each individual human being to peacefully pursue his own self-interest without fear of reprisal. Put a human in a zoo or in a straitjacket and his creative energies dissipate.

Why did Thomas Edison invent the light bulb? It was not because some central planner ordered him too!

Why don't slaves produce great works of art, Swiss watches, or jet airplanes? To the believer in freedom, the answer is obvious.

Take a look around the world today and you see the point I am driving at. Compare North Korea with South Korea, Red China with Taiwan or Hong Kong, or East Germany with West Germany.

One would think, with such overwhelming evidence against the record of socialism, that socialism would have few adherents. Yet there are many people here and abroad who cry for nationalization of industry, wage and price controls, confiscatory taxation, cradle to grave welfarism, and even outright abolition of private property. What does it take for them to see the light?

As I see it, the choice is an easy one. It is the choice between freedom and tyranny, between a moral society and an immoral one, between prosperity and poverty. I choose capitalism; how about you?

CHAPTER 14

The Case for Economic Freedom

by Benjamin A. Rogge

My economic philosophy is here offered with full knowledge that it is *not* generally accepted as the right one. On the contrary, my brand of economics has now become *Brand X*, the one that is never selected as the whitest by the housewife, the one that is said to be slow acting, the one that contains no miracle ingredient. It loses nine times out of ten in the popularity polls run on Election Day, and, in most elections, it doesn't even present a candidate.

I shall identify my brand of economics as that of economic freedom, and I shall define economic freedom as that set of economic arrangements that would exist in a society in which the government's only function would be to prevent one man from using force or fraud against another — including within this, of course, the task of national defense. So that there can be no misunderstanding here, let me say that this is pure, uncompromising *laissez faire* economics. It is not the mixed economy; it is the unmixed economy.

I readily admit that I do not expect to see such an economy in my lifetime or in anyone's lifetime in the infinity of years ahead of us. I present it rather as the ideal we should strive for and should be disappointed in never fully attaining. Human society is *not* destroyed by men who have ideals but find that they cannot, in their imperfection, always attain them; rather it is destroyed by men who have no ideals, by men who have no benchmarks against which to measure their own performances.

The tragedy of the classical socialist is that he has false ideals; the threat to society of the modern liberal is that so often he has *no* ideals, no guides to conduct, other than political expediency and a spurious realism. The man who insists that he will walk the middle of the road has his path determined for him by those who define the ditches, and never then takes a step of his own real choosing.

To put it another way: I am not frustrated by the fact that politicians often pass laws that do violence to the free market. I *am* frustrated by the fact that so many people do not *know* that vio-

---

From *The Freeman,* September 1963.

lence has been done, that so few feel any sense of uneasiness at the departure from the ideal.

I am convinced that we continue to move away from the free market because few of the leaders of opinion even know or understand the ideal of the free market, because the ideal itself is no longer accepted as a basic guide to action. We drift toward socialism, not because we consciously wish to go there, but because we no longer know or care where our own home is.

How has this come about? Who has done us in? The fact is, of course, that we have done ourselves in. We have *not* been betrayed by subversives. We have been betrayed by our own indolence, by our preoccupation with profiting individually from the government interventions we deplore, by our failure to prepare and present the case for economic freedom as powerfully and persuasively as possible. The cure must start within each of us individually and not with programs to reform everyone else.

Where do we find the most powerful and persuasive case for economic freedom? I don't know; probably it hasn't been prepared yet, and each concerned person should work at it himself. Certainly it is unlikely that the case I present is the definitive one. However, it is the one that is persuasive with me, that leads me to my own deep commitment to the free market. I present it as grist for your own mill and not as the divinely inspired last word on the subject.

The Moral Case

You will note as I develop my case that I attach relatively little importance to the demonstrated efficiency of the free market system in promoting economic growth, in raising levels of living. In fact, my central thesis is that *the most important part of the case for economic freedom is not its vaunted efficiency as a system for organizing resources, not its dramatic success in promoting economic growth, but rather its consistency with certain fundamental moral principles of life itself.*

I say, "the most important part of the case" for two reasons. First, the significance I attach to those moral principles would lead me to prefer the free enterprise system even if it were demonstrably less efficient than alternative systems, even if it were to produce a *slower* rate of economic growth than systems of central direction and control. Second, the great mass of the people of any country is never really going to understand the purely economic workings of *any* economic system, be it free enterprise or socialism. Hence, most people are going to judge an economic system by its consistency with their moral principles rather than by its purely scientific operating characteristics. If economic freedom survives in the years ahead, it will be only because a majority of the people accept its basic morality. The success of the system in bringing ever higher levels of living will be no more persuasive in the future than it has been in the past.

Let me illustrate: The doctrine of man held in general in nineteenth century America argued that each man was ultimately responsible for what happened to him, for his own salvation, both in the here and now and in the hereafter. Thus, whether a man prospered or failed in economic life was each man's individual responsibility: each man had a right to the rewards for success and, in the same sense, deserved the punishment that came with failure. It followed as well that it is explicitly immoral to use the power of government to take from one man to give to another, to legalize Robin Hood. This doctrine of man found its economic counterpart in the system of free enterprise and, hence, the system of free enterprise was accepted and respected by many who had no real understanding of its subtleties as a technique for organizing resources.

As this doctrine of man was replaced by one (largely reflecting Freudian psychology and sociology) which made of man a helpless victim of his subconscious and his environment — responsible for neither his successes nor his failures — the free enterprise system came to be rejected by many who still had no real understanding of its actual operating characteristics.

Basic Values Considered

Inasmuch as my own value systems and my own assumptions about human beings are so important to the case, I want to sketch them for you.

To begin with, the central value in my choice system is individual freedom. By freedom I mean exactly and only freedom from coercion by others. I do not mean the four freedoms of President Roosevelt, which are not freedoms at all, but only rhetorical devices to persuade people to give up some of their true freedom. In the Rogge system, each man must be free to do what is his duty as he defines it, so long as he does not use force against another.

Next, I believe each man to be ultimately responsible for what happens to him. True, he is influenced by his heredity, his environment, his subconscious, and by pure chance. But I insist that precisely what makes man man is his ability to rise above these influences, to change and determine his own destiny. If this be true, then, it follows that each of us is terribly and inevitably and forever responsible for everything he does. The answer to the question, "Who's to blame?" is always, *"Mea culpa,* I am."[1]

I believe as well that man is imperfect, now and forever. He is imperfect in his knowledge of the ultimate purpose of his life, imperfect in his choice of means to serve those purposes he does select, imperfect in the integrity with which he deals with himself and those around him, imperfect in his capacity to love his fellow man. If man is imperfect, then all of his constructs must be imperfect, and the choice is always among degrees and kinds of imperfection. The New Jerusalem is never going to be realized here on earth, and the man who insists that it is, is always lost unto freedom.

Moreover, man's imperfections are intensified as he acquires the power to coerce others; "power tends to corrupt and absolute power corrupts absolutely."

This completes the listing of my assumptions, and it should be clear that the list does not constitute a total philosophy of life. Most importantly, it does not define what I believe the free man's *duty* to be, or more specifically, what I believe my own duty to be and the source of the charge to me. However important these questions, I do not consider them relevant to the choice of an economic system.

Here, then, are two sections of the case for economic freedom as I would construct it. The first section presents economic freedom as an ultimate end in itself and the second presents it as a means to the preservation of the noneconomic elements in total freedom.

Individual Freedom of Choice

The first section of the case is made in the stating of it, if one accepts the fundamental premise:

Major premise: Each man should be free to take whatever *action* he wishes, so long as he does not use force or fraud against another;

Minor premise: All economic behavior is "action" as identified above;

Conclusion: Each man should be free to take whatever action he wishes in his economic behavior, so long as he does not use force or fraud against another.

In other words, economic freedom is a part of total freedom; *if freedom is an end in itself, as our society has traditionally asserted it to be, then economic freedom is an end in itself, to be valued for itself alone and not just for its instrumental value in serving other goals.*

---

[1] See my "Who's To Blame?" in *The Freeman*, January 1961.

If this thesis be accepted, then there must always exist a tremendous presumption against each and every proposal for governmental limitation of economic freedom. What is wrong with a state system of compulsory social security? It denies to the individual his *freedom,* his right to choose what he will do with his own money resources. What is wrong with a governmentally enforced minimum wage? It denies to the employer and the employee their individual freedom, their individual rights to enter into any voluntary relationship not involving force or fraud. What is wrong with government-to-government foreign economic aid? It denies to the individual freedom to choose, as his conscience dictates, whether to send aid or not. What is wrong with a tariff or an import quota? It denies to the individual consumer his right to buy what he wishes, wherever he wishes.

It is breathtaking to think what this simple approach would do to the apparatus of state control at all levels of government. Strike from the books all legislation that denies economic freedom to any individual and three-fourths of all the activities now undertaken by government would be eliminated.

I am no dreamer of empty dreams and I do not expect that the day will ever come when this principle of economic freedom as a part of total freedom will be fully accepted and applied. Yet I am convinced that unless this principle is given some standing, unless at least those who examine proposals for each new regulation of the individual by government look on this loss of freedom as a "cost" of the proposed legislation, the chances of free enterprise surviving are small indeed. The would-be controller can always find reasons why it might seem "expedient" to control the individual; and unless slowed down by some general feeling that it is immoral to do so, he will usually have his way.

Noneconomic Freedoms

So much for the first section of the case. Now for the second. The major premise here is the same, that is, the premise of the rightness of freedom. Here, though, the concern is with the noneconomic elements in total freedom — with freedom of speech, of religion, of the press, of personal behavior. My thesis is that these freedoms are not likely to be long preserved in a society that has denied economic freedom to its individual numbers.

Before developing this thesis, I wish to comment briefly on the importance of these noneconomic freedoms. I do so because we who are known as conservatives have often given too little attention to these freedoms or have even played a significant role in reducing them. The modern liberal is usually inconsistent in that he defends man's noneconomic freedoms, but is often quite indifferent to his economic freedom. The modern conservative is often inconsistent in that he defends man's economic freedom but is indifferent to his noneconomic freedoms. Why are there so few conservatives in the struggles over censorship, over denials of equality before the law for people of all races, over blue laws, and so on?

Why do we let the modern liberals dominate an organization such as the American Civil Liberties Union? The general purposes of this organization are completely consistent with, even necessary to, the truly free society. Its modern liberal leadership has led it to make mistakes but, in spite of those mistakes, I continue as a member of the organization. After all, it was the only organization to protest when Moise Tshombe was denied a visa to enter this country. It was the first organization to study the handling of General Walker in the Mississippi case, to see if his rights before the law were being denied. Undoubtedly there are leftists in the organization, but probably few more than in other groups with which I am involved, such as the American Economics Association, the Episcopal Church and, yes, the Republican Party.

Particularly in times of stress such as these, we must fight against the general pressure to curb the rights of individual human beings, even those whose ideas and actions we detest. Now is the time to remember the example of men such as David Ricardo, the London banker and economist of the Classical free market school in the first part of the last century. Born a Jew, turned Quaker, he devoted some part of his energy and his fortune to eliminating the legal discriminations against Catholics in the England of his day.

It is precisely because I believe these noneconomic freedoms to be so important that I believe economic freedom to be so important. The argument here could be drawn from the wisdom of the Bible and the statement that "where a man's treasure is, there will his heart be also." Give me control over a man's economic actions, and hence over his means of survival, and except for a few occasional heroes, I'll promise to deliver to you men who think and write and behave as you want them to.

The case is not difficult to make for the fully-controlled economy, the true socialistic state. Milton Friedman, in his book, *Capitalism and Freedom,* takes the case of a socialist society that has a sincere desire to preserve freedom of the press. The first problem would be that there would be no "private" capital, no private fortunes that could be used to subsidize an antisocialist, procapitalist press. Hence, the socialist state would have to do it. However, the men and women undertaking the task would have to be released from the socialist labor pool and would have to be assured that they would never be discriminated against in employment opportunities in the socialist apparatus if they were to wish to change occupations later. Then these procapitalist members of the socialist society would have to go to other functionaries of the state to secure the buildings, the presses, the paper, the skilled and unskilled workmen, and all the other components of a working newspaper. Then they would face the problem of finding distribution outlets, either creating their own (a frightening task) or using the same ones used by the official socialist propaganda organs. Finally, where would they find readers? How many men and women would risk showing up at their state-controlled jobs carrying copies of the *Daily Capitalist?*

There are so many unlikely steps in this process that the assumption that true freedom of the press could be maintained in a socialist society is so unrealistic as to be ludicrous.

Partly Socialized

Of course, we are not facing as yet a fully socialized America, but only one in which there is significant government intervention in a still predominantly private enterprise economy. Do these interventions pose any threat to the noneconomic freedoms? I believe they do.

First of all, the total of coercive devices now available to any administration of either party at the national level is so great that true freedom to work actively against the current administration (whatever it might be) is seriously reduced. For example, farmers have become captives of the government in such a way that they are forced into political alignments that seriously reduce their ability to protest that of which they do not approve. The new trade bill, though right in the principle of free trade, gives to the President enormous power to reward his friends and punish his critics.

Secondly, the form of these interventions is such as to threaten seriously one of the real cornerstones of all freedoms — equality before the law. For example, farmers and trade union members are now encouraged and assisted in doing precisely that for which businessmen are sent to jail (i.e., acting collusively to manipulate prices). The blindfolded Goddess of Justice has been encouraged to peek and she now says, with the jurists of the ancient regime, "First tell me who you are and then I'll tell you what your rights are." A society in which such gross inequalities before the law are encouraged in economic life is not likely to be one which preserves the principle of equality before the law generally.

We could go on to many specific illustrations. For example, the government uses its legislated monopoly to carry the mails as a means for imposing a censorship on what people send to each other in a completely voluntary relationship. A man and a woman who exchange obscene letters may not be making productive use of their time, but their correspondence is certainly no business of the government. Or to take an example from another country, Winston Churchill, as a critic of the Chamberlain government, was not permitted one minute of radio time on the government-owned and monopolized broadcasting system in the period from 1936 to the outbreak of the war he was predicting in 1939.

Each Step Leads to Another

Every act of intervention in the economic life of its citizens gives to a government additional power to shape and control the attitudes, the writings, the behavior of those citizens. Every such act is another break in the dike protecting the integrity of the individual as a free man or woman.

The free market protects the integrity of the individual by providing him with a host of decentralized alternatives rather than with one centralized opportunity. Even the known communist can readily find employment in capitalist America. The free market is politics-blind, religion-blind, and, yes, race-blind. Do you ask about the politics or the religion of the farmer who grew the potatoes you buy at the store? Do you ask about the color of the hands that helped produce the steel you use in your office building?

South Africa provides an interesting example of this. The South Africans, of course, provide a shocking picture of racial bigotry, shocking even to a country that has its own tragic race problems. South African law clearly separates the whites from the nonwhites. Orientals have traditionally been classed as nonwhites, but South African trade with Japan has become so important in the postwar period that the government of South Africa has declared the Japanese visitors to South Africa to be officially and legally "white." The free market is one of the really great forces making for tolerance and understanding among human beings. The controlled market gives man rein to express all those blind prejudices and intolerant beliefs to which he is forever subject.

Impersonality of the Market

To look at this another way: The free market is often said to be impersonal, and indeed it is. Rather than a vice, this is one of its great virtues. Because the relationships *are* substantially impersonal, they are not usually marked by bitter personal conflict. It is precisely because the labor union attempts to take the employment relationship *out* of the market place that bitter personal conflict so often marks union-management relationships. The intensely personal relationship is one that is civilized only by love, as between man and wife, and within the family. But man's capacity for love is severely limited by his imperfect nature. Far better, then, to economize on love, to reserve our dependence on it to those relationships where even our imperfect natures are capable of sustained action based on love. Far better, then, to build our economic system on largely impersonal relationships and on man's self-interest — a motive power with which he is generously supplied.

One need only study the history of such utopian experiments as our Indiana's New Harmony to realize that a social structure which ignores man's essential nature results in the dissension, conflict, disintegration, and dissolution of Robert Owen's New Harmony or the absolutism of Father Rapp's Harmony.

The "vulgar calculus of the market place," as its critics have described it, is still the most humane way man has yet found for solving those questions of economic allocation and division which are ubiquitous in human society.

By what must seem fortunate coincidence, it is also the system most likely to produce the affluent society, to move mankind above an existence in which life is mean, nasty, brutish, and short. But, of course, this is *not* just coincidence. Under economic freedom, only man's destructive instincts are curbed by law. All of his creative instincts are released and freed to work those wonders of which free men are capable. In the controlled society only the creativity of the few at the top can be utilized, and much of this creativity must be expended in maintaining control and in fending off rivals. In the free society, the creativity of every man can be expressed — and surely by now we know that we cannot predict who will prove to be the most creative.

You may be puzzled, then, that I do not rest my case for economic freedom on its productive achievements; on its buildings, its houses, its automobiles, its bathtubs, its wonder drugs, its television sets, its sirloin steaks and green salads with Roquefort dressings. I neither feel within myself nor do I hear in the testimony of others any evidence that man's search for purpose, his longing for fulfillment, is in any significant way relieved by these accomplishments. I do not scorn these accomplishments nor do I worship them. Nor do I find in the lives of those who do worship them any evidence that they find ultimate peace and justification in their idols.

I rest my case rather on the consistency of the free market with man's essential nature, on the basic morality of its system of rewards and punishments, on the protection it gives to the integrity of the individual.

The free market cannot produce the perfect world, but it can create an environment in which each imperfect man may conduct his lifelong search for purpose in his own way, in which each day he may order his life according to his own imperfect vision of his destiny, suffering both the agonies of his errors and the sweet pleasure of his successes. This freedom is what it means to be a man; this is the God-head, if you wish.

I give you, then, the free market, the economic expression of man's freedom itself and the guarantor of all his other freedoms.

CHAPTER 15

Legislated Security Is Bondage

by Samuel Gompers

There has never yet come down from any government any substantial improvement in the conditions of the masses of the people, unless it found its own initiative in the mind, the heart, and the courage of the people. Take from the people of our country the source of initiative and the opportunity to aspire and to struggle in order that that aspiration may become a reality, and though you couch your action in any sympathetic terms, it will fail of its purpose and be the undoing of the vital forces that go to make up a virile people. Look over all the world where you will, and see those governments where the features of compulsory benevolence have been established, and you will find the initiative taken from the hearts of the people.

Social insurance cannot even undertake to remove or prevent poverty. It is not fundamental and does not get at the causes of social injustice.

The first step in establishing compulsory social insurance is to divide people into groups, those eligible for benefits and those considered capable of caring for themselves. The division is based upon earning capacity. This governmental regulation must tend to fix the citizens of the country into classes, and a long-established insurance system would tend to make those classes rigid.

Governmental power grows upon that on which it feeds. Give an agency power, and it at once tries to reach out after more. Its effectiveness depends upon increasing power.

Recently a gentleman of the highest standing stated to me that during the time he was in Germany, and in a position to know, German workmen came to him seeking aid to get out of that country to the United States. They told him that by reason of the taxes which they were compelled to pay into compulsory social insurance schemes, they had no money left except for absolute necessities of life, and were unable to secure sufficient funds to come to

---

Excerpts from an address, December 5, 1916.

the United States even in the steerage. He said to me further that in Germany, where compulsory social insurance has been more extensively worked out than in any other country, the workmen of that country, by reason of their property interests in compulsory social insurance, have been compelled to remain in Germany and work under circumstances, wages, hours, and conditions of employment which forced them to endure conditions below standards of a living wage.

Is it not discernible that the payments required of workmen for this compulsory social insurance interfere very materially with mobility of labor, and constitute a very effectual barrier to the workers determining their whole lives?

Industrial freedom exists only when and where wage earners have complete control over their labor power. To delegate control over their labor power to an outside agency takes away from the economic power of those wage earners and creates another agency for power. Whoever has control of this new agency acquires some degree of control over the worker. There is nothing to guarantee control over that agency to employees. It may also be controlled by employers. In other words, giving the government control over industrial relations creates a fulcrum which means great power for an unknown user.

What Compulsion Means

The introduction of compulsory social insurance in cases of sickness, or compulsory social insurance in cases of unemployment, means that the workers must be subject to examinations, investigations, regulations, and limitations. Their activities must be regulated in accordance with the standards set by governmental agencies. To that we shall not stand idly by and give our assent.

Men and women, I trust I may not be sounding my warnings upon the empty air. I hope that they may find a lodgment in the minds and the hearts of my countrymen. I bid you have a care in all these attempts to regulate the personal relations and the normal personal activities of the citizenship of our country ere it be too late.

There is in the minds of many an absence of understanding of the fundamental essentials of freedom. They talk freedom, and yet would have bound upon their wrists the gyves that would tie them to everlasting bondage. And no matter how sympathetic or humanitarian is the gloss over the plan and the scheme, I again bid you beware. We know not when or how this great struggle going on in Europe will terminate, or what it shall mean for the future of those countries; but at least let the people of the United States hold their liberties in their own hands, for it may come to pass that our

America, the America whose institutions and ideals we so much revere, may be the one nation to hold the beacon light of freedom aloft, and thus aid in relighting the torch, rekindling the heart flame of the world's liberty.

For a mess of pottage, under the pretense of compulsory social insurance, let us not voluntarily surrender the fundamental principles of liberty and freedom, the hope of the Republic of the United States, the leader and teacher to the world of the significance of this great anthem chorus of humanity — liberty!

When We Are Free

CHAPTER 16

Liberty and Property: One and Inseparable

by William Henry Chamberlin

Two familiar left-wing clichés that are too often allowed to pass unexamined and unrefuted are that freedom under capitalism is freedom to starve and that human rights are superior to property rights. The implications are that people are most likely to go hungry under a system of free enterprise and private ownership and that there is a basic antagonism between human rights and property rights. Both assumptions are completely false and misleading.

Where have the great famines of the twentieth century occurred? There have been two in the Soviet Union, each costing millions of human lives, in 1921-22 and in 1932-33. Capitalism obviously cannot be blamed for either of these. The first was the product of a number of causes, drought, transportation breakdowns after years of fierce civil war, and last, but by no means least, the Soviet system of so-called war communism. Under this system the value of money was virtually abolished; the government requisitioned all the peasants' "surplus" produce and, in theory, gave him what he needed in clothing, machinery, and manufactured goods. But this theory was seldom translated into fact; what actually happened was that armed requisitioning bands scoured the villages, confiscating any food stocks they found and giving nothing in return. Under these circumstances there was an understandable unwillingness of the peasant to raise more than he required for his own subsistence.

At least the Soviet Government admitted the fact of this famine and welcomed foreign aid from the American Relief Agency, headed by Herbert Hoover, and various foreign religious and charitable organizations. Its responsibility for the second great famine, in 1932-33, is far more unmistakable and undivided. This famine, which devastated what are normally the most fertile areas of European Russia, the Ukraine, and the North Caucasus, was primarily political in character.

From *The Freeman*, January 1968.

Stalin was bringing all possible pressure to force the peasants to give up their individual holdings and accept regimentation in so-called collective farms, where they were completely under state control as regards what they should plant, how much they must surrender to the government, what prices they should receive. Weather conditions had been unfavorable and the peasants' will to produce had been paralyzed. Yields were naturally low and I still recall, from a trip in rural areas, the striking number of weeds in the collective farm fields. The Soviet authorities easily could have coped with the food shortage by drawing on reserve stocks or importing food from abroad. Instead, heavy requisitions were imposed and the peasants were left to starve, as several millions of them did. Foreign relief was not permitted; honest reporting of the famine, its background and causes, was not permitted.

Industrial Taj Mahals

Famine has also occurred in recent years in communist China and in India. In India, socialist state planning led to systematic neglect of agriculture in favor of building big new factories, which a prominent Indian economist, B. R. Shenoy, has called "industrial Taj Mahals," out of proportion to the needs and absorption capacities of the country. There can be no serious suggestion that capitalism is responsible for starvation in India. For the disastrous famines that have occurred in the Soviet Union, China, and India there is no parallel in any country with an economy based on private property relations.

There is an intermediate phase between the stark horror of downright famine, with thousands of human beings perishing from lack of food and the diseases that malnutrition always brings, and the contented satisfaction of needs enjoyed by shoppers in an American supermarket. In this phase people are not acutely hungry but are condemned to a drab, unappetizing diet, either because of rationing or because foodstuffs which they may desire are not available in the stores. This is the present situation in Russia and in the communist-ruled areas of Central and Eastern Europe. There has been nothing of the kind in the strongholds of free enterprise and private property, in North America and Western Europe — at least, not since Great Britain got rid of rationing, prolonged by Labor governments after it had been dropped on the continent and finally abolished by the Conservatives in the fifties.

So much for the old wheeze about "freedom to starve" under free enterprise. It is the overwhelming testimony of experience that anyone who wishes to eat as much as he wishes and as wide a variety of foods as he wishes should stay away from communist and socialist states.

Property Rights Are Human Rights

And the supposed antithesis between "human" rights and "property" rights is quite nonexistent. For the right to own property and use it in lawful ways is a very basic human right and when this right disappears, others also swiftly vanish. What are, after all, basic human freedoms? Security against arbitrary arrest, imprisonment, and execution is surely prominent on the list. So is the right, through an uncoerced vote, to exercise some share of control in government decisions. And the right to state one's views, in speech or writing, as an individual or in association with others. And to choose one's form of work and occupation, without external coercion. And to travel freely to foreign countries, and, if one chooses, to quit one's native country for residence in another. And to be secure against having letters opened and telephone conversations reported by snooping government agents. And to give up a job, or to change jobs without let or hindrance. And to publish newspapers and books, operate radio broadcasts, and generally communicate with one's fellows without official censorship.

Call the roll of this list of elementary human rights and liberties and examine how it stands up under various social and economic systems. No form of government or society is perfect; but by and large the above mentioned liberties are pretty well observed in countries where the rights of private property are most scrupulously respected. Most or all are disregarded under any form of dictatorship. But the denial of every one of these human rights is most complete, systematic, and irrevocable under the dictatorships which have gone furthest in abolishing the right to own and utilize private property.

The regimes that are now in power in the Soviet Union, in mainland China, and in Cuba grew out of revolutions that took place under differing circumstances and against differing national backgrounds. But all these tyrannies, as also those in East Germany, Poland, Hungary, Czechoslovakia, Romania, Yugoslavia, and Albania, have one negative trait in common. They recognize for the individual *no* right which the state may not arbitrarily withhold or deny.

Liberty is the first casualty after the wholesale nationalization and confiscation of property. This rule has been proven so often under so many circumstances in so many countries with such varied backgrounds that there can be no reasonable doubt as to its universal application.

The Communist Purge

Russia fifty years ago was the scene of the most thoroughgoing smashing of property rights ever witnessed. Land, factories, mines, banks, houses, stores, every imaginable form of tangible property, was taken over by the state. Such intangibles as stocks and bonds automatically became worthless, and this was also true as regards the prerevolutionary currency.

And along with this process went the systematic destruction of all the human rights and liberties that had been solemnly affirmed after the overthrow of the czarist regime a few months before. A secret police was set up with unlimited powers of arrest, sentence, and execution. This agency has several times changed its name and has operated sometimes more ruthlessly than at others; but it remains the ultimate sanction of Soviet dictatorship.

Voting became a farce, with only one set of candidates, handpicked by the ruling Communist Party, to vote for. Fifty years after the inauguration of the communist system there is not one organ of opinion in the Soviet Union that is free from state censorship and control. No meetings may be held, no clubs or societies formed, without official approval. To leave the country for travel abroad, a right casually exercised every year by millions of Americans and West Europeans, is for the Soviet citizen a rarely granted privilege. Foreigners resident in Moscow have long become accustomed to receiving letters which have quite obviously been opened. Foreign embassies take every precaution against the constant bugging of conversation within their walls and no Russian in his right mind speaks freely over the telephone.

Forced labor has been a prominent feature of the Soviet system, varying from the barbarous cruelty of concentration camps where millions of men and women were overworked and underfed in the Arctic climate of Northern Russia and Northern Siberia, to the milder constraint put upon university graduates in medicine, engineering, and teaching to accept assignment to remote localities for two years after graduation. And this same pattern of recognizing no inherent rights of the citizen, of treating him merely as a tool and chattel of an all-powerful state, has reappeared in China and in Castro's Cuba. During the last decade bitter hostility has developed between the Soviet and Chinese communist regimes. There have been instances of more or less suppressed friction between Moscow and its east European satellites. Fidel Castro as the first totalitarian ruler in Latin America has not operated under the same conditions, human and material, as Lenin, Stalin, and Mao Tse-tung.

And communism takes on differing national colorations, depending on the people on whom it is imposed. All the more significant, therefore, is the universal common trait of every communist regime, in Europe, in Asia, in Latin America. This is the denial of every basic individual liberty for the individual.

Locke: "Life, Liberty, and Property"

When England, after half a century of turmoil, civil war, religious and political persecution and proscriptions, reached its great compromise in the establishment of constitutional monarchy under William III in 1688, the greatest exponent of the new mood was the political scientist and philosopher, John Locke. By nature broad-minded and tolerant, Locke worked out a theoretical scheme well calculated to satisfy a people sick of the excesses of royal despotism, on one side, and of Puritan rule, embodied in Cromwell's personal dictatorship, on the other.

Locke, whose thought influenced the Founding Fathers of the American Republic as much as the leaders of his native England, strongly vindicated the rights of the individual citizen as against the state. For the old-fashioned theory of an anointed king ruling by divine right he substituted the conception of society as a body of individuals living together for mutual convenience and conferring on government only certain limited and specifically defined powers. He emphasized the "natural right of life, liberty, and property," properly regarding all three as closely associated. It was perhaps an accident that the Declaration of Independence did not restate Locke's formula, substituting for property the rather meaningless phrase: "pursuit of happiness." Property, in Locke's opinion, is "the great and chief end of men's uniting into commonwealths."

Progress in guaranteed individual liberty has marched side by side with assured guaranties of the right of the individual to accumulate and enjoy property. Great principles of ordered liberty were symbolized in John Hampden's resistance to the payment of "ship money," a tax imposed for a phony purpose by the arbitrary power of King Charles I, and in the actions of Hampden's successors, the rebellious colonists, in refusing to pay taxes on stamps and tea levied without American representation by the British Parliament.

It was because men like Hampden were prepared to stand up for their rights (including their property rights) that England until recent times was a lightly taxed country. And, of course, the conflicts over the stamp and tea taxes were the overture to the establishment of the American Republic.

Eternal Vigilance

Freedom in all its forms, including not least economic freedom, must always be defended, although the enemy changes with changing times. Absolute kings and emperors have disappeared into the archives of history and no longer constitute a threat. The principal threat to freedom now is the adoption of measures that in some countries have led and in others might lead to the modern-style demagogic dictatorship, which, in the name of abolishing exploitation, sets up a superstate with unrivaled powers for exploiting its subjects and invariably strikes down every other freedom as a sequel to eliminating economic freedom.

The surest brake on the tendency of government to exceed its proper functions and degenerate into tyranny is a strong propertied middle class. It was the emergence of such a class that sounded the death knell of absolutist monarchs and feudal barons. The destruction of such a class is the invariable first objective of the totalitarian communist revolution that exploits discontent, justified or unjustified, in order to set up a tyranny far worse than anything against which it rebelled.

One may paraphrase a famous oratorical climax of Daniel Webster, himself a stout defender of economic freedom, and sum up as follows the lesson to be drawn from all historical experience, past and present:

Liberty and Property. One and Inseparable. Now and Forever.

CHAPTER 17

The Man Who Defied Castro

by David Reed

On January 1, 1959, the city of Santiago de Cuba exploded with joy. Cuba's dictator, Fulgencio Batista, had capitulated to an army of bearded young guerrillas led by Fidel Castro. Among the *barbudos*, or bearded ones, who streamed into the city to a tumultuous welcome was Huber Matos. The dashingly handsome former schoolteacher and peasant farmer wore the gold star of a *comandante*, the highest rank in the rebel army. At 40, he was older than most of his comrades, but he radiated fitness and exceptional strength of character. As a guerrilla leader his bravery and skill had become legendary.

Castro asked Matos to become military chief of Camagüey Province. Matos agreed, feeling he had a duty to the revolution. Like many of his countrymen, he believed Castro would fulfill his promises to restore a democratic constitution and hold free elections. Jails filled with political prisoners and the practice of torture would be abolished. Or so Castro said.

After a few months in Camagüey, Matos began to have doubts about Castro. More and more, the rebel army newspaper espoused the communist line. Matos learned that communists were infiltrating rapidly into high government positions.

Matos went to Castro on several occasions. "We need to define the goals of our revolution," Matos told him. "It was fine, during the war, that you were the leader and gave the orders. But now we have to establish a government of laws, which is something that one man cannot do."

Each time Castro smiled and clapped Matos on the shoulder. "You're right," he said — but did nothing.

Despairing of being able to halt Cuba's march toward communism, Matos wrote a letter to Castro on October 19, 1959, resigning from the army and adding, "I do not wish to become an obstacle

---

Reprinted with permission from the April 1980 *Reader's Digest*. Copyright © 1980 by The Reader's Digest Assn., Inc.

to the revolution." In a separate statement, he said: "Once, Fidel, you trusted the people. When you rebelled against tyranny you called upon them to rise in the name of justice and reason, and they responded. Now, Fidel, you are destroying your work."

Castro exploded in rage. Matos was a formidable revolutionary figure, who had a wide following. Castro felt Matos was a potential threat, one that had to be destroyed. Flying to Camagüey, he assembled a crowd of 20,000, denounced Matos as a "traitor" and falsely accused him of plotting to overthrow the government.

"Waste" Box. On October 21, Matos was arrested and taken to El Morro Castle, overlooking Havana Harbor. There he was shoved into a punishment cell, one yard wide and three yards long, with a boarded-up window and no electric light. Weeks went by, and Matos sank into deep depression. Finally he rallied, deciding that he wanted, above all, to live to defend himself against Castro's charges, so the Cuban people would know that he was no traitor.

Finally, on December 9, Matos was put on trial in Havana. Some 1500 spectators were present, most of them rebel military men. Standing before five judges handpicked by Castro, Matos denied that he had planned a military revolt. When Matos finished testifying, several hundred soldiers rose and applauded. They were forced to leave (and later denounced by Castro as "degenerates and traitors" and dismissed from the army).

Then Castro strode in and harangued the spectators for seven hours. "Ours is not a communist revolution," Castro thundered. Matos knew that he would never get a chance to cross-examine his chief accuser, so he jumped up frequently to shout, "That's a lie!" Finally, Castro turned a pained face to the judges and said, "This man won't let me talk." The prosecutor demanded that Matos be condemned to death, but Castro must have had second thoughts. The judges sentenced Matos to 20 years in prison.

Matos was taken to a prison on the Isle of Pines, off the southwest coast of Cuba. He and another man were placed in a concrete box, seven feet long, six feet wide and just high enough to stand in. They never saw the sun, never were taken out for exercise. Food was shoved through a small space atop the door. Twice a day, a guard would bang a metal rod on the door and each man would have to respond, "I'm here." They never saw the guard's face and he never spoke to them. The two men remained in the box for a year. Prisoners call those boxes *pudrideros*, "rotteners." As Matos was to recall many years later: "You put men in. When you finally open the door, what you have is waste."

Matos struggled to retain his sanity. "I had some books," he recalls, "but I spent most of the day trying to survive." He kept telling himself that he was a patient man, with a strong will. He was determined not to be broken.

Punishment Chamber. After prison officials felt that Matos had been sufficiently softened up, they offered him a deal. "You can regain your liberty in stages if you join the rehabilitation program," they said. Matos would have to admit that he was a traitor. Moreover, he would have to "cooperate" with prison authorities. "No," Matos replied. "It was not I but Castro who betrayed the revolution."

By this time, Castro had dropped the mask. He proclaimed Cuba a communist dictatorship, amassing more power in his hands than Batista ever did. The free press, judiciary, universities and labor unions all were destroyed. A ubiquitous secret police, the Department of State Security, dealt ruthlessly with anyone suspected of dissent. Political prisoners numbered in the thousands. At least 5000 persons had perished at *el paredón*, the firing-squad wall.

In 1966, Matos was transferred to Havana's La Cabaña fortress. He was thrown into a large underground punishment chamber, called Gallery 23, which he shared with 12 other men — and cockroaches, lice, flies and mosquitoes. There was no circulation of air. Soot from oil fires in a kitchen overhead filtered into the gallery and, in summer, the heat was unbearable. Often, at night, men woke up screaming. Eventually, Matos contracted emphysema and chronic bronchitis from having to breathe the foul air. Normally men were confined to Gallery 23 for a week. Matos was to spend most of five years there.

Faced with rising world criticism, Castro decided to get rid of all his political prisoners by reclassifying them as common criminals. Told to exchange their yellow uniforms for blue ones worn by ordinary felons, Matos and other *plantados* ("those who remain steadfast," who spurned Castro's "rehabilitation" offers) refused. In retaliation, they were kept naked or clad only in undershorts for nearly a year.

Finally, in 1968, Matos wrote prison authorities protesting the cruel treatment. His letter ignored, Matos went on a hunger strike. Weakening rapidly, he was moved to State Security headquarters on a stretcher. The secret police demanded that he retract the letter. He refused.

On the 30th day of his hunger strike, Matos regained consciousness to find himself tied to a bed. He was being given a blood transfusion in an arm and force-fed through a tube in one nostril. Matos figured he was near death. Later, when he could touch his legs, he recoiled in horror. All he could feel was skin and bones, and he was reminded of photographs of prisoners in Nazi death camps. But, miraculously, he survived. After 135 days he was taken back to La Cabaña, given clothing and medical attention.

"You'll Never Leave Alive." Matos by this time had become one of the most famous political prisoners in the world — a symbol of resistance to oppression. All through the years, his wife, Maria Luisa Araluce, never gave up her efforts on her husband's behalf. Finally allowed to leave Cuba with her four children in 1963, she settled in Elizabeth, N. J., and got a job in a garment factory. To make ends meet, she spent evenings sewing clothing at home. She traveled frequently to Washington. Eventually, 47 sympathetic Senators and 120 Representatives signed letters urging Castro to release Matos. Mrs. Matos appealed many times to the Inter-American Commission on Human Rights, an arm of the Organization of American States. With money raised by the Cuban community in Elizabeth, she flew to Geneva to bring Matos' case to the United Nations Commission on Human Rights.

Castro, however, ignored all pleas to release Matos. The prisoner was allowed no visitors for 8½ years. His ailing father, Rogelio, then in his 80s, made many journeys to see him, but always got the same answer: "The prisoner does not wish to see anyone." Matos himself was told that no one came to see him. Hundreds of letters from his wife were never given to him.

Every few years, Matos was transferred to a different prison — standard practice to heighten feelings of anxiety among the *plantados*. For 16 agonizing years, he was isolated from other prisoners.

Officials kept asking Matos if he would accept "rehabilitation." Angered by his repeated refusals, they finally told him: "You'll never leave prison alive." Matos believed them.

In 1973, several State Security agents marched into his cell at El Principe Prison, carrying long metal bars. Like a pack of dogs, the men fell on Matos, hammering him to the floor with the bars. Matos jumped up, screaming insults at them. They beat him to the floor again. When he jumped up once more, they beat him until he was unconscious. After he revived, he realized that several ribs were broken and his left shoulder was severely damaged.

For days Matos lay on his cot, racked with pain. A year and a half after the beating, a surgeon finally examined him. It was too late for surgery, the doctor said. The shoulder had atrophied, and muscles and tendons had been severed.

In a letter smuggled out of prison in 1975, Matos wrote his wife: "I am a shadow of the man who entered prison in October 1959. Only 56 years old, I look like an old man. The good thing is that my spirit has no holes, nor will I allow them. Privation and suffering, however hard, cannot undermine my spirit."

Matos' sentence was to be completed on October 21, 1979. But his family and friends feared he might not be released. Matos' eldest son, Huber, Jr., a businessman in San José, Costa Rica, stepped up efforts on his father's behalf. Costa Rica's president agreed to send a delegation to Havana to plead for Matos' release.

On October 17, State Security agents came to Matos' cell and beat him savagely. Then they handcuffed him, taped his mouth and threw him on the floor of a car, with their feet on his face and chest. "The prisoner is rebelling," the agents radioed their headquarters. Matos was convinced that they were going to kill him, saying that he had tried to escape, to keep him from telling the world of the horrors of Castro's prisons.

When Matos reached police headquarters, he went wild with rage. He smashed furniture and screamed insults. Guards dragged him to an empty cell. Moaning in pain, Matos slumped to the floor.

Proud Symbol. At 7:30 a.m. on October 21, Matos was bundled into a car. Again he thought it would be his last ride. But the car pulled up in front of the Costa Rican mission in Havana. "You're under our protection now," a Costa Rican diplomat said. Later in the morning, Matos' father and sister, Salustina, arrived. Matos approached his father, now 94, blind and confined to a wheelchair. "Do you know who's here?" Matos asked. His father kept saying, over and over, "Huber, is it really you?"

At midnight, Matos, Salustina and Rogelio left for San José. When their plane landed, a tearful crowd, singing the Cuban national anthem of pre-Castro days, hailed Matos as a man "back from the dead." As if in a dream, Matos swept his wife into his arms. Four vaguely familiar faces appeared, his sons and daughters, Huber, Jr., 35, Rogelio, 33, Lucy, 29, and Carmen, 21. He had not seen them since they were children. Matos ran his fingers over the faces of his two daughters, as if in disbelief. One by one, ten grandchildren who had been born while he was in prison were presented to him.

Today, at 61, Matos scarcely resembles the dashing *barbudo* who entered Santiago de Cuba in triumph on New Year's Day 1959. His mind and spirit, however, are as strong as ever. He intends to devote himself to writing and speaking on behalf of the thousands of political prisoners, and especially the *plantados*, who remain in Castro's jails.

Proudly, just as he did 21 years ago, Huber Matos wears the star of a *comandante*. "I earned it fighting for my country and for liberty," he said. "No dictator can take it from me."

When We Are Free

CHAPTER 18

Getting Rid of Communism

by Leonard E. Read

Zealous opposition to communism appears to be on the increase, and growing numbers of sincere citizens ask FEE[1] how best to lend a hand. Many of the inquiries, however, reveal the popular notion that it's only a matter of identifying Peiping or Moscow-oriented Communists, and nullifying their efforts. Down with these people, goes the mischievous myth, and we will have purged the U.S.A. of communism.

Here at the outset is my shocking conclusion: Were every "card-carrying" Communist miraculously to disappear, from our own and every other country, the practice of communism would continue unabated.

Capital "C" Communists are, for the most part, agents of an avowed political enemy, and thus they are dangerous in a military sense — as are any enemy conspirators and spies. But they are not very effective carriers of communism as a philosophy! If anything, we are so revolted by those agents and their drunken display of power that we hate the very name, Communist! Indeed, so pronounced is our hate that we have made it illegal, that is, libelous to call anyone but a "card-carrying" Communist a Communist. In a word, the official "Reds" tend to turn us away from rather than toward communism; they serve more as a repellent than as a converting force.

Communism, by reason of its identity with a gang of dictators "on the make" who would take us over if they could, is a term of derision. But communism as a philosophy — if it be accurately defined — is more highly respected in our country today than is its opposite: the private property, free exchange, limited government way of life. Like these modern Genghis Khans who hoodwink their own people by calling their grab for power "the dictatorship of the proletariat," we fool ourselves by labeling American communism "social democracy," and by giving it numerous other nonrevealing

---

From *Notes from FEE*, Vol. XV, No. 3.
[1] Foundation for Economic Education.

nicknames. If we continue to confuse these terms of discourse we shall soon find ourselves in that complete communistic milieu we so vigorously deprecate.

Communism Is Forced Sharing

For the moment, let us put aside our blinding hatred for some of the practitioners of communism, thereby making it possible to view the matter as philosophers instead of as military strategists. Then it becomes crystal clear that communism, regardless of how well or evil intentioned its sponsorship, is an ideology. It is a set of ideas aiming at equalization by force. These are the ideas which we must first identify and then displace if we are to rid our nation of communism. Where are we to look for these ideas? Disheartening as it is, among teachers, preachers, workers, farmers, business and professional men and women, neighbors, friends; indeed, it is not amiss to take a look in the mirror! Honesty obliges us — all of us — to confess that this is far more a "we" than a "they" problem.

Now, just what do I mean by that remark? I mean that a vast percentage of Americans today subscribe to and support the tenets of the communistic philosophy. Does this make them small c Communists? They may apply this appelation to themselves, but, legally, no one else can.

Whether or not they accept the appelation, it is these people — pillars of our society — who support the philosophy and effectively spread communism. As carriers, they resemble "Typhoid Marys": they decry communism; they think of themselves and are regarded by others as anticommunists and, thus, are advertised as not infected themselves; yet, they unsuspectingly and unwittingly carry the ideological virus! By reason of their avowed Americanism, their social standing, and the high esteem in which they are held generally, these folks tend more to promote than to defeat communism.

Then, what, precisely, are communist ideas? That these are difficult to recognize is self-evident; otherwise, more of us than now would know one whenever it shows itself. The reason for this myopia? Once a communist idea has been Americanized for a short time, it becomes a part of the mores, the idea seems to lose its identity with communism and takes on a likeness of Americanism. And, why not? For what, actually, is Americanism? It is construed to be whatever Americans believe, and it makes not the slightest difference what the beliefs are. Thus, the term Americanism is meaningless for definitive purposes. Therefore, if we are to rid our country of communism, we must give ourselves repeated refresher courses on what the ideological virus is. And for this instruction why not begin with the source itself: *The Communist Manifesto?*

The Communist Program

This document was written over a century ago with English conditions in mind. It requires some astuteness in political economy, therefore, to make the translation and apply the Manifesto to developments which have occurred in the United States. Nonetheless, even a casually interested person can sense the alarming extent to which we, more or less naively, have adopted the tenets of Marx and Engels. The ten points:

No. 1. Abolition of property in land and application of all rents of land to public purposes.
No. 2. A heavy progressive or graduated income tax.
No. 3. Abolition of all rights of inheritance.
No. 4. Confiscation of the property of all emigrants and rebels.
No. 5. Centralization of credit in the hands of the State, by means of a national bank with State capital and an exclusive monoply.
No. 6. Centralization of the means of communication and transport in the hands of the State.
No. 7. Extension of factories and instruments of production owned by the State; the bringing into cultivation of waste lands, and the improvement of the soil generally in accordance with a common plan.
No. 8. Equal liability of all to labor. Establishment of industrial armies; especially for agriculture.
No. 9. Combination of agriculture with manufacturing industries; gradual abolition of the distinction between town and country, by a more equable distribution of the population over the country.
No. 10. Free education for all children in public schools. Abolition of children's factory labor in its present form, etc., etc.

Listing the above ten points is almost like recapping the events of old home week, so far toward the communistic ideology have we drifted, but with little recognition of what we have done. A revealing statement of the late Dean Inge comes to mind: "History seems to show that the powers of evil have won their greatest triumphs by capturing the organizations which were formed to defeat them, and that when the devil has thus changed the contents of the bottles, he never alters the labels. The fort may have been captured by the enemy, but it still flies the flag of its defenders."

To assist in correlating the above ten points with what a majority of Americans now support, observe the all too familiar terms:

Abolition of property; application of land rents to public purposes; progressive income tax; abolition of all rights; confiscation; centralization; State capital; exclusive monopoly; in the hands of the State; a common plan; industrial armies; equable distribution; free education.

As we reflect on these ten points and their familiar jargon, it becomes clear that communism is no more than the communization of the product of all by force; that is, State ownership and control of the means of production (the planned economy) and/or State ownership and control of the results of production (the Welfare State). If we substitute socialization or equalization or collectivization for communization, the meaning is in no way altered. Regardless of which of these terms we employ, the result is the same: ". . . state planning and control of the economy . . . suppression of individual liberties."

Our Pilgrim Fathers practiced socialism, egalitarianism, collectivism, communism — call it what you will — during their first three years after landing at Plymouth Rock. Everyone was compelled to put his produce into a common warehouse; the proceeds were doled out according to the authority's idea of "need." The point to be emphasized is that we do not despise the communism they initially practiced; we only feel sorry for the ones who starved or failed to prosper by the system which denied private property, freedom in exchange, and individual liberty.

Communism, by whatever name, should be judged not only by its sponsors and performance, but also by its morality. Then it should be embraced or thrown overboard in fact as well as in terminology. Is it meritorious or deleterious? That's the question! If we propose to endorse the principles of communism, why not use the label? We would then be at least as honest as those political gangsters who have seen fit to adopt the correct label as their trade mark.

When we thus fail to understand what we do, we deceive ourselves and do foolish things; ranting against communism as we promote it and warring against the gangsters while adopting their ways.

Each individual acts in response to what he is; he is what he believes; if his beliefs be contradictory, he must, of necessity, act against himself.

Communistic ideas are just as indestructible as freedom ideas. They can't be shot or shouted out of existence; they can only be relegated to a state of general disapproval. But this is possible only as superior ideas gain the ascendancy. In short, we have no way to combat the false doctrines and the raw violence of communism except as we come to understand and learn how to explain the common-consent ways of the free market, the ways of willing exchange, personal choice, self-responsibility, mutual respect for life and property, and government limited to keeping the peace. Such achievement is out of the question except for a dedicated student of liberty. Being such a student is the lowest price of admission even to get on the work force. That's how difficult getting rid of communism is!

When We Are Free

Unit IV: The Rise and Fall of Civilizations

It was Ben Franklin who once remarked, "Those who give up essential liberty to obtain a little temporary security deserve neither liberty nor security." Whether it was his intent to do so or not, Franklin distilled in that statement the essence of the decline of history's great civilizations.

That elusive goal of security — guaranteed by the State — is a major theme of this unit, which opens with a selection by Lois H. Sargent. She argues that, far from being a hindrance, *insecurity* is behind "most of the progress mankind has made." She regards it as a "condition of life," "an incentive," and "a challenge."

Pursuing a point developed by Roger Williams in Unit I, the author of this unit's second chapter reveals that, in every sense of the word, "civilizations" don't really rise and fall, only *individuals* do. What history records as the course of nations is actually the stories of billions of individuals, each of whom have progressed or regressed depending in large measure on the character of the ideas they held.

A unit with the title of this one would hardly be complete if it didn't mention those great and glorious people, the Romans. "The Fall of Rome and Modern Parallels" traces their course and reveals that the Romans "first lost their freedom and only then did they lose their lives." It was what any good historical coroner would label as a clear case of suicide. The chapter also draws some ominous parallels to events in recent American history.

One of the great lessons of the past is expressed in Kershner's Second Law: "Throughout history, periods of sound money have been marked by moral advance and prosperity. Conversely, periods of unsound money have been accompanied by moral decline." In "The Demonetization of Money," the author chronicles a few of the many periods of unsound money and urges Americans to restore honest money. The reader will see clearly what so many others sense — that big government, inflated money, and internal rot are closely related.

Sweden is a modern day counterpart to the welfare states of old and few people in America are better qualified to speak of that country than Eric Brodin. In "Why I Left Sweden," Brodin laments the tragic path his native land has chosen.

"The Last Candle" by Jack Schreiber ends the unit where it began. In caving in to the corrupting temptation of government-guaranteed "security," Americans, claims Schreiber, are threatening to extinguish "the last candle" of liberty. For the sake of humankind, that must not happen!

CHAPTER 19

In Defense of Insecurity

by Lois H. Sargent

We are constantly reading and hearing about security. Banks, investment firms, insurance companies build advertisements around the virtues of saving — for security. The liberal politicians and union heads plan their policies around an appeal to man's urge for security. Psychologists and counselors make use of the word in discussions of emotional stability. Security has become the frantic obsession of our age.

No one has a good word to say about insecurity.

Yet were it not for *insecurity* the human race probably would never have advanced beyond the mentality of the caveman.

It was his insecurity that prompted primitive man to find and invent instruments of self-protection and develop methods and tools for increasing his food supply. It was insecurity that led him to restrain an instinctive suspicion and distrust of his fellow men and to unite with them for greater safety and well-being.

Insecurity in some form is behind most of the progress mankind has made. Curiosity and ambition are strong driving forces in human nature, but the tension of insecurity is frequently needed to prod men into action. If "necessity is the mother of invention," insecurity is surely its father. Probably more work efforts and more ingenuity of ideas have been inspired by insecurity than by a comfortable environment and a life free of trouble.

It is the feeling of insecurity, not the ease of security that challenges a man to strive for prosperity and to prepare for the uncertainty of the future. Even the man of wealth who (apparently) would have no financial worry recognizes the need to protect his interests and prepare for possible reverses of fortune. Insecurity is not a comfortable or contentment-creating sensation, but it is one of the inevitable tensions of life. And it is this very discomfort that prompts whatever efforts we make to improve conditions.

What do we mean when we speak of security?

From *The Freeman*, August 1964.

The dictionary gives the following definitions: feelings of assurance of safety or certainty; freedom from fear, doubt, care, danger, or anxiety — a quality of being safe.

Is it possible to enjoy all of this safety?

Freedom from physical danger can be fairly well assured by the protective forces of the community in which we live and by our own common-sense safety precautions. This sort of security is attainable, or at least enough of it to eliminate haunting fears of danger. We do not dispute the desire for this aspect of security which, after all, is but a normal expression of man's self-protective instinct.

As promulgated today, the aspect of security most frequently emphasized relates to economic conditions and the psychological effects of financial well-being or want. The apparent aim of those who beat the drum for security is for a security that would remove all anxiety about the present and future. Such emphasis upon security is grist to the mill of the socialistic schemers and welfare statists. While the motives of some of these idealists may be sincere, they are encouraging the pursuit of a false goal when they picture a life of continuous ease. The power-hungry men who wish to build an all-powerful government deliberately arouse fear of insecurity and sell their programs under the guise of providing immutable security.

The Absence of Challenge

But is security immutable?

If, by security, we understand a permanent or continuous state of well-being, a life devoid of problems or obstacles, we are ascribing to security a permanence impossible to realize. Neither the capitalistic system nor the welfare state has been able to achieve this, nor are they likely to in the future because neither can eliminate change and uncertainty from life.

That tomorrow will come is a certainty. What it may bring by way of circumstances or events is an uncertainty. We may go along day after day in the same routine or existence, but any day an event may occur — with or without our personal instigation — which breaks into the pattern or which brings about a change in our affairs. It happens to someone, somewhere, every day.

To achieve and maintain an ideal state of economic security we would have to eliminate all uncertainty, all chance and change from life. We would have to deny what history and experience teaches — that uncertainty is always with us. The changes and uncertainties of weather which affect the produce of the earth, and the market fluctuations of business are the obvious examples. All the political programs conceived to offset these fluctuations have in practice merely created new problems and different kinds of anxiety and uncertainty.

When put to the test of logic, the idea of employment security is found to be equally irrational. Industry and business are too much affected by new inventions, new methods and by market fluctuations to ensure work opportunity to the entire employable population. The government may create jobs through bureaus or other make-work projects, but they cannot absorb all of the working classes.

All of this would appear to be so obvious to the intelligent reader that it is hardly necessary to state that security as an economic condition cannot be realized for everybody. Whatever *degree* of security it is possible for the individual to attain will be mainly through his own foresight and efforts, assuming that he has freedom to work out his own destiny.

Every Choice Involves a Risk

That insecurity is a powerful driving force in motivating human action would be hard to dispute. It is the awareness of insecurity that impels our plans and preparations for the future. We take out health and accident insurance, not as an assurance of good health or safety, but to be prepared for the possible unexpected emergency or misfortune. The desire for prosperity, while motivated by the urge to enjoy the advantages and comforts of living, also prompts most of us to save or invest part of that prosperity for the future so it will (we hope) continue to be available.

People face insecurity to accomplish a possible good. The early pioneers crossed the plains and mountains facing insecurity every mile of the way but went ahead courageously because they envisioned a new and better life at the end of the journey than the one they had left. It is doubtful that they thought of their adventure as a search for security, but they surely must have been aware of their insecurity.

Every man who establishes a new business or expands one already in operation takes a risk, however well he has allowed for emergencies or unexpected costs. But he knowingly and optimistically faces the insecurity of the situation to achieve his objectives.

Many farmers have begged for removal of government controls. They prefer their freedom to operate without restriction, with the insecurity of nature's whims and market fluctuations, with possible falling prices, to the false security of government subsidy with its controls and restrictions.

Psychologists often blame insecurity for deviations of personality and neuroses of various types. But it is only when a feeling of insecurity becomes a gnawing fear that it threatens emotional balance. This the layman does not always understand.

There are various causes of insecurity tensions; lack of money is but one of them. At the same time having plenty of the world's goods will not always ensure emotional stability. Many wealthy and famous persons have been driven to intemperance or suicide by feelings of insecurity which grew out of an unsolved personality problem. Behind the problem was the individual's failure to recognize or handle his own private insecurity.

As we pursue the analysis of security and its counterpart, insecurity, we are led to the conclusion that the effect of either will be determined by the mental attitude of the individual in his reaction to circumstances. Our purpose here has been to show that insecurity is a normal factor of life. As a condition of life, or as an emotion, it serves a purpose. It can be an incentive or a challenge. Seen in proper perspective, it can be a blessing in disguise.

CHAPTER 20

Impotent Abstractions — Potent Individuals

by Dale M. Haywood

In the human world there is no entity but the individual person. There is no force but individual energy.[1]

I believe the author of these lines, Rose Wilder Lane, is correct. And if she is correct, the power of a group of human beings to act physically, mentally, morally, or financially cannot be greater than the sum of the power of the individual members in that group. A human aggregation cannot have a force separate from the force of its individual members.

Why do we sometimes forget these truths about the nature of human aggregates? What happens when we lose sight of these facts and then attribute to a group power separate from the power of the group's constituents? The purpose of this article is to answer these two questions.

Human Abstractions

When referring to various groups of people, we often use abstractions. "Team," "society," "the country," and "civilization" are examples of such abstractions. These terms are simply proxies for the specific individuals to which they refer. However, when we repeatedly use an abstraction, we run a risk. We may forget what it stands for. We may begin to think that it is not a surrogate but a separate, independent entity — an entity in its own right.

When the group to which the term applies is quite small, there seems to be less chance of forgetting that the individual person is the only entity in the human world and that individual energy is the only force. For example, consider the *Midland* (Michigan) *Daily News* headline that announces: "Northmen defeat Wayne in tuneup for SVSC." More specifically, let's examine the human abstraction "Northmen."

As used in this headline, there may be considerable ambiguity as to what individuals "Northmen" refers to. For readers in the

---

[1] Rose Wilder Lane, *The Discovery of Freedom* (New York City: The John Day Company), 1943, page 5.

Midland area, the term might be the stand-in for all male students currently enrolled at Northwood Institute. There may still be some uncertainty in the mind of the person who notes that the headline appears in the sports section of the paper. For if the reader did not notice the date of the paper (February 13, 1981), he might be unsure of whether the Northmen are the football team or the basketball team. And even if he noticed the date, he probably couldn't be sure of whether the abstraction referred to the hockey team or the basketball team. Of course anyone who reads the article under the headline can finally determine that the Northmen in this case are members of Northwood Institute's current men's basketball team.

As newspaper accounts of basketball games customarily do, this one ends this way:

> WAYNE STATE — Bauer 0-0-0; E. Thorderson 0-0-0; Wicker 4-2-10; K. Thorderson 0-0-0; Visser 2-2-6; Scott 10-5-25; Cooks 4-5-13; Scollin 0-0-0; Monk 2-3-7; Cain 0-0-0; Totals 22-17-61.
> NORTHWOOD — Bartnick 2-1-5; Mann 7-0-14; Ruttle 8-5-21; Somers 5-5-15; Lewis 0-0-0; Taylor 2-2-6; Hardman 4-0-8; Totals 28-13-69.

Of course a tabulation of who made the scores in a game is a crude, incomplete record of the contributions individual team members made to the victory. Getting rebounds, blocking the opponent's shots, passing the ball to teammates who are in better scoring positions and stealing the ball from opposing players are examples of other important actions. Although these and other actions do not directly result in scores, they can indirectly contribute very significantly to a victory.

The main point of this illustration is, however, to note the direction the sportswriter is moving — away from "Northmen" toward specific individuals. *To help his readers get a better understanding of what happened in this game, the sportswriter deaggregates this particular human aggregate.* The writer thereby makes it very clear to the reader that "Northmen" is *not* an entity separate and independent from specific individuals.

Especially note that, in the final analysis, "Northmen" did not score a single field goal. "Northmen" did not block an opponent's shot. Because of the deaggregation of this human abstraction, we clearly see that "Northmen" does not have the power to score a single point, get even one rebound, or in any way contribute to the victory described in the article. *Abstractions are impotent.*

Larger Abstractions, Greater Perils

As the group to which an abstraction used as the stand-in for a human aggregate gets larger, there is greater risk. Because it is less practical to enumerate the members of larger groups, we enumerate them less frequently. If we enumerate them less frequently, the abstraction more frequently stands alone in our thinking, speaking, and writing. We get to the point where an abstraction that refers to a larger human aggregate is used by itself so often that we may unconsciously begin to think of it as a separate, independent entity. Yet, we may impute to that entity power that only human beings have.

This risk is especially great with such terms as "the nation." For nation may be used as a more encompassing aggregate on some occasions than on others. Sometimes the term refers to all of the people in a certain geographic area. At other times, nation may be expanded to include people *and* land *and* improvements built on that land and so on. When the abstraction is thus used more broadly, portions of what it refers to, e.g., land, *can* stand alone, independent of human beings. But the discussion in this article is limited to abstractions as they refer strictly to human aggregates.

As the group of individuals to which an abstraction refers gets larger, something else often happens. Although we may (incorrectly) attribute to that group a power that only individual human beings have, we may (correctly) ascribe mostly impersonal attributes to it. Groups such as "the country" may be practically depersonalized. For unlike North*men*, there is no apparent reference to humans in "the country." This probably contributes to the severance of this human aggregate's ties with individual men and women for whom it is the proxy.

But "So what?", you may ask, if we think of human aggregate abstractions as separate entities, attribute power to them that is uniquely individual human power, and yet largely depersonalize them. The short answer to your question is, *"We may further reduce what private property and individual liberty is left in the United States."*

Our A, B, C's

To understand my response, let's begin with this sentence which I found on page 21 of the February 5, 1981 issue of *The Wall Street Journal:*

> Dr. Richard M. Freeman, president of the National Kidney Foundation, argues that the country probably ought to provide kidney machines for all who need them.

On a quick, uncritical reading, I suspect many of us would feel a general sympathy for Dr. Freeman's position. That's if our focus is on his *goal*. Could any humane person possibly quarrel with the goal, i.e., kidney machines for all who need them? The "hook" in this statement is, of course, "the country." "The country" is the means of accomplishing Dr. Freeman's objective. Those of us who have lost sight of the true nature of human groups might not recognize that "the country" is the hook and thus might reason as follows:

If we think "the country" is a separate, independent entity, we look outside ourselves to find a point at which to start moving toward the goal of kidney machines for all who need them. Increasingly, that point seems to be Washington, D.C. Maybe we turn to state capitals. But wherever we turn, it is, more and more often, "elsewhere."

Then, if we think this independent entity has the power that individuals have, we expect it to provide kidney machines. After all, particular individuals have the power to make kidney machines. These individuals could provide them to many, if not all, those who need them. So "the country" should be able to provide them too.

Finally, those of us who have lost sight of the true nature of human groups find it very convenient largely to depersonalize "the country." For the impersonal does not have feelings. Particularly, the impersonal does not know pain of any sort. It knows nothing about rewards and incentives, nothing about punishment and penalties. To a depersonalized "country," there are no costs.

Focus on the Individual

This line of reasoning is, of course, just filled with errors. When we lose sight of the true nature of "the country," "civilization," and similar human aggregates, we are likely to make such errors. All of these errors could be eliminated by deaggregating the aggregates. If we did for "the country" what Ron Kirkwood, assistant sports editor for *The Midland Daily News*, did for "Northmen," we could greatly reduce the chance of making these mistakes. We could eliminate the errors in our reasoning by replacing ambiguous abstractions with specific individuals.

In the end, Mr. Kirkwood specified precisely what direct, score-contribution each of seven basketball players currently enrolled at Northwood Institute made toward the 69-61 victory over the Wayne State University team. Similarly, although it might not be practical, we could specify precisely what contribution, if any, each man, woman, and child in the United States is making in competition with (and in many cases victory over) hunger, ignorance, disease (including kidney disease), pain, boredom, and all other human perils. Now, with the deaggregated "the country" in mind, let's reconsider the position on kidney machines that a *Wall Street Journal* writer attributes to Dr. Freeman.

Now it's clear that we cannot look outside ourselves for kidney machines — or for any other economic good. The only place there is to turn is to ourselves.

There is no mystery now as to who has the power to make kidney machines. It is only the particular individuals who own and work in kidney machine manufacturing plants. We could visit them. We could measure each one's contribution to the total output of those plants.

It is in *re*personalizing "the country" that we bring Dr. Freeman's position into sharp focus. Now we can clearly see the true cost of realizing his goal of kidney machines for all who need them. For it is precisely the Dr. Freemans in the world and their sympathizers who William Graham Sumner, a Yale professor writing about one hundred years ago, was referring to when he wrote:

> The humanitarians, philanthropists, and reformers, looking at the facts of life as they present themselves, find enough which is sad and unpromising in the condition of many members of society. . . . They eagerly set about the attempt to account for what they see, and to devise schemes for remedying what they do not like. In their eagerness to recommend the less fortunate classes to pity and consideration *they forget all about the rights of other classes;* they gloss over all the faults of the classes in question, and they exaggerate their misfortunes and their virtues. They invent new theories of property, distorting rights and perpetuating injustice, as anyone is sure to do who sets about the readjustment of social relations with the interests of one group distinctly before his mind, and the interests of all other groups thrown into the background. . . . Their schemes, therefore, may always be reduced to this type — that A and B decide what C shall do for D . . . In all the discussions attention is concentrated on A and B, the noble social reformers, and on D, the "poor man." I call C the Forgotten Man, because I have never seen that any notice was taken of him in any of the discussions.[2] (Emphasis added.)

---

[2]William Graham Sumner, *What Social Classes Owe to Each Other* (Caldwell, Idaho: The Caxton Printers, Ltd., 1963), pages 20-22.

Dr. Freeman and his sympathizers correspond to A and B. All who need kidney machines correspond to D. There is no mention in the quotation that reports Dr. Freeman's position of anyone corresponding to C. Sure enough, C is the Forgotten Man. But because we have deaggregated "the country," we can recognize what the cost of kidney machines for all who need them is and identify who C is.

The cost of realizing Dr. Freeman's goal would be shifting investments and workers from the production of goods and services other than kidney machines to the production of kidney machines. The investors and workers thus affected correspond to the C in Professor Sumner's paradigm. Although this is a shift Dr. Freeman and his sympathizers believe *ought* to take place, we can be certain this is not a shift that the investors and workers themselves believe ought to be made. To the extent they are free, we can be sure that these investors and workers are already doing what they prefer to do. For where there is liberty, individuals will, when making investment and employment decisions, always act in ways that they believe are to their best advantage.

So *the cost of Dr. Freeman's and his sympathizers' goal is no less than the loss of human liberty.* The As and Bs of the world want to direct how C's property is used. Thus C would have less freedom to dispose of his property as he thinks best, i.e., there would be less *private* property if the As and Bs have their way. The As and Bs of the world want to decide how C uses his energy and talents. Thus C would have less freedom to channel his energy and talents as he believes is in his best interest. This is the cost of losing sight of the true nature of groups of people. To a libertarian, this is a prohibitively high cost.

But we have seen how we can avoid paying this terrible price. We must see through abstractions that refer to human aggregates. Each of us must persistently and consistently remind himself what "team," "society," "the country," and "civilization" stand for.

In the human world there is no entity but the individual person. There is no force but individual energy.

CHAPTER 21

The Fall of Rome and Modern Parallels

by Lawrence W. Reed

There's an old story worth retelling about a band of wild hogs which lived along a river in a secluded area of Georgia. These hogs were a stubborn, ornery, independent bunch. They had survived floods, fires, freezes, droughts, hunters, dogs, and everything else. No one thought they could ever be captured.

One day a stranger came into town not far from where the hogs lived and went into the general store. He asked the storekeeper, "Where can I find the hogs? I want to capture them." The storekeeper laughed at such a claim but pointed in the general direction. The stranger left with his one-horse wagon, an axe, and a few sacks of corn.

Two months later he returned, went back to the store and asked for help to bring the hogs out. He said he had them all penned up in the woods. People were amazed and came from miles around to hear him tell the story of how he did it.

"The first thing I did," the stranger said, "was to clear a small area of the woods with my axe. Then I put some corn in the center of the clearing. At first, none of the hogs would take the corn. Then after a few days, some of the young ones would come out, snatch some corn, and then scamper back into the underbrush. Then the older ones began taking the corn, probably figuring that if they didn't get it, some of the other ones would. Soon they were all eating the corn. They stopped grubbing for acorns and roots on their own.

"About that time, I started building a fence around the clearing, a little higher each day. At the right moment, I built a trap door and sprung it. Naturally, they squealed and hollered when they knew I had them, *but I can pen any animal on the face of the earth if I can first get him to depend on me for a free handout!*"

---

*This is the text of a speech delivered at Campbell University in Buies Creek, North Carolina, January 13, 1981.

When We Are Free

The moral to that story happens to be the connecting link between the course of ancient Rome and the path which America is taking today.

Roman civilization began many centuries ago. In those early days, Roman society was basically agricultural, made up of small farmers and shepherds. By the second century B.C., large-scale businesses made their appearance. Italy became urbanized. Immigration accelerated as people from many lands were attracted by the vibrant growth and great opportunities the Roman economy offered. The growing prosperity was made possible by a general climate of free enterprise, limited government, and respect for private property. Merchants and entrepreneurs were admired and emulated. Commerce and trade flourished and large investments were commonplace.

It is certainly true that some slavery existed in Rome. That's deplorable from a libertarian standpoint, of course. But to be fair to the Romans, it must be said that slavery was far more common and far more brutal in the rest of the world in those days.

Remarkable Achievements

Historians still talk today about the remarkable achievements Rome made in sanitation, public parks, banking, architecture, education, and administration. The city even had mass production of some consumer items and a stock market. With low taxes and low tariffs, free trade and private property, Rome became the center of the world's wealth.

At one time, the political and military power of Rome dominated Europe and the Mediterranean. Roman roads facilitated speed of travel and communication to a degree which would not be surpassed until the development of the railroad, the steamship, and the telegraph in the nineteenth century.

Roman law and justice enabled the traveler to journey throughout the empire with a considerable degree of safety.

All of this disappeared, however, by the fifth century A.D., and when it was gone, the world was plunged into darkness and despair, slavery and poverty. There are lessons to be learned from this course of Roman history.

Why did Rome decline and fall? The record is abundantly clear on this point. Rome fell because of a fundamental change in ideas on the part of the Roman people — ideas which relate primarily to personal responsibility and the source of personal income. In the early days of greatness, Romans regarded *themselves* as their chief source of income. Each individual looked to himself — what he could acquire voluntarily in the marketplace — as the source of his livelihood. Rome's decline began when the people discovered another source of income: the political process — *the State.*

When Romans abandoned self-responsibility and self-reliance and began to vote themselves benefits, to use government to rob Peter to pay Paul, to put their hands into other people's pockets, and to envy and covet the productive and their wealth, they set into motion Kershner's First Law: "When a self-governing people confer upon their government the power to take from some and give to others, the process will not stop until the last bone of the last taxpayer is picked bare."

The legalized plunder of the Roman Welfare State was undoubtedly sanctioned by people who wished to do good. But as Henry David Thoreau wrote, "If I knew for certain that a man was coming to my house to do me good, I would run for my life." Another person coined the phrase, "The road to hell is paved with good intentions." Nothing but evil can come from a society bent upon coercion, the confiscation of property, and the degradation of the productive.

Early in this process, a politician named Clodius ran for the office of tribune on a "free wheat for the masses" platform and won. Candidates for office began spending huge sums to win election and plundering the population afterwards to pay their campaign debts.

When Julius Caesar came to power in 48 B.C., he found 320,000 persons on government grain relief. Temporarily putting a dent in the Welfare State bandwagon, he ordered the rolls cut to 200,000. But forty-five years later, the rolls were back up to well over 300,000.

Government Bread

A real landmark in the course of events came in the year 274 A.D. Emperor Aurelian, wishing to provide cradle-to-grave care for the citizenry, declared the right to relief to be hereditary. Those whose parents received government benefits were entitled as a matter of right to benefits as well. And Aurelian gave welfare recipients government-baked bread (instead of the old practice of giving them wheat and letting them bake their own bread) and added free salt, pork, and olive oil. Not surprisingly, the ranks of the unproductive grew fatter, and the ranks of the productive grew thinner.

Surely, many Romans opposed the Welfare State and held fast to the old virtues of work, thrift, and self-reliance. But just as surely, some of these sturdy people gave in and began to feed at the public trough in the belief that if they didn't get it, somebody else would. That attitude only hastened the slide into bankruptcy.

The central government also assumed the responsibility of providing the people with entertainment. Elaborate circuses and gladiator duels were staged to keep the people happy. The equivalent of a hundred million dollars a year in the city of Rome alone is a moderate estimate of what was poured out on the games. It was, so to speak, a rough, ancient counterpart to the National Endowment for the Arts, administered and financed by the American government today.

Someone once remarked that the Welfare State is so named because in it, the politicians get well and *you* pay the fare! There is much truth in that statement. In Rome, the emperors were buying support with the people's money. After all, government can give only what it first takes. The emperors, in dishing out all these goodies, were in a position to manipulate public opinion. Alexander Hamilton observed, "Control of a man's subsistence is control of a man's will." Few people will bite the hand that feeds them!

By the second century A.D. many cities had spent themselves deeply into debt. Beginning with the emperor Hadrian, municipalities which got themselves into financial difficulties lost their independence as the central government placed them under the authority of imperial curators. The financial troubles of New York City and Cleveland of late are modern day echoes. More than half the budget of the city of Detroit is now provided (with strings attached) by the federal government.

High Taxes

Civil wars and conflict of all sorts increased as faction fought against faction to get control of the huge State apparatus and all its public loot. Of twenty-seven emperors or would-be emperors between 180 and 285 A.D., all but two met violent deaths. High taxes and burdensome regulations were the order of the day. Business enterprise was called upon to support the growing body of public parasites.

By the time of Emperor Antoninus Pius, who ruled from 138 to 161 A.D., the Roman bureaucracy was as all-embracing as that of modern times. The historian Trever wrote that by the third century, "the relentless system of taxation, requisition, and compulsory labour was administered by an army of military bureaucrats .... Everywhere were the ubiquitous personal agents of the emperors to spy out any remotest case of attempted strikes or evasion of taxes."

Another writer, W. G. Hardy, said several years ago that in later Rome, "what the soldiers or the barbarians spared, the emperors took in taxes." The crushing cost of the military, the top-heavy bureaucracy, and the public programs taxed the middle class out of existence.

Clearly, the State gradually became the prime source of income for an increasing number of Romans. The high taxes needed to finance this drove business into bankruptcy and then nationalization. Whole sectors of the economy came under government domination in this manner. The first industry in Rome to be taken over was transportation — shipping in particular. Interestingly, the first industry in America to suffer comprehensive control was also transportation — specifically, railroads.

Emperor Nero may have been the original architect of urban renewal legislation. In the tenth year of his reign (64 A.D.), a great fire left more than half of Rome in ashes. It was rumored then, and many historians now believe, that Nero had ordered the conflagration to be lighted in order to clear the ground for a rebuilding of the city.

In 91 A.D., the government became deeply involved in the business of agriculture. Emperor Domitian, to reduce the production and raise the price of wine, ordered the destruction of half the provincial vineyards.

As the old virtue of self-reliance gave way to political redistribution of income, priests, teachers, and intellectuals extolled the virtues of the almighty emperor, the Provider of all things. The interests of the individual were considered a distant second to the interests of the emperor and his legions. A spiritual vacuum ensued, which was filled partly by the rise of cults and oriental religions and partly by worship of the emperor. The latter reached its zenith under Emperor Diocletian in 285 A.D. No one could approach him without prostrating himself on the ground and kissing the hem of his garment. Formerly, the proud, free citizens of Rome had refused to render such servile adoration to any of their magistrates and rulers.

Natural Disasters

The Roman empire, amid this sickening spectacle of moral decay, fell victim to an unfortunate series of natural disasters and plagues. Earthquakes, volcanoes, and harsh storms caused great damage. By 200 A.D. at least one-fourth of the population of the whole empire, both civilian and military, had perished by a plague brought from the East. A later one, from 252 to 267 A.D., was nearly as bad. A morally righteous and strong people might have recovered and rebuilt, but these disasters only reinforced the growing despair of a desperate people. The fabric of Roman society was rotting away under the influence of government paternalism, bureaucracy, and spiritual malaise.

Rome also suffered from the bane of all Welfare States — inflation. The massive demands on the government to spend for this and that created pressures for the multiplication of money. The Roman coin, the denarius, was cheapened and debased by one emperor after another to help pay for the expensive programs. Once 94% silver, the denarius by 268 A.D. was little more than a piece of junk containing only .02% silver. (Sound familiar?)

Flooding the economy with all this new and cheapened money had predictable results: prices skyrocketed, savings were eroded, and the people became angry and frustrated. Businessmen were often blamed for the rising prices even as government continued its spendthrift ways.

The easy money policies produced periodic crises in the economy. The panic of 86 A.D. and a severe economic contraction of a few years later are examples. The government responded by imposing penalties for trading in gold, especially for exporting it, much as Franklin Roosevelt did in 1933.

Demanding relief from economic disorder, the people of Rome cried out for a strong man. They got him in the person of Diocletian who, in the year 301, imposed his famous "Edict of 301." This law established a system of comprehensive wage and price controls, to be enforced by a penalty of death. The chaos that followed inspired the contemporary historian Lactantius to write in 314: "After the many oppressions which he put into practice had brought a general dearth upon the empire, he then set himself to regulate the prices of all vendible things. There was much bloodshed upon very slight and trifling accounts; and the people brought provisions no more to market, since they could not get a reasonable price for them; and this increased the dearth so much that at last after many had died by it, the law itself was laid aside."

From Welfarism to Despotism

Diocletian also ordered that all offices, trades, and professions, in so far as possible, were to be made hereditary. Young men were forced to carry on in the trade of their fathers. There was no escape from this regimentation. The Welfare State had become a despotism.

This tyrant left his mark on history in other ways too. It was during his reign that fully half the men of the Empire were on the government payroll. And not only did he impose across-the-board wage and price controls in relative peacetime, he also resigned from office, in the year 305. (Shades of Richard Nixon?)

All this robbery and tyranny by the State was a reflection of the breakdown of moral law in Roman society. The people had lost all respect for the sanctity of private property. This author is reminded of the New York City blackout of 1977, when all it took was for the lights to go out for hundreds to go on a "shopping spree."

The Christians were the last to resist the tyranny of the Roman Welfare State. Until 313 A.D., they had been persecuted because of their faith and their unwillingness to worship the emperor. Under Diocletian, Christians were cast into dungeons, thrown to the wild beasts in the ampitheater, and put to death by every other mode of torture that ingenious cruelty could devise. In this year, Emperor Constantine granted them toleration in exchange for their acquiescence to his authority.

Constantine himself professed Christianity but his personal morality defied his word. Within three years of his announced conversion, he put a nephew to death, drowned his wife in a bath, and murdered his son.

Meanwhile, Constantine showered the Church with land, gifts, and patronage at taxpayer expense. Thus corrupted, the Church lost its old simplicity and high moral standards. It too had jumped aboard the gravy train.

In the year 380, a sadly-perverted Christianity became the official state religion under Emperor Theodosius. Rome's decline was like a falling rock from this point on.

Foreign Policy

In another arena, the foreign policy of Rome in the third, fourth and fifth centuries had become one of weakness and appeasement. Politicians, too busy buying votes at home with pie-in-the-sky programs, ignored the empire's defense. Barbarian "converts," whose loyalty was still suspect, were even permitted to hold important posts in the Roman military establishment.

In 410, Alaric the Goth and his primitive Germanic tribes — men assaulted the city and sacked its treasures. The once-proud Roman army, which had always repelled the barbarians before, now wilted in the face of opposition. Why risk life and limb to defend a corrupt and decaying society?

The end came, rather anti-climactically, in 476, when the German chieftain, Odoacer, pushed aside the last Roman emperor and made himself the new authority.

Some might say that Rome fell because of the attack by these foreigners. Such a claim overlooks what the Romans had done to themselves. When the Vandals, Goths, Huns and others reached Rome, many citizens actually welcomed them in the belief that anything was better than their own tax collectors and regulators. It is more accurate to say that Rome committed suicide. Like the wild hogs, Romans first lost their freedom, and only then did they lose their lives.

History does seem to have an uncanny knack of repeating itself now and then. America is surely making some of the same mistakes today that Rome made centuries ago. In a famous statement, paraphrased here, George Santayana warned, "Those who ignore history are condemned to repeat it."

No one reading this, however, should feel despair for the future. The decline of American influence and strength is not inevitable; it is not something beyond the control of the American people. It is, rather, the consequence of faulty ideas, which can change if only this message is carried forth by those who cherish liberty.

Most conservatives and libertarians oppose the Welfare State for moral, philosophical, and economic reasons. Now we must add another reason for our opposition: we understand the lessons of history! With such armaments, all we need now is faith in God, a commitment to victory, and the will to win.

CHAPTER 22

The Demonetization of Money

by Lawrence W. Reed

"Thy silver has become dross, thy wine mixed with water." — Isaiah 1:22

With that admonition, the prophet Isaiah condemned the Israelites and provided today's monetary historians with one of the earliest observations of a recurring economic phenomenon.

Inflation — debasement of currency — is almost as old as money itself. Hardly a civilization in the past has resisted the temptation to cheapen its money. What German Chancellor Erhard called a "burning, destructive, unpardonable, mortal sin of modern society" probably dates back to the first time some king seized control of his kingdom's medium of exchange. "The more things change," so goes the saying, "the more they remain the same."

Coinage was invented in the ancient kingdom of Lydia around 650 B.C. It represented a substantial improvement over primitive media of exchange and greatly accelerated the economic progress of the ancient world.

It wasn't long, however, before the Lydian kings discovered they could reduce the gold content of their coins, manufacture more (and adulterated) coins, and spend the new money themselves before the rest of the people caught on. Weakened by inflation, Lydia was conquered by Cyrus the Great of Persia around 550 B.C.

The ancient Greeks were also practitioners of the fine art of inflation. In his famed currency reform of 594 B.C., Solon devalued the "mina" by some 27%.

The currency cranks of modern times are echoes of ancient Rome, which made debasement a hallmark of the emperor's sovereignty. Up to the time of Nero (64 A.D.), the Roman coin was 94% pure silver; by the time of Aurelian (276 A.D.) only about .02% of the coin was silver — the rest was junk.

The Middle Ages were riddled with destructive inflations. In the year 805, Charlemagne declared a State monopoly of the mint and set the example for the rest of Europe. To clip, degrade, and debase the coinage became a hallowed right of the Crown. Is it any wonder that despotism and tyranny characterized the Middle Ages?

A particularly interesting case involves medieval Spain. After Christian kings conquered the country in the middle of the 13th Century, they clipped their gold coins until they became too small to circulate. Replacing them with silver coins, they proceeded to clip the new ones until they, too, vanished into oblivion.

The Chinese were the first to develop paper money. In the 13th Century, the Venetian Marco Polo wrote of the Mongol Dynasty's use of paper money made from mulberry bark. At first, the crudely-designed slips of paper were backed by precious metals. Then the government gradually removed the backing, inaugurating what we call today "fiat money." The money became worth whatever the emperor said it was worth, at least in theory. The rest of the story is what any good historian might expect — rampant inflation.

Printing Press Makes Inflation Easy

The invention of the printing press in the 1450s, with its movable type and mass production potential, was a godsend to inflating politicians. It made the process of inflation easy, inexpensive, and quick. Historical examples of its use as the instrument of debasement are legion: France, 1716-1720 — the schemes of currency crank John Law; America, 1775-1779 — the continental dollar; France, 1789-1796 — the assignats; America, 1861-1865 — the paper money of the Confederacy; Germany, 1914-1923 — perhaps the best-known of all hyperinflations; and many more too numerous to mention here.

Despite differences in nationality, personality, time, and circumstance, currency debasements of the past have had these features in common:

1) The inflating governments had an insatiable appetite for revenue.
2) The inflation was made possible by, and did not begin until, the government in each case assumed control over the production and quality of money.
3) The inflations lasted only until precious metals of honest weight were restored as money or backing for money, or the money lost all value in the marketplace.
4) While the inflation persisted, the people found refuge in precious metal investments. Their confidence in gold and silver was not shaken by the propaganda and subterfuge of the inflators.

When an inflation begins, officials scoff at the thought that it might some day get out of control. They argue that, in any case, it is necessary to pay for foreign adventures, build public projects, fight poverty, or keep the government's creditors at bay.

Manufacturing money is a great way to raise revenue without having to directly and visibly raise taxes. This temptation was eloquently revealed in the following statement by one of the delegates to America's Second Continental Congress in 1775: "Do you think, gentlemen, that I will consent to load my constituents with taxes when we can send to the printer, and get a wagon-load of money, one quire of which will pay for the whole?"

In another statement from that revolutionary era, Josiah Quincy wrote these words in a letter to George Washington:

> I am firmly of the opinion, and think it entirely defensible, that there never was a paper pound, a paper dollar, or a paper promise of any kind, that ever yet obtained a general currency, but by force or fraud, generally by both. [It is fact] That the army has been grossly cheated, that creditors have been infamously defrauded, that the widows and fatherless have been oppressively wronged and beggared; that the gray hairs of the aged and the innocent, for want of their just dues, have gone down with sorrow to their graves, in consequence of our disgraceful, depreciated paper currency.

Do we Americans of today have reason to believe that "it can't happen to us," that we are somehow different, that our inflation is something which we'll always be able to live with? He who assumes so flies in the face of centuries of experience. Surely, if we persist in pursuing the same policies of yesteryear, we must suffer the same consequences!

Politicians Assault the Dollar

Let us first realize that our inflation is not so different from those of the past. The federal government, beginning with the establishment of the Federal Reserve System in 1913, gradually removed all restraints on the multiplication of money. Gold was seized from the pockets of American citizens in 1933, silver was dropped from coinage in 1964, and President Nixon repudiated gold payments to foreign creditors in 1971. The American dollar has become a completely fiat currency, at the mercy of whichever band of big spenders is in power.

Meanwhile, as occurred with inflations past, real money — gold and silver — have been excellent barometers of and refuges from the depreciation of paper. Both metals have more than kept pace with inflation since 1970. All of the promises of so-called "inflation-fighters" in Washington, all of their assurances that inflation is manageable, all of their official condemnations of gold as a "barbarous relic" have not altered the verdicts of monetary history. There simply is no sound, logical, rational, or historical basis for trusting government with money. Period.

Let us understand clearly what is happening. The American dollar is being demonetized at double digit rates. Prices are rising because the money is falling in value. Because of the profligacy and corrupting power of government, we have conducted a kind of slow motion debasement which now threatens to move into high gear and make the dollar just another one of those many hyperinflated currencies of history.

To ward off such a fate requires concerted action by informed and committed individuals. The dollar *can* be saved if the following ideas are communicated to the American people:

1) The growth of government must not be simply slowed down or halted. It must be *reversed* with a program of repeal, dismantlement, and deregulation.
2) An unadulterated gold standard is the only policy which will spell the end to inflation. To make the dollar "as good as gold," the gold standard must once again become synonymous in people's minds with honesty, integrity, stability, and prosperity.
3) Americans must refrain from seeking handouts, subsidies, and other favors from others through government. Only then will the pressure for government to debase the monetary unit be eased.

Those of us who wish to accomplish these noble goals have a massive educational task before us. Winning converts and changing public policy has never been easy. We must undertake the task with no real guarantees of victory. But we know from history that, in the words of British statesman Edmund Burke, "All that is necessary for evil to triumph is for good men to do nothing."

CHAPTER 23

Why I Left Sweden

by Eric Brodin*

I LEFT SWEDEN because I wanted untrammeled freedom of religion. I wanted to escape the inevitable constraints of a state church with its special privileges. I no longer wanted to live in a society where the property of my church could be appropriated in the name of zoning laws or municipal expropriation, where the building of new churches is subjected to a special 25 percent tax because they are regarded as "non-utilitarian" structures, where there are no tax exemptions for donations to my church, but the state church is supported by my taxes, where only state-approved religious groups have access to radio and television time, and where the state church has become an instrument of political power, contributing to a secularization of life resulting in a disrespect for all religion.

I LEFT SWEDEN because I wanted to be free to choose the work I desired without being compelled to join a union and without being affiliated (and having to pay dues) to a political party chosen by that union, a party for which I may have no sympathy. I wanted to be able to enjoy the constitutional right of association, which also means freedom *from* association, but which is now being denied Swedish workers (more unionized than anywhere else in the world) by unions or by employers fearful of union retaliation.

I LEFT SWEDEN because I believe in the businessman's right to succeed, including the right to hire those whom he may deem suitable and the right not be compelled to take employees selected by a government agency. I believe in the employer's traditional right of directing and allocating work, now turned over to "worker's representatives," who may be union officials not connected with any firm. I think employers should have the right to fire those who steal goods or time, and I believe they should be able to announce vacancies anywhere and to use private employment

---

*Mr. Brodin, born in Sweden, is a naturalized U.S. citizen. In 1980, he made America his permanent home.

agencies to till those vacancies, a privilege now denied in my homeland.

I LEFT SWEDEN because I was, in a most concrete way, denied the fruits of my labor. Half of even a modest salary is taken in income taxes and progressive escalation can bring it up to nearly 100 percent. An employer in Sweden can be charged special "excess profits" taxes and "social charges" for employees, ranging from 40 percent to more than 60 percent of the salary. On top of all that, everyone must pay a 22.5 percent so-called "value-added tax," in effect a sales tax on all goods and services. In short, I saw half to two-thirds of my earnings being siphoned off to pay for a bloated public sector and in support of the increasing and increasingly indolent classes.

I LEFT SWEDEN because I was denied not only the right to inherit the well-earned results of my parents' hard work but also the right to bequeath to my children my own, due to a punitive inheritance tax, which in some cases would leave a mere 25 percent of my fortune to be given to my family.

I LEFT SWEDEN because I wanted to enjoy the time-honored right to own a bit of the land of my ancestral home — to own property. Yet, I saw the rights to property being everywhere circumscribed and defamed with a view toward eventual abolition. Those who own their own homes in Sweden suffer from unprecedented attack on state media and then are subjected to special tax rates, both of which cause a disrespect for property rights and result in the most widespread and indiscriminate vandalism known in the modern world.

I LEFT SWEDEN because, even though a formal freedom of assembly and speech remains, total government control of the radio and television stations guarantees little opportunity for the advocacy of unpopular views in the mass media. Access to the airways is denied even the largest of the free evangelical church bodies. Even if I were interviewed, there would be no legal protection against editing my words beyond recognition. With few exceptions, newspapers and magazines of opinion receive government subsidies, with all that that implies.

I LEFT SWEDEN because I sought for myself and for my children the right to choose our education. Practically all of education has been forced into the public sector — where parents are denied effective influence, in some cases not even being allowed to see the textbooks the children use; where an "activist" school will subject my child to outside political indoctrination; where my presence is prevented in order to reinforce the state's *in loco parentis*; where education has become a tool to transform the child into a cog

Why I Left Sweden

in the wheels of a socialist state; and where, in the interest of the "policy of leveling," grades are abolished and to excel is regarded as disloyal to the school.

I LEFT SWEDEN because I wanted to have the right and the freedom to choose my own physician and dentist, to choose the medical and social care which best suits my needs and wants. In Sweden, these rights are being denied as the socialization of the medical profession now amounts to 95 percent of the physicians, with but one private hospital left in all of Sweden. The remaining private dentists are being subjected to bureaucratic harassment (compulsory carpeted floors in waiting rooms, for example), denied new licensing, or subjected to tax raids without warrants, accompanied by vicious propaganda against "private profiteering from human ills" in the state-owned media.

I LEFT SWEDEN because I still believe in the sanctity of the family, one of the most essential guarantors for a healthy society. I believe in the words of a contemporary American religious leader: "No success in life can compensate for failure in the home." I wanted to leave a society where propaganda in the name of the new feminism and sexual equality, together with punitive forms of taxation, has brought 70 percent of the women from ages 16 to 74 into the employment sector, resulting in the world's loneliest children, one of the world's lowest birthrates, and alarming increases in divorce, abortions, and illegitimate births.

I LEFT SWEDEN because I wanted my child to be my own, not to be the property of a state, which "permits" me to rear it only for the first few years of life. I wanted to have the right to train my child according to my own ethical and religious convictions, without being deprived of my rights as a parent on the anonymous report by a neighbor that in scolding my child or restricting its movements in temporary punishment, I have made myself subject to a jail sentence. I wanted to escape a society which, in the name of "protector of the children," denies parents their fundamental rights, and where the courts will honor a "request for divorce" by a 16-year-old girl from her family, and where a 14-year-old girl, on the word of a school nurse, can have an abortion without her parents' knowledge or consent.

I LEFT SWEDEN because I could no longer tolerate the increasingly arbitrary actions by government agencies which have assumed powers unprecedented in nontotalitarian states. More than a third of the total working force is employed by government, 35,000 full and part-time inspectors review income tax returns, and raids against suspected tax evaders take the form of persecution.

I LEFT SWEDEN because I wanted to escape a society in

which even the courts have become politicized and forced into an ideological straitjacket of socialist and egalitarian provenance. Judges and laws now serve narrow ideological ends and the traditional concept that the "land should by *law* be governed" is dead. In a single decade, from 1969 to 1979, 12,286 laws and judicial judgments were passed, often as tools for the transformation of society because, as one spokesman said, "Laws should not be viewed with subservient respect. They are tools we use in order to reach political goals."

I LEFT SWEDEN, finally, because I wanted to be able to maintain my dignity as an individual. I wanted to be an uncommon man — of my own design. I wanted to feel that there is an essential connection between what I do and what happens; that there is an interdependence between my decisions and the results, between cause and effect; that if I commit a violation or make a mistake, I will suffer the consequences so that I might learn to avoid them in the future; that, in short, I will have the "right to fail." I wanted to be able to enjoy the fruits of my labor, to see the results of my work, to rejoice in the creation of my hands and mind, and to be regarded always as an individual, with values and merits and dignity in my own right, not merely as an adjunct to an impersonal Leviathan state or the by-product of a collectivized *Brave New World* anno *1984*.

These, then, are some of the reasons why I left Sweden and why I came to the shores of America, a nation which has welcomed millions of others who have sought freedom and opportunity in a land of promise. All of this is what motivated me to leave the beauties of my ancestral land, leaving behind a society perverted by the ideology of the big lie. I was not able to continue living in a country where truth, as I saw it, no longer had the power to make itself believed.

CHAPTER 24

The Last Candle

by Jack Schreiber

How much is it worth? How much is your personal freedom worth to you? How much would you be willing to sacrifice today, just to keep your freedom to worship God as you see fit? What price would you pay just to maintain your right to work at the business or profession of your choice; or your right to speak freely without fear of imprisonment? Have you ever stopped to think that men haven't always been this free? Since the beginning of time, most men through the centuries have been slaves or serfs. Personal freedom was granted as a gift by kings, or tyrants, only to a chosen few. Occasionally, history records, there were brief periods of personal freedom, but it finally took America for the world to realize the dream of all men — the inherent right of a man to be free.

We aren't free to do what we want to do, but rather, Jefferson said, we are free to do what we ought to do. In other words, the price of freedom is individual responsibility. So freedom isn't all free, you see, nor is it perpetual. Part of the American dream is that to each generation there falls a new responsibility to preserve that freedom which was established here by those early patriots. But it took more than just a philosophy of government. Those early Americans, wise beyond their years, also realized that government of, by, and for the people had to flourish in an economic system of free enterprise, with competition as the catalyst. So they established a structure of limited central government, permitting this newly won freedom to have unlimited possibilities.

One could assume, then, that we have it made. Never have any people, at any time, anywhere, had it so good. But in our present abundance and luxury something is wrong. People aren't happy. They don't walk down the streets of our cities smiling, or whistling a happy tune. There is discontent, and one can sense fear of the unknown. Overabundant Americans are jittery. There seems to be a tarnish on our golden Mecca. Our welfare lists are growing. We've

---

From *The Freeman*, July 1967.

created a new breed of men who won't work. And instead of the slogan, "God bless America," we now hear, "What have you done for me lately?" The signs aren't too hard to read. They are the signs of internal decay — the dry rot of apathy and indifference.

The symptoms of our disease of welfarism began some years ago when we began to penalize success by taxation. By using our tax dollars, government has relieved us of many of our own personal responsibilities, in exchange for our personal freedom. We have come to think of our early history and the men who made it as a kind of fairy tale instead of the greatest success story of all time. We have been flirting with a dangerous and clever seductive mistress called socialism. And for a time, since the depression days of the thirties, we have been toying with ideas which have proven a failure in most of those countries where they've been tried. It seems to me we are in the mess we're in for several reasons.

From Freedom to Barbarism

The first is the natural evolution of civilization. Lord Byron, in tracing the rise and fall of great nations, said that "people go from freedom to glory, from glory to wealth, from wealth to vice, from vice to corruption, and from corruption to barbarism."

The second reason for the beginning of the welfare state is temptation. We are being tempted as we have never been tempted before — tempted to let the government do it. From all sides of the Great Society comes the siren song. The government should provide free housing; the government should pay for college education; the government should take care of the aged; the government should provide beauty and culture; the government should guarantee jobs; and so it goes. It's not an easy thing being a free American, when all around us the misguided and the misinformed tell us the government owes us all these things which up to now we have been providing for ourselves.

There is a third reason why we are losing our freedom. Most of us accept the beginning of the welfare state, not because of our weakness, but rather because of one of our finest virtues — human compassion. Through our misguided love for humanity we have bought the idea that the mere spending of enormous sums of our own money, plus the creation of vast new bureaucracy to process and administer the complexities of the new social laws will, in themselves, solve the ills of the people. By passing the buck and surrendering our personal responsibilities into the hands of government, we solve our guilty consciences as a nation and as individuals.

And finally, we have begun our journey into the welfare state for another reason. For too long now, too many of us have been too willing to let someone else call the shots. We have been busy with things, which in the end don't count for much, and in our madness for materialism we have forgotten how to lead. We have been letting "George do it," and "George" has messed it up. For one shining, glorious moment of history we had the key and the open door and the way was there before us. Men threw off the yoke of centuries and thrust forward along that way with such hope and such brilliance that for a little while we were the light and the inspiration of the world. Now the key has been thrown carelessly aside — the door is closing — we are losing the way.

In summary then, we Americans have inherited the greatest nation in the world, but we're finding out it's not easy being a free American. We need to remind ourselves of the magic formula of free enterprise, operating in an environment of competition with limited central government. We must constantly remind ourselves, and each other, that our freedom is threatened by those who promise us security instead of opportunity. We do not have to go down the drain of the welfare state just because of a silly historic cycle. We can pass on the heritage of personal freedom to our children with the three keys of leadership, personal involvement in public affairs, and a recrudescence of the home and church. This we can do if enough of us will care enough to do enough.

Freedom, Self-Control, Human Dignity, and Limited Government

Once upon a time there was a young nation struggling in the community of nations to find her place in the sun. For this young country of brave people discovered that freedom is a God-given right. So impressed were they with this belief that they lit a candle to symbolize their freedom. But in their wisdom they knew that the flame could not burn alone, so they lit a second candle to symbolize man's right to govern himself. The third candle was lighted to signify that the rights of the individual were more important than the rights of the state. And finally they lit a fourth candle to show that government should not do for the people those things which people should do for themselves.

As the four candles of freedom burned brightly, the young nation prospered; and as they prospered, they grew fat; and as they grew fat, they got lazy. When they got lazy, they asked the government to do things for them which they had been doing for themselves, and one of the candles went out. As government became bigger, the people became littler and the government became all important and the rights of the individual were sacrificed to the all important rights of the state. Then the second candle went out. In their apathy and indifference they asked someone else to govern them, and someone else did and the third candle went out.

In the end, more than they wanted freedom, they wanted security, a comfortable life, and they lost all, comfort and security and freedom. For you see when the freedom they wanted most was freedom from responsibility — then Athens ceased to be free, and the Athenians of nearly two thousand years ago were never free again. The last candle was extinguished.

Unit V: The American Experiment

We think there is, in all of history, something special about the history of the United States. The purpose of this unit is to examine several of the especially distinctive and critical features of the history of this country. It is these distinctive and critical features that have contributed mightily to our greatness. However, they do not pass automatically from one generation to the next. They must be studied, understood, and lived by each new generation if the United States is to continue to be a country of great people.

In the first chapter in this unit, "The Thanksgiving Story," Charles Wolfe succinctly reminds us of some particularly valuable lessons we can learn from the Pilgrims. The lessons are very basic ones in religion, politics, and economics.

The next four chapters pertain primarily to the Constitution. "The American Experiment" and "Against All Enemies" deal with the Constitution very broadly and as a whole. "The American Experiment" is one chapter from a book by Robert LeFevre. We commend the entire book, also called *The American Experiment*, to you. One of the points that Robert Bearce discusses in "Against All Enemies" is the difference between a democracy and a republic. This discussion is most instructive.

The focus in "NOT in the Constitution" is on one small part of the Constitution, viz., the so-called "general welfare" clause. The misinterpretation of this clause is proving to be the source of considerable mischief.

"Not Yours to Give" provides a valuable moral lesson. Horatio Bunce, one of the central characters in this chapter, may serve as a life-long reminder to us of the political power, *in the United States*, of an individual. Note, however, that the political power of this individual is rooted in *his understanding of the Constitution*. For it was because he had this understanding that Mr. Bunce was able to challenge Davy Crockett with "... you gave a vote last winter which shows that either you have not capacity to understand the Constitution, or that you are wanting in the honesty and firmness to be guided by it." Oh, that each of us were similarly attentive to the politicians elected to represent us and equally qualified to rein in all of them who stray from the Constitution with this challenge!

The concluding chapter of this unit, "We the People," links the Constitution to the present day. It shows us where repeated government activity of the sort that Horatio Bunce (and, ultimately, Davy Crockett) denounced would lead us. But improvement, Ralph Bradford makes clear, *is* possible. The route to that improvement is not through others but rather through ourselves.

CHAPTER 25

The Thanksgiving Story

by Charles Hull Wolfe

Every schoolchild knows the story of the Pilgrims — how a band of somber, aging, black-suited Puritans landed at Plymouth Rock, made friends with the Indians, reaped a bountiful harvest, celebrated "the first Thanksgiving" — and lived happily ever after.

It's a beautiful story, only it isn't altogether true. To begin with, the Mayflower's passengers were not stern, strait-laced, middle-aged Puritans. They were a distinct group called Pilgrims — mainly young Elizabethans in their twenties and thirties, who liked colorful clothes and good times, but were determined to worship God in the simple, earnest ways called for in the Scriptures.

Convinced that religious reform had to start with individuals, they rejected the Puritan's coercive methods, separated from the Church of England, and formed their own church.

Following the covenant tradition of Old and New Testaments, the Pilgrims drew up a covenant or compact — the first such compact ever put in writing — for their own church self-government. While still aboard the ship that took them across the ocean to America, the Pilgrims took their Scrooby Compact for *church* self-government, and translated it into the Mayflower Compact for *civil* self-government — the first such written covenant and a forerunner of the United States Constitution.

Just as important, the Pilgrims' pattern for economic organization helped to shape our economic system.

The Pilgrims didn't have enough money themselves to rent and provision the Mayflower for its long ocean voyage. The only way the Pilgrims could finance their expedition was with the help of profit-seeking English businessmen. In their arrangement with London merchants, the Pilgrims were committed to work for the profit of a joint stock company consisting of themselves — investing their labor — and those merchants who invested their money.

Reprinted with permission from American Economic Foundation, 51 East 42nd Street, New York, N.Y. 10017.

Each of the Pilgrims was given a share of stock. Everything they produced was to go into a common fund. At the end of seven years they were to sell whatever was left, beyond the necessities of living. The remainder was to be the profit that would compensate the merchants for saving their money and risking its loss, in order to finance the expedition.

Due to the hardships in the wilderness, piracy of cargoes, and the burden of supporting later arrivals to the Colony, it was no easy matter to repay the debt, much less earn a profit. Yet for over twenty years the Pilgrims labored to pay off these obligations, until they reached a financial settlement in 1645.

From this experience come two lessons: 1) it takes sturdy individual character to meet the personal responsibilities of a free economy; 2) the profit system — which made the voyage possible — provides opportunities for progress that otherwise would not exist.

The London merchants saw no inconsistency between the fact that they operated as private profit-seeking businessmen, yet denied the Pilgrims the right to own their own land and work for direct benefit of their families.

The merchants demanded a communal arrangement with the intention of making a convenient distribution, after seven years, of the Colony's collective earnings. It was a "take it or leave it" proposition, and the Pilgrims reluctantly took it; but in 1621 and 1622 their crops were extremely poor. Much of the time the Pilgrims went hungry.

Convinced, finally, that the communal system failed to motivate the people to produce, Governor William Bradford concluded that "community of property was found to breed much confusion and discontent, and retard much employment which would have been to the general benefit and comfort."

Fruitage of Private Agriculture

And so, as the Governor wrote in his classic book, *Of Plymouth Plantation,* "at length after much debate" he "allowed each man to plant corn for his own household, and to trust themselves for that ... So every family was assigned a parcel of land, according to the proportion of their number ... This was very successful. It made all hands very industrious, so that much more corn was planted."

How much did productivity actually increase? The first year in Plymouth, 1621, the Pilgrims planted only 26 acres. The second year, still under the communal system, but keenly aware of the desperate need to plant all they could, they planted 60 acres. In

The Thanksgiving Story

1623, spurred on by individual enterprise, the Pilgrims laid out 184 acres — three times as much!

The peas, corn and barley which the Pilgrims brought with them from England would not grow in the poor Plymouth soil. It was the native corn that kept the Pilgrims alive. Soon the Pilgrims were planting, harvesting and grinding far more corn per capita than the Indians.

The Pilgrims, practicing individual enterprise on their private fields, were more motivated to be productive than the Indians, who practiced communal agriculture. More important, the Pilgrims had better, more efficient farm *tools* — tools that did more to multiply their energies. As the American Economic Foundation's formula for man's material welfare explains, "Man's material welfare equals natural resources *plus* human energy *multiplied* by tools."

The Pilgrims brought with them an assortment of English agricultural tools — hoes and mattocks, metal-sheathed shovels, weeding tongs and sickles. The Indians had only crude clamshells to scratch out weeds and cultivate the earth, and a stone mortar and pestle to grind the corn.

Investment in a Power Tool

The disparity between the Pilgrim and Indian tools at the time of the Pilgrims' landing soon increased. A ship arrived carrying farm horses and horse-drawn iron plows, and an entrepreneur named Stephen Deane. Deane had the capital and the know-how to build the Colony's first grist mill. Situated at the head of Plymouth Town Brook, it was powered by a big water wheel, which turned massive grinding stones.

Between the establishment of an orderly town self-government under the Mayflower Compact, the practice of the Pilgrim work ethic, the motivation provided by individual responsibility and the profit incentive, and the multiplication of human energy made possible by horse-drawn iron plows and a water-powered grist mill, soon the Pilgrim economy was on its way — a prototype of what was to become, in the 19th century, the world's freest, most productive economy.

Now, hundreds of years later, in a world where men and women still yearn to be free from oppression and hunger — but where there is little disciplined self-government and little appreciation of the productivity of private enterprise — thoughtful people everywhere could glean a great insight from the Pilgrim experience.

When We Are Free

CHAPTER 26

The American Experiment

by Robert LeFevre

When the American pioneers found themselves the victors after a war with England, they decided they must undertake the establishment of a form of government which was to be impervious to inner tyranny.

It is probable that at no other time or place in history had so many men, so well informed, so nobly motivated, ever convened for such a purpose. Few of the founders of our Constitution were politically ambitious. With high purpose and deep sincerity, they set about the task of providing a *form* of government which would stand the assaults of the mean and selfish.

They labored diligently and well. And when they finished, although they were far from unanimity, they had forged a document which was at once both wonderful and a political curiosity.

For the great distinction which set the American *form* apart from all others was that it was probably the most inefficient, cumbersome, and unwieldy government ever devised!

How well the founders knew that men with power could not be trusted. They set up a conflicting and enigmatic mechanism which was more notable for what it could not do than for what it could do.

There was an executive branch; but its functions were limited and contained. There was a legislative branch, equally frustrating. And, finally, a judicial branch, which was to watch the fulminations of the other two.

But this was not all. Having established three equal containers for power, they proclaimed that it was a *federated* government, with sovereignty residing both in the separate states and in the people generally. In short, what they had devised was *not* a government but the antithesis of government as it was normally contrived.

European politicians chortled with glee when they first heard the news. Here was an antirule rulership; a powerless powerhouse; a contradiction within an enigma. They opined that it would never

---

Extracted from *The American Experiment* by Robert LeFevre and reprinted here with permission from The Caxton Printers, Ltd., Caldwell, Idaho.

work. However, a few elevated mentalities glimpsed the ideal our pioneers had striven to attain and gasped at its daring and immensity.

And in large measure the European politicians who ridiculed the form were right. The American government did *not* perform with efficiency. It wasn't intended to. And the American people, finding themselves for the first time without a ruling despot, were hard pressed to know what to do. Consequently, unable to call upon their government for aid or guidance, they set to work themselves. Their energy, uncontrolled by living authority, changed the world. Their achievements, in a few short years altered all of history.

For the first time, freedom was proclaimed as a national policy, individualism was given full sway, and government was reduced to puppeteering functions.

It was delightful, while it lasted. Never was so much accomplished by so few, under such adverse conditions. Freedom was the big payoff. Men who do not have to kneel come to recognize divinity within themselves as individuals. Our ancestors were a stiff-necked lot. They bowed to none but God. Government could go hang for all of them.

We had done away with theocracy by delivering it a mortal blow. And even in our Bill of Rights it was ordained that the government could make no law affecting the practice of religion. Church and state were separated.

We had a republic which used a democratic process, which provided for a temporary aristocracy, which removed the priests, which put God into heaven and off the throne, which uncrowned the dictator or the king, which eliminated succession to power, and which generally disrupted every ordinary political practice.

For years it worked, because it didn't do too much. Our power was in the hands of the people.

But our founding fathers had seen that what they had done, even though it was a mechanism shorn of much power, still contained the seeds of tyranny. Therefore they provided that as time passed, changes could occur. And at least some of them fondly hoped that, by permitting change, still further reductions in governmental protocol would come.

An informed populace could learn the fallacy of even this much power remaining. For if the people individually learned to overcome their weakness, what need had they for an instrument of force?

The changes, provided for, came in due course. But the changes were not in the direction our most dedicated idealists had desired.

CHAPTER 27

Against All Enemies

by Robert Bearce

The elected and appointed officials of our federal government take an oath of office before undertaking their constitutional duties. Let's take a look at that oath, expressed as a question and answered by "I do."

Do you solemnly swear that you will support and defend the Constitution of the United States against all enemies, foreign and domestic; that you will bear true faith and allegiance to the same; that you take this obligation freely, without any mental reservation or purpose of evasion; and that you will well and faithfully discharge the duties of the office on which you are about to enter: So help you God?

In response to their oath of office, our Congressmen and Senators answer "I do," but do they really mean it?

Unfortunately for the cause of freedom, the oath of office has often become only a hollow formality. Too many members of the administrative, legislative, and judicial branches of the federal government have failed to "support and defend the Constitution of the United States" and "bear true faith and allegiance to the same."

The Constitution has been misinterpreted, abused, and subverted. As it continues to be violated, we should see how freedom is gradually being destroyed.

The word "destroyed" might appear to be somewhat harsh, but it is appropriate. We ought to heed a warning made by Patrick Henry in 1775, not long before the opening shots of the War for Independence were fired at Lexington and Concord. Henry clearly understood how freedom was being threatened by oppressive government rule. He warned against indifference, complacency, and apathy.

"It is natural to man to indulge in the illusions of hope. We are apt to shut our eyes against a painful truth, and listen to the song of that siren, till she transforms us into beasts. Is this the part of wise men, engaged in a great and arduous struggle for liberty? Are we

---

From *The Freeman*, September 1980.

disposed to be of the number of those who, having eyes, see not, and having ears, hear not, the things which so nearly concern their temporal salvation? For my part, whatever anguish of spirit it may cost, I am willing to know the whole truth; to know the worst and provide for it."

By "temporal salvation," Patrick Henry meant the preservation of freedom — the freedom to work and provide for our personal lives as we best see fit. Henry and other patriots believed that freedom meant individuals had the ability and responsibility to plan their own lives without unnecessary government intervention. That freedom was being threatened, and Henry was telling the colonists to wake up and confront the danger before them. His admonition applies to us today.

If we truly want to strengthen freedom and regain what we have already lost, we will pledge ourselves to defending the Constitution. We cannot support our Constitution, however, unless we face the fact that it is being continually ignored and betrayed. It is time that we give some serious thought to the Constitution.

Protection from Enemies — Foreign and Domestic

The Founding Fathers who framed our Constitution in 1787 knew that individuals have certain unalienable rights — "life, liberty, and the pursuit of happiness," as earlier expressed in the Declaration of Independence. These rights were God-given rights. No government or constitution gave them to the individual. Rather, the purpose of governments and constitutions was to protect these basic, God-given rights.

The Founding Fathers comprehended how and why people behave the way they do. Men like James Madison and Alexander Hamilton understood human nature. They saw that some human beings would always resort to force, deceit, war, stealing, and killing to get what they wanted. Thus, there was an obvious need for government — legitimate, just government to carry out two main functions:

(1) protecting free people from foreign enemies and invaders;
(2) protecting honest, self-responsible, hard-working citizens within the nation from domestic lawbreakers who would use coercion, fraud, or force to deprive others of "life, liberty, and the pursuit of happiness."

Good government would do the above, and the Founding Fathers outlined that kind of government in our Constitution. Just as they gave the government certain authority, they also placed limitations on government power. The framers of the Constitution realized that while government was needed to protect individual freedom, government itself had to be placed within limited, strictly defined boundaries. If government was not restrained, it would destroy individual liberty and lead to tyranny. Government had to be controlled. James Madison explained the matter:

> It may be a reflection on human nature that such devices should be necessary to control the abuses of government. But what is government itself but the greatest of all reflections on human nature? If men were angels, no government would be necessary. If angels were to govern men, neither external nor internal controls on government would be necessary. In framing a government which is to be administered by men over men, the great difficulty lies in this: you must first enable the government to control the governed, and in the next place oblige it to control itself.

When Madison wrote that government should "control the governed," he was thinking about necessary government laws required to maintain impartial law and order — law and order that protected individual liberty. This issue of defending individual rights and limiting the power of government is the central theme of the Constitution.

Preserving Personal Liberty

Four aspects of the Constitution show the Founding Fathers' concern for preserving personal liberty within the boundaries of limited government.

First, we have a *written* constitution. Having the powers of government and the rights of the citizenry spelled out in print is no assurance that freedom will be observed, but a written constitution does act as a safeguard to liberty. When the Constitution is snubbed or disregarded, we can at least hold up a warning hand and say something to the effect: "Stop, government bureaucrats! The law you have just passed is unconstitutional. The Fifth Amendment says . . ."

Second, our Constitution provides for a republic. That is, we have a republican form of government based upon the citizenry electing representatives to carry out the functions of government. The Founding Fathers did not frame a constitution that would set up a democracy — a kind of government where political power lay directly in the hands of the people. Under a pure democracy, the citizens of the state would exercise popular vote to decide what laws should be made. The majority view would be registered and then carried out by the administrative hand of the central government. There would be no representation (legislative branch of government) between the citizenry and the administrative branch of government.

A democracy might appear to be more "democratic" than a republic, but the authors of the Constitution knew that a democracy would lead to a loss of individual freedom . . . followed by anarchy or tyranny. While the Constitution was being considered for ratification by the Massachusetts Convention, Moses Ames observed:

> It has been said that a pure democracy is the best government for a small people who assemble in person . . . . It may be of some use in this argument . . . to consider, that it would be very burdensome, subject to faction and violence; decisions would often be made by surprise, in the precipitancy of passion, by men who either understand nothing or care nothing about the subject; or by interested men, or those who vote for their own indemnity. It would be a government not by laws, but by men.

The Dangers of Democracy

Seeing the dangers of a democracy, the Founding Fathers adopted a republican form of government. It is true that the history of our nation shows that a republic can suffer the very weaknesses of a democracy that Ames described, but the fact remains that a republic comes nearer to preserving individual rights than does a democracy.

Madison and others rejected popular vote as the method of making laws. Instead, Article I of the Constitution provides for representation through the election of Senators and Congressmen to the Senate and House of Representatives. These legislators would represent us and make laws — laws that should protect and promote individual freedom. The government was to be guided by clearly defined laws, not by direct majority rule, which would lead to oppression.

Although Thomas Jefferson did not participate in the work on the Constitution, he understood why a republic was superior to a democracy. He also knew what the basic purpose of a republic was: "The true foundation of republican government is the equal right of every citizen, in his person and property, and in their management."

A republic meant a government that allowed the people of the United States to work freely, associate freely, and otherwise plan their own lives in the way they pleased — equal rights shared by all citizens. Speaking of the national or central government of the United States, Article IV, Section 4 of the Constitution says: "The United States shall guarantee to every State in this Union a *Republican Form of Government*, and shall protect each of them against Invasion . . ." (emphasis added).

A third principle of our Constitution that defends individual liberty is federalism. When we speak today about the "federal government," we refer to the executive, legislative, and judicial branches of the central government located in Washington, D.C. In the minds of the Founding Fathers, though, federal government was an all-encompassing term used to describe a nation made up of sovereign states — a nation composed of a central or national government (the folks in Washington, D.C.) and state governments (Delaware, South Carolina, Connecticut, etc.).

Notice that the Constitution recognizes that the United States *are*, not "is," a union of sovereign states. Article III, Section 3 reads: "Treason against the United States, shall consist only in levying War against *them*, or in adhering to *their* Enemies . . ." (emphasis added). Although the Founding Fathers considered themselves as Americans and citizens of a unified nation, they also considered themselves citizens of separate, self-governing states. The United States were considered in the plural, not the singular. Thus, treason against the United States was against *them*, not *it*. This fact stresses the federalist nature of the government established by the Constitution.

The Separation of Powers to Protect the Citizenry

The Constitution provides for federalism that grants some powers to the national government and other powers to the states. This federal separation of powers acts as a safeguard to personal freedom. Federalism places the burden of law-making and political decisions upon power units close to the supervision of the citizenry. The Founding Fathers did not want the national government in Washington, D.C., telling the people of Virginia or North Carolina what to do.

Thus, political power was distributed among the different state, county, and local governments, enabling the people to govern themselves. This widespread distribution of authority makes it more difficult for one power unit to infringe upon the constitutional rights of the citizens.

The Founding Fathers provided for another form of separation of powers. This is the fourth aspect of the Constitution's defense of individual liberty. The national government, or, as we say, the federal government, was split up into three separate branches with each branch having distinct, limited powers.

Basically, the executive branch of government headed by the President and his Cabinet carries out constitutional laws and duties. The legislative branch made up of the Senate and House of Representatives make the laws, while the judicial branch (the Supreme Court and federal courts) decides whether or not laws have been violated in light of the Constitution.

Three Branches of Government

The authority and powers of the three branches of the federal government are balanced and checked by one another. For example, the President can veto laws passed by Congress. Congress, on the other hand, can withhold funds from executive agencies. Although Congress can pass legislation, the Supreme Court has the power to declare certain laws unconstitutional, making them null and void. The President appoints federal judges and various civil servants, but the Senate can refuse to ratify major appointments. The federal judiciary can find individuals guilty of crimes but the President has power to grant pardons and reprieves.

This separation of powers, like federalism, should act as a checks and balances system to keep government from going beyond the boundaries of its constitutional authority. No single branch of government should have the combined power to make, interpret, and enforce laws.

The United States Constitution is really a remarkable document. It is a monument to personal freedom. The Founding Fathers distrusted government, and they attempted to shackle political power when they adopted the Constitution. It restricts government to the primary responsibilities of providing for the common defense, maintaining domestic security and peace, and protecting individual rights.

The Bill of Rights

When we think of individual rights, we usually have in mind the first ten amendments of the Constitution, the Bill of Rights. Much has been written about the first eight amendments which include assurances of freedom of religion, speech, and press . . . the right to bear arms . . . the right to trial by jury, etc. Not enough is said, though, about the Ninth and Tenth Amendments.

The Ninth Amendment states that "The enumeration in the Constitution of certain rights, shall not be construed to deny or disparage others retained by the people."

This amendment assures the individual that he has other rights besides those listed in the Constitution and previous eight amendments. These unnamed rights cannot be taken away just because they are not mentioned in the Constitution. We have such rights as "the pursuit of happiness," not included in the Constitution but stated earlier in the Declaration of Independence.

Now look at the Tenth Amendment: "The powers not delegated to the United States by the Constitution, nor prohibited by it to the States, are reserved to the States respectively, or to the people."

This important amendment says that all powers not granted by the Constitution to the national government are retained either by the states or individual citizens. Likewise, all powers not prohibited by the Constitution to the states are left in the hands of the states or people themselves.

Unfortunately, many of our government officials today act as if the Ninth and Tenth Amendments do not exist. They have twisted the meaning of the Constitution and the role of government. They look upon the Bill of Rights as rights granted to us by a supposedly benevolent government. In reality, the first ten amendments are a list of prohibitions against government *interfering* with those rights. Our legislators should listen to Daniel Webster.

Webster was only a youngster when the Constitution was ratified in 1788, but in later years he earned the reputation of being "The Defender of the Constitution." During a Senate speech in 1830, he declared:

> The people, then, Sir, erected this government. They gave it a Constitution, and in that Constitution they have enumerated the powers which they bestow on it. They have made it a limited government. They have defined its authority. They have restrained it to the exercise of such powers as are granted; and all others, they declare, are reserved to the states or the people.

A Framework for Freedom

The Founding Fathers knew that the basic responsibility of government was to serve as a "watchdog" to maintain a free society of free individuals working together freely. Improved working conditions . . . better education . . . good health care . . . material progress — all of these are goals that people work toward. The purpose of government is to ensure the necessary freedom that will permit individuals to work for those goals through self-responsibility, individual initiative, the free market, and voluntary exchange. Government has the responsibility of providing a framework that will allow individuals to achieve prosperity and dignity on their own.

The Founding Fathers were not men who felt that the purpose of government was to plan, formulate, and then implement specific ways to achieve the goals of a nation. Government was not to be in the business of providing public housing or job training through its political, economic, or social legislation. Government was not to mold society but, instead, allow society to mold itself freely.

Let's consider some advice from Jefferson:

> . . . Still one thing more, fellow citizens — a wise and frugal Government, which shall restrain men from injuring one another, shall leave them otherwise free to regulate their own pursuits of industry and improvement, and shall not take from the mouth of labor the bread it has earned. This is the sum of good government. . . .

We need to see how far we have strayed away from the Constitution. Not only is government poking its bureaucratic nose into where it should not be, it is not fulfilling one of its primary constitutional responsibilities — deterring crime. Government is supposed to prevent, prosecute, and punish crime, but now government itself has become the lawbreaker of the Constitution.

The Enemy Within

Many of our public officials have broken their oath of office. They affirm or swear that they will support the Constitution and defend it "against all enemies, foreign and domestic." There is the foreign threat of Marxist subversion and aggression. More dangerous, however, are the domestic enemies — individuals whose actions and attitudes are corrupting the Constitution. Those individuals include some of the very government officials sworn to uphold the Constitution.

Actions by the executive, legislative, and judicial branches of the federal government have proven that many officeholders apparently do not understand the Constitution. If they do know what the Constitution stands for, then we should hold them responsible for willfully repudiating their oath of office.

Two tasks are before us. First, we must have a firm appreciation for the Constitution. Second, we must have a clear understanding how and why the Constitution is being defied. Until we face the truth, we will slide steadily towards the eventual destruction of freedom in the United States.

CHAPTER 28

NOT in the Constitution

by George W. Nilsson

In addition to the threats of danger from outside of the United States, and subversion within, the constitutional republic of the United States is being threatened by the concentration of power in the federal government in spite of, and contrary to, the "checks and balances" of the Constitution.

More and more power is being seized by, or surrendered to, the federal government under the guise of the alleged general welfare clause of Article I, Section 8, Clause 1 of the Constitution, which contains the following language:

> The Congress shall have power to lay and collect taxes, duties, imposts and excises, to pay the debts and provide for the common defense and general welfare of the United States...

This clause is followed by sixteen other clauses specifying the various powers of Congress — Clause 2, to borrow money; Clause 3, to regulate foreign and interstate commerce, etc.; then Clause 18 gives the Congress power "to make laws necessary to carry into execution the foregoing powers." This last clause would have been unnecessary if Clause 1 gave "general welfare power."

For 140 years it was generally recognized that the quotation from Clause 1 was not a grant of "general welfare power." Many Presidents vetoed acts passed by Congress for that reason.

Early in the 1930's some individual "discovered" that the clause granted "general welfare power," and more and more this has been used to pass legislation based solely on this alleged grant of general welfare power.

The rush to pass "welfare" legislation for various pressure groups calls to mind an item in the joke column of *Pay Dirt*, a mining magazine published in Phoenix, Arizona (unfortunately, it is more tragic than humorous):

From *The Freeman,* July 1961.

If a politician tries to buy votes with private money, he is a dirty crook; but if he tries to buy them with the people's own money, he's a great liberal.

On July 8, 1960, during the Democratic Convention at Los Angeles, the newspapers reported that the mayors of five substantial cities had appeared before the Democratic Platform Committee and requested a statement in the platform recommending the establishment in the federal government of a "Department of Urban Affairs" which would have jurisdiction over "such problems as inadequate housing, residential and industrial slums, double shift schools, inefficient mass transit systems, congested streets, water shortages, and sewage disposal."

Every one of these problems is purely local. If the local communities are unable to take care of them, that tragic conclusion is an acknowledgment that the people are unable to govern themselves, and that the principles stated in the Declaration of Independence, the Constitution, and the Bill of Rights are incorrect. With such a hypothesis no American lawyer will agree.

When the Constitution was completed and ready to be signed, Benjamin Franklin made a speech in the course of which he said:

> I think a General Government necessary for us, and *there is no form of government, but what may be a blessing to the people if well administered;* and believe further, that this is likely to be well administered for a course of years, and *can only end in despotism, as other forms have done before it, when the people shall become so corrupted as to need despotic government, being incapable of any other.*

There is a general rule of law that where the statement of a general proposition is followed by specific provisions, the latter prevail. This rule is stated by James Madison in *Federalist Paper* No. 41 and by Alexander Hamilton in *Federalist Paper* No. 83. It is applied by Mr. Justice Story to Article I, Section 8 of the Constitution, enumerating the powers of Congress, in his book on the Constitution in Sections 909, 910, and 911. He shows that by Clauses 2 to 17, inclusive, specific powers limit Clause 1, referring to general welfare. Section 910 reads in part:

> 910 . . . Nothing is more natural or common than first to use a general phrase, and then to qualify it by a recital of particulars. But the idea of an enumeration of particulars, which neither explain, nor qualify the general meaning, and can have

no other effect than to confound and mislead, is an absurdity which no one ought to charge on the enlightened authors of the Constitution. It would be to charge them either with premeditated folly or premeditated fraud.

Climate of Opinion in 1787

In 1787, when the Constitution was adopted, the colonists had been through eight years of war and four years of "a critical period." Knowing what led up to the war, and reading the charges in the Declaration of Independence, can anyone for a minute think that the colonists generally, and the members of the convention specifically, would have adopted a constitution which granted general welfare powers to the federal government?

The resistance to the adoption of the Constitution, which will be discussed hereafter, shows what the people generally felt.

This is summarized by Albert J. Beveridge in his great biography, *The Life of John Marshall*, in Volume I, Chapter 10, where he writes about the convention called in the State of Virginia for the purpose of discussing the ratification of the proposed United States Constitution. At page 371 he describes the general feeling of the people about a strong central government in these words:

> They [who resisted the Constitution] had on their side the fears of the people who, as has appeared, looked on all government with hostility, and on a great central Government as some distant and monstrous thing, too far away to be within their reach, too powerful to be resisted, too high and exalted for the good of the common man, too dangerous to be tried. It was, to the masses, something new, vague and awful; something to oppress the poor, the weak, the debtor, the settler; something to strengthen and enrich the already strong and opulent, the merchant, the creditor, the financial interests.
>
> True, the people had suffered by the loose arrangement under which they now lived; but, after all, had not they and their "liberties" survived? And surely they would suffer even more, they felt, under this stronger power; but would they and their "liberties" survive its "oppression"? They thought not.

Thomas Jefferson made the same point in a letter in 1823:

> I have been blamed for saying that a prevalence of the doctrine of consolidation would one day call for reformation or revolution. *I answer by asking if a single State of the Union would have agreed to the Constitution had it given all powers*

to the General Government? If the whole opposition to it did not proceed from the jealousy and fear of every State being subjected to the other States in matters merely its own? And also is there any reason to believe the States more disposed now than then to acquiesce to this general surrender of all their rights and powers to a consolidated government, one and undivided? [Italics added.]

Article VIII of the Articles of Confederation begins with the following language: "All charges of war and of expences that shall be incurred for the common defence and general welfare . . ."

James Madison pointed out in a letter to Edmund Pendleton, dated January 21, 1792, that the "general welfare clause" had been copied from the Articles of Confederation, and then said:

> . . . Where it was always understood as nothing more than a general caption to specific powers, and it is a fact that it was preferred in the new instrument for that very reason as less than any other to misconstruction. [See *Jefferson and Madison*, by Adrienne Koch, pages 128 and 129, and Irving Brant's *Madison*, Volume 3, *Father of the Constitution*, page 138.]

Constitutional Convention Debates

A summary of the day-by-day proceedings of the Constitutional Convention of 1787 is found in Charles Warren's book, *The Making of the Constitution.*

From a study of the records of the Convention, it will appear that from time to time efforts were made by some delegates to have the Constitution grant broad general powers to the federal government. Each time such proposal was advanced, it was rejected.

Beginning on page 464 is a discussion of "The Taxing Power and the General Welfare Clause." At page 474 occurs this statement:

> In Governor Livingston's Committee Report of August 21, these words had been used with reference to prior debts, and merely described them as having been incurred during the late war "for the common defense and general welfare . . ."

On page 475 Mr. Warren says:

> Some words evidently had to be added that would make clear the power of Congress to levy taxes *for all the National*

purposes set forth in the grants of power subsequently specified in this section. Evidently the Committee selected these words, "to provide for the common defence and general welfare," as comprising all the other purposes for which Congress was to be empowered to levy and collect taxes. *They selected these words as embracing all the subsequent limited grants of power which the Committee of Detail, in its Report of August 6, had specified as constituting that amount of common defence and general welfare which the National Government ought to control and as to which ought to have power of legislation.* In other words, the phrase "to provide for the general welfare" *is merely a general description of the amount of welfare which was to be accomplished by carrying out those enumerated and limited powers vested in Congress — and no others.* [Italics added.] [See also *James Madison* by Irving Brant, Volume 3, *Father of the Constitution,* Chapter 10, beginning at page 132, which is entitled "General Power or Enumeration."]

Debates in the Various States

History tells us that in 1787 there was great opposition to the adoption of the proposed new Constitution. As a matter of fact, it squeaked through by a very few votes in a number of states. For instance, Massachusetts 187 to 168, Virginia 89 to 79, and New York 30 to 27, and then only on condition that a Bill of Rights be added.

The *Federalist Papers* were written by Alexander Hamilton, James Madison, and John Jay in support of the adoption of the Constitution, principally in connection with the debates in New York, where there was strong opposition to the adoption of the Constitution.

In *Federalist Paper* No. 41, James Madison said (after pointing out the objections to the clause ". . . to raise money for the general welfare . . ."):

> *But what color can the objection have, when a specification of the objects alluded to by these general terms immediately follows, and is not even separated by a longer pause than a semicolon?* If the different parts of the same instrument ought to be so expounded, as to give meaning to every part which will bear it, shall one part of the same sentence be excluded altogether from a share in the meaning; and shall the more doubtful and indefinite terms be retained in their full extent, and the clear and precise expressions be denied any signification whatsoever? *For what purpose could the enum-*

eration of particular powers be inserted, if these and all others were meant to be included in the preceding general power? Nothing is more natural or common than first to use a general phrase, and then to explain and qualify it by a recital of particulars. [Italics added.]

Only Limited Powers

In considering the question of whether this "general welfare" clause of Article I, Section 8, Clause 1 is a grant of power, we must also remember that the powers granted to the federal government were few and defined. James Madison, in *Federalist Paper* No. 45, said:

> The *powers* delegated by the proposed Constitution to the Federal Government are *few and defined.* Those which are to remain to the State governments are numerous and indefinite. The former will be exercised principally on external objects, as war, peace, negotiations and foreign commerce; with which last the power of taxation will, for the most part, be connected. The powers reserved to the several States will extend to all the objects which, in the ordinary course of affairs, concern the *lives, liberties* and *properties* of the people, and the *internal order, improvement* and prosperity of the State. [Italics added.]

Alexander Hamilton, himself, who argued in the Constitutional Convention for general instead of particular enumeration of powers, nevertheless said in *Federalist Paper* No. 83:

> The plan of the Convention declares that the power of Congress or, in other words, of the "national legislature," shall extend to certain enumerated cases. *This specification of particulars evidently excluded all pretension to a general legislative authority, because an affirmative grant of special powers would be absurd, as well as useless, if a general authority was intended.* [Italics added.]

Since the people were persuaded to adopt the Constitution on the basis that the federal government was being given only limited and specified powers, how dare anyone, in good conscience, now take the position that the words "general welfare" give the federal government unlimited power?

This principle was restated by Franklin D. Roosevelt on March 2, 1930, while he was Governor of New York, in a speech which was entitled "An Address on State Rights" (Collected Papers, Volume I, page 569). He said in part:

> The preservation of this home rule by the states is a fundamental necessity if we are to remain a truly united country ... to bring about government by oligarchy masquerading as democracy it is fundamentally essential that practically all authority and control be centralized in our national government, the individual sovereignty of our states must first be destroyed ...
>
> We are safe from the danger of any such departure from the principles upon which this country was founded just so long as the individual home rule of the states is scrupulously preserved and fought for whenever they seem in danger. Thus it will be seen that this home rule is a most important thing — a most vital thing if we are to continue along the course on which we have so far progressed with such unprecedented success.

Bill of Rights

In many of the states, the Constitution was adopted only when it was accompanied by a resolution demanding that a Bill of Rights be added to the Constitution. If the people of the various states were satisfied with the Constitution as written, they certainly would not have demanded the added protection of the Bill of Rights.

As pointed out above, certainly no state would have adopted the Constitution if the Congress had been given *carte blanche* to pass any law or do anything which it desired or which it felt was for the "general welfare."

This demand for a Bill of Rights, therefore, should be sufficient to prove that the Constitution, and particularly Article I, Section 8, Clause I, did not grant general welfare power to the federal government.

True to his promise, James Madison, in the First Congress, which met in 1789, caused to be passed a Bill of Rights containing twelve sections, ten of which were adopted and went into effect December 15, 1791.

This Bill of Rights, and particularly the Ninth and Tenth Amendments, are further and conclusive proof that the clause that we are discussing did not grant any authority to the federal government to pass any laws based on "general welfare powers."

When We Are Free

Statements by Contemporaries

On December 5, 1791, Secretary of the Treasury Alexander Hamilton presented to the Congress his "Report on Manufactures."

Madison delivered an address in Congress against the Report, in which he said in part:

> If Congress can apply money indefinitely to the general welfare, and are the sole and supreme judges of the general welfare, they may take the care of religion into their own hands; they may establish teachers in every State, county and parish, and pay them out of the public Treasury; they may take into their own hands the education of children, establishing in like manner schools throughout the Union; they may undertake the regulation of all roads, other than post roads. In short, everything, from the highest object of State legislation, down to the most minute object of policy, would be thrown under the power of Congress; for every object I have mentioned would admit the application of money, and might be called, if Congress pleased, provisions for the general welfare.

The report was pigeonholed, the first major defeat for one of Hamilton's most cherished policies. (*Jefferson and Madison*, by Adrienne Koch, page 129.)

Further on the same question, James Madison, on January 1, 1792, in a letter to Henry Lee, Governor of Virginia, said in part:

> What think you of the commentary ... on the term "general welfare"? ... The federal government has been hitherto limited to the specified powers, by the Greatest Champions for Latitude in expounding those powers ... *If not only the means, but the objects are unlimited, the parchment had better be thrown into the fire at once.* [Italics added.]

And in a letter to Edmund Randolph (January 21, 1792), said:

> *If Congress can do whatever in their discretion can be done by money, and will promote the general welfare, the government is no longer one possessing enumerated powers, but an indefinite one subject to particular exceptions.* [Italics added.] [*Jefferson and Madison*, by Adrienne Koch, page 128.]

Thomas Jefferson had the same views. He wrote to Albert Gallatin in 1817, about the General Welfare Clause, of which he said:

You will have to learn that an act for internal improvement, after passing both houses, was negatived by the President. The act was founded, avowedly, on the principle that the phrase in the Constitution which authorizes the Congress "to lay taxes, to pay the debts and provide for the general welfare," *was an extension of the powers specifically enumerated to whatever would promote the general welfare; and this, you know, was the Federal doctrine.* Whereas our tenet ever was, and, indeed, it is almost the only landmark which now divides the Federalists and the Republicans, that Congress had not unlimited powers to provide for the *general welfare, but was restrained to those specifically enumerated;* and that, as it was never meant that they should provide for that welfare but the exercise of the enumerated powers, so it could not have meant that they should raise money for purposes which the enumeration did not place under their action; consequently, that the specification of powers is a limitation on the purposes for which they may raise money. [Italics added.] [See *Undermining the Constitution,* by Thomas James Norton, page 191.]

Conclusion

(a) In a book recently published, analyzing some of the decisions of the modern Supreme Court, the writer says: "Enthroned at last, were Hamilton's bold nationalistic views . . ."

To say these modern ideas of "general welfare power" are those of Alexander Hamilton is to malign him. Alexander Hamilton was a great patriot and statesman. His ideas of a new government were far different from those embodied in the Constitution, but after the Constitution was adopted, he faithfully and enthusiastically supported it. For instance, he wrote most of the *Federalist Papers.*

It is therefore clear from history, common sense, the records of the Constitutional Convention, the *Federalist Papers,* the debates in the state ratification conventions, and precedents followed for more than 140 years, that THERE IS NO GRANT OF GENERAL WELFARE POWER IN THE CONSTITUTION OF THE UNITED STATES.

(b) While it would seem that such general welfare power is not needed, if it should be determined that it is necessary, then the amending clause of the Constitution should be followed, as was pointed out by George Washington in his Farewell Address:

> If, in the opinion of the people, the distribution or modification of the constitutional powers be in any particular wrong,

let it be corrected by an amendment in the way which the Constitution designates. But let there be no change by usurpation; for though this in one instance may be the instrument for good, *it is the customary weapon by which free governments are destroyed.* The precedent must always greatly overbalance, in permanent evil, any partial or transient benefit which the use can at any time yield. [Italics added.]

The dire results of undermining the Constitution were pointed out by Daniel Webster in his eulogy of George Washington in 1832, where he said in part:

>   Other misfortunes may be borne, or their effects overcome . . .
>   *But who shall reconstruct the fabric of demolished government? Who shall rear again the well-proportioned columns of constitutional liberty?* Who shall frame together the skillful architecture which unites national sovereignty with State rights, individual security and Public prosperity?

(c) Every lawyer when he is admitted to the Bar takes an oath to "uphold, defend, and protect the Constitution of the United States."

Since the Constitution is being ignored, misconstrued, or bypassed by legislation, by court decisions, and by executive action, it is time that fundamental principles of the Constitution be re-examined, and that every citizen, as well as every lawyer, take his place on the battle line in a new crusade to re-establish the principles and the spirit of the Declaration of Independence, the Constitution, and the Bill of Rights.

CHAPTER 29

Not Yours to Give

by Edward S. Ellis

One day in the House of Representatives, a bill was taken up appropriating money for the benefit of a widow of a distinguished naval officer. Several beautiful speeches had been made in its support. The Speaker was just about to put the question when Crockett arose:
"Mr. Speaker — I have as much respect for the memory of the deceased, and as much sympathy for the sufferings of the living, if suffering there be, as any man in this House, but we must not permit our respect for the dead or our sympathy for a part of the living to lead us into an act of injustice to the balance of the living. I will not go into an argument to prove that Congress has no power to appropriate this money as an act of charity. Every member upon this floor knows it. We have the right, as individuals, to give away as much of our own money as we please in charity; but as members of Congress we have no right so to appropriate a dollar of the public money. Some eloquent appeals have been made to us upon the ground that it is a debt due the deceased. Mr. Speaker, the deceased lived long after the close of the war; he was in office to the day of his death, and I have never heard that the government was in arrears to him.
"Every man in this House knows it is not a debt. We cannot, without the grossest corruption, appropriate this money as the payment of a debt. We have not the semblance of authority to appropriate it as a charity. Mr. Speaker, I have said we have the right to give as much money of our own as we please. I am the poorest man on this floor. I cannot vote for this bill, but I will give one week's pay to the object, and if every member of Congress will do the same, it will amount to more than the bill asks."
He took his seat. Nobody replied. The bill was put upon its passage, and, instead of passing unanimously, as was generally supposed, and as, no doubt, it would, but for that speech, it received but few votes, and, of course, was lost.

From *The Life of Colonel David Crockett,* compiled by Edward S. Ellis (Philadelphia: Porter & Coates, 1884).

Government "Charity" Unconstitutional

Later, when asked by a friend why he had opposed the appropriation, Crockett gave this explanation:

"Several years ago I was one evening standing on the steps of the Capitol with some other members of Congress, when our attention was attracted by a great light over in Georgetown. It was evidently a large fire. We jumped into a hack and drove over as fast as we could. In spite of all that could be done, many houses were burned and many families made houseless, and, besides, some of them had lost all but the clothes they had on. The weather was very cold, and when I saw so many women and children suffering, I felt that something ought to be done for them. The next morning a bill was introduced appropriating $20,000 for their relief. We put aside all other business and rushed it through as soon as it could be done.

"The next summer, when it began to be time to think about the election, I concluded I would take a scout around among the boys of my district. I had no opposition there, but, as the election was some time off, I did not know what might turn up. When riding one day in a part of my district in which I was more of a stranger than any other, I saw a man in a field plowing and coming toward the road. I gauged my gait so that we should meet as he came to the fence. As he came up, I spoke to the man. He replied politely, but, as I thought, rather coldly.

"I began: 'Well, friend, I am one of those unfortunate beings called candidates, and —'

" 'Yes, I know you; you are Colonel Crockett. I have seen you once before, and voted for you the last time you were elected. I suppose you are out electioneering now, but you had better not waste your time or mine. I shall not vote for you again.'

"This was a sockdolager . . . I begged him to tell me what was the matter.

" 'Well, Colonel, it is hardly worth-while to waste time or words upon it. I do not see how it can be mended, but you gave a vote last winter which shows that either you have not capacity to understand the Constitution, or that you are wanting in the honesty and firmness to be guided by it. In either case you are not the man to represent me. But I beg your pardon for expressing it in that way. I did not intend to avail myself of the privilege of the constituent to speak plainly to a candidate for the purpose of insulting or wounding you. I intend by it only to say that your understanding of the Constitution is very different from mine; and I will say to you what, but for my rudeness, I should not have said, that I believe you to be honest. . . . But an understanding of the Constitution different from mine I cannot overlook, because the Constitution, to be worth anything, must be held sacred, and rigidly observed in all its provisions. The man who wields power and misinterprets it is the more dangerous the more honest he is.'

" 'I admit the truth of all you say, but there must be some mistake about it, for I do not remember that I gave any vote last winter upon any constitutional question.'

" 'No, Colonel, there's no mistake. Though I live here in the backwoods and seldom go from home, I take the papers from Washington and read very carefully all the proceedings of Congress. My papers say that last winter you voted for a bill to appropriate $20,000 to some sufferers by a fire in Georgetown. Is that true?'

" 'Well, my friend; I may as well own up. You have got me there. But certainly nobody will complain that a great and rich country like ours should give the insignificant sum of $20,000 to relieve its suffering women and children, particularly with a full and overflowing Treasury, and I am sure, if you had been there, you would have done just as I did.'

" 'It is not the amount, Colonel, that I complain of; it is the principle. In the first place, the government ought to have in the Treasury no more than enough for its legitimate purposes. But that has nothing to do with the question. The power of collecting and disbursing money at pleasure is the most dangerous power that can be intrusted to man, particularly under our system of collecting revenue by a tariff, which reaches every man in the country, no matter how poor he may be, and the poorer he is the more he pays in proportion to his means. What is worse, it presses upon him without his knowledge where the weight centers, for there is not a man in the United States who can ever guess how much he pays to the government. So you see, that while you are contributing to relieve one, you are drawing it from thousands who are even worse off than he. If you had the right to give anything, the amount was simply a matter of discretion with you, and you had as much right to give $20,000,000 as $20,000. If you have the right to give to one, you have the right to give to all; and, as the Constitution neither defines charity nor stipulates the amount, you are at liberty to give to any and everything which you may believe, or profess to believe, is a charity, and to any amount you may think proper. You will very easily perceive what a wide door this would open for fraud and corruption and favoritism, on the one hand, and for robbing the people on the other. No, Colonel, Congress has no right to give charity. Individual members may give as much of their own money as they please, but they have no right to touch a dollar of the public money for that purpose. If twice as many houses had been burned in this county as in Georgetown, neither you nor any other member of Congress would have thought of appropriating a dollar for our relief. There are about two hundred and forty members of Congress. If they had shown their sympathy for the sufferers by contributing each one week's pay, it would have made over $13,000. There are plenty of wealthy men in and around Washington who could have given $20,000 without depriving themselves of even a luxury of life. The congressmen chose to keep their own money, which, if reports be true, some of them spend not very creditably; and the people about Washington, no doubt, applauded you for relieving them from the necessity of giving by giving what was not yours to give. The people have delegated to Congress, by the Constitution, the power to do certain things. To do these, it is authorized to collect and pay moneys, and for nothing else. Everything beyond this is usurpation, and a violation of the Constitution.

" 'So you see, Colonel, you have violated the Constitution in what I consider a vital point. It is a precedent fraught with danger to the country, for when Congress once begins to stretch its power beyond the limits of the Constitution, there is no limit to it, and no security for the people. I have no doubt you acted honestly, but that does not make it any better, except as far as you are personally concerned, and you see that I cannot vote for you.'

Crockett Admits Wrong

"I tell you I felt streaked. I saw if I should have opposition, and this man should go to talking, he would set others to talking, and in that district I was a gone fawn-skin. I could not answer him, and the fact is, I was so fully convinced that he was right, I did not want to. But I must satisfy him, and I said to him:

" 'Well, my friend, you hit the nail upon the head when you said I had not sense enough to understand the Constitution. I intended to be guided by it, and thought I had studied it fully. I have heard many speeches in Congress about the powers of Congress, but what you have said here at your plow has got more hard, sound sense in it than all the fine speeches I ever heard. If I had ever taken the view of it that you have, I would have put my head into the fire before I would have given that vote; and if you will forgive me and vote for me again, if I ever vote for another unconstitutional law I wish I may be shot.'

"He laughingly replied: 'Yes, Colonel, you have sworn to that once before, but I will trust you again upon one condition. You say that you are convinced that your vote was wrong. Your acknowledgment of it will do more good than beating you for it. If, as you go around the district, you will tell people about this vote, and that you are satisfied it was wrong, I will not only vote for you, but will do what I can to keep down opposition, and, perhaps, I may exert some little influence in that way.'

" 'If I don't,' said I, 'I wish I may be shot; and to convince you that I am in earnest in what I say I will come back this way in a week or ten days, and if you will get up a gathering of the people, I will make a speech to them. Get up a barbecue, and I will pay for it.'

" 'No, Colonel, we are not rich people in this section, but we have plenty of provisions to contribute for a barbecue, and some to spare for those who have none. The push of crops will be over in a few days, and we can then afford a day for a barbecue. This is Thursday; I will see to getting it up on Saturday week. Come to my house on Friday, and we will go together, and I promise you a very respectable crowd to see and hear you.'

" 'Well, I will be here. But one thing more before I say good-by. I must know your name.'

" 'My name is Bunce.'

" 'Not Horatio Bunce?'

" 'Yes.'

" 'Well, Mr. Bunce, I never saw you before, though you say you have seen me, but I know you very well. I am glad I have met you, and very proud that I may hope to have you for my friend.'

Another Chance

"It was one of the luckiest hits of my life that I met him. He mingled but little with the public, but was widely known for his remarkable intelligence and incorruptible integrity, and for a heart brimful and running over with kindness and benevolence, which showed themselves not only in words but in acts. He was the oracle of the whole country around him, and his fame had extended far beyond the circle of his immediate acquaintance. Though I had never met him before, I had heard much of him, and but for this meeting it is very likely I should have had opposition, and had been beaten. One thing is very certain, no man could now stand up in that district under such a vote.

"At the appointed time I was at his house, having told our conversation to every crowd I had met, and to every man I stayed all night with, and I found that it gave the people an interest and a confidence in me stronger than I had ever seen manifested before.

"Though I was considerably fatigued when I reached his house, and, under ordinary circumstances, should have gone early to bed, I kept him up until midnight, talking about the principles and affairs of government, and got more real, true knowledge of them than I had got all my life before.

"I have known and seen much of him since, for I respect him — no, that is not the word — I reverence and love him more than any living man, and I go to see him two or three times every year; and I will tell you, sir, if every one who professes to be a Christian lived and acted and enjoyed it as he does, the religion of Christ would take the world by storm.

"But to return to my story. The next morning we went to the barbecue, and, to my surprise, found about a thousand men there. I met a good many whom I had not known before, and they and my friend introduced me around until I had got pretty well acquainted — at least, they all knew me.

"In due time notice was given that I would speak to them. They gathered up around a stand that had been erected. I opened my speech by saying:

Publicly Acknowledges His Error

" 'Fellow-citizens — I present myself before you today feeling like a new man. My eyes have lately been opened to truths which ignorance or prejudice, or both, had heretofore hidden from my view. I feel that I can today offer you the ability to render you more valuable service than I have ever been able to render before. I am here today more for the purpose of acknowledging my error than to seek your votes. That I should make this acknowledgment is due to myself as well as to you. Whether you will vote for me is a matter for your consideration only.'

"I went on to tell them about the fire and my vote for the appropriation and then told them why I was satisfied it was wrong. I closed by saying:

" 'And now, fellow-citizens, it remains only for me to tell you that the most of the speech you have listened to with so much interest was simply a repetition of the arguments by which your neighbor, Mr. Bunce, convinced me of my error.

" 'It is the best speech I ever made in my life, but he is entitled to the credit for it. And now I hope he is satisfied with his convert and that he will get up here and tell you so.'

"He came upon the stand and said:

" 'Fellow-citizens — It affords me great pleasure to comply with the request of Colonel Crockett. I have always considered him a thoroughly honest man, and I am satisfied that he will faithfully perform all that he has promised you today.'

"He went down, and there went up from that crowd such a shout for Davy Crockett as his name never called forth before.

"I am not much given to tears, but I was taken with a choking then and felt some big drops rolling down my cheeks. And I tell you now that the remembrance of those few words spoken by such a man, and the honest, hearty shout they produced, is worth more to me than all the honors I have received and all the reputation I have ever made, or ever shall make, as a member of Congress.

"Now, sir," concluded Crockett, "you know why I made that speech yesterday.

"There is one thing now to which I will call your attention. You remember that I proposed to give a week's pay. There are in that House many very wealthy men — men who think nothing of spending a week's pay, or a dozen of them, for a dinner or a wine party when they have something to accomplish by it. Some of those same men made beautiful speeches upon the great debt of gratitude which the country owed the deceased — a debt which could not be paid by money — and the insignificance and worthlessness of money, particularly so insignificant a sum as $10,000, when weighed against the honor of the nation. Yet not one of them responded to my proposition. Money with them is nothing but trash when it is to come out of the people. But it is the one great thing for which most of them are striving, and many of them sacrifice honor, integrity, and justice to obtain it."

When We Are Free

CHAPTER 30

We the People

by Ralph Bradford

When our fathers put themselves to the task of devising a fundamental law for the brand new nation they had created, they displayed great unity of purpose and breadth of vision. They did not, in class-conscious fashion, ask, What can we do for the benefit of agriculture? Or, How can we help labor? Or, What will be best for industry? No, their sights were on an altogether different sort of target — and they expressed the essence of it in the first three words of the Constitution they were so carefully and laboriously drafting: "We, the people."

Today, at a time when we are beset on all sides by the demands of this and that special interest, it would be fine if the leaders and exponents of all such groups would take a minute to read the one short paragraph that forms the preamble to that Constitution.

In passing, it is of interest to note that in a period of rather florid rhetoric the Founders restrained themselves remarkably at the really crucial moments. The Declaration of Independence, to be sure, is not an example of such reticence; but then, it was really a public relations production — a propaganda document, designed to tell the world why a certain action had been taken. It was prepared out of "a decent respect for the opinions of mankind." It had to go into considerable detail.

But the "action paper," the thing that did the trick, was a little 47-word resolution introduced by Richard Henry Lee, which asserted quite simply that the American colonies were, and of right ought to be, free and independent states. And it was so with the Constitution. Of course many words were required to spell out all its articles and sections; but when it came to setting down just what the basic law of the new nation was all about, the Founders laid it out fully in that one short paragraph.

They said it was to form a more perfect union; establish justice; insure domestic tranquility; provide for the common defense; promote the general welfare; and secure the blessings of liberty for themselves and their posterity.

From *The Freeman*, July 1978.

That was it. That's what they said it was all about — and it ought to be required reading to offset somewhat the recurrent proposals for the addition of this or that million-dollar bureau to bring this or that alleged billion-dollar "benefit" to this or that group — or for the creation of this or that agency to regulate and control the minutiae of our lives.

And I now suddenly realize that the paragraph I have just written contains an example of the kind of compulsion I'm given to complaining about! Okay — so I will let it stand for that reason. Look: *"It ought to be required reading."* I know, I know — that's a common conversational stereotype, but its use illustrates the innate attitude toward compulsion that is at the root of supergovernmentalism. I think, or my particular elite group thinks, that the preamble is important — therefore everybody should be *required* to read it!

But to return to the Founders, in addition to being sure of their aims, they were very conscious of the source of their authority. When they set down a principle, or even a procedure, they knew who, ultimately, was speaking. It was "we, the people."

Of course the great issues of statism versus freedom were not posed to our colonial forebears in the explicit terms of privilege and preference such as we now hear. But the Founders were not ignorant of either history or human nature. They knew that a time would come when there would be demands for governmental favors, preferences, largesse; and they made no place for them, except inadvertently, perhaps, in the much-tortured general welfare clause; and the anticipated demands for such extensions of government were answered once for all by Jefferson's simple phrase: "The best governed are the least governed."

The Growth of Bureaucracy

History shows that it is the seemingly ineradicable tendency of men to vacillate between the extremes of government — from Jeffersonian simplicity to the imagined benefits (and inevitable restrictions) of complete statism. It is not argued in these paragraphs that we can return to the simple governmental forms that sufficed for our colonial and agrarian periods. We are a vast and complicated aggregation of aims, interests, economic problems, political processes and social responsibilities. But through the years we have erected in Washington and throughout the states a bureaucratic monstrosity that is devouring our savings, crippling our economy, and stifling our initiative.

To some extent the cost and repressions of such overextension of government were felt in colonial times, and they aroused the anger of our sires, perhaps even more than the British denial of representative government had done. Jefferson himself was testy about it. As a philosophical statesman he was concerned about life, liberty and the pursuit of happiness; but as a taxpaying citizen he was both concerned and angered because the London bureaucracy had "sent hither a swarm of officers to harass our people and eat out their substance."

What does that sentence signify in terms of present-day American experience? Well, wholly apart from the several vast and ramified Departments of the Federal establishment — State, Commerce, Labor, Justice and so on — there are now sixty-one so-called Independent Agencies, plus seventy Boards, Committees and Commissions, that have been created by the Congress. I have no figures on the number of people employed in them, but it is of course very large; and for the government as a whole, not counting those in the several military services, there are now very close to three million people on the Federal payroll!

A Costly Army

No question is here raised about the efficiency of those people, or their honesty and devotion. They are citizens, employed to do work projected by the Congress. But they *do*, "eat out our substance." They *do* cost money — millions, billions of it in the aggregate. And they do contribute to the accumulation of a debt that now exceeds the utterly incomprehensible figure of 1 *trillion* dollars.

Who owes that debt, and must finally pay it, one way or another? The government? Not really. The ultimate debtor: We, the people!

But the materiality of such dollar-statistics is really not what I am reaching for. Rather, I am trying to express the proper relationship of the citizen to his government and vice versa; and that relationship is not expressible ideally in terms of dollars or the cost of bread. To be sure, man *does* live by bread and the nutrients it symbolizes — not alone, of course, for there is a higher nourishment; but food and shelter are important needs, and even our moments of purest philosophy and warmest philanthropy are influenced and modified by the shape and size — and cost! — of our physical and political environment. Pseudo social scientists who envision the Superstate as the Mother-Father image of the future seem happily unaware that a shattering blow can be dealt to both economic and political theorizing by such a crass bit of realism as the price of beans!

When We Are Free

It is a far cry, from our present-day, Washington-centered politico-economic set up, back to the ideals of the Founders. It is the fashion these days in leftward circles to assume that the vast spate of so-called social legislation, and the resultant enormous cost and sprawling bureaucracy, is all in keeping with the "revolutionary" ideas of the men who wrote the Constitution. Especially during these past two or three years, when we were in a Bicentennial euphoria, we have heard a lot of cant about the "radicals" and "revolutionaries" who sparked the American War for Independence and devised the American form of government. A great deal of this maudlin output was either grossly overdrawn or flatly and ludicrously false.

What, after all, was the aim of those men who directed the American destinies for some years before, and during, that fateful summer of 1787 when the Constitution was being drafted? Certainly it was not "revolution" in the modern sense of the term. Indeed, that word does not occur in the Declaration of Independence; and so far as I can discover, it was little used in the literature and oratory of the period. Even Patrick Henry's impassioned plea was not for revolution, but for liberty. And when the term "revolution" was employed, it referred not so much to the act of separation from the mother country, as to the evolution of thinking among the American people — as when John Adams, years later, wrote that "the Revolution was in the minds and hearts of the people." No, the Founders were not aiming at revolution, but reason; they were not out to destroy, but to build.

They had reluctantly fought an unwanted war — a war which, judged either by logic or logistics, they hadn't a chance of winning. In that desperate gamble they were well served by the tenacity, cunning and superb generalship of the man from Mount Vernon, plus the wiles of Benjamin Franklin in luring France into the conflict. But now that was all past. Now they were on their own in the big world of nations. The makeshift, ramshackle machinery of the old Confederation, which had haltingly enabled them to ride out the war years, was a totally inadequate craft for the waters upon which they were now embarked.

They started out, first of all, with a healthy fear of the very institution they were charged with creating — namely, government. Recognizing the imperative need for it in the regulation of human affairs, they were nevertheless fully aware of its potential threat to the self-same liberties it was designed to preserve. They were, for the most part, men of considerable scholarship, versed in history and familiar with the writings of social and political philosophers like Locke, Montesquieu, and Blackstone.

Moreover, Adam Smith's long-awaited *Wealth of Nations* had been published in 1776, and by the summer of 1787, when the Constitution was being hammered out in Philadelphia, the Scotchman's masterpiece had been widely read in America, as it had in England and on the Continent. The framers of the Constitution were almost certainly familiar with its major premises. They were not all paragons of wisdom and virtue. They could and did play politics, quarrel, impute motives, take advantage. Bitter wrangling developed between those who represented the smaller states like Delaware, Maryland and New Jersey and their opposite numbers from such big commonwealths as New York, Pennsylvania, Massachusetts and Virginia. In other words, they were a convention of men. But they were enlightened men; and with all their differences they were devotedly committed to the task of making a nation.

They knew first of all that government, of some kind, is necessary. The ideal thing would be for men to live together in harmony, without need of control or direction. Indeed, one of the delegates was soon to express this, in the so-called Federalist papers, published to win support for the Constitution. "If men were angels," he wrote, "no government would be necessary." And he went on: "In forming a government which is to be administered by men over men, the great difficulty lies in this: you must first enable the government to control the governed; and in the next place, oblige it to control itself."

Limited Government

But men, alas, are not angels; and even if they were, conflicts might arise — witness Lucifer's revolt, as chronicled at considerable length by John Milton. But let's not be facetious. Men being fallible creatures, we confront the simple fact that they need to be protected — first of all, from one another! Also the mechanics of their civilization, as they have matured through the centuries, layer by layer and culture by culture, on the several world stages — those mechanics, or rather mechanisms, require to be guarded, protected from abuse, and, to a minimal degree, regulated. Hence government.

Once in a whimsical moment I fabulated in verse the origin of one such civilizing mechanism. In my fable a primitive hunter, back from a wearying chase with a haunch of venison over his hairy shoulder, was downcast because he had shattered his last flint-head spear, and must spend much time and effort to fashion another. But his neighbor, a cripple who could not go afield to hunt, had several flint heads all chipped out — but no meat in his cave. So, in a great flash, it came to them that they could swap and each be the gainer. Thus trade was born; and I summarized its essence in two lines:

> Each gave the thing he least required,
> And gained the thing he most desired!

It was that simple principle, applied across the broad spectrum of man's physical needs, which developed into the socio-economic mechanisms that came to be known by such names as the division of labor, specialization, craftsmanship, industry, exchange, money — in short, the implements of trade, the Great Civilizer.

For it was not alone to physical comforts and necessities that the principle of exchange was applied beneficially. If it could enable the hunter, the fisherman, the tanner, the spinner, the weaver and a hundred other specialists to develop and ply their crafts through the trading of skill for skill as expressed in product, it could also make possible a like extension in things of the mind. It could and did lead to the development of science and art and literature. The great principle of exchange, like a shuttle in the loom of time, helped weave the fabric of civilization.

Remove the Restrictions

By 1783 the new country was, of course, heavily involved in all the ramifications of a commercial, industrial and agricultural economy. Under the restrictive British bureaucracy the rights of the Colonials in all these areas had often been impeded and at times ruthlessly restricted. Those charged with devising the new government were aware that the greatest possible spirit of individual enterprise and initiative should be encouraged — not by subsidy from public funds, nor by the relaxation of vigilance in upholding necessary laws, but by the removal or nonimposition of all unneeded restrictions.

They wanted, it seems clear, a government under which Americans could pursue their respective interests through peaceful production and exchange in the open market — buyers and sellers, producers and consumers, suppliers and customers, in a beneficial interchange.

Freedom! That was what they were after; not just relief from whimsical bureaucratic restrictions, but freedom to make, produce, trade, sell, buy, invent, invest, build, save, spend — freedom, in short, to live the sort of life that is natural and normal to an industrious, inventive, adventurous and acquisitive people.

Acquisitive? Whoa there a minute! Better be careful here. Better tread softly. You see, to acquire is to get; and in certain overdelicate circles acquisition is equated with something like social piracy, as though "getting" anything is always done at someone else's expense. And indeed it sometimes may be done so — and that's where the State, represented by the Law, comes in. In a negative sense, that's what the State is for. But while Webster's says that to acquire is to gain "by any means," it adds, "usually by one's own exertions." And in that sense we have indeed been an acquisitive people — and three rousing cheers for it! Home ownership, competence, security, stability, industry, application, independence — these are at once the products and the motivation of acquisition. They are also the foundation stones of responsible government.

By creating a governmental environment favorable to personal initiative, the Founders laid the foundation for our greatness as a nation. Despite the drain of several wars — the long-felt burden of debt from the War of Independence itself, the ghastly toll of the Civil War, and the staggering outlays for the first and second World Wars — despite these colossal burdens, the nation grew, expanded and developed into the globe's greatest power. And at the same time it exceeded all others in the material welfare of its people.

The big question now is: Where do we, the people, go from here? No account has been taken in these paragraphs of our more recent performances on the world stage and in our domestic economy, nor of the added debt, bitterness and loss of prestige that have resulted. That is an article — a book, *a library!* — in itself.

The American problem today is not what we do about the world, but what we do about us, the people, and about us, the nation. Shall we resume our travels on a path of destiny — travels that have made us great and strong and useful in the world? Shall we rid ourselves of smothering debt through sufficient self-denial? Shall we once again be solvent as well as sovereign? Shall we halt the march to national bankruptcy? Shall we avoid the killing inflation that wipes out savings, destroys credit, and brings chaos?

If we do, who will benefit? If we do not, who will pay?

To both questions the answer is: We, the people.

When We Are Free

Unit VI: The Role of the Marketplace

We have chosen several articles by Leonard E. Read for inclusion in this book. None deserves more the honor of being known as a classic than the famous "I, Pencil." It first appeared a generation ago — 1958 — and has been reprinted countless times since.

In this most entertaining selection Mr. Read demonstrates that "not a single person on the face of the earth knows how to make" a pencil. As the story unfolds, the miraculous workings of the marketplace become apparent. What a perfect way to open this unit!

Thomas W. Hazlett, in "The Success of Failure," illustrates an important feature of the market — the right to fail. "It is the economic failure," he maintains, that allows us to *see* our mistakes and motivates us to *correct* them."

Success and failure are elements of the two selections from *The Wall Street Journal*, "A Matter of Taste" by Lawrence Ingrassia and "Procter and Gamble: A Good Listener" by John A. Prestbo. Ingrassia and Prestbo both bring out another vital point as well — that the consumer rules the marketplace and determines the fate of every business enterprise.

The role of the market in easing the drudgery of day to day life is the theme of "The Liberation of Women" by Bettina Bien Greaves. Citing evidence of hardship gleaned from old cookbooks, Mrs. Greaves concludes that it was capitalism "which liberated women from their traditional household chores."

On another matter, a very potent force for good in the marketplace is competition. It keeps businessmen "on their toes." As long as the economy is kept free, men will compete for the patronage of the consumer.

Competition can be short-circuited, however, when free men turn to government for protection from it. It is important to understand that when this happens, the marketplace is contaminated; its performance deteriorates. In "The Parable of the Parking Lots," Henry Manne illustrates that very point in a fictitious, yet entirely plausible, tale of a parking lot business.

CHAPTER 31

I, Pencil

My Family Tree as told to Leonard E. Read

I am a lead pencil — the ordinary wooden pencil familiar to all boys and girls and adults who can read and write.[1]

Writing is both my vocation and my avocation; that's all I do.

You may wonder why I should write a genealogy. Well, to begin with, my story is interesting. And, next, I am a mystery — more so than a tree or a sunset or even a flash of lightning. But, sadly, I am taken for granted by those who use me, as if I were a mere incident and without background. This supercilious attitude relegates me to the level of the commonplace. This is a species of the grievous error in which mankind cannot too long persist without peril. For, as a wise man observed, "We are perishing for want of wonder, not for want of wonders."[2]

I, Pencil, simple though I appear to be, merit your wonder and awe, a claim I shall attempt to prove. In fact, if you can understand me — no, that's too much to ask of anyone — if you can become aware of the miraculousness which I symbolize, you can help save the freedom mankind is so unhappily losing. I have a profound lesson to teach. And I can teach this lesson better than can an automobile or an airplane or a mechanical dishwasher because — well, because I am seemingly so simple.

Simple? Yet, *not a single person on the face of this earth knows how to make me*. This sounds fantastic, doesn't it? Especially when it is realized that there are about one and one-half billion of my kind produced in the U.S.A. each year.

Pick me up and look me over. What do you see? Not much meets the eye — there's some wood, lacquer, the printed labeling, graphite lead, a bit of metal, and an eraser.

From *The Freeman*, December 1958.

[1] My official name is "Mongol 482." My many ingredients are assembled, fabricated, and finished by Eberhard Faber Pencil Company, Wilkes-Barre, Pennsylvania.

[2] G. K. Chesterton

Innumerable Antecedents

Just as you cannot trace your family tree back very far, so is it impossible for me to name and explain all my antecedents. But I would like to suggest enough of them to impress upon you the richness and complexity of my background.

My family tree begins with what in fact is a tree, a cedar of straight grain that grows in Northern California and Oregon. Now contemplate all the saws and trucks and rope and the countless other gear used in harvesting and carting the cedar logs to the railroad siding. Think of all the persons and the numberless skills that went into their fabrication: the mining of ore, the making of steel and its refinement into saws, axes, motors; the growing of hemp and bringing it through all the stages to heavy and strong rope; the logging camps with their beds and mess halls, the cookery and the raising of all the foods. Why, untold thousands of persons had a hand in every cup of coffee the loggers drink!

The logs are shipped to a mill in San Leandro, California. Can you imagine the individuals who make flat cars and rails and railroad engines and who construct and install the communication systems incidental thereto? These legions are among my antecedents.

Consider the millwork in San Leandro. The cedar logs are cut into small, pencil-length slats less than one-fourth of an inch in thickness. These are kiln dried and then tinted for the same reason women put rouge on their faces. People prefer that I look pretty, not a pallid white. The slats are waxed and kiln dried again. How many skills went into the making of the tint and the kilns, into supplying the heat, the light and power, the belts, motors, and all the other things a mill requires? Sweepers in the mill among my ancestors? Yes, and included are the men who poured the concrete for the dam of a Pacific Gas & Electric Company hydroplant which supplies the mill's power!

Don't overlook the ancestors present and distant who have a hand in transporting sixty carloads of slats across the nation from California to Wilkes-Barre!

Complicated Machinery

Once in the pencil factory — $4,000,000 in machinery and building, all capital accumulated by thrifty and saving parents of mine — each slat is given eight grooves by a complex machine, after which another machine lays leads in every other slat, applies glue, and places another slat atop — a lead sandwich, so to speak. Seven brothers and I are mechanically carved from this "wood-clinched" sandwich.

My "lead" itself — it contains no lead at all — is complex. The graphite is mined in Ceylon. Consider these miners and those who make their many tools and the makers of the paper sacks in which the graphite is shipped and those who make the string that ties the sacks and those who put them aboard ships and those who make the ships. Even the lighthouse keepers along the way assisted in my birth — and the harbor pilots.

The graphite is mixed with clay from Mississippi in which ammonium hydroxide is used in the refining process. Then wetting agents are added such as sulfonated tallow — animal fats chemically reacted with sulfuric acid. After passing through numerous machines, the mixture finally appears as endless extrusions — as from a sausage grinder — cut to size, dried, and baked for several hours at 1,850 degrees Fahrenheit. To increase their strength and smoothness the leads are then treated with a hot mixture which includes candelilla wax from Mexico, paraffin wax, and hydrogenated natural fats.

My cedar receives six coats of lacquer. Do you know all of the ingredients of lacquer? Who would think that the growers of castor beans and the refiners of castor oil are a part of it? They are. Why, even the processes by which the lacquer is made a beautiful yellow involves the skills of more persons than one can enumerate!

Observe the labeling. That's a film formed by applying heat to carbon black mixed with resins. How do you make resins and what, pray, is carbon black?

My bit of metal — the ferrule — is brass. Think of all the persons who mine zinc and copper and those who have the skills to make shiny sheet brass from these products of nature. Those black rings on my ferrule are black nickel. What is black nickel and how is it applied? The complete story of why the center of my ferrule has no black nickel on it would take pages to explain.

Then there's my crowning glory, inelegantly referred to in the trade as "the plug," the part man uses to erase the errors he makes with me. An ingredient called "factice" is what does the erasing. It is a rubber-like product made by reacting rape seed oil from the Dutch East Indies with sulfur chloride. Rubber, contrary to the common notion, is only for binding purposes. Then, too, there are numerous vulcanizing and accelerating agents. The pumice comes from Italy; and the pigment which gives "the plug" its color is cadmium sulfide.

No One Knows

Does anyone wish to challenge my earlier assertion that no single person on the face of this earth knows how to make me?

Actually, millions of human beings have had a hand in my creation, no one of whom even knows more than a very few of the others. Now, you may say that I go too far in relating the picker of a coffee berry in far off Brazil and food growers elsewhere to my creation; that this is an extreme position. I shall stand by my claim. There isn't a single person in all these millions, including the president of the pencil company, who contributes more than a tiny, infinitesimal bit of know-how. From the standpoint of know-how the only difference between the miner of graphite in Ceylon and the logger in Oregon is in the *type* of know-how. Neither the miner nor the logger can be dispensed with, any more than can the chemist at the factory or the worker in the oil field — paraffin being a by-product of petroleum.

Here is an astounding fact: Neither the worker in the oil field nor the chemist nor the digger of graphite or clay nor any who mans or makes the ships or trains or trucks nor the one who runs the machine that does the knurling on my bit of metal nor the president of the company performs his singular task because he wants me. Each one wants me less, perhaps, than does a child in the first grade. Indeed, there are some among this vast multitude who never saw a pencil nor would they know how to use one. Their motivation is other than me. Perhaps it is something like this: Each of these millions sees that he can thus exchange his tiny know-how for the goods and services he needs or wants. I may or may not be among these items.

No Master Mind

There is a fact still more astounding: The absence of a master mind, of anyone dictating or forcibly directing these countless actions which bring me into being. No trace of such a person can be found. Instead, we find the Invisible Hand at work. This is the mystery to which I earlier referred.

It has been said that "only God can make a tree." Why do we agree with this? Isn't it because we realize that we ourselves could not make one? Indeed, can we even describe a tree? We cannot, except in superficial terms. We can say, for instance, that a certain molecular configuration manifests itself as a tree. But what mind is there among men that could even record, let alone direct, the constant changes in molecules that transpire in the life span of a tree? Such a feat is utterly unthinkable!

I, Pencil, am a complex combination of miracles: a tree, zinc, copper, graphite, and so on. But to these miracles which manifest themselves in Nature an even more extraordinary miracle has been added: the configuration of creative human energies — millions of tiny know-hows configurating naturally and spontaneously in response to human necessity and desire and *in the absence of any human master-minding!* Since only God can make a tree, I insist that only God could make me. Man can no more direct these millions of know-hows to bring me into being than he can put molecules together to create a tree.

The above is what I meant when writing, "If you can become aware of the miraculousness which I symbolize, you can help save the freedom mankind is so unhappily losing." For, if one is aware that these know-hows will naturally, yes, automatically, arrange themselves into creative and productive patterns in reponse to human necessity and demand — that is, in the absence of governmental or any other coercive master-minding — then one will possess an absolutely essential ingredient for freedom: *a faith in free men*. Freedom is impossible without this faith.

Once government has had a monopoly of a creative activity such, for instance, as the delivery of the mails, most individuals will believe that the mails could not be efficiently delivered by men acting freely. And here is the reason: Each one acknowledges that he himself doesn't know how to do all the things incident to mail delivery. He also recognizes that no other individual could do it. These assumptions are correct. No individual possesses enough know-how to perform a nation's mail delivery any more than any individual possesses enough know-how to make a pencil. Now, in the absence of a faith in free men — in the unawareness that millions of tiny know-hows would naturally and miraculously form and cooperate to satisfy this necessity — the individual cannot help but reach the erroneous conclusion that mail can be delivered only by governmental "master-minding."

Testimony Galore

If I, Pencil, were the only item that could offer testimony on what men can accomplish when free to try, then those with little faith would have a fair case. However, there is testimony galore; it's all about us and on every hand. Mail delivery is exceedingly simple when compared, for instance, to the making of an automobile or a calculating machine or a grain combine or a milling machine or to tens of thousands of other things. Delivery? Why, in this area where men have been left free to try, they deliver the human voice around the world in less than one second; they deliver an event visually and in motion to any person's home when it is happening; they deliver 150 passengers from Seattle to Baltimore in less than four hours; they deliver gas from Texas to one's range or furnace in New York at unbelievably low rates and without subsidy; they deliver each four pounds of oil from the Persian Gulf to our Eastern Seaboard — halfway around the world — for less money than the government charges for delivering a one-ounce letter across the street!

Leave Men Free

The lesson I have to teach is this: *Leave all creative energies uninhibited.* Merely organize society to act in harmony with this lesson. Let society's legal apparatus remove all obstacles the best it can. Permit these creative know-hows freely to flow. Have faith that free men will respond to the Invisible Hand. This faith will be confirmed. I, Pencil, seemingly simple though I am, offer the miracle of my creation as testimony that this is a practical faith, as practical as the sun, the rain, a cedar tree, the good earth.

CHAPTER 32

The Success of Failure

by Thomas W. Hazlett

Without failure we'd be in big trouble.

"Learning from our mistakes" is far more than a worn cliche, it is the gateway to an enormous truth about our entire economic system. Only by allowing our failures to run their due course may we ever chance to come by better ways of providing for our desires.

So much of the discussion of "failure" has turned to the mere exchanging of shibboleths. Everyday discourse is loaded with paeans to braving the chances for failure, accepting great challenges, the noble nature of "sink or swim," and warnings that "nothing ventured, nothing gained." There seems to be an instantaneous acceptance that individuals must, in their private affairs, be willing to risk something to make a showing in life. Not many would hedge on the idea that, if you take away the chance to flop, you simultaneously withdraw the opportunity to soar.

Yet, in extending this simple morality to larger spheres, there looms a dichotomy. While the challenge of life's game is hearty for the individual soul, the goal of social institutions is to demolish all possible exceptions to a pre-programmed "success." Security, the professed aim of scores of government programs, seeks to place a prohibition on all deviations from the politically-determined "success norm."

Now, from the individual's perspective, security is a decent sort of thing to strive for and a happy one to achieve. People who are far from being millionaires take reasonable measures to enhance their own security by purchasing insurance, getting an education (read: income security), joining a union, working on a contractual basis, getting married and, let's not forget, having children (could we call this a form of genetic social security?).

The distinctive characteristics of "private" security are that a person acts either to "pool" his risks voluntarily with others, as in buying insurance, or he takes positive action to lessen the uncertainty surrounding his circumstances, as in gaining an education.

From *The Freeman*, August 1978.

"Public" security will be pursued from a diametrically different angle: simply shifting the burden of failure from one group to another.

Forcibly Shifting the Burden

If we look at any government bureaucracy we can see the nature of the problem. When the government establishes "job security" via tenure rules (accompanied by cost-of-living escalators) the government is not "pooling" the risks of the workers nor is it taking positive action to reduce the uncertainty confronting the work force. It is forcibly transferring risks of failure from one group (government workers) to another group (private sector workers).

Now, from a moral view, this is a nasty break for the latter; the so-called civil servants are neither very servile nor very civil for inflicting this injustice. But this is only the visible damage of the deal. The most pernicious effects are to be found in the economic results of this redistribution of risk.

Just as a man can only find success by winding his way through — and past — failure, an economic system must depend on its failings to signal its path of success. This process is certainly more important for our system as a whole for, whereas a man may follow the examples of those who have gone before, a system has no model to emulate. It must break its ground in darkness.

Economic failings include many distasteful possibilities: people getting fired or laid-off, companies or individuals going bankrupt, product lines being discontinued, capital lying idle, stock equities falling in value, ad infinitum. All such disturbances are the result of some miscalculation in the plans of the economy's agents. People, businesses and governments cannot foresee the future, and so every unexpected change in our circumstances — even if it is, on the whole, a very favorable one — will cause some people to end up in less fortunate conditions than they had anticipated.

Change May Be Painful

Even when our society eagerly greeted the innovation of the automobile, for example, there were the poor blacksmiths being thrown out of work. And, in a recent movie, Woody Allen reminisces about an entire family that was wiped out by the introduction of automatic pinsetters. And, just as we pray for the cure for cancer, we know that, when it comes, we will see some bad economic news for the cobalt radiation industry.

These economic "failings" are tremendously important clues that, far from being swept under the rug, should be utilized as efficiently as possible for the value they contain. This value is both informational and motivational. It is the economic failure that allows us to *see* our mistakes and motivates us to *correct* them.

Failures are the "symptoms" of the economic organism. As the body of any living thing locates and cures its maladies by responding to its itches, aches and throbs, so the economy must behave to adjust to its unemployments, malinvestments and inefficiencies. Professor Axel Leijonhufvud discusses this organistic parallel by citing a biologist's description of a biological system:

> An *organism* is an integrated unit of structure and functions. In an *organism*, all *molecules* have to work in harmony. Each *molecule* has to know what the other *molecules* are doing. Each *molecule* must be able to receive messages and must be disciplined enough to obey orders. How has the *organism* solved the problem of inter*molecular* communication?

Professor Leijonhufvud suggests that, in the above passage, we simply substitute the word "economy" for "organism" and the word "transactors" for "molecules." Re-read the passage this way.

Thus, do we arrive at the essence of the co-ordination problem.

Adjust or Perish

If a living organism attempted to ignore certain biochemical signals it would soon degenerate into multitudinous plagues and perish. And when an economic system fails, as Prof. Leijonhufvud is fond of saying, to "mend its ways" in response to signs of ill health, it will likewise degenerate into economic anemia and witness economic diseases immensely greater in magnitude than the initial symptoms.

The ease with which our society has let this helpful analogy slip past is demonstrated by the single statistic that, for all of 1977, for all of the federal government, just 223 workers were fired. Out of two million federal job-holders, that represents about one out of every ten thousand employees. You'd probably have a better chance of being assaulted by a lightning bolt in Palm Springs or of receiving Sophia Loren's phone number from Computer Date.

More than the lack of individual failure in government is the absence of any way for departments and agencies of government to fail. When a public bureaucracy falls short of some assigned goal it is not driven to a cheap merger or bankruptcy as in the "ruthless" competition of the market place. Indeed, gross failures on the part of particular bureaucracies often send out enormously beneficial signals for the individual bureaucrats.

Witness the incredible failure of the Federal Energy Administration. Founded as a "temporary" agency to cushion the effects of the Arab oil embargo in 1973-74, the Agency was given the goal of Project Independence. The idea was to lessen oil imports over the years until, by 1985, we were to be completely — and patriotically — self-sufficient in energy.

The FEA went about this goal in rather bizarre fashion. It promptly slapped a "crude-oil equalization" tax on domestic producers, and used the resultant revenues to subsidize oil imports. But, let us not quibble over methodology; let us simply look at the results. When the FEA was born in 1973, the U.S. imported 1/3 of its oil; today we import 1/2.

By 1976 the President's Task Force on FEA Regulations was led to conclude:

> FEA regulations, as they now exist, confer few if any benefits upon the public ... In return for this lack of benefits and sense of false security, the American businessman, the taxpayer, and the petroleum consumer, must incur higher costs than might otherwise be the case. Indeed, continuation of the present regulatory mechanism will result in long-run inefficiencies for the American economy.

Failure may not come in a more plainly marked wrapper than the Federal Energy Administration. So how does the government cleanse us of the FEA burden? By exponential expansion!

Bureaucratic Growth

In 1977 the FEA opened its new offices with "Department of Energy" on the marquee. It has now attained full cabinet rank and boasts 20,000 full-timers "economizing" our energy with a ten billion dollar budget. Apart from its institutional successes, FEA officionados have scored well. The Agency's first director went on to become Secretary of the Treasury, the second has gone on to an esteemed academic post, and the third and present director, now a cabinet member, sits at the right hand of our President (1978).

In contrast to the artificial serenity of the public sphere, there were over 200,000 bankruptcies, individual and corporate, in 1977 and several millions of workers were forced to switch jobs in the private sector. As much as we would like to minimize such disruptions and failures (particularly the bankruptcy figures which are influenced by laws extremely generous to defaulters), we do not want to eliminate real errors of judgment and competence by "assuming them away." We want to "bleed" our system, purge the failing, and find a better way tomorrow.

Government bureaucracy has delivered a Brave New World to its protected clients: do not fear the future for it contains no failure. The job security of the public sector precludes any adjustment process whereby we purge the bad and try something new. "Government without failure" can only bring about "institutions without success."

Upon reflection, when *was* the last time that a government bureaucracy was closed and cleared away due to its failing to meet the needs of the consumers? The private market place displays a veritable barrage of such leapfrogging, with bankruptcies, mergers, corporate takeovers and shake-ups, proxy fights, "inside information" and all the "ravages" of "dog-eat-dog" competition. Yet it is this constant, relentless panic to discover today's failure and to gobble it up at a bargain price that promotes an incessant tendency toward most efficiently reaching for the consumer's dollar.

The Test at the Market

To illustrate the respective mechanisms of the market and the bureaucracy, it is interesting to review the *Wall Street Journal* on any given day. Look at the incredible information just on the stock market alone. Here we have the relative values, as judged by millions of traders, of the earning power of thousands of companies. A mistake (or unsolicited disaster) accruing to any of these firms reflects itself to the entire market in the price of the stock in a matter of — amazingly — seconds. No government study. No environmental impact statement. No six-year lawsuit. A private company can flunk the market test in seconds.

Look around the rest of the *Journal*. Articles on quarterly earnings reports, new product lines, management personnel shuffles, changes in corporate profit strategies, in technologies, in marketing techniques. All are based on the quest of private persons to meet the challenge of market competition, to best deliver the stockholders the highest sales at the lowest cost. In other words, to avoid flunking that market test. And here there is no room for pontification. Speech writers don't produce profit statements — accountants do.

The state has no room, no need, and no desire for a competitive test of its economic programs. Its motivation is to gain *political* efficiency, and this brand of activity takes on characteristics quite distinct from those required for *economic* efficiency. The appeal of the market solution is that, in the famous words of Adam Smith, each individual "neither intends to promote the public interest, nor knows how much he is promoting it . . . he intends only his own gain and he is in this . . . led by an invisible hand to promote an end which was no part of his intention. By pursuing his own interest he frequently promotes that of society more effectually than when he really intends to promote it."

The Political Test

Conversely, the drive for *political* efficiency can result in the most wasteful and fraudulent of activities and may foster the emergence of regimented, bureaucratic systems which are totally unresponsive to the public and which suffocate our spontaneous forces for creativity. As Professor Milton Friedman comments on the inverse of Smith's economic "invisible hand":

> The invisible hand in politics is as potent a force for harm as the invisible hand in economics is for good. In politics, men who intend only to promote the public interest, as they conceive it, are "led by an invisible hand to promote an end that was no part of their intention." They become front-men for special interests they would never knowingly serve. They end up sacrificing the public interest to the special interest, the interest of consumers to that of producers, the interest of the masses who never go to college to that of those who attend college, the interest of the poor working-class saddled with employment taxes to that of the middle class who get disproportionate benefits from social security, and so on down the line.

The rewards of success can only be fully effective where the risks from failure are real. Success and failure must be two sides of an indivisible coin. And it is only when we toss this coin fairly, without precluding the chance it may come up tails, can we gain the knowledge to steer ourselves toward a better way of doing things. The game of life is, naturally, a trial and error process, and only by allowing ourselves to face our failings and to correct our bearings will we move progressively.

How Protectionism Betrays and Destroys the Individual

Some of our best emotions nudge us to fudge. We want to do whatever "must" be done to cover up the downside risks of contemporary society. But if we are loyal to these "best emotions" when it comes to our public institutions we may well betray our "best judgment." There is a most compelling argument against such state action to directly outlaw social problems. For by such "protectionism" we seal ourselves off from the phenomenal dynamism of individual initiative that will, when all is said and done, still be the attribute of man that brings home the bread. As F. A. Hayek reveals:

> To the ambitious and impatient reformer, filled with indignation at a particular evil, nothing short of the complete abolition of that evil by the quickest and most direct means will seem adequate. If every person now suffering from unemployment, ill health, or inadequate provision for his old age is at once to be relieved of his cares, nothing short of an all-comprehensive and compulsory scheme will suffice. But if, in our impatience to solve such problems immediately, we give government exclusive and monopolistic powers, we may find that we have been short-sighted. If the quickest way to a now visible solution becomes the only permissible one and all alternative experimentation is precluded, and if what now seems the best method of satisfying a need is made the sole starting point for all future development, we may perhaps reach our present goal sooner, but we shall probably at the same time prevent the emergence of more effective alternative solutions. It is often those who are most anxious to use our existing knowledge and powers to the full that do most to impair the future growth of knowledge by the methods they use. The controlled single-channel development toward which impatience and administrative convenience have frequently inclined the reformer and which, especially in the field of social insurance, has become characteristic of the modern welfare state may well become the chief obstacle to future improvement.

At bottom, the price of synthetic success today will surely be the loss of opportunity for authentic success tomorrow.

When We Are Free

CHAPTER 33

A Matter of Taste

by Lawrence Ingrassia

Appleasy looked like a winner when it was whipped up in Pillsbury Co.'s test kitchen.

The new dessert — apples in cinnamon sauce with a crunchy streusel topping — was the product of three years of exhaustive research. It was cheap, easy to fix and fast.

There was just one problem: Not very many people liked it. There weren't enough apples, the cinnamon was overpowering and the topping was too sweet. "It was a magnificent flop," says one Pillsbury executive.

Appleasy went the way of most new food products — down the drain. The failure rate has always been enough to give food company executives indigestion, and it is getting worse. More than 60% of all new grocery products introduced into test markets in 1977 failed, compared with about 50% in 1971, according to A. C. Nielsen Co. And the failure rate is well over eight in 10 counting all the products scrapped in the test kitchen before they are marketed.

Batteries of tests and surveys are conducted to discern what shoppers want, to develop and refine recipes, to choose brand names and even to design packages for new products, but all these efforts have been to little avail. There still isn't a foolproof method of telling what will succeed. "If anybody really knew, the failure rate wouldn't be so high," says Edward Tauber, research director at the Dancer Fitzgerald Sample Inc. advertising agency.

A new food product needs a lot more going for it to succeed these days. Since grocery unit volume has been practically flat for several years, a new product has to bump something else off the supermarket shelf. And because of higher advertising costs, it is harder for a new product to pay for itself and turn a profit. But a real winner can mean millions of dollars in business for years — and more than pay for some losers.

With the success rate dropping and costs increasing, food companies have been more cautious in introducing new brands in the

---

Reprinted by permission of *The Wall Street Journal* (2/26/80) Dow Jones & Company, Inc., 1980. All Rights Reserved.

past couple of years. After topping 1,000 a year in the mid-1970s, the number of new-brand introductions slumped to 744 in 1978 and recovered only somewhat to 912 last year, according to A. C. Nielsen.

There have been some changes in strategy, too. Companies are dishing up more variations of old favorites. You now can buy Honey Nut Cheerios and Honey and Nut Corn Flakes, and there is Log Cabin Pancake and Waffle Mix to go with Log Cabin Syrup. Companies also are taking fewer chances with long shots. "They're less likely to play the dartboard game — throwing out a product and seeing if it sticks," Mr. Tauber says.

Solving Problems

By and large, though, the way new products are developed hasn't changed. "You have to look at the consumer, find out what problems he's encountering and try to devise a new product which presents a better solution than the old product," says Marc C. Particelli, a vice president at the Booz, Allen & Hamilton management-consultant office in Chicago.

That isn't easy, though. New food products today have to combine quality and convenience without costing too much. A look at some products cooked up in Pillsbury's test kitchen in the past few years shows how difficult it is to get all the ingredients for success into a single product.

At Pillsbury, most ideas come from marketing or research and development executives. The vast majority of ideas are discarded early because they don't pass cost-analysis or technical-feasibility studies. Others are dropped after market studies and taste tests. Only a handful are made into products each year.

Unfortunately, this laborious process doesn't guarantee success on the supermarket shelf. "This isn't a science; almost anything can go wrong," says Edgar T. Mertz, until recently vice president of Pillsbury's consumer-products group. "Whenever we have something we think is going to set the world on fire, I have a drawer full of things to remind me of the losers."

Some food products fail because they simply don't taste good enough. No one sets out to make a bad product, of course. But in an effort to make a product convenient and inexpensive, too much quality can be sacrificed. That apparently was Appleasy's downfall.

Pillsbury began looking for an easy-to-prepare dessert in June 1975. Initial ideas ranged from instant yogurt to Boston cream pie to fudge sauce with a brownie topping. But a fruit dessert emerged as the favorite in "focus group" discussions with consumers.

A Matter of Taste

Pillsbury chose apple because "the majority of consumers eat and perceive apples to be good; you know, 'An apple a day keeps the doctor away'," explains Allan A. McCusker, a marketing executive who joined Pillsbury after Appleasy was developed. Pillsbury's test kitchen, which is a cross between a laboratory and a kitchen, came up with a recipe using freeze-dried apples. All you had to do was add boiling water, stir, wait five minutes and eat.

Consumer panels were interviewed to help pick a name. The early choice, Hot Apple'n Crunch, was dropped because Appleasy conveyed the convenience image better. After consumer taste tests had been completed, however, Pillsbury began skimping on apples because the price of apples more than doubled. Appleasy was introduced in April 1978 and failed.

"The product became less Appleasy and more starch and sugar," Mr. McCusker says. He adds, "A lot of people tried it but didn't come back for seconds. There was no problem with convenience, but lots of problems with quality." Pillsbury won't say exactly how much it lost on Appleasy, but the figure was well over $1 million.

Some ideas sound good at the time but just misfire. One product the people at Green Giant would rather forget is vegetable yogurt. Green Giant, which was acquired by Pillsbury last year, went into a joint venture with Hawthorn Mellody Inc. in 1975 in an effort to cash in on the yogurt craze with something different. Different they were; the yogurt flavors were cucumber, beet, tomato and garden salad.

Vegetable yogurt was introduced in Cleveland to test consumer response. It bombed. "We lasted about six weeks before the supermarkets threw us out," recalls a Green Giant executive.

Even products that taste good may fail, often because market research doesn't measure consumer attitudes correctly. Green Giant executives thought they had a certain success in Oven Crock baked beans, which came already sweetened in the can. "We did a series of blind taste tests and had a significant winner over bland pork and beans by a 3-to-1 or 4-to-1 preference margin," says John M. Stafford, now an executive vice president at Pillsbury.

But Oven Crock was a disaster in a test market. Surveys later showed that people who ate heavily flavored baked beans added their own fixings to the bland variety and didn't want somebody to do it for them. "Our beans were terrific, but they were a solution to no known problem." Mr. Stafford says.

Scrapping a Croissant

Because of high advertising costs, Pillsbury is trying harder than ever to weed out new products that show little promise in the grocery market. "Market research and product research is the cheapest part of the ritual," explains Mr. Mertz. Advertising is the most expensive. Pillsbury recently dropped plans to market a high-quality frozen croissant even though it got high scores in consumer taste tests.

"The problem was that people didn't know when to eat it," says Thomas R. McBurney, a Pillsbury vice president. "The reaction was, 'It sure tastes good, but I don't know what it is. Do I eat it for dinner or breakfast?' " Pillsbury decided not to undertake the expense of trying to educate the public about croissant consumption.

In the food business, one big winner can make up for all the losers, and Pillsbury came up with one of its biggest ever in Totino's Crisp Crust Frozen Pizza. Like many successful new products, Crisp Crust Pizza satisfied a specific desire expressed by consumers. "Crisp Crust is a textbook story of how you ought to do things," says Kent C. Larson, vice president of frozen foods at Pillsbury.

In early 1976, Pillsbury held focus-group discussions around the U.S. and handed out 2,000 questionnaires to find out what consumers didn't like about frozen pizza. The response was overwhelming; about 60% hated the crust, which many said tasted like cardboard. "We know we could be head and shoulders above everybody else with a good crust," Mr. Larson says. The problem was sent to the test kitchen.

Baking the crust, the conventional method of making it, was scrapped. Instead, Pillsbury decided to fry the crust, using an old family recipe of Rose Totino, a Pillsbury vice president. But what worked in her kitchen at home didn't work right away in Pillsbury's test kitchen. "The sudden heat from frying caused the dough to grow in every direction," says James R. Behnke, vice president of R&D. "They came out contorted and all puffed up. When you're running a commercial frozen-pizza operation, there's a carton at the end of the production line and the pizza has to fit into it."

It took several months to control the size (the process now is patented). Pillsbury took special precautions to keep the project a secret from competitors. When trial production runs were held, the frozen crusts were shredded into small pieces and dumped into a landfill.

Consumer taste tests convinced Pillsbury that it had a winner. "People liked it so much that they said, 'I don't believe it's fro-

A Matter of Taste

zen,'" Mr. Behnke says. In choosing an advertising strategy, Pillsbury decided to avoid the common mistake of promising the consumer too much. "Many advertising campaigns for frozen pizza said, 'We're as good as pizzeria,'" Mr. Larson says. "That promise is totally unbelievable to the consumer." Pillsbury's ad campaign was direct, saying that the Totino's frozen-pizza crust didn't taste like cardboard.

Crisp Crust pizza was introduced in August 1978, and Pillsbury hasn't been able to keep up with demand. Crisp Crust has made Totino's the best-selling frozen pizza, with a 30% market share, up from 18% with the old Totino's pizza. With about $700 million of frozen pizza sold each year, the success of Crisp Crust pizza project means additional sales of about $60 million a year for Pillsbury.

When We Are Free

CHAPTER 34

Procter & Gamble: A Good Listener

by John A. Prestbo

One day in 1879, a workman in Procter & Gamble's soap factory went to lunch and forgot to turn off his mixing machine. When he came back, he found a frothy concoction that he considered throwing out. But he and his supervisor decided that the soap hadn't really been spoiled; so the batch was made into bars and sold.

A month later, consumers along the Ohio River who had ended up with this soap began pestering their storekeepers to reorder. "Give us more floating soap," the merchants told P&G, which traced those particular shipments back to the workman's mistake and determined that air bubbles whipped into the molten soap caused it to float.

Thus, Ivory soap was born. And so also began a dialogue between P&G and its customers that not only continues a century later but is growing tremendously. Giant P&G carefully nurtures this rapport with consumers not to keep the Ralph Naders off its back but to stay the nation's biggest maker of everyday consumer products — including, besides Ivory, such well-known brands as Folger's coffee, Crest toothpaste, Pampers disposable diapers and Tide detergent. The company promotes these brands with what is believed to be the largest advertising budget of any U.S. company. P&G declines to disclose any figures, although Broadcast Advertisers Reports Inc. puts the company's 1979 outlays on television ads alone at $463.4 million.

No Big Secret

"A lot of people think P&G 'buys' its way into the market with big ad and promotion budgets, or has some other secret to its success," says Leonard S. Matthews, president of the American Asso-

---

Reprinted by permission of *The Wall Street Journal* (4/29/80) Dow Jones & Company, Inc., 1980. All Rights Reserved.

ciation of Advertising Agencies and a former executive on P&G ad accounts. "I don't think there's much secret to it. The company simply is tuned in to what consumers want, and it does a good job of making products to satisfy those wants."

To tune itself in, P&G draws heavily on consumers' views, both solicited and unsolicited. P&G considers its consumer dialogue an essential ingredient of its success formula, albeit one usually unnoticed by those who try to dope out what makes the company prosper.

And prosper it does. So far in the 20th Century, the 143-year-old company has, on average, nearly doubled its earnings every decade, and in the past 10 years its profit has tripled. In the fiscal nine months ended March 31, P&G's earnings rose 13% from a year earlier to $521.5 million, or $6.31 a share, and its sales climbed 16% to $8.08 billion.

"There's no doubt in my mind that we wouldn't be the company we are if we didn't have our close contact with consumers," a top officer says. "We've never added it up, but I'm sure the feedback we get from consumers saves us many millions of dollars a year."

This consumer dialogue works pretty much the same now as it did a century ago. After P&G heard from consumers wanting more "floating soap," it investigated and found that they weren't merely amused by the novelty. They did a lot of washing and bathing in murky Ohio River water, and the floating bar saved them from groping for submerged soap.

Nowadays, this dialogue is conducted on a scale commensurate with P&G's size. The company is the nation's 23rd largest industrial concern, and it does business more frequently with American consumers — about 17 million transactions a day, it estimates — than any other corporation.

This year, it will receive and answer upwards of 250,000 calls and letters from customers. Half of these communications will be requests for information, a sixth will be expressions of praise, and a third will be complaints of all kinds, including those about products, ads and even the plots of soap operas that the company sponsors on TV.

But P&G is so hungry for more volunteered comment that it is expanding its toll-free telephone operation to make it easier for customers to contact the company. By year-end, all of P&G's 80 brands, including six in test-marketing, will carry a toll-free phone number on the package or label so that people can call in immediately their thoughts about them. P&G expects that by next year 500,000 customers will have contacted the company.

Much Research

Also, P&G will phone or visit some 1.5 million people this year in connection with about 1,000 research projects. That's up from 250,000 such interviews six years ago. These people are questioned extensively on their likes and dislikes about P&G products including their names, packaging and hundreds of other details. In addition, P&G does an unusual amount of continuing "basic" research into how people go about washing clothes, preparing meals, doing the dishes and other household tasks.

Generating this mountain of information is only half the process. It's what P&G does with it that really sets the company apart from the corporate pack. The data is funneled monthly to every major segment of the company — including the executive suite — where it is sifted and resifted for implications for P&G's marketing, advertising, manufacturing and research-and-development operations.

"In our business, we are forever trying to see what lies around the corner," says Edward G. Harness, P&G's chairman. "We study the ever-changing consumer and try to identify new trends in tastes, needs, environment and living habits. We study changes in the marketplace and try to assess their likely impact on our brands. We study our competition. Competitive brands are continually offering new benefits and new ideas to the consumer, and we must stay ahead of this."

Despite all the study, some P&G products have flopped over the years, of course — occasionally because the company didn't listen to consumers as well as it usually does. One such case was a product called Fling. Test-marketed in 1965, it was a roll of disposable, detergent-filled dishcloths made of tough, flexible paper. Even with P&G's ad and promotional blitz, Fling bombed.

"We were so enamored with our technical ability to put dish soap in a paper towel that we didn't research the concept well enough," says Jack Henry, manager of P&G's market research department. "When we went back and did what we should have in the first place, we found people were happy enough with the dishcloths they had. There simply wasn't a need for the product."

Inquiries, complaints and other contacts initiated by consumers are handled by the consumer services department. The basic job of the staff's 60 employes — up from 50 a year ago — is to help keep customers happy. That's important to P&G, which strives to build and hold hefty market shares through brand loyalty.

"If people have a problem with one of our products, we'd rather they tell us about it than switch to a competitor's product or say bad things about ours over the backyard fence," says Dorothy Puccini, head of P&G's consumer services department.

A recent study sponsored by the U.S. Office for Consumer Affairs supports this approach: "Many managers view complaints as a nuisance that wastes valuable corporate resources. However, the survey data suggest that complaints may instead be a valuable marketing asset. . . . Responsive companies were rewarded by the greatest degree of continued brand loyalty."

Slow and Deliberate

As it does with almost everything it tries, P&G proceeded slowly but deliberately with the toll-free telephone program. It started in 1974 with a number on Duncan Hines brownie-mix packages.

"We learned that people in high-altitude areas needed special instructions for baking, and these were soon added to the packages," Miss Puccini says. "We also found that one of the recipes on a box label was confusing, so we changed it. And we spotted a pattern of people complaining that they couldn't get the last bit of toothpaste out of the tube without it breaking; the tubes were strengthened."

As the toll-free phone numbers were put on other products, Miss Puccini and others became convinced they were getting a lot more consumer response, and calming more potentially disaffected customers, than if they had continued to depend solely on people who were mad enough, or had time enough, to write letters.

One call that couldn't have been dealt with by letter came from a woman who at the moment was giving her friend a home permanent with P&G's Lilt. Her friend was hanging her head in the sink and the woman said she had just discovered that the neutralizer, which "locks in" the curl and offsets the alkalinity of the waving solution, was missing from the Lilt kit. What to do? Rinse your friend's hair thoroughly, was the answer, apply a solution of one part water to one part vinegar or lemon juice and then rinse again. To compensate the women for the inconvenience, P&G mailed them a coupon for a free kit.

Back to the Plant

But P&G didn't stop there. The Lilt plant that made the faulty kit (identified by a product code on the caller's package) was told of the incident. Plant personnel checked the production lines and inspection methods to determine whether they were at fault — a standard procedure in such complaints. In this case, they found nothing amiss at the plant and concluded that the neutralizer may have been pilfered from the package as it sat on a store shelf.

The company doesn't always get off so easily, however. Last fall, for instance, a spate of calls informed P&G that the plastic tops on Downy fabric-softener bottles were splintering when twisted on and off — raising the danger of punctured fingers. P&G quickly identified the supplier of the fragile caps and found out that the supplier recently had changed its formula for making the plastic in the caps, which in time became unexpectedly brittle.

"Because of our early-warning system, we were able to get to the problem before it became widespread," a top P&G official says. "Most of the bad caps were still at the factory, and we simply replaced them." If the consumer reaction had been monitored less closely, the bad caps could have caused real problems. P&G hasn't ever had a product recall.

Consumers' calls and letters are used in other parts of P&G, too. Testimonials, for instance, are forwarded to the ad agencies, where they are scanned for insights into why people like the product. Several P&G ad campaigns have been based on unsolicited consumer comments.

Ideas Sent In

Consumers also send P&G some 4,000 ideas for new products each year, but nothing much comes of them. To protect against legal repercussions, a separate staff sorts through these ideas and almost always politely turns the sender down.

But the feedback itself sometimes suggests new products. For example, some people caring for incontinent teen-agers and adults said they wished P&G offered a bigger version of its Pampers diapers. P&G took the hint and now is test-marketing adult-size disposable diapers, called Attends, mainly to hospitals, nursing homes and medical-supply concerns.

Many more consumer-generated new product ideas come from the other part of P&G's consumer dialogue, which it initiates by asking questions. Much of this is standard market research, used by most major consumer-goods companies. But P&G goes beyond the consumer-oriented market research and studies consumers' habits. Researchers periodically follow housewives around as they do the laundry, for instance, and note how they sort the clothes, how many loads they do and a myriad other details. Over time, this research uncovers consumer-behavior trends that suggest products to P&G.

During the 1960s, for example, P&G noticed that the average household's loads of laundry increased to 7.6 a week from 6.4 and that the average temperature of the wash water dropped 15 degrees.

The reason: Clothes were being made of many more kinds of fabrics, especially synthetics and blends of synthetics and natural fibers, and they all presented different washing problems. Some of them required washing separately in cold or lukewarm rather than hot water.

So P&G developed a detergent that works in all levels of water temperature and on many different fabrics. Beginning in 1969, it was marketed as Cheer and was aimed at people who wanted one detergent capable of handling almost all their laundry. P&G says Cheer is selling very well.

At least once a year, P&G conducts market research on each of its brands. Frequently, these surveys turn up consumer attitudes that prompt the company to tinker even with its best-selling products — perhaps because consumers don't like something specific about the P&G brand or prefer a rival product. Tide detergent, one of P&G's biggest sellers, has been changed significantly 57 times since it was introduced in 1947, Mr. Harness, the chairman, says.

Sometimes a consumer gripe about one product can't be solved directly, but instead leads to another product. In its Downy fabric-softener research, P&G learned that people disliked having to run down to their washing machine on every rinse cycle to pour in Downy. P&G couldn't solve the problem by changing Downy, but it instead came up with Bounce, a nonwoven rayon sheet impregnated with softener that is tossed into the dryer with the clothes.

CHAPTER 35

The Liberation of Women

by Bettina Bien Greaves

"Vive la différence," say the French in referring to the difference between the sexes due to physical and physiological causes. This difference can be a source of delight to those free to enjoy it, but can generate ill-feeling and friction between the sexes if they are compelled by law to ignore it.[1] Our physical and physiological characteristics are bound to have economic consequences, which will persist so long as human life continues as we know it.

Legal and political rights, without distinction as to sex, have been recognized gradually by the governments of most civilized nations of the world. By legislation and common law decisions, women have acquired freedom on a par with men to act, own property, and make contracts in their own behalf. (This freedom is being eroded by the present trend toward socialism — to the disadvantage of both men and women. Special government privileges and subsidies, progressive taxation, legislation limiting the right of contract, hours of work, and so on, have already seriously interfered with the rights of property owners and the freedom of contract. But this is another story.) For all practical purposes, laws now deal with men and women pretty much the same.

In recent decades, economic and professional opportunities have been opened to women. Step-by-step, insofar as social customs have permitted, and within the limitations imposed by the "différence" between the sexes which at least the French appreciate, women in this country are relatively free. They may now compete with men, each to the extent of her abilities, in seeking their chosen goals — economically and professionally.

The tremendous advances, which have made it possible for women to achieve recognition as persons — legally, politically, economically, and professionally — are undoubtedly due in large part to capitalistic contributions. Savers, inventors, and producers,

---

From *The Freeman*, February 1971.

[1] For a discussion of some effects of prohibiting discrimination on the basis of sex in economic dealings, see Gary North's "The Feminine Mistake: The Economics of Women's Liberation," *The Freeman*, January 1971.

operating in a relatively free market economy risking their own private property in the hope of profit, supplied the goods and services which have freed women from the daily drudgery and heavy manual labor expected of them for centuries simply to fulfill their roles as sexual companions, mothers to their children, and homemakers for their families. The improved production and preparation of food, more efficient transport, better retail outlets, and inventions of modern household appliances have given women more time to pursue interests outside the home.

In this day of push button kitchens, automatic timers, electric refrigeration, home freezers, mechanical beaters and choppers, prepared foods and instant mixes, a housewife cannot begin to conceive of the many strenuous chores her grandmothers and great-grandmothers coped with daily. Imagine a home without heat or electricity. Imagine a kitchen without a stove, refrigerator, or running water. Suppose there were no corner stores or supermarkets with milk, butter, bread, meat, vegetables, or soap. Think of a life when each family had to grow its own food, gather the fuel to cook it, tote all water, produce the textiles, and sew, patch, and mend the family clothing.

Early Household Hints

Early cookbooks offer helpful hints to save the housewife's time and energy, hints which no modern bride need consider. For instance, keep kettles of water, both hot and cold, handy always in the kitchen. Pine wood is an economical fuel for heating ovens but hard wood makes much hotter coals. Lamps will have a less disagreeable smell if you dip your wick-yarn in strong hot vinegar, and dry it. Teach children to prepare and braid straw for their own bonnets, and their brothers' hats. Fresh meat brought into the house should be carefully covered from the flies, put in the coldest place in the cellar, and then cooked promptly — especially in summer. Save all the nice pieces of fat to make lard, and put those that are not so nice into the soap grease.

The earliest cookbooks and housekeeping manuals appeared only about 200 years ago. Few women could read before then; and how-to-do-it information, so much of which was needed to run a household smoothly, was passed along by example and by word-of-mouth.

Firing the Oven

One early cookbook published in this country was *The American Frugal Housewife* by Mrs. Lydia Maria Childs (12th ed., 1832).

The Liberation of Women

The housewife of that day cooked over an open fire, roasted meat on a spit, or baked in a reflecting oven before the fire or in a brick oven built in the chimney. To fire up the oven was such a chore that one or two days a week were set aside just for baking. With good planning, five successive bakings could be done in the oven with one heating: "The bread first — then the puddings — afterward pastry — then cake and gingerbread — and lastly, custards." This last suggestion comes from Mrs. M. H. Cornelius, whose book, *The Young Housekeeper's Friend,* appeared in 1859. At the time she wrote, brick ovens were going out, cooking stoves and ranges coming in. Yet, boiled dinners, stews, soups, and steamed cakes and puddings prepared on top of the stove were still more popular with the cooks than cakes which called for firing up the oven.

In 1832, Mrs. Childs wrote for the rural housewife who had her own vegetable garden, a few fruit trees, and chickens. The whole family shared in the household chores, of course, and most housewives had extra help from a hired girl or a female relative living with the family. Yet, the responsibility for the work was the housewife's. She grew the herbs for flavoring, gathered the eggs, and ofttimes milked the cow. She baked with yeast of her own making, or used eggs or baking soda and cream of tartar for leavening — baking powder was not for sale until about 1850. She did the family's cooking, and did it all with crude utensils. She beat eggs with a fork or a wire whisk, and elbow grease — the rotary egg beater did not come into general use until the second half of the nineteenth century.

Housewives had to bake the family's bread regularly. This meant mixing the dough, usually in the evening, setting it to rise overnight, and kneading it "very thoroughly." Mrs. Cornelius wrote, "A half an hour is the least time to be given to kneading a baking of bread, unless you prefer, after having done this till it ceases to stick to your hands, to chop it with a chopping-knife four or five hundred strokes. An hour's kneading is not too much." Bread was the staff of life and good bread was a source of pride to the housewife.

Lack of refrigeration was a continual challenge. The housewife took care to use things before they spoiled or to find satisfactory ways to preserve them. Before the canning industry developed in the late 1800's, she had to preserve fruits and vegetables in season to be assured of provisions year round. In 1859, Mrs. Cornelius advised putting preserves in wide-necked bottles, pasting paper over the tops, and then brushing egg white over the paper with a feather to seal the bottles and discourage mold.

First, Get a Cow

The nineteenth century housewife had to be a Jill of all trades. The industrial revolution with its increased specialization and division of labor barely ruffled the surface of traditional housekeeping practices. The 1859 housewife purchased a few more household items than her grandmother could have in 1832. But she still had to kill her own fowl, cut up the family's meat, salt it, smoke it, or otherwise cure it and keep it safe from bugs and animals. To be sure of good dairy products, she was told: "The first requisite is to have a good cow." Keeping a cow added to the household chores. Someone had to feed the cow and milk her, day in and day out, set the milk for the cream to rise, and churn butter at least twice a week. Without refrigeration, keeping milk, cream, butter, and dairy products sweet was a continual worry. Now that dairy products are sold in stores, packaged and ready to use, men do most of this heavy manual labor on a mass production basis, using methods developed and equipment produced with the aid of increased savings and investments.

Doing the family wash was another backbreaking chore in the nineteenth century. First the soap had to be prepared from lye made out of wood ashes, and fat and grease saved from·cooking. The water had to be toted and heated, heavy wash tubs filled, with countless trips back and forth to the stove. After the clothes were sorted, the finest and less soiled things were washed first, the coarser and dirtier items later in the same water. Most pieces were scrubbed by hand on a washboard. The white things were boiled. After washing, rinsing, boiling, wringing, bluing, and starching as necessary, the clothes were wrung and hung outdoors on a line. Doing the family wash took another full day of the housewife's time.

Ironing consumed most of a third day each week. The flat irons and special "polishing irons" for final touchups had to be heated on the stove and reheated again and again as they cooled.

Then Came Automation

The kitchen stove or range using wood or coal gradually came into use in the mid-nineteenth century. These had advantages over the open fireplace and the brick oven. With the use of gas and the construction of gas lines in the late 1800's, new cooking jets became available — gas ovens came considerably later — making meal preparations a little easier. The development of electricity, refrigeration, large scale specialized farming, improved transportation, professional bakeries, and the expansion of retail outlets have further liberated women from the grueling household labor which had been their lot in life. Automatic washing machines and dryers have taken the drudgery out of doing the family wash. Mothproofed woolens and new miracle fibers have simplified the care of the family's clothing. Vacuum cleaners, floor polishers, and local dry cleaning establishments help to keep homes and their furnishings clean the year round, doing away with the need to scour the house and everything in it from top to bottom spring and fall. Refrigeration and other effective ways of preserving foods have freed the family menu from dependence on the season. When compared with her nineteenth century counterpart, the modern housewife is truly liberated from grinding household drudgery and endless kitchen chores.

When a housewife presses a button or turns a switch on a modern household appliance, she has at her command the labor of countless specialists — savers, investors, inventors, producers, and merchants — each of whom then helps with her daily chores. In effect, they help tote the wood when she turns up the thermostat. A twist of the faucet draws the water. Turning a dial will fire the oven. A push-button machine will wash, rinse, and wring the weekly wash. With a trip to a grocery store, the housewife can in effect grow the family's food, milk the cow, churn the butter, make the cheese, gather the eggs, knead and bake the bread, grind the spices, kill the poultry, cure the meat, preserve fruits and vegetables, and make the soap.

Capital, the Key

Each person in the world differs from every other person. Thanks to these differences, everyone benefits if each of us is free to concentrate in the field of his (or her) greatest aptitude and interest. There is some specialization and division of labor even in small groups and primitive communities. But under capitalism, with private property and the freedom to move, invest, and exchange goods and services throughout large areas and among increasingly large populations, it has been possible to develop and exploit our differences more fully than ever before, to everyone's advantage. It was this complex economic system, developed on the basis of highly specialized division of labor, which liberated women from their traditional household chores.

Women are different from men — and always will be. The woman of the 1980's has gained recognition as an individual under law. She may own property, make contracts and, thanks to the development of capitalism, now has time to pursue her special aptitudes and interests outside the home and thus compete with men economically and professionally. Rather than trying to compel denial by law of the physical and physiological differences between the sexes, let's acknowledge and accept them philosophically as the French do: "Vive la différence."

CHAPTER 36

The Parable of the Parking Lots

by Henry G. Manne

In a city not far away there was a large football stadium. It was used from time to time for various events, but the principal use was for football games played Saturday afternoons by the local college team. The games were tremendously popular and people drove hundreds of miles to watch them. Parking was done in the usual way. People who arrived early were able to park free on the streets, and latecomers had to pay to park in regular and improvised lots.

There were, at distances ranging from 5 to 12 blocks from the stadium, approximately 25 commercial parking lots all of which received some business from Saturday afternoon football games. The lots closer to the stadium naturally received more football business than those further away, and some of the very close lots actually raised their price on Saturday afternoons. But they did not raise the price much, and most did not change prices at all. The reason was not hard to find.

For something else happened on football afternoons. A lot of people who during the week were students, lawyers, school teachers, plumbers, factory workers, and even stock brokers went into the parking lot business. It was not a difficult thing to do. Typically a young boy would put up a crude, homemade sign saying "Parking $3." He would direct a couple of cars into his parents' driveway, tell the driver to take the key, and collect the three dollars. If the driveway was larger or there was yard space to park in, an older brother, an uncle, or the head of the household would direct the operation, sometimes asking drivers to leave their keys so that shifts could be made if necessary.

Some part-time parking lot operators who lived very close to the stadium charged as much as $5.00 to park in their driveways. But as the residences-turned-parking-lots were located further from the stadium (and incidentally closer to the commercial parking lots), the price charged at game time declined. In fact houses at some distance from the stadium charged less than the adjacent

---

Reprinted with permission of the author from: *The Public Interest,* No. 23 (Spring 1971).
© 1971 by National Affairs. Inc.

commercial lots. The whole system seemed to work fairly smoothly, and though traffic just after a big game was terrible, there were no significant delays parking cars or retrieving parked cars.

But one day the owner of a chain of parking lots called a meeting of all the commercial parking lot owners in the general vicinity of the stadium. They formed an organization known as the Association of Professional Parking Lot Employers, or APPLE. And they were very concerned about the Saturday parking business. One man who owned four parking lots pointed out that honest parking lot owners had heavy capital investments in their businesses, that they paid taxes, and that they employed individuals who supported families. There was no reason, he alleged, why these lots should not handle all the cars coming into the area for special events like football games. "It is unethical," he said, "to engage in cutthroat competition with irresponsible fender benders. After all, parking cars is a profession, not a business." This last remark drew loud applause.

A "Statesmanlike" Position

Thus emboldened he continued, stating that commercial parking lot owners recognize their responsibility to serve the public's needs. Ethical car parkers, he said, understand their obligations not to dent fenders, to employ only trustworthy car parkers, to pay decent wages, and generally to care for their customers' automobiles as they would the corpus of a trust. His statement was hailed by others attending the meeting as being very statesmanlike.

Others at the meeting related various tales of horror about non-professional car parkers. One homeowner, it was said, actually allowed his fifteen-year-old son to move other peoples' cars around. Another said that he had seen an $18,000 Cadillac parked on a dirt lawn where it would have become mired in mud had it rained that day. Still another pointed out that a great deal of the problem came on the side of the stadium with the lower-priced houses, where there were more driveways per block than on the wealthier side of the stadium. He pointed out that these poor people would rarely be able to afford to pay for damage to other peoples' automobiles or to pay insurance premiums to cover such losses. He felt that a professional group such as APPLE had a duty to protect the public from their folly in using those parking spaces.

Finally another speaker reminded the audience that these "marginal, fly-by-night" parking lot operators generally parked a string of cars in their driveways so that a driver had to wait until all cars behind his had been removed before he could get his out. This, he pointed out, was quite unlike the situation in commercial lots

The Parable of the Parking Lots

where, during a normal business day, people had to be assured of ready access to their automobiles at any time. The commercial parking lots either had to hire more attendants to shift cars around, or they had to park them so that any car was always accessible, even though this meant that fewer cars could park than the total space would actually hold. "Clearly," he said, "driveway parking constitutes unfair competition."

Emotions ran high at this meeting, and every member of APPLE pledged $1 per parking space for something mysteriously called a "slush fund." It was never made clear exactly whose slush would be bought with these funds, but several months later a resolution was adopted by the city council requiring licensing for anyone in the parking lot business.

The preamble to the new ordinance read like the speeches at the earlier meeting. It said that this measure was designed to protect the public against unscrupulous, unprofessional and under capitalized parking lot operators. It required, *inter alia*, that anyone parking cars for a fee must have a minimum capital devoted to the parking lot business of $25,000, liability insurance in an amount not less than $500,000, bonding for each car parker, and a special driving test for these parkers (which incidentally would be designed and administered by APPLE). The ordinance also required, again in the public's interest, that every lot charge a single posted price for parking and that any change in the posted price be approved in advance by the city council. Incidentally, most members were able to raise their fees by about 20 per cent before the first posting.

Calling the Cops

Then a funny thing happened to drivers on their way to the stadium for the next big game. They discovered city police in unusually large numbers informing them that it was illegal to pay a non-licensed parking lot operator for the right to park a car. These policemen also reminded parents that if their children were found in violation of this ordinance it could result in a misdemeanor charge being brought against the parents and possible juvenile court proceedings for the children. There were no driveway parking lots that day.

Back at the commercial parking lots, another funny thing occurred. Proceeding from the entrance of each of these parking lots within twelve blocks of the stadium were long lines of cars waiting to park. The line got larger as the lot was closer to the stadium. Many drivers had to wait so long or walk so far that they missed the entire first quarter of the big game.

At the end of the game it was even worse. The confusion was massive. The lot attendants could not cope with the jam up, and some cars were actually not retrieved until the next day. It was even rumored about town that some automobiles had been lost forever and that considerable liabilities might result for some operators. Industry spokesmen denied this, however.

Naturally there was a lot of grumbling, but there was no agreement on what had caused the difficulty. At first everyone said there were merely some "bugs" in the system that would have to be ironed out. But the only "bug" ironed out was a Volkswagen which was flattened by a careless lot attendant in a Cadillac Eldorado.

The Mess Worsens

The situation did not improve at subsequent games. The members of APPLE did not hire additional employees to park cars, and operators near the stadium were not careful to follow their previous practice of parking cars in such a way as to have them immediately accessible. Employees seemed to become more surly, and the number of dented-fender claims mounted rapidly.

Little by little, too, cars began appearing in residential driveways again. For instance, one enterprising youth regularly went into the car wash business on football afternoons, promising that his wash job would take at least two hours. He charged five dollars, and got it — even on rainy days — in fact, especially on rainy days. Another homeowner offered to take cars on consignment for three hours to sell them at prices fixed by the owner. He charged $4.00 for this "service," but his subterfuge was quickly squelched by the authorities. The parking situation remained "critical."

Political pressures on the city council began to mount to "do something" about the inordinate delays in parking and retrieving cars on football afternoons. The city council sent a stern note of warning to APPLE, and APPLE appointed a special study group recruited from the local university's computer science department to look into the matter. This group reported that the managerial and administrative machinery in the parking lot business was archaic. What was needed, the study group said, was less goose quills and stand-up desks and more computers and conveyor belts. It was also suggested that all members of APPLE be hooked into one computer so that cars could readily be shifted to the most accessible spaces.

More Regulation a Threat

Spokesmen for the industry took up the cry of administrative modernization. Subtle warnings appeared in the local papers suggesting that if the industry did not get its own house in order, heavy-handed regulation could be anticipated. The city council asked for reports on failures to deliver cars and decreed that this would include any failure to put a driver in his car within five minutes of demand without a new dent.

Some of the professional operators actually installed computer equipment to handle their ticketing and parking logistics problems. And some added second stories to their parking lots. Others bought up additional space, thereby raising the value of vacant lots in the area. But many simply added a few additional car parkers and hoped that the problem would go away without a substantial investment of capital.

The commercial operators also began arguing that they needed higher parking fees because of their higher operating costs. Everyone agreed that costs for operating a parking lot were certainly higher than before the licensing ordinance. So the city council granted a request for an across-the-board ten per cent hike in fees. The local newspaper editorially hoped that this would ease the problem without still higher fees being necessary. In a way, it did. A lot of people stopped driving. They began using city buses, or they chartered private buses for the game. Some stayed home and watched the game on TV. A new study group on fees was appointed.

Unexpected Developments

Just about then several other blows fell on the parking lot business. Bus transportation to the area near the stadium was improved with a federal subsidy to the municipal bus company. And several new suburban shopping centers caused a loss of automobile traffic in the older areas of town. But most dramatic of all, the local university, under severe pressure from its students and faculty, dropped intercollegiate football altogether and converted the stadium into a park for underprivileged children.

The impact of these events on the commercial parking lots was swift. Income declined drastically. The companies that had borrowed money to finance the expansion everyone wanted earlier were hardest hit. Two declared bankruptcy, and many had to be absorbed by financially stronger companies. Layoffs among car parkers were enormous, and APPLE actually petitioned the city council to guarantee the premiums on their liability insurance policies so that people would not be afraid to park commercially. This idea was suggested to APPLE by recent Congressional legislation creating an insurance program for stock brokers.

A spokesman for APPLE made the following public statement: "New organizations or arrangements may be necessary to straighten out this problem. There has been a failure in both the structure of the industry and the regulatory scheme. New and better regulation is clearly demanded. A sound parking lot business is necessary for a healthy urban economy." The statement was hailed by the industry as being very statesmanlike, though everyone speculated about what he really meant.

Others in the industry demanded that the city bus service be curtailed during the emergency. The city council granted every rate increase the lots requested. There were no requests for rate decreases, but the weaker lots began offering prizes and other subtle or covert rebates to private bus companies who would park with them. In fact, this problem became so serious and uncontrollable that one owner of a large chain proclaimed that old-fashioned price competition for this business would be desirable. This again was hailed as statesmanlike, but everyone assumed that he really meant something else. No one proposed repeal of the licensing ordinance.

One other thing happened. Under pressure from APPLE, the city council decreed that henceforth no parking would be allowed on any streets in the downtown area of town. The local merchants were extremely unhappy with this, however, and the council rescinded the ordinance at the next meeting, citing a computer error as the basis for the earlier restriction.

The ultimate resolution of the "new" parking problem is not in sight. The parking lot industry in this town not very far from here is now said to be a depressed business, even a sick one. Everyone looks to the city council for a solution, but things will probably limp along as they are for quite a while, picking up with an occasional professional football game and dropping low with bad weather.

MORAL: If you risk your lot under an apple tree, you may get hit in the head.

Unit VII: Entrepreneurship

The graham crackers and pudding can be in the cupboard and eggs can be in the refrigerator, but that's not enough to make a lemon meringue pie. There must be a *doer*. There must be someone who sees the potential of these ingredients and who takes *action*. Units I through VI of this book deal primarily with the ingredients of a vital, productive society or, more precisely, of a *potentially* vital and productive society. In this seventh unit, the focus is on the specific men and women who, when these ingredients are present, *do* something with them.

There is a name for the individual who is the catalyst in converting the potential for progress and success into actual progress and success — entrepreneur. Webster's New World Dictionary defines the term as "a person who organizes and manages a business undertaking, assuming the risk for the sake of the profit." Although this is a useful starting notion of who an entrepreneur is, we think he is more than this.

To us, the entrepreneur is the individual man or woman who sees things other people don't see. He is the person who has ability — *and* the courage *and* the gumption to *do* something with his talents. He applies his talents and energy so as to try to profit from what he sees that others don't. In the process, he *adds* to the world's stock of goods and he *performs* services not previously performed. And as long as he does this in freedom, he gains and others gain.

The first chapter in this unit is "If Men Were Free to Try." Like Leonard Read's "I Pencil," this piece by John Sparks is a classic. Sparks contends that "We never do think creatively on any activity preempted by government." It is individual freedom which gives birth to creative thought.

The remaining chapters in this unit are among the most concrete chapters in this book. Our objective is to show you entrepreneurs in action. As the action proceeds, we try to get it closer and closer to home. By so doing, we hope you will identify ever more closely with the specific entrepreneurs you read about. Perhaps you will be inspired to join their ranks!

The action starts with "Self-Interest at Work," a case study about manufacturing a unique type of sailboat in California. In "The Entrepreneur as Hero," the action shifts to constructing buildings in booming Houston, Texas where there are no inhibiting zoning laws. "Food From Thought" is a delightful potpourri of anecdotes about the origins, in many different parts of the United States, of a whole host of familiar foods. The foods range from Jell-O to chocolate chips, from Grape Nuts to peanut butter.

Finally, in the last two chapters, the action shifts to Michigan. The scene of "A Story of Apples and Entrepreneurship" is what was once just an apple orchard about fifteen miles from Northwood's Michigan campus. Dr. David Fry, Chancellor of Northwood Institute, is the author of "A College That Became the Partner of Business." This chapter is about Northwood Institute itself. The purpose of these two chapters is to bring as close to home as possible the idea that it is specific, identifiable, enterprising individuals like John and Joan Bintz, Arthur Turner, and Gary Stauffer who, when left free, accomplish a great deal — for themselves, yes, but at the same time for literally thousands of other individuals too.

CHAPTER 37

If Men Were Free to Try

by John C. Sparks

Private ownership, private initiative, the hope of reward, and the expectation of achievement have always been primarily responsible for the advancement of mankind. Continued progress — be it spiritual, mental, or material — rests squarely upon a better understanding of the idea of individual freedom of choice and action, with personal responsibility for one's own decisions.

For the purpose of illustrating this idea, let us suppose you had lived in 1900 and somehow were confronted with the problem of seeking a solution to any *one* of the following problems:

1. To build and maintain roads adequate for use of conveyances, their operators, and passengers.
2. To increase the average span of life by 30 years.
3. To convey instantly the sound of a voice speaking at one place to any other point or any number of points around the world.
4. To convey instantly the visual replica of an action, such as a presidential inauguration, to men and women in their living rooms all over America.
5. To develop a medical preventive against death from pneumonia.
6. To transport physically a person from Los Angeles to New York in less than four hours.
7. To build a horseless carriage of the qualities and capabilities described in the latest advertising folder of any automobile manufacturer.

Without much doubt you would have selected the first problem as the one easiest of solution. In fact, the other problems would have seemed fantastic and quite likely would have been rejected as the figments of someone's wild imagination.

Now, let us see which of these problems has been solved to date. Has the easiest problem been solved? No. Have the seemingly fantastic problems been solved? Yes, and we hardly give them a second thought.

From *The Freeman,* February 1977.

It is not accidental that solutions have been found wherever the atmosphere of freedom and private ownership has prevailed wherein men could try out their ideas and succeed or fail on their own worthiness. Nor is it accidental that the coercive force of government — when hooked up to a creative field such as transportation — has been slow, plodding, and unimaginative in maintaining and replacing its facilities.

Does it not seem odd that a privately-owned automobile company found it expedient to sponsor a national contest with tremendous prizes and to conduct its own search in order to correct the faults of the publicly-owned and inadequate highway system? The highway dilemma has become more and more acute until someone other than the public owner has sought an answer. If the points of ownership had been reversed in 1900 — that is, motorcar development in the hands of the government, and highways left to private individuals — we would have likely participated in a contest sponsored by the privately-owned highway companies to suggest how to improve the government's horseless carriage so that it would keep pace with the fine and more-than-adequate highways.

How could roads be built and operated privately? I do not know. This is a subject to which none of us directs his creative attention. We never do think creatively on any activity preempted by government. It is not until an activity has been freed from monopoly that creative thought comes into play.

But go back to 1900. Could any of us then have told how to solve the six problems to which solutions have been found? Suppose, for instance, that someone could at that time have described the looks and performance of the latest model automobile. Could any of us have told him how to make it? No, no more than we can describe how privately to build and operate highways today.

What accounts, then, for the present automobile and other "fantastic" accomplishments? Government did not preempt these activities! Instead, these have been left to the area of free, uninhibited, creative thinking. Millions of man-hours of technically skilled, inventive thought have been at work. And the end is not yet. Nor will there be an end as long as the inhibitory influence of government is confined to its proper functions of protecting equally the life, liberty, and property of all citizens; as long as men are free to try their ideas in a competitive and voluntary market.

CHAPTER 38

Self-Interest at Work

by Dale M. Haywood

There is no need to apologize for the self-interest of human beings and the desire to earn a good living that follows from it. This is simply the way we are.

In a free enterprise system based on private property and the profit and loss system, earning a good living very frequently translates into efficiently performing a service or manufacturing a product which others value and for which they are willing and able to pay.

This was pointed out by Adam Smith more than 200 years ago in *An Inquiry Into the Nature and Causes of the Wealth of Nations:* "Every individual necessarily labours to render the annual revenue of the society as great as he can. He generally, indeed, neither intends to promote the public interest, nor knows how much he is promoting it . . . he intends only his own gain, and he is in this, as in many other cases, led by an invisible hand to promote an end which was no part of his intention."

In sum, most, if not all, new businesses start with someone motivated by self-interest being alert to some problem that others face. A new business then requires someone with imagination, ability, and courage to follow through with practical solutions to that problem. This was precisely the case with Roger and Mary Lou MacGregor's business.

The MacGregor Yacht Corporation

The time was about twenty years ago. The place was Costa Mesa, California. The "problems" that Roger MacGregor saw were rising sailboat prices and rising docking rentals.

For most of his life, Roger had been around sailboats — building them and sailing them. Sailboats were his hobby. While a student at Stanford University, he conceived a new kind of cruising sailboat with a retractable keel. The boater who owns a cruising sailboat with a retractable keel can tow his boat on a trailer behind his car. Thus, he can store his boat in his own back yard, thereby saving the cost of docking and slip rentals.

Starting a new business requires capital, money with which to buy (or rent) a building and machinery. The MacGregors started their business with $5,000 of their own savings. It is significant that the initial investment was *their* savings. In a private property, profit and loss system, the owners of private property at risk normally tend to look after that property very closely. Investors proceed cautiously when it is their savings that are at stake, for any losses will be *their* losses.

There was no guarantee that prospective cruising sailboat buyers would actually buy the kind of sailboat that Roger conceived and that the MacGregors' firm manufactured. As long as consumers are free to patronize whomever they please, there *cannot* be any such guarantee. In a free enterprise system, it is the consumers who are the ultimate judges of goods and services. Through their buying or not buying a particular product or service, consumers determine which businesses will earn profits and which businesses will suffer losses. The consumer is king. It is not the producer, it is not the wealthy, who guide the economy. Rather, it is the consumer who is in the driver's seat.

A Better Product at a Lower Price

The MacGregors knew there was competition in the sailboat manufacturing business. They knew that the way to woo customers was to come up with a superior boat at a lower price. And they understood that if a firm is to sell its products for less than the competition, it must have lower costs.

The MacGregors believed that the retractable keel feature of their boat made it a better boat than the competition's. They sought to cut costs, and thus to cut the selling prices of their boats, through the application of assembly line techniques and the standardization of parts in the fabrication of their sailboats. Neither the assembly line process nor the standardization of parts is new, of course. But the MacGregors made a new application of these familiar techniques, for historically the cruising sailboat manufacturing business has been a custom work business.

Reflect on what is happening here. In pursuing their own interests, the MacGregors were quietly transforming, in a small way, an industry geared to serving a select few to an industry geared more toward serving a less-select larger group. Characteristically, this is how many businesses and industries get started and grow in a free enterprise system.

Division of Labor

Initially, only Mary Lou devoted full time to Roger's hobby that was turning into a business. Roger kept his job at Ford Aerospace and Communications Corporation. But the MacGregors had correctly judged the demand for less expensive cruising sailboats with retractable keels. Consumers bought more and more of their boats. When production reached ten boats per week, Roger quit his job at Ford Aerospace and joined his wife full time. His hobby was no longer a hobby. It became a full-fledged business — the MacGregor Yacht Corporation.

As their business has grown, the MacGregors have split up some of its major functions. Roger has responsibility for production and sales. Mary Lou is responsible for finance and administration. Economists call this a *division of labor*.

The basis for a division of labor is the difference in the abilities and the interests of the individuals involved. Each individual does what he or she is relatively more interested in and better able to do. Such specialization usually leads to each specialist becoming even more proficient in handling his part of the business. The greater proficiency leads to greater productivity. And relatively high productivity is what it takes to survive in a competitive free market.

Retained Earnings Finance Growth

The MacGregors' business is profitable. Thus, it has survived. The profits retained in the business have provided much of the financing for the growth of the firm. This is typical of many businesses.

The bulk of the profits of business do not go for the owner's personal consumption. Rather, most of those profits go to finance the growth of business. And it is thus that the wealth of many wealthy people gets tied up in assets that provide jobs, in assets that multiply the productivity of the people who use them, in assets that help generate still more goods and services for consumers. In the free enterprise system, much of the wealth of wealthy people is in forms that serve the masses. And the wealthy person who wants to preserve or increase his wealth has an ongoing obligation to see to it that his wealth continues to be in forms that serve the masses.

But relatively high profit margins are short-lived in a system where there is private property, a free market, and a profit and loss system. The top of the heap is a precarious position. For example, as competitors also adopt the assembly line and standardization of parts techniques that the MacGregors pioneered in the sailboat manufacturing business, the competitors will be able to cut their costs too. Then, they also can cut their selling prices. And so the MacGregors will lose whatever competitive advantage they had because they were the first to apply these cost-cutting techniques to the cruising sailboat manufacturing business.

Thus, to hold, to say nothing of increasing, their share of the market for cruising sailboats, the MacGregors are continuously "under the gun." To maintain relatively high profit margins in a free market, it is not enough to come up with one or two new products. It is not enough to come up with one or two new ideas or new applications of ideas for cutting costs. No, to maintain above average profit margins in a free market, a businessman must *repeatedly* come up with new products that solve problems or in some other way appeal to consumers. The businessman must *repeatedly* come up with cost-cutting techniques. And he must do all of this *ahead* of the competition. Thus we see why the free enterprise system is such a powerful engine for economic progress.

The Uncertainty and Insecurity in Freedom

The MacGregor Yacht Corporation has had a healthy birth and infancy. Will this business continue to prosper and grow? As long as consumers are free to buy someone else's boats (or other goods altogether), no one can say for sure. The MacGregor boats with retractable keels may inspire another generation of sailboats. Who will have the inspiration? There is no way of knowing in advance. The MacGregor cost-cutting techniques may spark another round of cost-cutting. Who will have this spark? There is no way of knowing this in advance either.

Clearly there is a large element of uncertainty about this firm's future. In a free society, there is uncertainty about the future of all businesses. But this uncertainty and attendant insecurity are simply the consequences of freedom — freedom of the consumer to buy or not to buy from a given business; freedom of existing or potential producers to begin, expand, or halt the production of any item they believe there is a market for.

Not knowing exactly when or where or from whom the next idea for a new or improved product or new cost-cutting technique will come has been the source of both much mischief and of much good.

Not knowing the source of the next surge of progress tempts some individuals to call for central planning, for government planning of our economic affairs. Some individuals seem to think that not knowing exactly how the next spark of progress will come makes life unnecessarily chancy. Isn't it, they contend, more rational to "improve" on this chancy situation by methodical central planning? This line of reasoning is the source of much mischief.

History has repeatedly shown us what happens when government central planning is substituted for planning by individual consumers and producers. Central planning stifles the self-interest motive. It constricts the spirit inside us that urges us to strive for the "good life." This kind of planning is at odds with the nature of man. Although on the surface it appears that in theory political central planning should eliminate some of the uncertainty in freedom and accelerate economic progress, history clearly shows that in fact it is a source of instability and that in fact it retards progress.

Those among us who are tempted to endorse central planning, because it appears to be the more methodical way to progress, might profitably reflect on the life insurance industry. For there is an element of uncertainty in the life insurance industry that is in some ways like the uncertainty of the origins of progress in a free society.

Predictable Results

The most capable actuary cannot specify which particular sixty-year-old men will die next year. But the actuary studies history. Specifically, he studies the history of male deaths. He learns from history. He develops mortality tables. Equipped with the information in these mortality tables, that actuary can very accurately forecast the percentage of sixty-year-old men in a large population who will die next year. Knowing this percentage for sixty-year-old men and the corresponding percentages for men and women of all ages, he can help his company confidently proceed with its business of insuring the lives of men and women whatever their ages.

Similarly, a study of the history of free men and women enables us confidently to proceed in freedom. Although we cannot accurately forecast details of *how* the free society will progress, we can confidently forecast *that* it will progress. Free men and women will progress because of the good feature of insecurity.

The good feature of insecurity is that it is a powerful stimulus. For the best way to cope with insecurity is to become competent. By ably serving consumers day in and day out, productive individuals can do much to reduce insecurity. Then, in a society in which there are large numbers of individuals busy trying to become more competent and more productive, the average level of ability and the average output of the individuals in that society rises tremendously. Indeed, the average ability and output can rise to the point where the "poor" person in a free society is much better off than the "rich" person in a society that is not free.

Can the MacGregors, specifically, sustain their "track record?" Time will tell. But as for the record of free men and women generally, time has already told. That record is decisive. Freedom is a condition required for maximum human progress.

CHAPTER 39

The Entrepreneur as Hero

by Dick Bjornseth

Rosalie Gurka lived in Houston's redeveloping Montrose area, next door to a converted three-unit apartment building: "converted" to a "nude show" establishment. In 1973 she was asked by a national planning publication for her view of Houston's unique lack of zoning. "I don't feel anyone should be made to do anything. If I don't like the area becoming commercial, then I can move. I don't believe in zoning deals . . . This is a free country. Besides, this area is about 70 years old; it's time for a change."

An elementary school teacher, also a resident of the Montrose area, Mrs. Mary Smith, was quoted in the same article as saying, "I like to see new things coming in. We're sort of excited around here because downtown is moving into our neighborhood."

While the opinions of these two individuals are not universally held by all residents in Houston, the last zoning proposal (in 1962) was solidly defeated: 57% to 43% in a referendum. In the 15 years since the defeat of zoning, no politician has been able to gain enough support to again submit zoning.

Since the 1973 article, the Montrose area and several other older central neighborhoods in Houston have continued to redevelop and thrive. The interesting aspect is that this is happening without federal funds and central planning. It is a direct result of an "uncontrolled" private sector and its "selfish" motivation: profit.

The private sector redevelopment in Houston and other parts of the country suggests that entrepreneurs may be the "heroes" and not the "villains" of central city redevelopment.

Failure of Government Approach

Profit and self-oriented individual action are not the public goals that inspire the planning and architecture professions, who typically see the solution in more government regulations, expenditures, and power. After 50 years of the subsidy/regulation approach to central city redevelopment, let's look at the record. New York

---

From *New Guard*, March-April 1978

City adopted the country's first zoning ordinance in 1916 and every major city eventually followed suit (except Houston). The New York ordinance originally had six zoning classifications — it now has over 60. A half century of zoning in New York City has hardly made New York a model place to live and work.

The federal "urban renewal" program is another good example of a perhaps well-intended effort yielding contrary results. In his controversial yet well-respected book *The Federal Bulldozer*, Martin Anderson came to some starting conclusions. In the heyday of the federal urban renewal program between 1950 and 1960, about 126,000 mostly low-rent housing units were destroyed to make room for less than one quarter that number of mostly high-rent units. Recently New York City and others have expanded their regulations with such "innovative" approaches as rent control which, according to John McClaughry, president of the Institute for Liberty and Community, is "an absolute sure-fire, guaranteed way to destroy housing stock, especially decent housing stock," since it results in deferred maintenance accumulating into urban blight.

There is nothing economically or socially inevitable about the decay of our cities, according to the well-known author and urban critic Jane Jacobs. She states, "On the contrary, no other aspect of our economy and society has been more purposefully manipulated for a full quarter century to achieve precisely what we are getting. Extraordinary governmental financial incentives have been required to achieve this degree of monotony, sterility, and vulgarity. Decades of preaching, writing and exhorting by experts have gone into convincing us and our legislators that mush like this must be good for us . . ."

There Must Be a Better Way

As technology, individual tastes, and the economy have changed over the years, many neighborhoods have found themselves unable to meet the changing demands. Zoning and other governmental regulations have tended to preserve the status quo and thereby force many neighborhoods even further out of pace with the changing modern city. The adaptability of the marketplace is needed to save the central cities, not the slow, cumbersome, and bureaucratic operations of the public sector. The following additional traits of the private sector promise a practical and proven alternative to government action: (Ironically, these are the same traits that are used to defend government involvement.)

1. *Assumption of high risk*. Even a novice investor will soon realize the correlation between risk and profit potential. Low-risk investments such as insured savings accounts bring a low rate of

return. As the risk factor increases such as with bonds, stocks, and commodities, the profit (and loss) potential also increases. Yet this increasing risk does not mean that only government is suited to the task. Quite the contrary is true; the increased profit potential of high-risk investments draws vast amounts of money and entrepreneurial skills to these markets. The same investment principles used in the stock and commodity markets, including the advice "buy low — sell high," apply to redevelopment of the central city. As certain neighborhoods or buildings decline in value relative to the rest of the city, they can become more attractive for redevelopment. The lower in price they fall, the greater the potential profit in redevelopment.

One of the best examples of private redevelopment is Creative Restorations, Inc. in Houston. Steven J. Rudy is principal partner of this young, highly successful company specializing in buying, restoring, and managing older residential properties in the central city of unzoned Houston. His firm has already successfully restored about 50 buildings, mostly small apartment projects. He does not look for the fancy Victorian structures with obvious visual appeal, but for buildings which are "... plain block square ... have no design, are two dimensional, and completely rundown buildings that nobody else wants." Their low price tags, combined with entrepreneurial imagination and skill, allow Rudy to rehabilitate these into attractive and highly profitable projects. He is now undertaking a large multi-block renovation project of five apartment projects (totaling 390 apartments) and a 58,000 square foot retail center. This planned renovation is being done to a group of deteriorating projects that were constructed in central Houston during the late 50's and early 60's (that's "old" in Houston). The apartment units were popular with the singles and "swingers" in the early 60's and became known as "Sin Alley." Rudy states, however, that the apartments were gradually allowed to deteriorate "falling below their economic potential."

Whereas a government planner typically views such declining situations as justification for urgent public involvement and subsidy, Rudy sees them as low-cost structures presenting unique opportunities for private redevelopment.

Rudy makes no apologies for his motivation — profit — and points out that all his projects are private and being accomplished without governmental assistance. His projects have already had a highly visible impact on Houston's inner city redevelopment and his single firm can be credited with renovating more units than all the city and federal efforts in Houston combined.

Similar independent private redevelopment efforts are quietly taking place in central city neighborhoods around the country. Planners have either expediently ignored them or, once the trend has become too obvious to ignore, have scrambled to climb the band wagon by proposing a joint public/private partnership to salvage the neighborhood.

2. *Responsive to minority and special interests.* While public officials undertake the task of meeting the rather vague preferences of the majority, the interests and concerns of the minorities are lost in the shuffle. The private marketplace, on the other hand, does not depend on a 50%-plus-one majority to exist and operate. Only a very few American companies are able to claim 50% or more of their market. Yet thousands of businesses and entrepreneurs thrive by meeting the special demands of small special markets — often amounting to less than 1% of the population. While public planning typically represents some middle-class planner's idea of the good society, it many times ignores the needs of minority and special interests. Variety is something that planners find difficult to centrally plan.

In Austin, Texas, entrepreneur Terry Parker has successfully organized the nation's first two "clothes optional" (includes nudists) apartment projects. It's hard to imagine a public-sponsored development tailored to the needs of such a small minority — especially one whose lifestyle would seem so contrary to the majority of voters.

Behind the sensational aspects of Parker's projects (which he admits "have been getting a lot of exposure lately") lies a very serious potential for urban redevelopment. Parker explains that the laws of supply and demand also apply to the market demand for "freedom" and that the freedom in his projects' environment does have a dollar value. Because of his ability to meet this specialized market, he is able to rent his units for an estimated 10% to 15% more than similar housing in Austin.

This extra profit potential made it economically feasible to successfully redevelop the two formerly marginal projects, including a previously run-down 78-unit complex located in a depressed high-crime neighborhood. It has been turned around from a nearly vacant, unprofitable facility harboring criminals and vandals to a remodeled, clean, and safe environment with a private security force and even a private elementary school for the children of 150 liberated tenants. While Parker's projects have benefited the adjoining neighborhood with a reduced crime rate, he explains that his prime motivation is to "make a buck," and he does just that by successfully responding to the needs of a small minority — "liberated individuals."

3. *Cooperation and Coordination.* The large number of diverse, competing property owners and interests in the central city points to the need for some sort of central planning — at least according to the municipal planner. However, the cooperative spirit of private property owners acting in a mutually beneficial manner is often able to accomplish much more than would be feasible through government-sponsored action.

A walking tour of downtown Houston's pedestrian tunnel system would be illustrative. Connecting over 30 major buildings and parking facilities, this privately planned and financed system has grown into the second largest tunnel system in the country (behind New York City's, which is tied in great part to the public subway system). A look at the factors that have contributed to this amazing aspect of downtown Houston's growth and development reveals a couple of unique circumstances.

When Houston was surveyed in the mid 1800's, property owners within the area originally platted (now the downtown area) retained ownership of the land to the center of the street. An easement for streets and utilities was granted to the city, but the private property owner retained the complete ownership and control of land below (and above) the streets and utilities. As a result of this early survey decision, downtown property owners have recently had the unique opportunity to develop this extensive subterranean pedestrian system and an entire lower level of shops and services. The city's role, however, has been very important: it has kept out of the way. *Minimal* regulatory intervention (through the enforcement of standard building codes and an annual city inspection of each tunnel link) has allowed the private tunnel system to develop to its present size and profitable attractiveness that allows it to continue to expand.

The motivation for the private cooperation is again quite simple: extra profit. The owners of office buildings with connections to the tunnel system are able to advertise this as an extra amenity and get higher rents for their office towers above the streets. In addition, they are now able to lease out their basements with access to the tunnel as a new retail level. At present there are over a dozen restaurants, a half dozen banking and service centers, a like number of barber and beauty shops, several florists and plant stores, and dozens of other businesses including drug stores, office supply stores, camera shops, and travel agencies.

The climate-controlled, clean, and convenient tunnel system with private security has served as one of the important reasons that the Houston Central Business District has been rebuilding and prospering while the downtowns of most other large American cities struggle unsuccessfully to compete with new suburban development.

4. *Large Scale Financing and Planning.* A popular misconception is that only government (in particular the federal government) is big enough and powerful enough to handle large-scale central city development. Large-scale private redevelopment projects in Houston and elsewhere indicate, though, that the private sector is quite willing and able to undertake inner city redevelopment at a massive scale — even by government megabuck terminology. Two large private redevelopment efforts in Houston illustrate this:

Greenway Plaza today is a modern mixed-land use development in central Houston located about five miles west of downtown. In 1969, Century Development purchased three entire residential subdivisions in this area containing 237 homes. On the 1962 proposed zoning map (the latest one to be defeated at the polls) the area in which Greenway Plaza is being built would have been restricted to mostly R-1 (single family) and A (apartments) with only a small amount of commercial property. Instead, the land was acquired privately by offering each property owner the market price of his home plus 10%; rent-free occupancy for five more years; and even the owner's option to remove the structure itself for any desired salvage value. Century Development told the property owners that if there were any hold-outs, they would not move ahead with the project. Century got 99.9% acceptance! (Even with the single hold-out who several years later got several hundred thousand dollars for his home, the total real estate costs for this billion dollar project did not increase significantly.)

Another example of massive private redevelopment is Houston Center, now being developed by Texas Eastern Transmission. This project will be even larger than Greenway Plaza. It's located on the edge of downtown in a once marginally developed district of mixed warehouses and small businesses. Texas Eastern quietly assembled 32 square blocks through a dozen front companies over a period of years. In the non-zoned Houston situation, the developer was unlimited in the potential development and the project is claimed to be the largest and most costly private urban development project ever undertaken in the United States. The project is well underway with the completion of the 40-story Two Houston Center Building and the recent topping out of the 47-story One Houston Center.

One of the amazing things about the Greenway Plaza and Houston Center projects is that both involved the assembly and acquisition of literally hundreds of individual parcels and were accomplished within the marketplace without the government's power of eminent domain.

Public Vs. Private Planning

Planners will continue to mutter about the dangers of a laissez-faire approach to development and redevelopment while ignoring Houston, which is thriving on non-zoning and a policy of minimum taxes and a small public sector. The message should be clear: an expanded public sector with higher taxes, greater controls, and greater public expenditures leads inevitably to a New York City condition of stagnation, oppression, and waste.

As previously shown, the private sector is assuming redevelopment roles where planners claim only the government can succeed. The private entrepreneur's success in redevelopment lies in his ability to: (1) assume high levels of risk; (2) respond to minority and special interests; (3) coordinate a variety of private interests; and (4) provide large-scale planning and finance expertise.

While the self-appointed guardian of the public interests, the planner, tries to paint a self-portrait as the unselfish hero of the central city, the evidence is mounting to suggest the opposite. The real unsung hero of urban redevelopment is the entrepreneur — motivated primarily by profit, not by a misguided charity with other people's money and the presumption of knowing what is best for everyone.

When We Are Free

CHAPTER 40

Food From Thought

by Charles W. Williams

Important events in the exciting history of food have interesting, divergent, and often accidental beginnings.

In 1856 a boy in Pittsburgh grew some extra horseradish in his mother's garden. He borrowed a wheelbarrow, which he filled with bottles of ground horseradish and sold to local grocers. The boy was Henry Heinz; and from this first bottle of horseradish sauce grew the intricate world-wide business of the H. J. Heinz Company. Before 1900 that one variety had grown to 57, which today numbers close to 570 in this far-flung food empire.

In 1904 Thomas Sullivan, a tea merchant, sent samples of his various blends of tea to a few of his customers packed in little, hand-sewn silk bags. To his amazement, orders began pouring in by the hundreds for his tea put up in bags. His customers had discovered that tea could be made quickly without muss or fuss by pouring boiling water over tea bags in cups. Thus, quite by accident, was the start of a million-dollar innovation in the sale of tea.

In 1890 a salesman living in Johnstown, New York, while watching the time it took his wife to make some calf's-foot jelly, decided that powdering gelatin would save a lot of time in the kitchen. Charles B. Knox put his idea into operation, hired salesmen to go into peoples' homes to show how easily his gelatin could be dissolved in water and used. His wife worked out recipes for aspics and desserts to be given away with each package. This was the beginning of Knox Gelatine known today by every American housewife.

Peter Cooper, the inventor of the "Tom Thumb" locomotives, also invented a process for mixing powdered gelatin, sugar, and fruit flavors. This was fifty years before it began to appear on grocers' shelves as Jell-O. He was too early; merchandising methods had not been developed to convince housewives of the need for ready prepared foods. Just before the beginning of this century spectacular advertising for its day pointed out how many desserts could be prepared from this inexpensive, neat, clean package of

---

From *The Freeman*, November 1968.

Jell-O. Recipe booklets were distributed by the millions, as many as 15 million in one year, unheard of in that day. Another billion-dollar food business was launched.

Count Rumford, born in Massachusetts, who later migrated to England, was a leading physicist of the nineteenth century. He built the first kitchen range designed for use in a prison in Munich. This proved so efficient and workable that many wealthy people commissioned Count Rumford to replace their open hearth type of cooking apparatus with these new contraptions in their manor kitchens. By 1850 many American manufacturers had adapted Rumford's invention and were producing cast iron ranges in many sizes and shapes, lavishly decorated. From an experimental prison range, the modern stove industry was born.

In 1914 a young scientist from Brooklyn, New York, named Clarence Birdseye joined a scientific expedition to Labrador. He was also an avid sportsman, so he lost no time. He cut a hole in the thick arctic ice to try his hand at fishing. The fish froze as soon as they were exposed to the subfreezing air, often before he had them off the hook. To his surprise, the fish could be kept frozen for weeks and then defrosted and cooked like a fresh fish without any loss of texture or flavor. After returning to the United States, Birdseye made the same discovery while hunting caribou. The steaks from the quick-frozen caribou could later be broiled to a juicy, flavorsome rareness. Because of World War I, he had to drop many additional experiments in quick-freezing all kinds of food. After the war he went into the fishery business in Gloucester, Massachusetts, and experimented with fast freezing on the side. With a tremendous amount of good salesmanship, he raised money for the first quick-frozen food company. The first Birdseye package went on sale to the public in 1930. It would have been difficult to believe, at that time, that within a relatively few years almost every segment of our giant American food industry would be in quick freezing.

From Lumpy Pudding to Tapioca

In Boston in 1894 a boardinghouse keeper was criticized by a sailor in her rooming house because her puddings were lumpy. Insulted at first, she became interested when he explained that the South Sea island natives pounded tapioca to a smooth consistency and suggested that she experiment by running some through her coffee grinder. Sure enough from then on her puddings were as smooth as silk. Soon she was putting up her finely ground tapioca in bags and selling them to her neighbors. She chose a very magic name — "Minute Tapioca" — and soon found a big business on her hands. Many quickly prepared foods have since copied the word

Food From Thought

"minute," but today a minute does not seem fast enough and has been replaced by "instant."

Many people wonder how the Aunt Jemima trademark began. Chris L. Rutt, with a partner, had purchased a flour mill. After some experimenting they developed a packaged pancake mix to use the flours they produced. Then one evening in 1889, Rutt attended a vaudeville show. There he got the idea for a name that reflected the festive spirit long associated with pancakes. A tune called Aunt Jemima, which accompanied a New Orleans style cake walk, inspired the name of the first ready pancake mix.

Chiffon cake was billed in huge cake mix ads in the 1940's as the "first really new cake in a hundred years." Harry Baker was a professional baker and owned a pastry shop in Hollywood, California. For years celebrities had flocked to his store and raved about his cakes. Many cooks feel that their personal recipes should be very valuable to some big food manufacturer but are shocked to find that variations of nearly every recipe have already been tried in the research kitchens. Harry Baker was one of the lucky ones; he sold his recipes for many thousands of dollars to General Mills. The valuable secret of his chiffon cake was that instead of shortening he used salad oil.

Going back many years to 1520, Cortez, the Spanish conqueror of Mexico, observed native Mayan Indians treating tough meat with the juice of the papaya, a common fruit in most tropical lands. He noted this in his writings about his conquest. Strangely enough, this find lay dormant until recent years, when the tenderizing element in papayas was turned into a powder, put up in jars ready to sprinkle on the surface of meat to make chuck and round steaks as tender as sirloin and porterhouse. From this long-forgotten idea came Adolph's Meat Tenderizer, a necessity in many homes.

In 1824 a German doctor living in Venezuela had a Spanish wife who had been sickly for years. Determined to cure her, he worked for over a year on a formula of herbs and spices until he invented a tonic that he claimed brought her back to health. Sailors stopping at the little port of Angostura found that this blend of herbs, spices, and the blossoms of the blue Gentian plant would cure seasickness. They spread the fame of Angostura bitters around the world, the process being speeded when they learned to add it to their ration of rum. When it became an essential part of a Manhattan cocktail, its place in our lives was further assured. Later, it was found to be an excellent addition in many food recipes, and today Angostura Bitters is found on almost everyone's food shelf.

Early traveling merchants from the city of Hamburg, Germany, learned from the Tartars in the Baltic Sea area how to scrape raw meat, season it with salt, pepper, and onion juice to make what is still called tartar steak. The people of Hamburg soon adopted the tartar steak. After many years some unknown Hamburg cook made patties out of the raw meat and broiled them brown on the outside and still pretty raw on the inside — a true hamburger. Today in the butcher shops of America, ground hamburger meat accounts for 30 per cent of all the beef sold to consumers.

Toll House Cookies

The Toll House was a country inn in Massachusetts noted for good food. In the early 1940's Ruth Wakefield, who was then mistress of the inn, started serving a crisp little cookie studded with bits of chocolate. Miss Wakefield readily gave her customers the recipe, and all of a sudden, bars of semi-sweet chocolate began vanishing from the shelves of the stores in the area. It didn't take long for the Nestle Company, and later Hershey, to smoke out the fact that everyone was making the cookie recipe from the Toll House; and soon they were selling millions of packages of chocolate bits specifically so people could make these wonderful cookies. Today it is America's most popular cookie, available frozen, in ready-to-use cookie mixes, and already made in packages.

The early Chinese found that seaweed dried and ground into a powder and added like salt to food had a magical effect on meats and vegetables — all their natural flavor was enhanced. That's why Chinese food became so popular all over the world. Eventually our chemists discovered the flavor-enhancing element and called it glutamate. Today this product, monosodium glutamate, made from beet sugar waste, soy beans, or wheat, is a staple item in every market. It is known to American shoppers as Ac'cent.

Gail Borden, the son of a frontiersman, went to London in 1852 to sell a dehydrated meat biscuit at the International Exposition being held in England. He used all his money trying to put over his idea and had to travel steerage to get home. He was appalled at the crowded, miserable conditions imposed on the immigrant families coming to America. During the trip several infants died in their mothers' arms from milk from infected cows, which were carried on board most passenger vessels to furnish milk, cream, and butter for the passengers. Borden was sure there was a way to preserve milk for long voyages; but many before him had tried and failed, including Pasteur. After four years of intensive research, Borden perfected a process of condensing milk. In 1856 his patent was approved in Washington. After much work selling the idea to skeptics, the first canned milk was introduced to the American market and formed the cornerstone of the vast and diversified Borden Company.

In Battle Creek, Michigan, Ellen Gould White had a dream one night in which she was told by the Lord that man should eat no meat, use no tobacco, tea, coffee, or alcoholic beverages. As a Seventh Day Adventist she established the "Health Reform Institute," a sort of sanitarium, where her guests ate nuts disguised as meat and drank a cereal beverage. This beverage was the creation of one of her guests named Charles William Post, who was suffering from ulcers. He named his beverage Postum. Post also invented the first dry breakfast cereal, which he called "Elijah's Manna." He decided to go into business producing his inventions; but the name Elijah's Manna ran into consumer resistance, so he changed it to "Grape Nuts."

In this same sanitarium was a surgeon named Dr. Harvey Kellogg, whose name along with Post's was destined to be on millions of cereal packages every year. One of Dr. Kellogg's patients had broken her false teeth on a piece of zwiebach, so he invented a paper-thin flake cereal from corn. Breakfast cereals immediately became a rage, and at one time there were as many as forty different companies in Battle Creek competing for this new health food business. So began the vast cereal business of today.

Margaret Rudkin was the wife of a stock broker and her son suffered from allergies. She made an old-fashioned loaf of bread from stone-milled whole wheat flour, hoping to build up her son's health. The bread helped her son; so her doctor persuaded her to bake the bread for some of his patients, and soon she was in business. When this bread was introduced in the thirties, it competed at 25¢ against the spongy white variety selling at 10¢. Within 10 years, Maggie Rudkin's Pepperidge Farm Bread was in demand all over the East Coast and other bakers were making similar loaves — another small beginning for a nationally-known company, Pepperidge Farms.

One night Teddy Roosevelt, who had been visiting the home of President Andrew Jackson, stopped for dinner at the Maxwell House, a famous eating place nearby. Roosevelt, a great extrovert, was so delighted with the coffee that when he finished he replaced the cup in the saucer with a formal gesture and cried out heartily, "that was good to the last drop," a phrase destined to make quite famous the coffee named after the Maxwell House.

St Louis, Missouri, was the site of two important developments in the realm of food. In 1904 an Englishman was tending a booth at the St. Louis International Exposition demonstrating the virtues of a hot cup of tea. This was an insurmountable task during the hot

When We Are Free

July days in the Mid-West. Our Englishman, Richard Blechynden, disparagingly wiped the perspiration from his face as he watched the crowds pass him by. Finally, in desperation, he threw some ice into the hot tea urn and the crowds began to swarm around his booth. The drink was a sensation, and iced tea quickly became one of America's most popular thirst quenchers.

Still in St. Louis, but back in 1890, a physician ground and pounded peanuts to provide an easily-digested form of protein for his patients. The result was peanut butter, which was quickly and rightly adopted by food faddists all over the country. Today it is a staple found in almost every American kitchen. It's a rare mother who isn't thankful for healthful peanut butter when nothing else seems to tempt her children's appetites.

So, with these anecdotes, one can see that almost every great food company or food idea had a small but fascinating beginning. Some came quite by accident, others from diligent perseverance, reflecting the drive and ingenuity of the human race — free enterprise among free men.

CHAPTER 41

A Story of Apples and Entrepreneurship

by Lawrence W. Reed

When this book was just a vision, my colleague, Professor Dale Haywood, and I were convinced that one theme would have to be made clear to the student: the importance of entrepreneurship. After meeting the two people to whom this chapter is dedicated, we are more convinced than ever that America is great because of the *un*common people who conceive ideas, struggle to make them reality, and in the process, show others what the word accomplishment is all about.

Theodore Roosevelt may have had this message in mind when he said, "Far better it is to dare mighty things, to win glorious triumphs, even though checkered by failure, than to take rank with those poor spirits who neither enjoy much nor suffer much, because they live in the gray twilight that knows not victory nor defeat."

Another observer once said that there are only three classes of people in all the world — a very small minority which makes things happen, a somewhat larger minority which watches things happen, and the vast majority of people *who never know what happened.*

This is the story of two people who made things happen, who dared mighty things, who sketched a dream and stuck with it. It is a story of two entrepreneurs in the best American tradition, whose examples of hard work, dedication, and enterprise are a living inspiration for the rest of us. This is the story of John and Joan Bintz of Freeland, Michigan.

The Bintzes are a charming, middle-aged couple, modest and unassuming. They are proud of what they have accomplished but they tell their story in a quiet, simple, folksy manner. As we listened over dinner on two separate occasions, Dr. Haywood and I felt like others might feel if they were invited to have breakfast with the President of the United States. Here we were, being entertained by two people who have been to the mountaintop (literally, in this case) of success — two entrepreneurs responsible for *creating* something, rather than just redistributing someone else's creation, as politicians are fond of doing.

By now you are asking, I am sure, just what is it that these people did? Well, for starters, they built a mountain. A ski mountain. *In the middle of the flattest territory in the state of Michigan.* More than that, they made this seemingly impossible venture work! In fact, the Bintz "Apple Mountain" is today only a part of the total operation, which includes a gift shop, a bakery, a cyder mill, an apple farm, an entire ski resort, a restaurant, and two sporting goods stores. Sure, it's not Rockefeller Center or General Motors, but it's a feat nonetheless, and the kind of thing that makes America's free enterprise system so inspiring.

An Early Lesson

Much has been written in praise of the Bintz operation. Articles have appeared in such publications as *Time, Reader's Digest,* and *Congressional Record.* John Bintz has been called "the area's greatest living legend." But it was not always that way. The story really begins with an experience John had as a young man.

Upon returning home from high school one day, young John showed his mother one of his textbooks. The title was, *How to Get a Living.*

His mother was incensed at that title and promptly lectured John on the virtues of hard work and paying your own way. "*How to Earn a Living* should be the title," she stressed. That lesson, and others like it coming from wise and thoughtful parents, had its impact on John.

In 1949, John's father decided to become a farmer and purchased 80 acres of land south of Freeland, Michigan. He and young John planted 1300 two-foot apple trees on the land and waited for them to mature.

Meanwhile, John attended college and graduated in 1955 with a degree in horticulture. After two years in the army, he returned to the family farm. Shortly thereafter, his father passed away and John shouldered the responsibility for marketing the apples. By that time, the family operation included a small gift shop and country store. A cyder mill (the Bintzes prefer this spelling) was added a little later.

Putting all one's eggs (or apples) in one basket can be risky business, however. As John puts it, "What used to scare me were those cold nights in the spring. I was afraid the whole farm would go. That's what prompted me to diversify."

And that's when John — who knew nothing about skiing except that it was becoming very popular in hillier parts of the country — hit upon the idea of building a mountain. When he told his brother-in-law of his earthshaking project, he heard for the first time what soon would be a familiar refrain: "You're crazy!"

Undaunted, John did his own market research and sketched

A Story of Apples and Entrepreneurship

out the grand design. Sir Edmund Hillary, when asked why he climbed a mountain, said, "Because it's there." John Bintz, when asked why he built a mountain, replied, "Because it wasn't there."

Getting the money to finance the building of the mountain was not easy. The Bintzes went from bank to bank seeking a loan, only to be turned down by understandably skeptical bankers. Finally, one banker had faith in the project and granted a loan. That money plus the family savings got the thing off the ground.

Dr. Haywood and I asked John how confident he was back then that the venture would succeed. Smiling, he told us that he built a barn for ski equipment "which would accommodate apple crates in case the thing didn't work." Still, dogged determination prevailed.

Ski magazine, in November 1968, described those early days:

> Once he decided where to put his mountain, he simply bought some tractors and hired enough men to operate them 24 hours a day, summer and winter, for the next four years. The first hitch came when the men discovered they weren't moving earth — it was blue clay, which when wet became blue glue. And, unfortunately, Apple country experienced a monsoon for most of the spring and summer that first year. The tractors stuck or slid in the mud; temporary power poles toppled over like sticks in hot Good Humor; one of the earth-moving machines fell in the lake that was created by the mountain-makers.

In that first year, what once was a wheat field adjacent to the Bintz apple orchard had become a man-made mountain all of 30 feet in height. When it opened for skiing on December 21, 1961, "Bintz's Bump," as some called it, was 60 feet high and had two feet of man-made snow on it. Since then, the mountain has grown to a height of 201 feet and boasts runs of a thousand feet and eight rope tows.

Later Additions

As they added to the mountain's height from year to year, John and Joan had other brainstorms too. They had visions of a great complex built around the "apple" theme.

The A-frame "Apple Mountain Steak House" was added in 1968. It was a family endeavor, with the Bintz children pitching in, even pouring cement when necessary. Joan put her talents to work as an interior decorator for the restaurant and for the cyder mill, the bakery, and the gift shop.

With a college degree in speech and experience in radio and television, Joan took on advertising and promotional activities. She organized one-hour educational tours of the farm for area school groups. It was a "long-run thing" for Joan, who displays her entrepreneurial foresight by noting that the tours were "a good marketing tool because eventually the kids become our customers."

Whether it is the ski resort, the restaurant, the cyder mill, the bakery, the gift shop, or the sporting goods stores which came later, the Bintzes have always held their patrons in high esteem. "I have always worried about the customers," says John, "because they pay our bills."

What about competition? "Stay one step ahead of them," John advises. He understands, of course, that his competition is not just other ski resorts in the hilly part of northern Michigan — it's any other activity which people seeking a good time might engage in! And that involves many enterprises of much greater size than Bintz Apple Mountain.

John reads voraciously to keep up on new developments in the industry, travels widely and conducts research to get "a feel" for the market, and always welcomes the comments and suggestions of anyone willing to offer them. Presently, he is making plans to install a chair lift for old folks who do not want to ride the tow ropes — all in an effort to keep the customer happy and coming back for more. That's free enterprise in its very essence!

Expansion is Continuing

When the Bintzes began their work, there was John, Joan, a few family members, and a hired hand. Today, the entire operation provides employment for from 110 to 210 people, depending on the season. John personally interviews and hires all managers and lets them hire their employees. A bonus system for the managers gives them added incentive to hire the very best people, keep costs down, and satisfy the consumer.

And the end of expansion is not yet in sight. The entrepreneurial spirit in John and Joan Bintz is just as alive today as it was twenty years ago. Both have many new projects in mind, including a golf course. The only cloud on their horizon, as they see it, is "the uncertainty and expense of government interference." This is a problem, John notes, which hangs over every business enterprise, and he is one businessman who actively speaks out on behalf of the free enterprise system.

"What motivates you two?" we asked John and Joan. Their reply: "Financial rewards from a profitable operation, a sense of accomplishment, a sense of 'moving ahead,' and being able to provide something good for our children." We couldn't summarize more concisely the "American way of life."

A Story of Apples and Entrepreneurship

All across this land are monuments to celebrated politicians. Every state capital is full of them. The nation's capital is so cluttered with them that a foreign visitor easily gets the impression that politicians are what America is all about.

Well, I submit that the greatness of this country more appropriately rests with the spirits of entrepreneurs like John and Joan Bintz. Behind theirs and every enterprise is a story of great risk, hard work, and perseverance. The industrial might of America didn't just happen; the millions of products and services that sustain life and that provide happiness every day didn't just appear with a wave of a wand; men and women with vision and foresight, with ideas and the courage to act upon them, carved out of this former wilderness the highest level of living on this earth. All they needed was faith in themselves and a system which gave them the freedom to try.

When We Are Free

CHAPTER 42

A College That Became the Partner of Business

by David E. Fry

Undergraduate, post-secondary education in the United States is overwhelmingly "traditional." In spite of claims to the contrary, the vast majority of colleges and universities are structured similarly to perform similarly.

Not so, at a college called Northwood Institute, where two Michigan educators struck out on their own to answer a call few others in academe were even hearing.

It was the late 1950s and America was in trauma. The Soviets had just orbited Sputnik and the educational establishment responded with a sustained change in emphasis to hard sciences. Arthur Turner and Gary Stauffer were concerned because they could see that there were many students who wanted specialized programs in business management — students not cut out to be scientists. But where were they to go?

Responding to an Opportunity

Turner and Stauffer saw an opportunity to serve in that confluence of events. What seemed obvious to them took other educators another twenty years to fully realize:
  (1) The future of our society depended on the ability of our private sector to perform.
  (2) Young people wanted, and needed, programs to help them be productive in that private sector.
  (3) The private sector desperately needed to be "listened to," seriously, by people who could help educate young people for management professions.

Out of that combination of factors grew Northwood Institute. It started in Alma, Michigan, in the spring of 1959. The first class had fewer than 100 students and the college operated out of a former residence in the small Michigan city. In 1962 Northwood Institute moved to Midland, then added campuses in Indiana and Texas in the mid-60s and is currently building an educational center in Florida as well as operating international programs in Europe and elsewhere.

Northwood Institute is a singular success story because of the vision of two men who believed in free enterprise, listened to business and industry, and believed that serious, quality-focused education could be provided to young people by paying attention to *real needs*.

Today, Northwood enrolls almost 2500 students in on-campus programs on three campuses and another 3,000 students in extension centers, in continuing education programs and in a unique external degree program. The college has grown in influence and ability to the extent that several major industries now consider it "their college" — the only college offering specialized curricula built for their industries and focused on the future.

Programs for Private Enterprise

While maintaining a strictly private nature, refusing to accept or apply for a dime of federal or state assistance in its development, Northwood Institute developed specially designed programs in Business Management, Automotive Marketing, Accounting, Fashion Merchandising, as well as more than a dozen other business fields.

The college designed a "2 + 2" system. A student spends the first two years intensively pursuing general education, general business disciplines and a concentration in one of fourteen specialty business fields, culminating in an Associate of Arts degree in that specialty. Then, the student may continue for an additional two years earning the Bachelor of Business Administration degree with functional majors in either management, marketing or accounting.

Free enterprise thought is embedded in every course and in every curriculum throughout the college. The arts and humanities are also strongly emphasized.

The faculty is composed of two-thirds traditional academics with a dedication to the private sector and one-third former business professionals who teach students in the fields where they themselves excelled.

Business and industry have been generous in their support. The three campuses grew and flourished through the generosity of individuals willing and eager to invest in the future of their society through young minds.

Today, more than 10,000 alumni all over the world are involved in more than 100 different fields and management disciplines. But to understand the growth and success of the college is to recognize the tenacity and vision of its founders.

A College That Became the Partner of Business

Turner and Stauffer

Turner and Stauffer were risk-takers in the entrepreneurial mold. What they saw was nothing others couldn't see as well. But what they did was different.

They listened to business.

They designed curricula to meet real needs.

They collected about themselves a faculty committed to a vision of a strong, private, free society.

They walked out on a very long, thin limb to build a college to serve those needs.

They were aggressive in seeking out young people who were serious about building for their future.

They were aggressive in telling their story to business and industry. They made the point that here was a college which would listen and respond.

The Northwood Idea wasn't long in attracting advocates. Key executives from the automotive sector, the advertising field, banking and finance, retailing and others were quickly attracted.

Dr. Turner, now Chairman of the Board of Trustees, and Dr. Stauffer, now Chairman of the College, continue to be the driving forces in this twenty-one year old idea which turned into a vibrant institution. "The first twenty years were the most exciting," comments Turner, "but the second twenty will be even better. We are going to help more than 30,000 men and women enter the productive, private sector of our society during that time. We are going to be a factor in the success of our society. We intend to be leaders in its success. We wanted to have an impact on our society, and it looks as if, with the help of good people from all over the earth, we have been endowed with the tools to do that job. No one could ask for more."

Northwood Institute's success makes the point that even in a tradition bound area, given the freedom to innovate and an entrepreneurial spirit, good ideas flourish, grow and benefit mankind.

When We Are Free

Unit VIII: Myths About Free Markets

Is there no end to the myths and misconceptions about free markets? They seem to be as plentiful as dandelions in springtime. Needless to say, we can afford to deal with only a few of the more common ones here.

Camille P. Castorina attacks the myths of the English Industrial Revolution. This profound event in man's development was hardly a horror story. It was a marvelous achievement which lifted from the backs of men and women much of the burden of crushing toil which characterized pre-industrial days.

"But what about evil, rapacious, capitalist monopolies?" the free market critic asks. The monopoly issue is featured in "Witch-Hunting for Robber Barons: The Standard Oil Story." Special emphasis is given to John D. Rockefeller's company, which is the Number One Bogeyman for many anti-capitalist mythmongers. The reader will also find in this piece a great deal of ammunition regarding competition and monopoly in general.

Timothy G. Nash, at the time of this writing a student at Northwood Institute, defends profit from hostile and misinformed commentators. In the chapter titled "In Defense of Profit," Nash explains that profit is not a rip-off but is a catalyst for production and a barometer of efficiency.

The question of conservation comes up in Ruth Shallcross Maynard's "Who Conserves Our Resources?" The charge is often made that the free market is not a very good steward of the earth's riches. Mrs. Maynard thinks otherwise: "Natural resources are best utilized and conserved where they meet specific economic requirements in the most efficient way as determined by competition in the free market."

Surely, racial discrimination thrives when men are free. Not so! declares George Leef, one of our faculty colleagues at Northwood

Institute. In his chapter, Leef argues that capitalism "is a ruthless foe of all uneconomic prejudices." Government policies, not free markets, actually *cause* discrimination!

Finally, "Am I My Brother's Keeper?" challenges the myths that welfarism is moral and capitalism is immoral. Freedom, William Henry Chamberlin claims, gives rise to a spirit of independence. Being "kept" by another, especially if that "other" is the State, produces an instinctive revulsion in people. That theme reminds us of the old saying, "Give me a fish and I eat for a day; teach me to fish and I eat for a lifetime."

CHAPTER 43

Capitalism and Its Industrial Revolution

by Camille P. Castorina

Two issues are raised in the Industrial Revolution debate by the opponents of capitalism. First, it is alleged that the age *before* the Industrial Revolution was cleaner and better for the common man. Second, it is alleged that there was increasing misery *during* the Industrial Revolution, caused by the expansion of capitalism.

It is advanced, either directly or by inference — in novels and manifestos — that previous to the Industrial Revolution, which began in England, the workers lived in a "golden age" of pastoral life. The Britons lived in lovely thatched cottages in a green countryside and danced around the Maypole. Then the evil capitalist factory owners forced them into disease-ridden cities to live among untold horrors where they choked in newly-created slums and worked long hours.

Let us examine the pre-industrial "golden age." First of all, the workers left the countryside *by choice*. If life was better there than in the cities, why did they leave? "People vote with their feet," contrary to all the pronouncements of government leaders and ideologues. Furthermore, the pre-industrial era was the era of the "highwaymen" — men who preyed on travelers along the roads of England. Countless thousands risked hanging on the gallows for crimes related to their needs — to feed their families. The British jails were so overcrowded that the tales of horrors of prison life live on.

The misery of pre-industrial times occurred because the government imposed restrictions upon enterprise. There was no free market. Instead, there was a vast network of tariffs, taxes, regulations, and government monopolies.

If a woman's husband or father died, where could she turn for livelihood for herself or her children before the Industrial Revolution? Without the factory system, for many the only choice besides charity was prostitution or the convent. One may guess which occupation a woman with four children would choose. Ah, for the good old days before capitalism!

These situations were evident throughout Europe as well, and generally worse. In most other areas before 1750, serfdom was in effect and peasants were completely at the whim of the lord of the manor.

Many of the "horrors" attributed to the Industrial Revolution were really a creation of government control. For example, one hears the lament, "Oh, the poor people in factories, they had no windows." If there *were* not enough windows, it was because the British government had a tax on windows into the early years of the Industrial Revolution!

Why does the myth of a pre-industrial "golden age" persist? Some authors, novelists in particular, had some erroneous notions of earlier days being filled with knights in shining armor. This may have sold novels, but it was bad economic history. Others who wanted to push socialism, to make England a "workers paradise," seized upon this "golden age" story as quite convenient.

The Technology of the Revolution

Why was there a swift march of technological discoveries, inventions, and innovations after 1750? Government slowly but surely lifted its own tyrannical practices of earlier centuries. Regulations had been so extensive that under one monarch, a particular Lord was granted an exclusive right for making playing cards. With the abolition of many controls, men of enterprise and genius began losing their fears of expropriation and were thus encouraged to intensify their efforts.

Clothmaking was a significant British occupation, especially wool and cotton. In the 18th century came an invention for faster weaving. This in turn gave rise to the invention of better looms, and thus demand for better spinning devices which were soon forthcoming. Iron implements had formally been too expensive for the common man, who had to subsist with more primitive wooden devices. Abraham Darby devised a process for the mass production of iron and put that product into the hands of thousands. With iron available at low prices, James Watt could finally invent a steam engine.

With industrialization and its factories, more was produced for *mass* consumption. Who was buying the *mass* produced goods but the masses — the workers themselves! The wealthy still preferred expensive, handmade items.

The truth is that the Industrial Revolution did more to relieve poverty and distress than any previous age. Though some "authorities" deny the benefits of the degree of economic liberty which gave birth to the Industrial Revolution, there has been fine work done by scholars showing the tremendous benefits of laissez faire.

One observer wrote the following after Parliament in 1846 finally abolished the old Corn Laws, which were tariffs on the importation of grain:

> A feeling of anxiety which almost amounted to despair gave way to hopefulness. Business began to expand, our commerce increased, and there was soon plenty of employment for everybody. The staple food and the people were changed ... At the same time, new kinds of food, hitherto shut out, began to appear in our markets and many articles which till then had been considered luxuries, were soon within the reach of all.[1]

Hundreds of other duties were abolished. The wealth of the nation immensely increased. The standards of living skyrocketed. Savings banks emerged where none existed before. The national debt was rapidly diminished. Great Britain became the envy of most of the world because of these and similar developments.

It is significant to note that the European revolutions of 1848 never spread to England. Why, if there was such "misery" in England, didn't a revolt take place? If there were hordes of discontented workers in England, why was there no revolt? This was because the 1846 Corn Law repeal was a symbol of the peaceful destruction of government restrictions and the British people themselves saw their living standards increase. Others in feudal systems revolted, but capitalist Britain had better things to do.

Evidence of Improvement

Real wages in England in the second half of the 19th century increased tremendously. Wages were rising to higher levels because workers had better machines and thus produced more. This wage increase in factory areas pushed agricultural workers' wages up as well. All this with a virtual absence of unions! It was precisely because of increased wages, however, that more vocal complaints about suffering were made. The increased standards brought a heightened awareness of the issue of relative poverty and the need for further improvement.

Capitalism brought with it upward social and economic mobility. A large percentage of factory owners and managers had once

---

[1] Henry Duckley, "The Jubilee of Free Trade," in *Richard Cobden and the Jubilee of Free Trade* (London: T. Fisher Unwin, 1896), p. 44.

been workers themselves. Gone was the era of feudalism when position in life was dictated by birth.

Many of the horror stories about children working in factories came from parliamentary committees. Actually, there were two committees; one of them concluding that the factories made children *better* off. The other one, in 1816, concluded that children were indeed "exploited." Of nine doctors who testified before that committee, however, most later admitted they knew nothing of factories or had never visited one; one stated he was in a factory as a young man in times past; another was a personal friend of an agricultural protectionist leader trying to make factory owners look bad; and another contradicted the evidence of all the others![2]

Some opponents of the Industrial Revolution like to show that many children in factories were smaller, thinner, and more sickly than farm children. However, where this was the case it was not because of factory exploitation but because in those days farm work demanded long hours of intense physical labor, and sickly children could never survive. The factories gave them a chance.

Parents found positions in factories, and in the earlier days of industrialization (especially before 1846) this income was not sufficient without children working. It seems only logical that the parents would prefer their children with them in the same room at the factory than in another part of the country working under some farmer under conditions not under their scrutiny. It must be noted as well that with increased productivity and the expansion of capitalism there was less and less of a need for children to work.

The Views of Cobden

Perhaps the spirit of capitalism and the Industrial Revolution is best captured by English laissez faire leader Richard Cobden and his many followers in the 1840's. They saw that the way to alleviate suffering was to expand capitalism, not diminish it. Only by capitalism's rapid expansion would the poverty that still existed — especially before the 1846 Corn Law repeal — be alleviated. In fighting to free the economy from the restrictions of government intervention, Cobden challenged the members of parliament:

> Can you by legislation add one farthing to the wealth of the country? You may by legislation, in one evening, destroy the fruits and accumulations of a century of labor, but I defy you to show me how, by the legislation of the House, you can add one

---
[2] See Friedrich Hayek, ed., *Capitalism and the Historians* (Chicago University Press, 1954).

farthing to the wealth of the country. That springs from the industry and intelligence of the people of the country . . . If you attempt by legislation to give direction to trade or industry, it is a thousand to one that you are doing wrong; and if you happen to be right . . . the parties for whom you legislate would go right on without you . . . I want you to put an end, from conviction, to an evil system.[3]

Richard Cobden knew what so many enemies of capitalism fail to see — that any process (such as industrialization) which leaves people alone to produce will generate higher standards of living. Platitudes or ranting will not feed people, but capitalism with its productive methods will — and did.

With regard to Third World nations today, they do not lack "government planning." They sure have plenty of that. What they lack is enough liberty.

The problems of our time are critical. The increase in living standards of the last two hundred years is now threatened. But history can *assist us* in plotting a hopeful future. As Cobden proclaimed in Parliament:

> Time and truth against all the world . . . and that time which destroys everything else only establishes truth.[4]

---

[3]Richard Cobden, Speech, House of Commons, Feb. 27, 1846. *Speeches on Questions of Public Policy* (London: Macmillan, 1903), p. 198.
[4]Richard Cobden, Speech, House of Commons, October 19, 1843 in Ibid., p. 198.

When We Are Free

CHAPTER 44

Witch-Hunting for Robber Barons: The Standard Oil Story

by Lawrence W. Reed

Among the great misconceptions of the free economy is the widely-held belief that "laissez faire" embodies a natural tendency toward monopoly concentration. Under unfettered capitalism, so goes the familiar refrain, large firms would systematically devour smaller ones, corner markets, and stamp out competition until every inhabitant of the land fell victim to their power. Just as popular is the notion that John D. Rockefeller's Standard Oil Company of the late 1800s gave substance to such an evil course of events.

Regarding Standard Oil's chief executive, one noted historian writes, "He (Rockefeller) iron-handedly ruined competitors by cutting prices until his victim went bankrupt or sold out, whereupon higher prices would be likely to return."[1]

Two other historians, co-authors of a popular college text, opine that "Rockefeller was a ruthless operator who did not hesitate to crush his competitors by harsh and unfair methods."[2]

In 1899, Standard refined 90 per cent of America's oil — the peak of the company's dominance of the refining business. Though that market share was steadily siphoned off by competitors after 1899, the company nonetheless has been branded ever since as "an industrial octopus."

Does the story of Standard Oil really present a case *against* the free market? In my opinion, it most emphatically does not. Furthermore, setting the record straight on this issue must become an important weapon in every free market advocate's intellectual arsenal. That's the purpose of the following remarks.

Theoretically, there are two kinds of monopoly: coercive and efficiency. A coercive monopoly results from, in the words of Adam

---

From *The Freeman*, March 1980

[1]Thomas A. Bailey, *The American Pageant: A History of the Republic*, 2 vols., 8th ed. (Boston: D. C. Heath and Company, 1966), 2:532.

[2]Gilbert C. Fite and Jim E. Reese, *An Economic History of the United States*, 2nd ed. (Boston: Houghton Mifflin Company, 1965), p. 367.

Smith, "a government grant of exclusive privilege." Government, in effect, must take sides in the market in order to give birth to a coercive monopoly. It must make it difficult, costly, or impossible for anyone but the favored firm to do business.

The United States Postal Service is an example of this kind of monopoly. By law, no one can deliver first class mail except the USPS. Fines and imprisonment (coercion) await all those daring enough to compete.

In some other cases, the government may not ban competition outright, but simply bestow privileges, immunities, or subsidies on one firm while imposing costly requirements on all others. Regardless of the method, a firm which enjoys a coercive monopoly is in a position to harm the consumer and get away with it.

An efficiency monopoly, on the other hand, earns a high share of a market because it does the best job. It receives no special favors from the law to account for its size. Others are free to compete and, if consumers so will it, to grow as big as the "monopoly."

An efficiency monopoly has no legal power to compel people to deal with it or to protect itself from the consequences of its unethical practices. It can only attain bigness through its excellence in satisfying customers and by the economy of its operations. An efficiency monopoly which turns its back on the very performance which produced its success would be posting a sign, "COMPETITORS WANTED." The market rewards excellence and exacts a toll on mediocrity.

It is my contention that the historical record casts the Standard Oil Company in the role of efficiency monopoly — a firm to which consumers repeatedly awarded their votes of confidence.

The oil rush began with the discovery of oil by Colonel Edwin Drake at Titusville, Pennsylvania in 1859. Northwestern Pennsylvania soon "was overrun with businessmen, speculators, misfits, horse dealers, drillers, bankers, and just plain hell-raisers. Dirt-poor farmers leased land at fantastic prices, and rigs began blackening the landscape. Existing towns jammed full overnight with 'strangers,' and new towns appeared almost as quickly."[3]

In the midst of chaos emerged young John D. Rockefeller. An exceptionally hard-working and thrifty man, Rockefeller transformed his early interest in oil into a partnership in the refinery stage of the business in 1865.

Five years later, Rockefeller formed the Standard Oil Company with 4 per cent of the refining market. Less than thirty years later,

---

[3] D. T. Armentano, *The Myths of Antitrust: Economic Theory and Legal Cases* (New Rochelle, N.Y.: Arlington House, 1972), p. 64.

he reached that all-time high of 90 per cent. What accounts for such stunning success?

On December 30, 1899, Rockefeller was asked that very question before a governmental investigating body called the Industrial Commission. He replied:

> I ascribe the success of the Standard to its consistent policy to make the volume of its business large through the merits and cheapness of its products. It has spared no expense in finding, securing, and utilizing the best and cheapest methods of manufacture. It has sought for the best superintendents and workmen and paid the best wages. It has not hesitated to sacrifice old machinery and old plants for new and better ones. It has placed its manufactories at the points where they could supply markets at the least expense. It has not only sought markets for its principal products, but for all possible by-products, sparing no expense in introducing them to the public. It has not hesitated to invest millions of dollars in methods of cheapening the gathering and distribution of oils by pipe lines, special cars, tank steamers, and tank wagons. It has erected tank stations at every important railroad station to cheapen the storage and delivery of its products. It has spared no expense in forcing its products into the markets of the world among people civilized and uncivilized. It has had faith in American oil, and has brought together millions of money for the purpose of making it what it is, and holding its markets against the competition of Russia and all the many countries which are producers of oil and competitors against American oil.[4]

A Master Organizer of Men and Materials

Rockefeller was a managerial genius — a master organizer of men as well as of materials. He had a gift for bringing devoted, brilliant, and hard-working young men into his organization. Among his most outstanding associates were H. H. Rogers, John D. Archbold, Stephen V. Harkness, Samuel Andrews, and Henry M. Flagler. Together they emphasized efficient economic operation, research, and sound financial practices. The economic excellence of their performance is described by economist D. T. Armentano:

---

[4]Thomas G. Manning, E. David Cronon, and Howard R. Lamar, *The Standard Oil Company: The Rise of a National Monopoly*, part 3: *Government and the American Economy: 1870 to the Present*, revised (New York: Henry Holt and Company, 1960), p. 19.

Instead of buying oil from jobbers, they made the jobbers' profit by sending their own purchasing men into the oil region. In addition, they made their own sulfuric acid, their own barrels, their own lumber, their own wagons, and their own glue. They kept minute and accurate records of every item from rivets to barrel bungs. They built elaborate storage facilities near their refineries. Rockefeller bargained as shrewdly for crude as anyone before or since. And Sam Andrews coaxed more kerosene from a barrel of crude than could the competition. In addition, the Rockefeller firm put out the cleanest-burning kerosene, and managed to dispose of most of the residues like lubricating oil, paraffin, and vaseline at a profit.[5]

Even muckraker Ida Tarbell, one of Standard's critics, admired the company's streamlined processes of production:

Not far away from the canning works, on Newton Creek, is an oil refinery. This oil runs to the canning works, and, as the newmade cans come down by a chute from the works above, where they have just been finished, they are filled, twelve at a time, with the oil made a few miles away. The filling apparatus is admirable. As the newmade cans come down the chute they are distributed, twelve in a row, along one side of a turn-table. The turn-table is revolved, and the cans come directly under twelve measures, each holding five gallons of oil — a turn of a valve, and the cans are full. The table is turned a quarter, and while twelve more cans are filled and twelve fresh ones are distributed, four men with soldering cappers put the caps on the first set. Another quarter turn, and men stand ready to take the cans from the filler and while they do this, twelve more are having caps put on, twelve are filling, and twelve are coming to their place from the chute. The cans are placed at once in wooden boxes standing ready, and, after a twenty-four-hour wait for discovering leaks, are nailed up and carted to a nearby door. This door opens on the river, and there at anchor by the side of the factory is a vessel chartered for South America or China or where not — waiting to receive the cans which a little more than twenty-four hours before were tin sheets lying on flatboxes. It is a marvelous example of economy, not only in materials, but in time and in footsteps.[6]

---

[5] Armentano, *Myths of Antitrust*, p. 67.
[6] Ida M. Tarbell, *The History of the Standard Oil Company*, 2 vols. in 1 (Gloucester, Mass.: Peter Smith, 1950), p. 240-241.

Witch-Hunting for Robber Barons: The Standard Oil Story

Market Competition Protects the Public

Socialist historian Gabriel Kolko, who argues in *The Triumph of Conservatism* that the forces of competition in the free market of the late 1800s were too potent to allow Standard to cheat the public, stresses that "Standard treated the consumer with deference. Crude and refined oil prices for consumers declined during the period Standard exercised greatest control of the industry . . ."[7]

Standard's service to the consumer in the form of lower prices is well-documented. To quote from Professor Armentano again:

> Between 1870 and 1885 the price of refined kerosene dropped from 26 cents to 8 cents per gallon. In the same period, the Standard Oil Company reduced the [refining] costs per gallon from almost 3 cents in 1870 to .452 cents in 1885. Clearly, the firm was relatively efficient, and its efficiency was being translated to the consumer in the form of lower prices for a much improved product, and to the firm in the form of additional profits.[8]

That story continued for the remainder of the century, with the price of kerosene to the consumer falling to 5.91 cents per gallon in 1897. Armentano concludes from the record that "at the very pinnacle of Standard's industry 'control,' *the costs and the prices for refined oil reached their lowest levels in the history of the petroleum industry.*"[9]

John D. Rockefeller's success, then, was a consequence of his superior performance. He derived his impressive market share not from sloppiness, coercion, or government favors but rather from aggressive courting of the consumer. Standard Oil is one of history's classic efficiency monoplies.

But what about the many serious charges leveled against Standard? Predatory price cutting? Buying out competitors? Conspiracy? Railroad rebates? Charging any price it wanted? Greed? Each of these can be viewed as an assault not just on Standard Oil but on the free market in general. They can and must be answered.

---

[7] Gabriel Kolko, *The Triumph of Conservatism: A Reinterpretation of American History, 1900-1916* (New York: The Macmillan Company, 1963; reprint ed., Chicago: Quadrangle Books, 1967), p. 39.

[8] Armentano, *Myths of Antitrust*, p. 70.

[9] *Ibid.*, p. 77.

A. Predatory Price Cutting

Predatory price cutting is "the practice of deliberately underselling rivals in certain markets to drive them out of business, and then raising prices to exploit a market devoid of competition."[10]

Professor John S. McGee, writing in the *Journal of Law and Economics* for October 1958, stripped this charge of any intellectual substance. Describing it as "logically deficient," he concluded, "I can find little or no evidence to support it."[11]

In his extraordinary article, McGee scrutinized the testimony of Rockefeller's competitors who claimed to have been victims of predatory price cutting. He found their claims to be shallow and misdirected. McGee pointed out that some of these very people later opened new refineries and successfully challenged Standard again.

Beyond the actual record, economic theory also argues against a winning policy of predatory price cutting in a free market for the following reasons:

1. *Price is only one aspect of competition.* Firms compete in a variety of ways: service, location, packaging, marketing, even courtesy. For price alone to draw customers away from the competition, the predator would have to cut substantially — enough to outweigh all the other competitive pressures the others can throw at him. That means suffering losses on every unit sold. If the predator has a war-chest of "monopoly profits" to draw upon in such a battle, then the predatory price cutting theorist must explain how he was able to achieve such ability in the absence of this practice in the first place!
2. *The large firm stands to lose the most.* By definition, the large firm is already selling the most units. As a predator, it must actually step up its production if it is to have any effect on competitors. As Professor McGee observed, "To lure customers away from somebody, he (the predator) must be prepared to serve them himself. The monopolizer thus finds himself in the position of selling more — and therefore losing more — than his competitors."[12]
3. *Consumers will increase their purchases at the "bargain prices."* This factor causes the predator to step up produc-

---

[10] *Ibid.*, p. 73.
[11] John S. McGee, "Predatory Price Cutting: The Standard Oil (N.J.) Case," *Journal of Law and Economics*, I (October, 1958), p. 138.
[12] *Ibid.*, p. 140.

tion even further. It also puts off the day when he can "cash in" on his hoped-for victory because consumers will be in a position to refrain from purchasing at higher prices, consuming their stockpiles instead.
4. *The length of the battle is always uncertain.* The predator does not know how long he must suffer losses before his competitors quit. It may take weeks, months, or even years. Meanwhile, consumers are "cleaning up" at his expense!
5. *Any "beaten" firms may reopen.* Competitors may scale down production or close only temporarily as they "wait out the storm." When the predator raises prices, they enter the market again. Conceivably, a "beaten" firm might be bought up by someone for a "song," and then, under fresh management and with relatively low capital costs, face the predator with an actual competitive cost advantage.
6. *High prices encourage newcomers.* Even if the predator drives everyone else from the market, raising prices will attract competition from people heretofore not even in the industry. The higher the prices go, the more powerful that attraction.
7. *The predator would lose the favor of consumers.* Predatory price cutting is simply not good public relations. Once known, it would swiftly erode the public's faith and good will. It might even evoke consumer boycotts and a backlash of sympathy for the firm's competitors.

In summary, let me quote Professor McGee once again:

> Judging from the Record, Standard Oil did not use predatory price discrimination to drive out competing refiners, nor did its pricing practice have that effect. Whereas there may be a very few cases in which retail kerosene peddlers or dealers went out of business after or during price cutting, there is no real proof that Standard's pricing policies were responsible. I am convinced that Standard did not systematically, if ever, use local price cutting in retailing, or anywhere else, to reduce competition. To do so would have been foolish; and, whatever else has been said about them, the old Standard organization was seldom criticized for making less money when it could readily have made more.[13]

---

[13] *Ibid.*, p. 168.

B. Buying Out Competitors

The intent of this practice, the critics say, was to stifle competitors by absorbing them.

First, it must be said that Standard had no legal power to coerce a competitor into selling. For a purchase to occur, Rockefeller had to pay the *market* price for an oil refinery. And evidence abounds that he often hired the very people whose operations he purchased. "Victimized ex-rivals," wrote McGee, "might be expected to make poor employees and dissident or unwilling shareholders."[14]

Kolko writes that "Standard attained its control of the refinery business primarily by mergers, not price wars; and most refinery owners were anxious to sell out to it. Some of these refinery owners later reopened new plants after selling to Standard."[15]

Buying out competitors can be a wise move if achieving economy of scale is the intent. Buying out competitors merely to eliminate them from the market can be a futile, expensive, and never-ending policy. It appears that Rockefeller's mergers were designed with the first motive in mind.

Even so, other people found it profitable to go into the business of building refineries and selling to Standard. David P. Reighard managed to build and sell three successive refineries to Rockefeller, all on excellent terms.

A firm which adopts a policy of absorbing others solely to stifle competition embarks upon the impossible adventure of putting out the recurring and unpredictable prairie fires of competition.

C. Conspiracy to Fix Prices

This accusation holds that Standard secured secret agreements with competitors to carve up markets and fix prices at higher-than-market levels.

I will not contend here that Rockefeller never attempted this policy. His experiment with the South Improvement Company in 1872 provides at least some evidence that he did. I do argue, however, that all such attempts were failures from the start and no harm to the consumer occurred.

Standard's price performance, cited extensively above, supports my argument. Prices fell steadily on an improving product. Some conspiracy!

From the perspective of economic theory, collusion to raise and/or fix prices is a practice doomed to failure in a free market for these reasons:

---

[14] *Ibid.*, p. 145.
[15] Kolko, *Triumph of Conservatism*, p. 40.

1. *Internal pressures.* Conspiring firms must resolve the dilemma of production. To exact a higher price than the market currently permits, production must be curtailed. Otherwise, in the face of a fall in demand, the firms will be stuck with a quantity of unsold goods. Who will cut their production and by how much? Will the conspirators accept an equal reduction for all when it is likely that each faces a unique constellation of cost and distribution advantages and disadvantages?

   Assuming a formula for restricting production is agreed upon, it then becomes highly profitable for any member of the cartel to quietly cheat on the agreement. By offering secret rebates or discounts or other "deals" to his competitors' customers, any conspirator can undercut the cartel price, earn an increasing share of the market and make a lot of money. When the others get wind of this, they must quickly break the agreement or lose their market shares to the "cheater." The very reason for the conspiracy in the first place — higher profits — proves to be its undoing!

2. *External pressures.* This comes from competitors who are not parties to the secret agreement. They feel under no obligation to abide by the cartel price and actually use their somewhat lower price as a selling point to customers. The higher the cartel price, the more this external competition pays. The conspiracy must either convince all outsiders to join the cartel (making it increasingly likely that somebody will cheat) or else dissolve the cartel to meet the competition.

I would once again call the reader's attention to Kolko's *The Triumph of Conservatism*, which documents the tendency for collusive agreements to break apart, sometimes even before the ink is dry.

D. Railroad Rebates

John D. Rockefeller received substantial rebates from railroads who hauled his oil, a factor which critics claim gave him an unfair advantage over other refiners.

The fact is that *most* refiners received rebates from railroads. This practice was simply evidence of stiff competition among the rails for the business of hauling oil and oil products. Standard got the biggest rebates because Rockefeller was a shrewd bargainer and because he offered the railroads large volume on a regular basis. He also provided his own insurance for oil in transport.

This charge is even less credible when one considers that Rockefeller increasingly relied on his own pipelines, not railroads, to transport his oil.

E. The Power to Change Any Price Wanted

According to the notion that Standard's size gave it the power to charge any price it wanted, bigness itself immunizes the firm from competition and consumer sovereignty.

As an "efficiency monopoly," Standard could not coercively prevent others from competing with it. And others did, so much so that the company's share of the market declined dramatically after 1899. As the economy shifted from kerosene to electricity, from the horse to the automobile, and from oil production in the East to production in the Gulf States, Rockefeller found himself losing ground to younger, more aggressive men.

Neither did Standard have the power to compel people to buy its products. It had to rely on its own excellence to attract and keep customers.

In a totally free market, the following factors insure that no firm, regardless of size, can charge and get "any price it wants":

1. *Free entry.* Potential competition is encouraged by any firm's abuse of the consumer. In describing entry into the oil business, Rockefeller once remarked that "all sorts of people . . . the butcher, the baker, and the candlestick maker began to refine oil."[16]
2. *Foreign competition.* As long as government doesn't hamper international trade, this is always a potent force.
3. *Competition of substitutes.* People are often able to substitute a product different from yet similar to the "monopolist's."
4. *Competition of all goods for the consumer's dollar.* Every businessman is in competition with every other businessman to get consumers to spend their limited dollars on him.
5. *Elasticity of demand.* At higher prices, people will simply buy less.

It makes sense to view competition in a free market not as a static phenomenon, but as a dynamic, never-ending, leap-frog process by which the leader today might become the follower tomorrow.

---

[16] John A. Garraty, *The American Nation*, vol. 2: *A History of the United States Since 1865*, 3rd ed. (New York: Harper and Row, 1975), p. 499.

F. Rockefeller Was Greedy

The charge that John D. Rockefeller was a "greedy" man is the most meaningless of all the attacks on him but nonetheless echoes constantly in the history books.

If Rockefeller wanted to make a lot of money (and there is no doubting he did), he certainly discovered the free market solution to his problem: produce and sell something that consumers will buy and buy again. One of the great attributes of the free market is that it channels greed into constructive directions. One cannot accumulate wealth without offering something in exchange!

At this point the reader might rightly wonder about the dissolution of the Standard Oil Trust in 1911. Didn't the Supreme Court find Standard guilty of successfully employing anti-competitive practices?

Interestingly, a careful reading of the decision reveals that no attempt was made by the Court to examine Standard's conduct or performance. The justices did not sift through the conflicting evidence concerning any of the government's allegations against the company. No specific finding of guilt was made with regard to those charges. Although the record clearly indicates that "prices fell, costs fell, outputs expanded, product quality improved, and hundreds of firms at one time or another produced and sold refined petroleum products in competition with Standard Oil,"[17] the Supreme Court ruled against the company. The justices argued simply that the competition between some of the divisions of Standard Oil was less than the competition that existed between them when they were separate companies before merging with Standard!

In 1915, Charles W. Eliot, president of Harvard, observed: "The organization of the great business of taking petroleum out of the earth, piping the oil over great distances, distilling and refining it, and distributing it in tank steamers, tank wagons, and cans all over the earth, was an American invention."[18] Let the facts record that the great Standard Oil Company, more than any other firm, and John D. Rockefeller, more than any other man, were responsible for this amazing development.

---

[17] Armentano, *Myths of Antitrust*, p. 83.
[18] Fite and Reese, *An Economic History*, p. 366.

When We Are Free

CHAPTER 45

In Defense of Profits

by Timothy G. Nash

Here is an old story with an important message. It is entitled, "I'm for People, not for Profit."

Once upon a time there was a Little Red Hen who scratched about and uncovered some grains of wheat. She called her barnyard neighbors and said, "If we work together and plant this wheat we will have some fine bread to eat. Who will help me plant the wheat?"

"Not I," said the Cow. "Not I," said the Duck. "Not I," said the Goose. "Then I will," said the Little Red Hen and she did.

After the wheat started growing, the ground turned dry and there was no rain in sight. "Who will help me water the wheat?" said the Little Red Hen.

"Not I," said the Cow. "Not I," said the Duck. "Not I," said the Pig. "Equal rights," said the Goose. "Then I will," said the Little Red Hen and she did.

The wheat grew tall and ripened into golden grain. "Who will help me reap the wheat?" asked the Little Red Hen.

"Not I," said the Cow. "Not I," said the Duck. "Out of my classification," said the Pig. "I'd lose my ADC," said the Goose. "Then I will," said the Little Red Hen and she did.

When it came time to grind the flour, "Not I," said the Cow. "I'd lose my unemployment compensation," said the Duck.

When it came time to bake the bread, "That's overtime for me," said the Cow. "I'm a dropout and never learned how," said the Duck. "I'd lose my welfare benefits," said the Pig. "If I'm the only one helping, that's discrimination," said the Goose.

"Then I will," said the Little Red Hen — and she did.

She baked five loaves of fine bread and held them up for her neighbors to see.

"I want some," said the Cow. "I want some," said the Duck. "I want some," said the Pig. "I demand my share!" said the Goose.

"No," said the Little Red Hen. "I can rest for awhile and eat the five loaves myself."

"Excess profits!" cried the Cow. "Capitalistic leech!" screamed the Duck. "Company fink!" grunted the Pig. "Equal rights!" screamed the Goose.

And they hurriedly painted picket signs and marched around the Little Red Hen singing, "We shall overcome." And they did.

For when the Farmer came to investigate the commotion, he said, "You must not be greedy, Little Red Hen. Look at the oppressed Cow. Look at the disadvantaged Duck. Look at the underprivileged Pig. Look at the less-fortunate Goose. You are guilty of making second-class citizens of them."

"But — but — but — I earned the bread." said the Little Red Hen.

"Exactly," the wise farmer said. "That is the wonderful free enterprise system; anybody in the barnyard can earn as much as he wants. You should be happy to have this freedom; in other barnyards, you would have to give all five loaves to the Farmer. Here you only have to give four loaves to your suffering neighbors."

The Little Red Hen obliged and walked away in silence . . . .

It has been some time since the Farmer's lecture. The barnyard is now dilapidated, the animals are always hungry, and the Little Red Hen, well, she left some time ago.

The hostility toward the Little Red Hen's success was based on greed and ignorance. Today, those who defend the profit motive face the same obstacles. Too many people are either envious of a profitable business, and/or just don't understand profit.

We Should Be Thankful for Profit

We are awakened in the morning by an alarm clock which was made for a profit. Practically everything we come into contact with from that moment on was made by people seeking profit.

The breakfast we eat, the clothes we wear, the house we live in, are all made possible by profit.

The car we drive to work, our jobs, our paychecks, are all based on profit.

The lunches and dinners we eat outside the home are made possible only because someone can prepare them at a profit. The trip to the amusement park, or that late night snack; once again, profit.

In the free world, most of our wants and needs from vacations in the Bahamas, to blankets for babies, are made possible by profit.

Profit makes the world go round!

Profit in a free economy is the reward for satisfying the consumer with a product or service. It is awarded to the producer by the customer through his patronage.

Profits in a free market economy are a barometer of efficiency. More efficient companies will earn larger profits. The companies that are making a profit will grow; they will continue to find new ways to offer the public what it wants at the lowest possible price. The individuals who earn profits must never forget that competition — actual and potential — threatens at all times to take those profits away. The profit-seeker must keep mistakes to a minimum or the consumer will take his business elsewhere. This is the idea of "consumer sovereignty."

We consumers decide whether Exxon, General Motors, or any other firm, will be successful from year to year. If producers do not satisfy the consumer, they will be here today but gone tomorrow. Their profits will turn into losses. The consumer is hard to please and does not settle for second best.

It is quite clear that in a truly free market, the customer is king. The producer is his servant and only if the servant serves competently will royalty (the consumer) bestow upon him profit.

The Alleged Evils of Profit

It is common today to read in the newspapers across the land that corporations are unfeeling entities who don't care about the employees. Their only goal is profit. Professor Ludwig Von Mises, in an article, "The Elite Under Capitalism," examines this charge: "If one deplores the businessman's unfeeling preoccupation with profit-seeking, one has to realize two things. First, that this attitude is prescribed to the entrepreneur by the consumers who are not prepared to accept any excuse for poor service. Secondly, that it is precisely this neglect of the 'human angle' that prevents arbitrariness and partiality from affecting the employer-employee nexus."[1]

Another argument commonly presented (by people who do not understand profit) is that "Business must be limited to a fair profit." These people will organize consumer groups to lobby in Washington in order to convince the bureaucracy to enact laws allowing only a fair profit. New regulations, windfall profits taxation, rebates, are all byproducts of this mentality. Just what is a "fair" profit, meanwhile, is never clearly explained.

One industry that has suffered greatly, as have its customers, from this narrow view, is the oil industry. The average return on profits in all of manufacturing has been about 5.5%, or 5.5 cents on every dollar of sales. When oil profits recently went from 4.5 cents

---

[1] Ludwig von Mises, "The Elite Under Capitalism," *The Freeman*, January 1962.

on the dollar (below the average for all manufacturing), in the third quarter of 1978 to 6.5% on the dollar in a later quarter, the media depicted this as an astronomical percentage increase.

A most flagrant example of this was when a news commentator announced one evening that the profits of Amerada Hess, an oil company, had risen 290% from 3rd quarter 1978 to 3rd quarter 1979. What the broadcaster failed to include was that Amerada Hess had had a dismally low 3rd quarter profit margin in 1978 of 2.7% on sales. It had subsequently managed to raise profits to 7.6% on sales by third quarter 1979. Amerada Hess did not even make 8 cents on the sales dollar and yet that night the public heard "Amerada Hess had increased profits by 290% in just one year."

It is when facts and figures are thus twisted and used against them that many businessmen must wonder if it might be better to place all their assets in Treasury bills that pay 12% (or better), and go on permanent vacation.

It is time people realize that the only fair system is the market system. All that any person is entitled to in the market place — businessman or wage earner — is what others will offer in willing exchange. If both parties to an exchange did not expect to benefit, the exchange simply would not happen.

Profit-Seeking Businessmen

Adam Smith put the actions of profit-seeking businessmen into proper perspective in his classic work, *The Wealth of Nations*: "By directing that industry in such a manner as its produce may be of the greatest value, he intends only his own gain . . . . He is in this, as in many other cases, led by an invisible hand to promote an end which was no part of his intention . . . . By pursuing his own interests, he frequently promotes that of the society more efficiently than when he really intends to promote it."

John D. Rockefeller was a successful businessman at an age when most men of today would be in college. Rockefeller was considered a greedy "robber baron," who took risks only because there was a potential for profit; the result being the Standard Oil Corporation. Even if it is true that Rockefeller was motivated by greed, so what! For every thousand dollars J. D. Rockefeller spent on himself, he spent hundreds of thousands creating jobs and providing the consumer with the best product at the lowest possible cost.

Henry Ford, driven by the desire for profit, built a great American "empire." But when Ford became complacent and adopted the theory that the consumer should have any color of car he wanted, "as long as it was black," he attracted the competition of other profit-seekers. Alfred P. Sloan, head of General Motors, felt he could increase sagging profits and put GM back on its feet by offering the consumer a quality car in a choice of colors on easy credit terms. The public loved the idea and within a few years, General Motors was the country's largest manufacturer of automobiles. It has been that way ever since. So it is that profit is not only a reward for services rendered to the consumer, but an incentive to compete as well.

A Lesson to be Learned

William E. Simon explains the role of our profit-seeking *Entrepreneurial* Founding Fathers, in this excerpt from *A Time For Truth*: "Productivity and the growth of productivity must be the *first* economic consideration at all times; not the last. That is the source of technological innovation, jobs and wealth. This means that profits needed for investment must be considered a great social blessing, not a social evil."[2]

We can learn an important lesson from the Industrial Revolution. The United States of America rose to greatness on the strength of the profit motive. In 1749, death from disease and malnutrition claimed over 50% of children before the age of five. Today, because of the science and the production made possible by profit, America has an infant death rate that is a fraction of a percent. We have goods and services and a standard of living that people would not have conceived of in their wildest imagination two hundred years ago — all because of the lure of profit.

Today, we are at a crossroads; we will decide whether America will continue to be the land of opportunity and growth or a stagnant, decaying, once-great has-been.

I am convinced that if we strive to be like the Little Red Hen instead of emulating the Cows, Ducks, Pigs, and Geese of this land, America will once again be great.

Personally, I cast my vote for profit, *because* I'm for people.

---

[2]William E. Simon, *A Time For Truth* (New York: Reader's Digest Press, McGraw-Hill Book Company, 1978), p. 219.

When We Are Free

CHAPTER 46

Who Conserves Our Resources?

by Ruth Shallcross Maynard

"Who should conserve our resources?" If a poll were taken, a large majority probably would answer: "Our federal and state governments." And if one were to ask why this view is so widely held, he would find among other "reasons" the following:

(1) that the free market is chaotic, gives profits to the few, and is unmindful of the great "waste" of our diminishing limited resources;
(2) that "people's rights" are above "private or special interests" and only the government can properly serve the public interest;
(3) that government has access to more funds;
(4) that government has the power and facilities to obtain all the necessary data and to do the research needed for the best "scientific" decisions on resource conservation;
(5) that the price system does not operate in the interests of conservation because of the "unrestrained pursuit of self-interest;"
(6) that the concentration of power in some corporations further threatens our dwindling resources and must be regulated by government.

Refuting the "Reasons"

These "reasons," of course, do not indicate how a government agency would go about attempting a solution to the conservation problem — this is always just assumed — but consider them briefly:

(1a) The free market is anything but chaotic. Competing natural market forces reflect in prices the wishes of both buyers and sellers — millions of individuals, separately accountable and responsible for their own actions in their own field of economic activity. All persons seek their own advantage when allowed a choice,

---

From *The Freeman*, July 1962, with appropriate updating of figures.

but in the free market a producer cannot profit unless he pleases consumers better than his competitor does. Since he must think of efficiency and lowered costs in order to survive, it is false to assume that he alone profits from the use of natural resources from which are made the products wanted by consumers. All gain who use the resulting products.

(2a) Can there be "people's rights" superior to the rights of individuals? All individuals have special and private interests and rights. Therefore, the "people" cannot have rights except individually; and the right to life carries with it the right to maintain it by private and special means.

(3a) The government has no funds that have not been taken from the people by force, whereas many a large private undertaking has come forth from voluntarily contributed funds. In fact, the entire industrial development in this country has been a continuous example of this voluntary way of creating the facilities for production by giving the consumer what he wants at the price he is willing to pay in competition.

(4a) Offhand it would seem that a government might have access to more data about scarce resources than would a private enterpriser. But government cannot bring forth the detailed information so vital to sound decision. The kind of detailed knowledge needed simply isn't "given to anyone in its totality," as Hayek has pointed out.[1] "Knowledge of the circumstances of which we must make use never exists in concentrated or integrated form," he states, "but solely as dispersed bits of incomplete and frequently contradictory knowledge which all the separate individuals possess." Yet, producers need such information before they can decide how to act. The chief communicator of this knowledge is free price movements. If the price of a given resource continues upward, this tells producers all they need to know about its increasing scarcity and signals them to conserve it, to use it sparingly and for the most valuable products. Advocates of government planning never seem to grasp how this works, for they are constantly tampering with market forces, distorting the delicate price signals that could otherwise guide them. Thus, government planners must rely on using *general* data obtained by crude polling methods which are unreliable for action in specific economic areas and are out of date before they can be collected, analyzed, and summarized. Moreover, such studies cannot tell the government controller as much as free price movements tell individuals acting in a particular market as buyers or sellers.

---

[1] F. A. Hayek, "The Use of Knowledge in Society," *The American Economic Review*, Vol. XXXV, No. 4, September 1945.

(5a) The role that prices play in the free economy is so little understood that many people believe government must set prices lest they reflect only the "selfish interests" of the producers. The price system not only tells producers and consumers when scarcity of a product exists (prices rise) or when it has become more plentiful (prices drop); it also supplies the incentive to act in the interests of conservation by seeking a substitute for the high-priced scarce material. Competitive prices allocate scarce resources to those who will *pay* more (not those who *have* more, as is alleged) for the right to try to serve consumers efficiently and profitably.

(6a) If concentration of power in corporations is too great to be permitted, what about the ultimate concentration of power in a government institution beyond the regulation of market forces? Government is unaccountable in the sense that it is not obliged to please consumers in order to stay in business. If it does not show a profit, its losses can be covered by tax money. Big corporations can behave in monopolistic fashion only if they enjoy government privileges of some kind. Potential competition, substitution, and elasticity of demand force them to keep prices close to the competitive level.[2]

When Government Controls

The foregoing arguments, however, do not touch upon the basic problem involved in the conservation of resources. Let us assume that Congress passes a conservation law setting up "The Federal Bureau of Conservation." Tax money must then be appropriated for this bureau. The director, a political appointee, must find a building and hire a staff large enough to justify his salary. To investigate and collect data on what is being done is a time-and tax-consuming job.

Turning the conservation problems over to an agency with police power does not mean solution, however. It only means that the director has been given the authority to find a solution and to force it on those individuals who are in the market for natural resources. This does not assure the public that the director has any special grant of wisdom concerning the problems involved, or that he will even know what they are. This appointment would lead him to assume that individual enterprisers were not doing their jobs well. He would undoubtedly define his task as one of finding what individual enterprisers are doing wrong and stopping it. Such interference could only prevent private individuals from utilizing their

---

[2] Hans Sennholz, "The Phantom Called Monopoly," *The Freeman*, March 1960.

creativity and energy in seeking a solution to both immediate and long-run conservation problems. Having stopped this flow of creative endeavor, he would need to find a "positive" solution — such as stockpiling by force certain quantities of those materials deemed most scarce.

Difficult Decisions

But for whom would the director be stockpiling? Would he sacrifice the present generation to future ones? And, if so, which ones? The next generation, the one after that, those living a hundred years from now, or whom? And how could he possibly know what those generations would want or need? Moreover, he would have the problem of what quantities to stockpile and what grades (best or worst) to save. Would some items have alternative uses? Would he plan for possible added or new uses in the future? These questions never seem to be asked by the authors of books and articles on conservation, whose specialty is to condemn private enterprise.

Stockpiling only aggravates the very scarcity given as the reason for stockpiling. The more scarce a stockpiled item, the higher the price, and the more complaints to be heard from the users. Whereupon, the director probably would seek power to fix prices lower than market levels. This, of course, could only lead to increased demand and pressure on prices, leading to black markets or government rationing, or both. Allocation by rationing would present the problem of whom to favor and whom to slight. His authority to discriminate would subject the director to strong political pressures. If not by political favoritism, the director could select by personal preference, or first come, first favored. Any system is discriminatory. The system of government planning implies arbitrary discrimination by one man with police power who decides who shall get what. Without personal favoritism, the free market "discriminates" *against* those who would waste scarce materials — it lets their businesses fail — and "discriminates" *for* those who would most efficiently use the resource to serve consumers — their profit depends on their capacity to conserve the scarce resource.

The government system is based on arbitrary decisions of man over man, with strong probability of political influence; the free market system is influenced by nonpolitical and nonpersonal forces. There is no other alternative. The first system leads to static conditions which cannot meet the changing needs and desires of consumers, the "people" most involved and presumably those whom a conservation agency ought to protect. The business way encourages search for substitutes when price rises indicate growing scarcity. This not only aids conservation but also affords the consuming public more reasonably priced alternatives in times of scarcity. When prices are fixed below market levels by the government director, this discourages conservation and gives a false signal as to the degree of scarcity all the way from the natural resource level to the final consumer.

Private Enterprisers Conserve What Is Worth Saving

Until someone discovers that a resource has a specific use, it has no value for which it should be conserved. Alexander the Great had no use for the reservoir of oil beneath his domain. The underdeveloped countries do not lack resources. But they have not yet found the key (personal saving and competitive private enterprise) by which to utilize the resources to meet the people's needs. Private enterprisers are constantly trying to find new materials and new uses for known resources, always looking ahead to see which ones will be available and how efficiently they can be utilized. Pick up any trade journal and note the articles on how to cut costs, utilize waste materials, be more efficient. Because the government told them to? No. The hope of profits acts as a powerful compulsion to be efficient, to improve, to conserve. The following examples show how private enterprisers eliminate waste and utilize natural resources to meet the needs of the consuming public.

Until natural gas was known to be useful as a fuel, petroleum producers burned it to get rid of it. Until ways were found of storing and transporting gas with safety, it had only local use. Competition forced the search for further uses and wider markets, and profits rewarded those who best served consumers. As ways were found to handle gas beyond local markets, consumers elsewhere gained a wider choice of fuel, and other fuels were thereby conserved.

Reliance on Hindsight

Accusations of waste in private industry are always based on hindsight. Any statistics of inadequate use of natural resources are history. When a new method or new use is discovered, it is easy to point out past waste and misuse. The assumption is that industrialists are wasteful if they haven't seen in advance all possible uses for all materials.

The meat-packing industry over the last century has used all but the squeal of the pig. But this did not come all at once. Nor did or could it have come from government decrees. It came slowly through individual efforts to cut costs and increase profits in competition with others.

In the lumber and pulp-paper industries, uses have been found for virtually all of a tree, including the bark, branches, and sawdust which were formerly "wasted." The "waste" lignin, after removal of the carbohydrates, has been the concern of many a pulp company as well as scientists at The Institute of Paper Chemistry, who have yet to find a use that will meet adequately the competitive market test of consumer choice.

With the increasing scarcity of pure water, the pulp and paper industry has used less and less of it per ton of product. When wood became scarce in Wisconsin, the "Trees-for-Tomorrow" program was instigated, encouraging farmers to grow trees as an added cash crop. As salt cake from Saskatchewan grew scarce, the Southern kraft-pulp mills learned how to reclaim it and cut the amount needed per ton of pulp by two-thirds or more. Could such a conservation measure have been forced by government decree? It is most doubtful.

In the agricultural field are many illustrations of continuous improvement: of tools (the history of the plow alone would make an impressive volume); of methods of utilizing land, fertilizers, insecticides, and seeds; of knowledge of genetics, hydroponics, and radioactive materials. All of these have played a vital part in getting better farm products to the people with fewer manhours and at less cost. These all conserve time.

Time also is a resource. Conserving time can save lives from starvation, give relief from backbreaking jobs, enable individuals to further achieve their respective purposes. Improved tools have won time for more leisure, for increasing recreational, cultural, educational, and religious activities.

Individual Improvement

Improvement of the well-being of individuals, rather than conservation, is the chief goal in the utilization of resources. Absolute conservation could lead to the absurdity of not utilizing our resources at all, and thus conserving to no purpose — no freedom and no improvement of our lives. J. S. Mill has expressed it thus: "The only unfailing and permanent source of improvement is liberty, since by it there are as many possible independent centers of improvement as there are individuals." The energy of the police force of a government agency must by its very nature be negative. Enterprisers are positive, constantly trying to solve specific problems. It is impossible to force the release of the creative energy of millions of individuals who, if free, are each highly motivated to release it in trying to improve their status. Thus, force only inhibits the real sources of improvement.

Because individuals have been free to find the best use of land resources, the American farmer today feeds himself and at least 40 others. In our early history food production was the principal occupation, and in some countries today as high as 90 per cent of the population still spends long hours of backbreaking work farming for a bare subsistence.

Who Is Responsible for Waste?

The real waste in resources comes from government policies. It is seen especially in wartime, but more and more in peacetime programs. The government farm program has encouraged waste of land, seeds, fertilizers, labor, and capital by subsidizing the production of surpluses to be stored in bins that dot the countryside. The foreign aid program has wasted various resources, sending them to countries where little if any use has been or could be made of them. Waste occurs in such projects as the TVA that floods permanently many fertile acres which formerly provided millions of dollars worth of food products and which the Army Engineers have estimated would not be flooded by the natural forces of the Tennessee River in 500 years.

Rising taxes also promote waste. The corporate income tax of 46 per cent of earnings, for example, encourages industrialists to engage in questionable and wasteful projects which appear justified only when purchased with a 54-cent dollar. This is not in the interests of conservation.

However, the errors individuals make and their waste of resources are small and inconsequential compared with those made by government agents in controlling a major supply of a scarce resource. Those in civil service positions are rarely dismissed or otherwise held accountable for their errors. A private individual stands to lose personally if he wastes resources in his field of economic activity, and has a built-in motivation for attempting to correct his mistakes as soon as they are reflected in rising costs or decreasing demand. A government agent, however, risks no personal loss when he misuses resources, he cannot recognize mistakes by rising costs when prices are fixed arbitrarily, nor is he motivated to correct his mistakes even when recognized.

Natural resources are best utilized and conserved where they meet specific economic requirements in the most efficient way as determined by competition in the free market. Government control of natural resources reduces the freedom of choice of producers in using these materials and this affects adversely the freedom of choice of consumers who buy the final products made from them. There is no effective method of determining the economic requirements of the people when the free market is not allowed to reflect them, nor can force solve the problem of conservation. It is a false panacea that is centuries old, advocated by those who desire power over others whom they neither trust nor respect. Conservation will take place in the best sense where individuals are allowed to seek solutions to their own personal problems as they arise. Necessity is the mother not only of invention but of conservation as well.

CHAPTER 47

The Economics and Politics of Discrimination

by George C. Leef

It is widely believed that capitalism, to the extent that it is still allowed to function, is responsible for our problem of racial discrimination. Blacks, Hispanics, and other ethnic groups are seen to be "underutilized" by business, and therefore many people conclude that the cause must be that businessmen are guilty of racial discrimination. Having arrived at this conclusion, the solution is simple and obvious: Merely compel businesses to hire more individuals from these groups. Mandate "affirmative action" programs, "goals" or quotas in hiring and promotion, enforce these with a federal bureaucracy and the courts, and everything will be fair and equal. A closer examination will show, however, that racial discrimination, far from being caused by capitalism, is in fact the result of governmental interferences with capitalism. We shall see that the proper response to the problems of blacks and other ethnic minorities in society is not more governmental coercion, but to eliminate that which we now have.

Businessmen are in business to make money. They are engaged in a continuous struggle to increase revenues and decrease costs. The first crucial point we must grasp is that racial discrimination imposes costs upon businessmen who practice it. For example, purchasing decisions are generally made upon the criteria of least cost and best service. If a businessman refuses to deal with a black supplier who could offer the lowest price and/or best service, he has imposed additional costs upon himself. Similarly, to refuse to hire qualified persons because of their skin color means that the businessman must devote more time and resources to searching for a person to fill the job, and perhaps having to settle for a less well qualified candidate.

The Price of Prejudice

Not many businessmen prefer prejudice to profits. As economist Milton Friedman puts it, "A businessman or an entre-

From *The Freeman*, February 1981

preneur who expresses preferences in his business activities that are not related to productive efficiency is at a disadvantage compared to other individuals who do not. Such an individual is in effect imposing higher costs on himself than are other individuals who do not have such preferences. Hence, in a free market, they will tend to drive him out." (*Capitalism and Freedom*, pp. 109-110)

In theory, therefore, we would expect to find little discrimination in a free market because of the self-interest of businessmen. This theory finds strong support from historical evidence. First, the Jim Crow laws of the states of the South specified that certain jobs in industry could be done only by white workers. But if the industrialists were intent upon discriminating, why did this preference have to be enacted into law? The answer is that to preserve the status of the white worker, there had to be a legal restraint upon employers. In the absence of the law, competition from nondiscriminating employers would have urged all to hire and promote blacks and whites on the basis of economic value, not race.

A second piece of evidence comes to us from South Africa, and again shows the power of business competition to reduce racial discrimination. The reason for the adoption of the policy of Apartheid in the 1930s was that white workers were incensed that so many blacks were being hired and were competing with them in pay and promotions. Therefore, they persuaded the government to restrict the better-paying jobs to whites only. Once more, we see that business was the enemy of discrimination, government the cause.

Further evidence on the relationship between capitalism and discrimination is found in the considerable affluence many "free persons of color" in the antebellum South were able to achieve. These were free blacks who had no political power at all, but could own property and do business as they wished. For example, in pre-Civil War New Orleans, free Negroes owned one-fifth of the total taxable property in the city. (*Race and Economics* by Thomas Sowell, p. 40) Thus, even while the government discriminated against these people, according them no political power, capitalism gave them economic power restricted only by their abilities to satisfy the wants of consumers.

Conditions Have Changed

Next, let us examine the experience of other ethnic groups which have migrated to the urban centers of the United States in search of economic progress. Jews, Italians, Chinese, Irish, Japanese, and many others settled here and were usually despised and subjected to legal harassment for decades after their arrival. Nevertheless, members of these groups have been highly successful in moving into the mainstream, and frequently into the highest strata of American life. Discrimination did not keep them depressed. Why were they able to advance whereas today's bottom-of-the-ladder minorities seem to be permanently stuck there? Have conditions changed in some way which would explain the difference? The answer is yes.

The great influx of blacks into the cities began after World War II. Prior to that time, most of the country's black population had lived on farms in the rural South. With the movement to the cities, the process of economic advancement began for the majority of the black population, just as it had for the Jews, Italians, Chinese and others in the previous century. What factors are militating against blacks now that did not hinder the progress of the earlier groups? A rather large number of such factors could be identified, but I wish to concentrate on three of the most significant.

Minimum Wage Laws

The first difference to which we can point is the existence of minimum wage laws. The minimum wage came into existence as a part of the Fair Labor Standards Act, passed during the New Deal. It sets a wage floor below which an employer may not pay. The stated reason for this law was to raise the income of poor workers. (The real reason was that labor union leaders hoped that it would stifle competition from lower-wage areas, such as the South. For this reason, the minimum wage bears a kinship to the Jim Crow laws discussed above.) What the legislators either did not see or chose to ignore is that the amount of one's pay depends upon his economic value to his employer. If the law says that you, the employer, cannot pay anyone less than $2.00 per hour, you are not going to hire people who, because of lack of skills and work experience, cannot produce at least $2.00 worth of revenue per hour for you.

What the minimum wage does, then, is to prevent people from getting a start. It prevents a person from going to an employer and saying, "I know I don't have any job skills, and I don't have a work record to prove my reliability, but I'm willing to start at a low wage. All I would like is a chance." That is exactly how the earlier immigrant groups began their climb up the economic ladder; but today that option is gone. Because they cannot find work, millions of young blacks, Hispanics, and others remain unemployed and unemployable. Frequently they turn to crime; if not, a life of indolence on welfare awaits them. It is not capitalism that caused this. It is the government.

New Businesses Thwarted

A second reason why economic advancement is more difficult today than it was for ethnic groups in the past is the obstacles which have been placed in the way of entrepreneurs who desire to open businesses. In the last century, one of the chief sources of employment for newly-arrived Jews, Italians, Chinese, and others, was in small businesses started by other members of their own ethnic group. Opening a bakery, tailor shop, or laundry was easy. If you could come up with the monthly rent, you could get a store-front location; if you wanted to hire someone, you simply put him on the payroll. There were virtually no government regulations, licenses, taxes, or inspectors.

Things are vastly different today, of course. The would-be entrepreneur is now faced with a maze of costly paperwork, usually requiring the high-priced services of lawyers and accountants before he can even make his first sale. There are also numerous taxes which he must collect and pay, and volumes of regulations with which he must comply. No wonder that more than 80 per cent of new businesses fail every year, and that many who might have attempted to start new businesses are deterred by the slim prospects for success. So here is a second reason why economic advancement is more difficult today — the hindrance of small business. Is this the fault of capitalism? No. It is the fault of government.

Educational Shortcomings

Lastly, let us consider education. In the previous century, schools concentrated on the "3R's." The student who completed work at even the junior high school level was equipped with the language and math skills he needed to function in the business world. Jewish immigrants made particularly good use of the educational opportunities available to them, quickly rising in such verbal-oriented professions as banking and the law. In contrast, what can we say about the possibilities of learning the language and math skills one needs to succeed in business today? It is close to impossible to learn them in the typical inner-city school. The environment in such schools is not conducive to learning, replete with disturbances and distractions from students who are there only because they are forced to attend.

Even without the problems of violence, unruliness, apathy, and drugs, it would still be nearly impossible for today's inner-city high school student to learn the skills needed in business, for the simple reason that those skills are not being taught. The public education bureaucracy no longer attaches much importance to such matters as precision in speech and writing. Rather than teach the mental discipline necessary for intelligible sentence structure and critical analysis of written passages, contemporary "English" courses usually revolve around getting the student to express how he "feels" about something he has attempted to read. Young people routinely graduate from such schools without even the reading and writing skills of the third grader of the nineteenth century. Is business to be blamed for not hiring as insurance adjustors people who have great trouble in reading and writing reports, or not hiring as cost accountants people who struggle with addition and subtraction? Clearly not. The blame is to be placed upon the government which runs the public education monopoly.

The foregoing analysis has discussed only a few of the important ways in which the government has made it difficult for blacks and other groups now attempting to improve their economic condition to do so. The elimination of these governmentally-erected barriers to progress is the only true solution. The minimum wage should be repealed. The plethora of taxes, regulations, and paperwork which now prevent the formation of small businesses should be swept away. The monopoly which public schools enjoy ought to be broken through the granting of tuition tax credits to parents who choose to send their children to private schools. Eventually, tax-supported schools should be phased out completely. This is the course of action which will enable minority group members to develop and sell the skills for which businesses compete.

Why Coercive Affirmative Action Programs Cannot Succeed

But what of the other "solution" to this problem, namely affirmative action programs to compel the hiring of minority group members? Should that policy not be used to speed the process? The answer is no, for three reasons.

First, to compel an employer to hire according to government dictates violates the employer's freedom of contract and association. Good ends do not justify bad means.

Second, it is no favor to the unqualified individual to obtain a job in which he will be constantly pressured and frustrated by his lack of preparation for it.

Third, the history of governmental activism on behalf of specified minority groups leads one to conclude that this course makes matters worse rather than better. The economist Thomas

Sowell has pointed out that economic advances for blacks have slowed or retrogressed during periods of greatest governmental efforts to assist them. (*Race and Economics*, pp. 51-55) Moreover, Sowell also finds that there is an inverse relationship between the extent of a group's economic progress and the extent of its political power. Blacks, Irish, and American Indians, groups which have relied heavily upon political power to improve their conditions, have advanced the most slowly, while Jews and Orientals, who never had much political power and thus had to rely upon their individual abilities, have done by far the best. Therefore, either by diverting attention from the true solutions, arousing antagonism, or both, the current policy of governmental activism is likely to make matters worse.

Let Self-Interest Take Its Course in the Open Market

In this brief essay, I have argued that the belief that racial discrimination is the fault of prejudice-blinded businessmen who refuse to hire minority group members is entirely wrong. There is probably no institution in society where color is as irrelevant as in the free market. In the commercial world, making money is what counts, and discrimination gets in the way of doing that. Many ethnic groups have come to this country and met poverty and prejudice. In the past, such people were able to advance economically by acquiring the skills which made them valuable to businessmen. Unfortunately, conditions are different now. Due to a variety of governmental actions, those ethnic groups which are presently attempting to rise in the economy have had the deck stacked against them. Instead of following the foolish course of believing that the way to rectify the undesirable results of past governmental interferences with freedom is through yet more interferences with freedom, we must see that the only escape from our difficulties is to let freedom work. Do so, and a lot of self-interested businessmen will make short work of racial discrimination.

CHAPTER 48

"Am I My Brother's Keeper?"

by William Henry Chamberlin

Is there sound warrant for assuming the moral superiority of a collectivist to an individualist economic system, for imparting religious sanction to welfare state policies?

The answer is No.

All the great religious and ethical systems emphasize the moral obligations of compassion and charity: the virtue that accrues when an individual foregoes a part of his wealth to help someone less fortunate or to promote some desirable cause in such fields as education, health, and general well-being. Incidentally, Americans, sometimes dismissed as materialistic, have been more responsive to this kind of moral appeal than any people in the world. Nowhere is there a quicker and warmer response to the call for relief from distress. There is nothing in Europe to compare with the Rockefeller, Carnegie, and Ford Foundations; nowhere have men of wealth shown such willingness voluntarily to give up a vast share of their wealth.

Nor is there any parallel to the number of American colleges and universities which owe their existence to private donations, not to state aid but to the generosity with which such institutions are supported by their alumni and friends. Nor is American willingness to extend the boundaries of health and education restricted to the boundaries of the United States. In far-off cities which few Americans have ever seen, in Istanbul, Beirut, Teheran, Salonika, colleges and schools founded by American initiative and supported to a considerable extent by American contributions have broadened considerably the educational opportunities in the countries where they are located.

The Far East was a prominent field of American missionary effort, with important educational and health by-products. This is still true as regards Japan and Taiwan. China, before the communist take-over, was dotted with American-founded colleges, schools, hospitals, research institutions; and the schools and colleges for

---

Excerpted from "Is God a Keynesian?" *The Freeman*, February 1965

many young Chinese eased the transition to study abroad in the United States and other foreign countries.

None of the Great Religions Endorses the Welfare State

Individual prosperity does pose moral challenges and Americans have met these challenges on a much larger scale than many European or Oriental peoples whose wealthier representatives are apt to let generosity stop at the limits of the family.

But where is the moral element when the state transforms taxation from an instrument of raising revenue into an instrument for reallocating income, for pillaging the thrifty for the benefit of the thriftless?

One will find in the Bible, in the Koran, in the writings of Buddha, Confucius, and other religious prophets, moralists, and sages many injunctions to practice charity and make voluntary sacrifices for the common good. What one does not find is any endorsement of a communist or collectivist form of society, anything that could reasonably be construed as a divine commandment in favor of the welfare state. On the contrary, the assumption is always that the individual enjoys enough of the fruits of his own labor to be able to share these, in one form or another, with those less fortunate.

And a very good case can be made, on moral as well as economic grounds, for a system in which the individual is required to stand on his own feet, not to lean on the state for handouts. Character, resourcefulness, capacity are formed and developed in struggle with obstacles, not in waiting passively for benefits from outside. Not the least of the causes of the juvenile delinquency which sometimes spills over into senseless and brutal riots is a sense of boredom, of having "nothing to do." This complaint could scarcely be voiced in earlier times when young people expected and were expected to earn their livelihoods, instead of having these furnished on a silver platter.

For the individual to be intelligently generous with his own money is a meritorious and enriching side of life in a free political and economic system. For designing politicians and empire-building bureaucrats to be generous with other people's money is something quite different. The more Federal, state, and local agencies exact in taxation, the more limited is the scope of private beneficence. And an individual gift is much more likely to be well spent than a government grant.

So, there is no warrant in logic or morals for trying to place the authority of religion behind measures of social and economic collectivism. Indeed, there is a much stronger case for arguing that the sense of individual responsibility — which is a key indispensable factor in making it possible for the individual to distinguish between right and wrong — is best assured under a system in which the human being is mainly committed to his own care and required to make his own decisions, instead of being shaped and molded in line with some scheme of bureaucratic planners.

Misinterpretation of Biblical Reference to "Brother's Keeper"

It has been said that the Devil can quote Scripture. And a biblical reference that is often used completely out of context, and for collectivist ends, is the reference in Genesis to "my brother's keeper." There is a widespread attempt to twist Cain's reply, "Am I my brother's keeper?" when Jehovah interrogates him about the whereabouts of his brother Abel, as a divine injunction of all human beings to play the role of "brother's keepers"; that is, to assume responsibility for and, by implication, direction of enormous numbers of strangers, from riotous juvenile delinquents at home to feuding cannibals in the Congo.

It should be noted that the use of the phrase in Genesis carries no such implication. "Am I my brother's keeper?" is not a divine injunction for all human beings. It is the guilty Cain, taking the Fifth Amendment when charged with murder. And the whole idea of men and nations playing in relation to each other the role of "brother's keeper" carries more than a little suggestion of condescension, even of insult. Among the dictionary definitions of the verb "keep" are "guard," "manage," "conduct," "detain," "confine" — a rather ominous series of connotations. A "keeper" may be a warden in a prison, a supervisor of animals in a zoo.

A person of spirit and independence would give the rough edge of his tongue to anyone who tried to play the role of "keeper" by intruding into the concerns of his private life. And this is just as true for nations as for men. There is something naive in the surprised distress with which some Americans receive the not infrequent news that a mob in the capital of some country which has been on the handout list for foreign aid has pulled down the American flag or smashed the handsome quarters of the United States information agency.

Foreign Aid Resented

Behind such episodes is often an element of communist instigation. But this is by no means the whole story. No matter how poor a people may be, they have an instinctive revulsion against the idea of being "kept" by another. Here is one psychological explanation of why American aid has so often been met by brickbats, not bouquets. Another irritant is the large number of Americans in diplomatic and related establishments and the visibly lavish style in which they live. The poorer and more undeveloped the country economically, the more noticeable is this sort of thing.

There has been much anguished discussion, with the aid of high-power psychology and opinion polls, of the question why Americans are not better liked abroad. One of the reasons, beyond reasonable doubt, is America's self-assumed role as "brother's keeper" for a vast number of peoples in foreign lands, many with profoundly different traditions, cultures, tastes, and habits. Even the most tactfully proffered advice can easily be resented as intrusion and interference; and the sudden injection of large numbers of free-spending Americans has sometimes created awkward financial and trade problems.

Looking back to the far-off days when the political systems and the economies of distant lands in Asia, Africa, and Latin America were regarded as the concern of the natives of those lands, when government-to-government grants were unknown, when Americans were content to invest and do business in countries where they were welcome and to stay away from those where they were not, when the United States Government considered its first task as one of protecting the security and legitimate interests of its citizens abroad, one wonders whether Americans were not just as well or perhaps better liked when their government was not trying to play beneficent Big Brother to the rest of the world. And behind this lies still another question.

Is it so important to be a winner in an international popularity contest? In the age of Britain's greatest international power and prestige, in the nineteenth century, there is no evidence that the British Government or individual traveling Britons cared very much about the "national image" or attached undue importance to the question whether they were liked or not.

Perhaps respect is a more reasonable and feasible goal than liking, which is sometimes least achieved when most pursued. No doubt many individual Americans have won esteem for themselves and, incidentally, for their country by striking out as pioneers of some new project in economic development, or health, or education in a foreign country. But there is precious little indication that the bureaucrats who shovel out foreign aid have won a place in the hearts of the natives of the countries to which they have been assigned.

The "brother's keeper" philosophy, with its false interpretation of Scripture, is just as inapplicable in dealings between individuals as in relations between nations. Meddlers in other people's affairs, however good their intentions, seldom win much thanks for their pains. Sometimes the theory of collective responsibility is carried to truly absurd lengths.

It was by no means common, after the assassination of President Kennedy, for orators in and out of pulpits to put forward the idea that the whole American people was responsible for this tragedy. This is sheer nonsense. According to all evidence collected by painstaking search of a government commission, supplemented by the private investigations of many journalists and publicists, a single unbalanced person conceived and executed the assassination, without accomplices, without instigation. How in the name of reason and common sense, can the whole American people be regarded as participants in the demented act of this person?

More Harm Than Good

Throughout history the efforts of religious spokesmen to take sides and pronounce judgments on secular, political and economic issues have probably wrought more harm than good. It is the primary function of religion to elevate the soul and improve the conduct of the individuals who respond to its teachings. There is no reason to assume that there is a divine sanction for any form of collectivist economics.

And an international society of self-respecting peoples and a national society of self-reliant individuals who would vigorously resent the idea that anyone had the right to act as their "keepers," are far more attractive than the idea of some individuals and some nations assuming the impossible and undesirable burden of minding everyone else's business. *No human being, no people worthy of its salt, has the slightest desire to submit to the ministrations, however benevolent in design, of a self-appointed "keeper."*

When We Are Free

Unit IX: Solving Problems in Freedom

Men and women have repeatedly proved that they can accomplish great things when left free. It is not possible to forecast future accomplishments in detail. But, because of the historical record that we have to go on, we can be confident that they will be vast — where there is human liberty.

Despite the excellent record of free people, however, some individuals seem unwilling to resist the temptation to endorse government's using a little of its force here and there to "solve" particular problems. Short-term personal gain and the desire to "do good" are probably the most common motives of these individuals. The authors of the six chapters in this unit examine various aspects of just a few of the great many occasions where some individuals have endorsed, and others have not successfully resisted, government intervention in our lives. But all of these authors come to the same conclusion: The offensive use of coercion *is not* the route to the betterment of humankind; liberty *is*.

Though many of us in the United States *profess* to favor freedom for all, there are probably more people who favor restricted immigration than who support unrestricted immigration into this country. In "Open the Doors!" Donald Carpenter makes the case for no restrictions, a policy clearly consistent with liberty.

Fortunately, our immigration policy did not keep Petr Beckmann, a 1963 immigrant from Czechoslovakia, out of the United States. Dr. Beckmann has added incalculably to our understanding of energy — a field where there presently seems to be much more heat than light. In his "Pages From U. S. Energy History," he pens this gem: "The successful resolution of the first American oil crisis was in no small measure due to a major contribution by the U. S. government: *It kept out of the way!*"

Whereas a policy of restricted immigration tends to reduce competition in many fields, the policies covered in "What to do about the Post Office," "Medicine and the State," and "Regulation — Political or Market?" reduce competition in specific fields. These three chapters deal with interference in the delivery of first class mail, medical care, and the installation of electrical apparatus, respectively.

United States Congressman Ron Paul from Texas is the author of the last chapter in this unit, "A Free Market Foreign Policy." In this piece Congressman Paul makes the case for a foreign policy of *"neutrality, with a policy of non-intervention in the internal affairs of other nations, plus all the armed strength necessary to protect America."* This is a foreign policy that is consistent with government strictly limited to a defense function. And it is a foreign policy that is consistent with maximum liberty for the people of this country.

A unit which sets out to do what this one does must be woefully inadequate to the task. Problems are certainly not scarce, but neither are the solutions, we believe, if we rely on that great "mainspring of human progress" — liberty. With a consistent application of its principles, liberty stands a better chance of resolving problems than any other societal arrangement — all the promises of the State notwithstanding.

CHAPTER 49

Open the Doors!

by Donald H. Carpenter

The immigration issue is one of the few before us today on which there is little division of opinion. Newspaper editorials vigorously attack the "illegal immigrant," politicians denounce him, and liberal and conservative columnists rail against him at great length. Civic organizations and labor leaders hold him responsible for social and economic problems across the board, from violent crime to drug dealing to rising prices to massive unemployment.

In the midst of this uproar, the immigrant can expect to find very few defenders. He has never been popular, if for no other reason than that he is different. And yet, recently, that unpopularity has been growing steadily, and the wariness and hatred of him has become more intense. As many of the consequences of government intervention, such as inflation, labor violence, and unemployment, become evident, a general frustration sets in. No one is willing to accept the blame, and a scapegoat must be found. The immigrant is not the only victim of this witch-hunt, but he is an outstanding example.

But underneath all the vicious verbal assaults, there are many good arguments for opening our borders and allowing *unrestricted immigration*. In the course of presenting those arguments, I will make no distinction between legal and illegal immigrants. The only reason we have so many *illegal* immigrants is because current restrictions are so tight that the number of persons who are allowed to immigrate legally is far below the total of those who actually wish to immigrate. So far below, in fact, that many decide to enter without regard for the law. How many enter illegally is anybody's guess, but some estimates run as high as 1 million per year.

The First Myth

Many myths exist concerning this subject, and one which needs to be discarded is that which says large-scale immigration causes unemployment. Organized labor is chiefly responsible for

---

From *New Guard,* July-August 1978

this fiction, which holds that foreigners often displace Americans from their jobs, and force them into idleness. Thus, pressure from organized labor contributed to the passage of the Chinese Exclusion Act of 1882, essentially the first immigration barrier in the United States, which forbade any Chinese entry into this country. Since then, labor leaders have been in the forefront of virtually every battle to restrict immigration, and have at times openly advocated shutting the borders completely, allowing no entry by any ethnic group.

Many factors contribute to unemployment, but perhaps the most important of these is government action which, directly or indirectly, forces wage rates above their free-market level. The most prominent example is probably the minimum wage, which forces many unskilled workers out of a job because their services are not worth the wage that employers would have to pay for them. Laws which grant labor unions a virtual monopoly on the sale of labor services, allowing them to restrict the supply of workers and gain special bargaining privileges in dealing with businesses, have the same general effect, although usually at a higher wage level. The workers who survive the slide into unemployment benefit from these policies, through higher wage rates, only at the expense of those who are forced into a lower-paying job or out of work completely.

Under these conditions, it is possible that massive immigration may aggravate the unemployment picture, but it is by no means the cause of the problem. In the free-market economy, other factors being equal, labor will tend to migrate to those areas where wage rates are highest, just as capital will tend to flow to areas where wages are low. Labor, like all other goods, is scarce, and therefore always in demand at its appropriate free-market price. As with any form of price control, attempts by government to impose artificially low or artifically high wage rates will always result in either a shortage, or a surplus, of labor.

Employee Selection

It is true that an immigrant may displace a native worker from a particular job, and this raises an interesting, and controversial question: Should a native worker be given preference in hiring over a foreign worker? Although the prevailing answer nowadays would be yes, I would have to say no. Within the borders of the United States, a native worker already has the freedom to move from city to city, or from state to state. He can move from the bayous of Louisiana to the Adirondacks in upstate New York, or from Seattle to Miami. He may be born to the owner of a small hardware store in Maine, but he can still migrate to Texas and work in the oil industry. Why should someone born in Mexico, Poland, or Japan be prevented from moving to, and working in, the United States?

I can see no rational justification for such a position. About the only rational criteria in employee selection is: Of what value is this person to the employer? What is he or she worth to the business? Worth, in this case, is not always measured purely in monetary terms.

The above point needs a bit of clarification. In the free-market economy, an employer may hire whomever he wishes, for whatever reason, whether the reason be rational or irrational. Thus, he may choose to hire only redheads, or Filipinos, or persons over six feet tall; on the other hand, he may choose to hire a mixture of persons based on his opinion of their value to his enterprise. To be consistent, therefore, any advocate of the free market must oppose laws which seek to tell an employer whom he can or cannot hire.

Three Other Arguments

As with unemployment, the charge made by some that immigrants commit a disproportionate number of crimes cannot be substantiated. Perhaps isolated groups of them will, but there is no reason for immigrants in general to do so. Like native Americans, each immigrant is a distinct individual who must be judged according to his own particular actions.

Many have said that the immigrants are a drain on the taxpayers, that they pay little in taxes while receiving free social services. Yet there is little to indicate this is true. For the most part, those who decide to immigrate are the most talented, the most educated, the most ambitious; they are anxious to get ahead in life and make something of themselves. In short, they are looking for a better life than was available to them in their homeland. They will benefit from their decision to immigrate, but so will the country which receives them, and it is high time to recognize that which is so obvious.

Many native Americans pay little or nothing in taxes, yet they live almost entirely off of government expenditures, or receive numerous government services. This is primarily the fault of our high taxation rates and bloated welfare programs, which subsidize leisure and penalize work. Under any system of taxation, some will necessarily be *tax-consumers*, paying less in taxes than they receive in expenditures and services; others will be *taxpayers*, paying more in taxes than they get from the government. If this condition did not exist, everyone would receive from the government exactly what he had paid in taxes, and there would be no justification for taxation.

Another charge brought against the immigrants is that they tend to cluster into distinct groups, to segregate themselves, according to nationality, from the rest of the population. This is probably true, but I suspect it has more to do with the attitudes of the natives toward the immigrants than vice versa. It is far less likely to happen in an open society, where immigrants are treated as equals and not looked down upon or discriminated against, simply because they were born in a foreign land. Education, over a period of time, is probably the only remedy for this problem, if indeed it is a problem. We still retain, in the United States, some remnants of a right of association (or disassociation, as the case may be).

Up to now I have tried to refute what I consider to be the major arguments against unrestricted immigration, and the reader must decide for himself whether or not I have done so in a convincing manner. For if there are no good reasons for opposing immigration, it logically follows that such opposition is an unworthy goal.

Reasons *For* Immigration

However, aside from criticisms of the opposing arguments, there are some very positive reasons for allowing unrestricted immigration.

First, there is the question of property rights. Suppose a person born in Mexico decides to immigrate to the United States. Suppose further that he finds someone who is willing to hire him, and someone else who will sell him shelter, either an apartment or a home. Doesn't it logically follow that any law or edict which prohibits this voluntary arrangement is in actuality a serious violation of property rights?

Just as price controls violate the rights of the businessman, by forcing him to sell his products below the market rate; just as the Social Security Act violates the rights of the individual workers, by requiring him to invest his earnings in an unsound financial system; so the immigration laws violate the rights of the person born in a foreign land, by preventing him from establishing his residence in this country and earning his livelihood here. To abolish restrictions on immigration would be a reassuring first step toward restoring our long eroded property rights.

Secondly, an influx of immigrants could provide a lift to the economy. As mentioned above, labor is scarce, and always in demand, at least in the free (or even semi-free) economy; thus, more workers means more production, more capital invested, and a greater division of labor. Greater competition among workers should bring labor prices, and ultimately consumer prices, down.

Labor leaders might object that this surge in competition might reduce the high wage rates enjoyed by union members, and they are probably right. But it is a curious moral doctrine which seeks to gain a great level of prosperity for one segment of the population, only at the expense of many others who are denied the same economic opportunities. This, of course, is why labor leaders not only oppose immigration, but also support a tightly restrictive entry policy for the unions, restrictive even for native American workers. In this regard, they are better economists than most people, at least in the short run. It is toward their peculiar brand of ethics that criticism must be directed.

Thirdly, immigration allows foreigners to escape from oppressive nations, be they Communist, socialist, fascist, or whatever. America, the land of opportunity, should welcome these refugees with open arms. The alternative is shutting the doors, thus condemning them to a life of sheer mental and physical torture, with death as the only way out.

One very fortunate consequence of this kind of immigration would be the weakening of the oppressive countries, since those most likely to immigrate are generally the most daring, the most able, the ones who will contribute the most to a free society. Our gain is the oppressor's loss. This simply cannot be ignored, especially today, when liberty is vanishing rapidly from almost every corner of the globe.

Finally, immigration adds variety to a community, in the form of new ideas, new cultural trends, new styles of living and working. Diversity is always good, provided one is free to pick and choose from among the various factors.

These are not the only reasons, of course, for allowing immigration, but they are the most important, because they deal with issues which touch us daily.

Immigrants are individuals, born in one country, who move to another in search of better conditions. Their reasons may be chiefly economic, political, or religious. Despite its faults, for most of them the United States still stands out as the land of promise. Can we afford to keep them out any longer?

When We Are Free

CHAPTER 50

Pages from U.S. Energy History

by Petr Beckmann

History floats on strange undercurrents that often go unrecognized for a considerable time.

Until quite recently, for example, historians did not ponder the puzzle of the conquest of Central and South America; yet it *was* a puzzle how Cortez, with less than 600 men, 17 horses and 10 cannon, was able to subdue the millions of the Aztec empire and (even more puzzling) make their religion utterly disappear. Moreover, it soon happened again in Peru, when Pizarro and a handful of Spaniards conquered the Inca empire.

By all the rules of logic, Montezuma should have had no difficulty in overpowering Cortez' little band and driving it out of Mexico City. As a matter of fact, on the night of June 30, 1520, he did; but he failed to follow up and annihilate the intruders. For this turn of events and the entire miraculous conquest of Central and South America, the Aztecs, Incas and Spaniards had the same explanation: The White Man's God was superior.

Couched in only slightly different terms, that was also, until quite recently, the explanation given by most historians. Thus, in *An Encyclopaedia of World History* (1952 edition), a Harvard professor writes: "The military triumphs of the Spaniards over incredible odds was the triumph of indomitable representatives of a more highly developed society over those of a lesser."

But what the indomitable representatives of a more highly developed society had left behind in Mexico City on that June night in 1520 was a smallpox epidemic, a disease to which the Spaniards had grown more resistant than the Indians who had never been exposed to it before. What marched before the *conquistadores* was not the White Man's superior God, but the germ of the smallpox.

Historians had, of course, always known about plagues and other epidemics; but they had simply taken them as random interruptions of the "normal" course of history. Only quite recently did historian W. H. McNeill pioneer the study of the circulation, pooling and evolution of diseases to investigate their *systematic* impact on history.[1]

Nothing nearly so dramatic is attempted in the following pages, which relate a handful of historical episodes involving the U.S. energy supply.

Yet it could be that energy sources are among the undercurrents of modern history that deserve more attention in interpreting its course.

Until modern times, of course, the main energy source was human and animal muscle power, both of which come from the food yielded by the land. To say that history revolved round "energy" in those days, therefore, is trivial. But with the rise of large-scale industries, particularly metal smelting, an increasing role was taken on by wood, coal, and water power. (That windmills never did amount to very much is one of history's unlearned lessons.)

In a round-about way, wood and coal were deeply involved in the founding of the American colonies.

A 17th Century Energy Crisis

If things always continued the way they start, this article would be written in Spanish or French, for the English (let alone Scots) made little effort to colonize America for the first 100 years after its discovery.

The Crown had done no more than lay claim to a part of Newfoundland after John Cabot's voyage in 1497-98, and even private Englishmen such as Sir Francis Drake or Sir Walter Raleigh preferred to extract gold and other goodies from homebound Spanish ships rather than from the continent itself; the few attempts at colonization (such as Roanoke Island in 1585) failed quite ingloriously.

Not until 1606 did the English crown grant a charter to the Virginia Company, a century after the Spanish and French crowns had been in the business of colonization.

What took them so long?

Not people's desire for religious freedom, or for adventure, or for starting a new life — these reasons had been there all along. But after defeating the Spanish Armada in 1588, England was able to turn to colonization because her government had become stable, and her navy was strong.

And Navy was the key word: It could not have remained strong without American timber. With hindsight, we know that England's

---

[1] W. H. McNeill, *Plagues and Peoples*, Doubleday, New York, 1976. McNeill does not, of course, claim that disease is the *only* factor affecting history.

Navy was about to become the world's supreme navy for the next three and a half centuries; yet at the time Jamestown, Virginia, was founded (1607), its future was threatened: There was imminent lack of timber for building ships in Britain. Much of its woodlands had been cleared for agriculture, and much had been burned as fuel, particularly by Britain's expanding iron smelting industry. The woodlands receded ever further from the cities, raising the price of fuel wood ever higher (a phenomenon observable today in some Third World countries). And that was just fuel wood.

But England's navy did not need fuel wood; the timber it needed was the kind of wood that is, as James I put it in a Royal Proclamation of 1615, "not only great and large in height and bulk, but hath also that toughness and heart, as is not subject to rive or cleave, and thereby of excellent use of shipping, as if God Almightie, which had ordained this Nation to be mighty by Sea and navigation, had in his providence indued the same with the principall materiall conducing therunto."

By 1662, English deforestation had gone so far that the commissioners of the Royal Navy, realizing that its future was in jeopardy, asked the fledgling Royal Society (Britain's highest scientific body) for assistance in finding remedies.

For fuel, Britain simply switched to coal, this time permanently.[2]

But for shipbuilding, British statesmen and admirals had not waited for the fuel crisis of the 1650's; they had been looking to America for timber. The principal object of English colonization in America had, in fact, been the development of a shipbuilding industry where the timber was, so that the Royal Navy would not be dependent on Swedish and other European timber for its ships.

And American timber was not only plentiful, it turned out to be incomparable. The tall straight New England pines, many of them reserved for the navy by the King's broad arrow as they grew, were made into masts; oaks provided the other ship timber. North Carolina's pines were richly productive in "naval stores" — pitch, tar and resin — which were placed on the "enumerated list" in 1705, so that they were for sale only in England and the colonies.

The sawmills of the new American lumber industry were placed amidst virgin timber along streams and rivers, which provided both water power and transportation. Water power, in fact,

---

[2] In previous fuel crises, London had used coal imported by sea from Newcastle, but its use ran into opposition from forerunners of the Friends of the Earth, who charged that its smoke was "poisoning the very fish in the Thames." See W. H. Te Brake, "Air Pollution and Fuel Crises in Preindustrial London," 1250-1650, *Technology and Culture*, vol. 16, no.3, pp.337-359, July 1975.

remained the principal U.S. source of machine-driving energy into the mid-19th century; steam came much later than in Europe, and did not, as it did there, usher in the Industrial Revolution, which was by that time well on the way in the U.S.

The abundance of fuel wood also led to an extraordinarily high per-capita energy consumption, far above that of traditional societies, from the time the first white settlers reached the continent. The first available statistics (1850) show the per-capita fuel wood consumption well above 100 million BTU's per year; in 1977, the *total* energy consumption per capita, though it is headed for the highest in the nation's (and the world's) history, will not even quadruple that figure.

Having nearly depleted her own forests, England's intent of safeguarding her navy with American timber succeeded extraordinarily well: By 1776 about a third of all shipping under the British flag was of colonial construction.

Britannia ruled the waves with American timber.

When the Iron Industry Ran Out of Fuel

By all the rules of the Sierra Club, the deforestation of Britain should have ended in doom, death and disaster. The selfish rape of the forests by the British iron smelters left future generations without iron or steel (didn't it?).

What happened in reality was that Britain became the number one iron and steel manufacturer, and the workshop of the world, for much of the 18th, and all of the 19th century; and that if you have some scrap iron today, it is you who must pay to have it taken off your hands. Nevertheless, the rising price of wood did have the English iron smelters in a pinch for a while. Two agents resolved the crisis: America and coal.

Conscious of the threat to the Royal Navy by the destruction of Britain's oak timber, British admirals and statesmen looked to America not only for a substitute timber supply, but also as a place for an iron industry, which had chiefly been responsible for depleting Britain's forests.

More to the point, perhaps, British entrepreneurs recognized the profitable possibilities of an iron industry in America. Production of iron ore from American ores and forests was one of the express purposes of Sir Walter Raleigh's expedition in 1585, and when Virginia was founded in 1607, one furnace and two forges were set up at Falling Creek, 66 miles above Jamestown.

In Britain, meanwhile, the high price of wood provided a spur to new technology. Coal could not simply be substituted for wood (or charcoal) in an open fire in metal smelting or most other processes, because coal fumes would damage the product; but the reverberatory furnace enabled coal to be used for smelting nonferrous metals, and by the end of the 18th century only the production of pig and bar iron remained dependent on wood.[3] But in 1709, in what some historians consider one of the most momentous discoveries, Abraham Darby the elder used coke to smelt iron ore in his blast furnace, opening the way to the Industrial Revolution. The process was further improved by Abraham Darby II in 1745, and by Abraham Darby III in 1775; and finally Henry Cort in 1788 invented the puddling process, at last freeing iron and steel production completely of any wooden fuel.

As late as 1750, however, the British parliament passed the Iron Act, seeking to encourage the importation of pig iron from the colonies, yet restricting colonial manufacture of finished iron products in favor of British industry. Trade was something to be legislated, not to be left to free competition, believed the mercantilists of the time; Adam Smith's *Wealth of Nations* was still 26 years away (an excuse not open to the AFL-CIO and other protectionist advocates of our time). The act turned out to be quite superfluous — British forests were now safe, by 1788 British pig iron production exceeded importation, and by that time Americans weren't asking what they were allowed to manufacture.

In America, iron smelting in charcoal kilns lingered on until the late 19th century; but neither in Britain nor in the U.S. were the forests totally depleted. No resource has ever completely run out; its price just rises beyond the point where it is economical to use. When the first white settlers arrived in America, about 40% of the area was covered by forest; and few will guess how much of it was still covered in 1970 — 33.28%! So much for resource depletion.

The First American Oil Crisis

Until the Civil War, most Americans probably used tallow candles for lighting; but those who were better off burned whale oil and sperm oil in their lamps. Both products were derived from whales, which were getting harder to find during the first half of the 19th century. As whaling voyages grew longer, eventually extending up to five years, prices of whale and sperm oil soared: Sperm oil rose from 43¢ a gallon in 1823 to $2.25 a gallon, and whale oil rose from 23¢ in 1832 to $1.45 a gallon.

---

[3] See J. Nef, "An early Energy Crisis and Its Consequences," *Scientific American*, November 1977, pp. 140-151.

The price explosion triggered the development of a number of substitutes: first camphene (derived from vegetable oils) and lard oil, later coal gas. By 1850, all of these were being pushed out by kerosene, then made from coal and called coal oil.

But coal oil did not dominate the market for long. The discovery of petroleum provided a new source of kerosene — crude oil. By 1861 its price had fallen to 10¢ a barrel, and within two years kerosene had pushed out all other lighting fuels from the market, including tallow candles (as a permanent source of light). Though not everyone had been able to afford whale oil, practically everyone was able to buy kerosene. Indeed, kerosene lamps made way only to electric bulbs, and even as late as 1941, more than half of the farm families in the country still used kerosene for lighting.

The first American oil crisis, then, was solved purely by market forces, and in a way that greatly benefited the consumer. Both the more affluent, who had been using whale oil, and the less well off, who had been using tallow candles, ended up using a better and more convenient fuel, kerosene, and they did so by their own choice. There was no National Energy Policy, and no president appealed to the country to turn down the lights.

In this, as in so many other episodes, history had widely disregarded the preachings of the Natural Resources Defense Council and other fountains of wisdom who regard resources as "finite," as if they were in a barrel and once the bottom has been scraped, there is no more, The supply of whales was no more depleted than the forests were — the price went up until a substitute became more economical. (Whales are still in danger from Soviet and Japanese harpoons, but hardly as a source of illumination.)

By contrast, in the oil crisis of the late 1970's, there is no reliable way of knowing whether gasification and liquification of coal is an economic, or even a necessary, substitute for oil and gas: price controls not only cause a shortage of these fuels, but they also artificially keep other fuels uncompetitive.

On the other hand, the successful resolution of the first American oil crisis was in no small measure due to a major contribution by the U.S. government: *It kept out of the way!*

Scaring the Ignorant

When smallpox inoculation was first introduced in the 1720's the infection was transferred by introducing matter from a smallpox pustule into a slight wound made in the patient's skin. The receiver would then usually develop a very mild form of the disease and thereafter became immune to it; however, occasionally a receiver would develop a severe case of smallpox, and sometimes even die of it. No wonder people were afraid of inoculation, and there was widespread opposition to the practice.

Yet people realized that the risks of inoculation were far smaller than those of *not* being inoculated, and smallpox inoculation was accepted in the American colonies in the early 18th century far quicker than in Europe.[4]

The fear of the unknown is understandable, but it does not hold up progress for long unless it is artificially fanned by vested interests. Very fortunately, there were no interests vested in the smallpox.

Alas, the same has not been true of energy.

In U.S. energy history, there have been three cases when fear of the unknown was shamelessly exploited by vested interests to obstruct progress for the great majority: the railroads, AC electricity, and nuclear power. In all three cases, the scaremongers were able to delay the benefits of technical innovation for some time; in the first two, they passed through ridicule into oblivion, and that, it is to be hoped, is what awaits them in the third case, too.

America entered the 19th century with a formidable network of turnpikes, reaching a total length of 11,000 miles by 1830. By that time turnpikes had surrendered their leading role for freight transport to a system of waterways, of which, by 1850, no less than 4,000 miles were hand-dug artificial canals.[5] They, in turn, yielded to the railroads.

But not easily.

They were fought tooth and nail, ostensibly on the "safety issue," by those who had much to lose by a better form of transportation.

The *Stourbridge Lion* made a trial run over 3 miles of track built by the Chesapeake & Ohio Canal Co. in 1829, in which the 4-ton locomotive bent the rails out of alignment. However, the practicability of hauling freight and passengers over long distances was proven by the Baltimore & Ohio and the Charleston & Hamburg railroads (the latter completed in 1833, and with 136 miles the

---

[4] Perhaps because of the frequent demonstrations of lethal epidemics among the Indians, perhaps due to the efforts of Cotton Mather (1663-1728), Massachusetts Congregational minister, founder of Yale University, and Salem witch hunter, who endorsed inoculation against smallpox. In Europe, smallpox vaccination was not widely accepted until after 1798, when immunization was effected by cowpox, a disease not dangerous to humans.

[5] For detailed statistics and history, see L. E. Davis *et al.*, *American Economic Growth*, Harper & Row, 1972; R. M. Robertson, *History of the American Economy*, Harcourt, Brace, Jovanovich, 1973; H. S. Drago, *Canal Days in America*, Bramhall House, 1972.

longest railroad in the world at the time). Nevertheless, it took the railroads another 20 years to overcome public antipathy, rooted in ignorance and liberally fomented by the interests vested in canals, highways, and associated industries such as taverns. Even farmers growing horsefeed suddenly became enthusiastic safety advocates.

But much of the hostility was openly economic, sparing the public the present-day hypocrisy of safety, enviromentalism, security, peace-keeping and whatever other masquerades contemporary anti-technologists can lay their hands on.

Legislation Against Railroads

At least one town in Massachusetts instructed its representatives in the state legislature to prevent "so great a calamity to our town as must be the location of any railroad through it." Several states limited railroad traffic to passengers, or to freight hauled only during the months when canal operations ceased. Some railroads were required to pay a tonnage tax supporting the operation of canals, and one Ohio railroad had to pay for any loss in canal traffic attributed to railroad competition.[6]*

The economic interests had no difficulty in scaring the public with horror stories of what the railroads were going to do to them; who could, at the time, convincingly deny that speeds of 20 and even 30 miles per hour might be physically harmful to passengers?

Much of the propaganda was purely emotional, appealing for "the lives of your little ones," as in the anti-nuke campaign of the 1970's.

Electricity, of course, is far more mysterious to people than railroads ever were, and it was correspondingly easier to scare them. And when it comes to scaremongering, all the news unfit to print could usually be found in the *New York Times*, for a hundred years ago that august paper wallowed in the same type of puerile alarmism as it does today. Thus, on December 30, 1878, it editorialized:

---

[6]The same general picture emerged in Europe. In Austria-Hungary, the wagoneers' lobby (in the interests of health and safety, of course) pushed through a law requiring railroad stations to be built at least a mile from the community served. Since then, towns have grown around the stations, and many tracks have been re-laid, but to this day trains in Bohemia often stop at stations in the open country, and passengers must change to road transportation (or walk) to reach the village the railroad is supposed to serve.

*Editors' note: On the other hand, many railroads were recipients of government favors, such as grants of land and money. The free market believer is opposed to subsidies as well as restrictive legislation.

Pages from U.S. Energy History

> Some curious facts regarding the properties of electric light have become familiar to experts, which raise the question whether it may prove physiologically injurious. One of them is the very high penetrating power of an illumination generated by the incandescence of metals or by their slow combustion . . .
>
> The retina of the human eye is habituated to a certain given intensity of illumination which is many degrees below that of electricity, and any very material advance in intensity must necessarily prove very irritating. [This] raises the point whether the properties of electric light are such as to render it a safe and wholesome substitute for the light produced by combustion.

Note, however, that 100 years ago the *New York Times* had the integrity to compare (even if ineptly) the dangers of electric light with those of the then current "light produced by combustion." Such honesty (or competence) is entirely alien to the Tom Wickers and Gladwin Hills who fan the anti-nuclear hysteria in the pages of the *New York Times* today, carefully brushing any comparison with present power sources under the carpet.

Perhaps the following editorial of December 25, 1883, more fittingly foreshadows the days of Tom Wicker-type journalism:

> No one seems to have thought of the pleasant surprise that the electric light companies which use currents of dangerous intensity have prepared for us in readiness for the first winter rainstorm. Every few winters we have a rainstorm in freezing weather when every drop of rain that falls on the telegraph wires freezes, and the ice accumulates until the wires break . . . The next time this happens the electric wires will have their share in making the scene a very lively one. No one will be able to tell which one of thousands of broken wires is charged with a current strong enough to kill, or at least stun the man who touches it . . .
>
> The streets will soon be rendered impassable by stunned or killed horses, and every attempt to better the condition of affairs will lead to fresh casualties among the workmen . . .

A Ralph Nader of the 1880's

The first of the *New York Times* editorials above was a reaction to Thomas Alva Edison's invention of the electric light bulb; the second was provoked by the first successful central electric lighting system that Edison put into operation in New York in September 1882.

By 1887, his system had 121 central generating stations with a total capacity of some 325,000 lamps. The decade from 1885 on was one of explosive growth for electric power — new ways of generating, transmitting, and utilizing it.

Edison's lighting system worked on direct current (flowing always in the same direction), but in 1885, George Westinghouse realized the possibilities of alternating (oscillating) currents which could be transformed to high voltages for efficient transmission and then to low voltages for distribution to consumers. The Westinghouse system, originally based in Great Barrington, Mass., grew quickly and was considerably spurred by a sharp rise in copper prices in 1887, for as a high-voltage system it needed significantly less copper than Edison's. By the summer of 1888, Westinghouse had not only bought Tesla's patents for the AC motor, but had secured the services of the famous engineer himself. In that same year, Westinghouse's chief engineer O. B. Shallenberger also invented a superior consumption meter, eliminating one of the few then remaining disadvantages of AC.

Westinghouse, in short, had much the better system. Edison was licked and should have known it; instead he chose to concentrate on a single issue of the then ongoing AC-DC debate, the safety issue, for he (mistakenly) believed AC to be more dangerous.

This stance may have been brought about by the activity of one Harold P. Brown, a self-educated engineer who wrote an open letter to the New York Board of Electrical Control, published in the *Evening Post* on June 5, 1888, in which he claimed low voltage DC "such as used by the Edison Company for incandescent lights" to be "safe as far as life risk is concerned," while AC was deadly, dangerous, and he concluded, "can be described by no adjective less forcible than damnable."

Harold Brown claimed to be unconnected with the Edison Co., and while this may have been true originally, Edison and his company subsequently made financial support and laboratory facilities available to him. Brown, in any case, unleashed a campaign of horror propaganda against AC, in part based on unsound experiments, in part on one-sided evidence, and most often involving the killing of dogs and horses by high AC voltage.[7]

The most memorable of Brown's stunts came in 1890, when he turned the first execution in the electric chair into another publicity

---

[7] They could equally well have been killed by high DC voltages. How Brown evaded this point in a public demonstration is described in *George Westinghouse* by H. Thomas (Putnam, 1960); however, this is a brief and partly fictionalized biography, and it is not clear to what extent the episode described there is historically authentic.

victory for DC. Brown had convinced the authorities of the greater deadliness of AC, and had even secured a Westinghouse alternator for the execution. George Westinghouse's efforts to prevent its use proved to no avail: On August 6, 1890, at Auburn Prison, New York, the first legal electrocution was performed by deadly, damnable AC.[8]

Now Brown was a demagogue of near Naderite proportions, but it would be nice to think that Edison himself had nothing to do with distorting evidence to fit his own prejudices and the technology used by his company. Unfortunately, his article *The Dangers of Electric Lighting*[9] does little for taking such a charitable view. After expressing his personal desire to prohibit entirely the use of alternating currents, he claims that the 220 volts DC [of his own system] "will force so weak a current through the human body that it can barely be detected."

To which Westinghouse replies "I have witnessed the roasting of a large piece of beef by direct continuous current of less than 100 volts within two minutes," and gives directions on how to steam and cook beef on the 200 V Edison system. Westinghouse also coolly explodes the many other of Edison's inconsistencies, finally presenting the verdict of the ultimate judge — the free choice of the consumer:

> [I]t is worthy of note that for three years past the purchasers of apparatus for electric lighting, who are at perfect liberty to buy from any company, have, for the most part, preferred to use the alternating system, so that to-day the extension of that system ... is at least five times as great as that of the direct current. If the opinion of these persons who can have no interest except to purchase that which they believe to be the best, is of any value, then the alternating system has been demonstrated to be the one which can give to the public that which they so much desire — a safe, cheap, efficient, and universally applicable system of incandescent electric lighting.

The clash of the two giants, Edison and Westinghouse, makes interesting reading. Westinghouse's dignified reply to Edison's attack abounds in watertight arguments and examples of convincing evidence. It is, however, noteworthy that he left the point quoted

---

[8] T.S. Reynolds and T. Bernstein, "The damnable alternating current," *Proc. IEEE*, vol. 64, no. 9, pp. 1339-43, Sept. 1976; also T. Bernstein, "A grand success: The first legal eletrocution ... ," *IEEE Spectrum*, vol. 10, no. 2, pp. 54-58, Feb. 1973.

[9] *North American Review*, vol. 109, no. 396, pp. 625-634, 1889; George Westinghouse's reply is in no. 397, pp. 653-654, 1889.

above, the consumer's verdict, for the conclusion of his reply; evidently he considered this point the strongest.

This is interesting in view of today's "consumer advocates," who reject expert opinion and force their doctrines (as well as their high price) on the consumer by legislation, or more often, by administrative action of an unelected bureaucracy. The one thing that has these vicarious consumer advocates scared more than anything else is what George Westinghouse put his finger on: the consumer's free choice.

Edison's stubbornness over AC soon led to his loss of all influence over the electric power industry, including his own company, which merged with the second-largest company (after Westinghouse Corp.) producing AC machinery, and emerged as a new company (General Electric) with which he was no longer connected.

"As for Brown," write Reynolds and Bernstein (see footnote on p. 337), "he was one of those figures seen occasionally in the course of history, who rises suddenly from obscurity, enjoys a few fleeting moments of notoriety, and then returns from whence he came."

The Interests Vested in Energy

Neither the canal owners who opposed the railroads, nor the shareholders of the Edison Electric Company who opposed alternating current, had the slightest difficulty in convincing themselves that they were driven only by the noble spirit of neighborly love and safety.

Nor is there, in this respect, the slightest difficulty for those who today oppose any kind of large-scale energy conversion, economic growth, individual mobility (whether on the roads or in society), free enterprise, and all but "appropriate" (pitiful) technology.

They do not have a vested interest in anything as easily come by as stocks or direct financial benefits from a particular enterprise. Their vested interest is the preservation of the privileged, tone-setting position of an elite that fears nothing so much as mass prosperity.

They have had no difficulty in kidding themselves that their actions, which grievously injure safety, health, environment and public interest, are justified by the purest motives of safety, health, environment and public interest — plus sensitivity, awareness, societal relevance and further buzzwords *ad infinitum.*

Pages from U.S. Energy History

Over centuries, energy sources and means of transportation have changed; but human nature has not.

To defend liberty and abundance against the vested interests of the sanctimonious, we will have to make the most of the lessons of history.

When We Are Free

CHAPTER 51

What to do about the Post Office

by Scott W. Bixler

The Founding Fathers anticipated a postal monopoly, every country has a postal monopoly, and Congress is permitted to do anything to insure that postal monopoly.[1]

For many years this view has been the justification for outlawing competition in mail delivery. Today, however, a number of signs indicate that this idea is losing much of its appeal. Huge deficits, reductions in the frequency of pickups and deliveries, and numerous horror stories about outrageously slow mail delivery make us realize that something is clearly wrong.

Almost no one doubts the need for mail service. But why is it generally believed that a government monopoly is the only possible means of providing this service?

In this essay, we shall first take a brief look at the history of mail service in the United States — up to the time Congress granted the Post Office a legal monopoly. Then, we shall examine several of the arguments presented by those who favor the government's retention of the postal monopoly. Our objective will be to attempt to answer the question: Should the federal government continue to have a monopoly on mail delivery?

A Short History

The Constitution empowered Congress to put government in the postal business. George Washington declared that the Post Office was the "unbroken chain that holds the nation together." This illustrates the Founding Fathers' belief that the Post Office was necessary for "national unity."

Throughout the 1800's, Congress held firm to the belief that government had a duty to provide service to all. Of course that included service to frontier and rural areas. In providing service to remote areas, the Post Office resorted to a *cross subsidy*. That is, it

---

[1] Gerald J. Houlihan, quoted in "A Private Mail Service Challenges the Post Office," *Free Enterprise*, February 1978, p. 16.

used the profits it made on routes in populous areas to offset the losses it incurred on rural routes.

Some individuals argued that entrusting mail delivery to private carriers was undesirable because the private firms would provide service only to populous areas. By serving just those areas, they could make profits. But they would not fulfill the obligation to provide nationwide service. Thus, the private carriers would *skim the cream*, leaving the Post Office with the unprofitable routes.

Hundreds of private carriers did indeed successfully compete with the United States Post Office. By 1843, Boston alone had at least twenty private postal operators.[2] Private carriers were so successful that in 1844 a senator from Rhode Island stated that "on the express routes, twenty letters are sent outside the mail for the one that is carried by the mail."[3] By 1845, they carried an estimated one-third of the nation's letters.[4]

There was concern in Washington as the success for the private carriers meant deficits for the Post Office. For supporters of the Post Office, this situation was intolerable. So in 1845 Congress passed the Private Express Statutes which prohibited private firms from carrying first class mail. Congress thereby granted a *legal* monopoly to the United States Post Office. The nation's Representatives and Senators were, in effect, admitting that the Post Office was unable to match the efficiency of the private carriers. The government had to resort to threats of arrest and criminal prosecution in order to establish its monopoly.

Let's now turn to several of the arguments advanced by some of the people who favor the government's keeping that monopoly.

The Natural Monopoly Argument

Some individuals contend that mail delivery is a natural monopoly. This is the notion that the cost of providing mail service, because of characteristics inherent in this service, will be lowest if there is just one firm providing it. Because of this, these individuals argue, competition in this business is self-destructive and thus incompatible with the public interest. Thus, those people who subscribe to the natural monopoly argument contend competition should be outlawed.

---

[2]William C. Wooldridge, *Uncle Sam the Monopoly Man* (Arlington House, New Rochelle, N.Y., 1970), pp. 11-13.

[3]George L. Priest, "The History of the Postal Monopoly in the United States," *Journal of Law and Economics*, April, 1975, p. 59.

[4]Wooldridge, pp. 11-31.

The natural monopoly argument is simply not valid with regard to the delivery of mail. For the natural monopoly argument to be valid, there must be large economies of scale in the economic activity to which the argument applies. "Independent economic studies have shown no evidence of large economies of scale in mail delivery."[5]

If a firm has a genuine natural monopoly, there is no need to prohibit entry. By definition, that entrenched firm will always be able to undersell potential competitors and thus keep them out. The true monopoly can undersell potential competitors because it has the lowest costs. If the United States Post Office is actually the lowest cost mail deliverer, the government would not have to crush prospective competitors with threats and actual competitors with criminal indictments.

Furthermore, if the United States Post Office as a legal monopoly can provide its patrons with first class mail delivery at the lowest cost, why haven't steps been taken to prohibit delivery of *all* categories of mail — including second, third, and fourth classes? Wouldn't this broader prohibition provide the greatest possible benefit to society? Yet there has never been any attempt to do this. Congress seems content to allow the Post Office to confine its monopoly to first class mail, i.e., "letters."

The definition of letters has been frequently broadened. It now includes bills, price lists, and punched hole cards. This is interesting because the use of electronic mail (e.g., in the direct deposit of Social Security checks) has been steadily increasing to the point where it is estimated that by 1985 nearly 60 per cent of all bills, receipts, checks, and computer cards will be sent outside the postal system. Private companies have for some time taken advantage of the cheaper and more efficient electronic mail. Still there is no serious attempt to prosecute these firms. Some individuals have suggested that the government allows limited competition in some areas where it could legally prosecute in order to quiet opposition that might otherwise pressure Congress into repealing the Private Express Statutes.[6]

The Uniform Rates Argument

A second argument advanced by those defending the postal monopoly is that private carriers, if permitted, would serve a limited clientele and would not charge uniform rates. The United

---

[5]John C. Goodman and Edwin G. Dolan, *Economics of Public Policy* (St. Paul, Minnesota: West Publishing Company, 1979), p. 141.

[6]Priest, p. 76.

States Post Office, on the other hand, has uniform prices for administrative convenience and for the benefit of everyone.

Those who advance this argument contend that a varied price structure would cause public confusion and unnecessary red tape. But this hardly seems a valid reason for prohibiting competition. If the competitors could manage the alleged confusion and red tape caused by a variety of rates, the Post Office should also be able to contend with them — even more effectively if it is truly a natural monopoly.

The present uniform rate system compels cross-town mailers to subsidize cross-continent mailers. It is difficult to see the virtue in this practice. In the final analysis, it seems only fair for people to pay for what they receive. If economic justice requires different rates, isn't that a powerful argument *for* different rates?

The Alternatives

Neither the natural monopoly argument nor the uniform rates argument seems to be a very persuasive argument for perpetuating the government's present monopoly. But what are the alternatives?

To reduce or eliminate the Postal Service's deficits, there are those who advise higher rates, fewer pickups, and fewer deliveries. A number of politicians, many members of the Union of Postal Employees, and many members of the National Association of Postmasters recommend these alternatives. Their recommendations are, of course, predicated on the federal government's maintaining its monopoly.

But isn't there a better alternative? Why don't we simply repeal the Private Express Statutes and immediately stop all subsidies to the Postal Service?[7] *Let anyone who wants to deliver mail deliver it for whomever he pleases and on whatever terms are mutually agreeable to him and his patrons.*

If the United States Postal Service can survive without the protection of the Private Express Statutes, without subsidies, and without any other special consideration, fine. If it can't survive under these circumstances, it doesn't deserve to.

If there were a free market in mail delivery, it seems likely that the federal government would benefit in several ways. The government would no longer have to make up the Postal Service's deficits. And profitable private mail carriers would *pay* federal income taxes, not *drain* them.

---

[7]Technically, with the Postal Reorganization Act in 1970, the Post Office became the United States Postal Service — a semi-independent publicly owned corporation. However, the Postal Service has the same monopoly privileges that the Post Office had.

What to do about the Post Office

Judging from the advances in other forms of communication (e.g., in television) where there has been a free (or, at least, freer) market all along, we have good reason to believe the consumer of mail service would benefit greatly from a free market in mail delivery. As to the precise forms progress in mail delivery would come, Paul Poirot wisely observes:

> To speculate on how the mail might be delivered if anyone were free to try, would be foolish. No one can possibly imagine what innovations might spring from the unrestricted imaginations of everyone in search of better ways to serve consumers.[8]

What should we do about the Postal Service? Surely, to the objective observer this last alternative is the best alternative. Subject the Postal Service to the rigors of competition. What does that require? Freedom — simply freedom.

---

[8] Paul L. Poirot, "A Monopoly — And How to Break It," *The Freeman,* June 1970, p. 352.

When We Are Free

CHAPTER 52

Medicine and the State

by John C. Goodman

That there is a crisis in the American health care system seems to be almost universally acknowledged. The charge has been echoed and re-echoed by the news media, by politicians, by academicians and even by members of the medical community.

Much of what is considered a "crisis" in our health care system, however, is not really a crisis at all. The fact that we are spending more of our national income on health care than ever before is hardly surprising. It is natural and inevitable that as we become more wealthy, we will want to spend more of our income on health care. This is a historical phenomenon that has been observed in all countries through time. Nor is it surprising that what we casually refer to as "health care" is becoming more expensive. New innovations and inventions in medical science have expanded the range of services which doctors and hospitals can offer. Frequently, the real cost of this new technology is quite high. But the advent of new medical technology can hardly be described as a "crisis." These developments in no way make us worse off — they do not destroy old options; they merely create new ones.

Nonetheless there is a genuine crisis, or at least a major problem, in the health care marketplace. The problem is: we do not get our money's worth for the health care dollars we spend. Under a different set of institutions, we could get more health care for the dollars we are now spending; or, put alternatively, we could obtain the same quantity and quality of health care we now receive at a lower cost.

Why does this problem exist? Most public discussions of the issue imply that the failures of our health care system are failures inherent in a free market for medical care. Such a conclusion inevitably points in the direction of an age-old "solution": more government regulation.

Editors' note: Dr. Goodman, Director of the Center for Health Policy Research at the University of Dallas, is an emerging national authority on the subject of this article. We have extracted this from a larger work.

My thesis is quite different: most of the problems we encounter in the market for health care arise not because the free market has failed, but because it is not being tried.

Controls on the Form of Delivery: The Hospital

In 1910, approximately 56% of all hospitals in the United States were proprietary, or for-profit, hospitals. Today, less than 11% of all hospitals are proprietary, and they account for only 8% of all admissions and only 4% of all out-patient visits. This decline in the role of proprietary hospitals is puzzling in view of both theoretical and empirical evidence which suggests that for-profit hospitals are more efficient producers of health care services than either non-profit or state-owned hospitals.

The answer to the puzzle is that the decline of the proprietary hospital in the U.S. is not the result of competition in a free market. It is the result of explicit government policies. Some states have outlawed proprietaries altogether. In states which allow them, proprietary hospitals suffer from a number of government-imposed competitive disadvantages: First, proprietary hospitals pay real property and corporate income taxes, whereas non-profit hospitals do not. Second, non-profit hospitals have received enormous subsidies under the Hill-Burton Hospital Construction Act of 1946; proprietary hospitals were excluded from this program. Third, charitable contributions, which comprise a substantial portion of the funds most hospitals receive, are deductible under federal income tax laws if the hospital is non-profit; contributions to proprietary hospitals are not deductible.

A number of states impose regulatory restrictions on proprietaries which do not apply to non-profit hospitals. In addition, regulatory agencies often discriminate against proprietary hospitals. In most cities, the opening of a new hospital, expansion of an existing one, and even the purchase of a large piece of equipment require the permission of a local planning agency. Yet these agencies are often dominated by the interest of existing non-profit institutions which feel threatened by innovative entrepreneurs who are trying to cut costs and aggressively compete for patients.

It is not known what role was played by organized medicine in the demise of proprietary hospitals in the 20th century. What is known is that proprietary hospitals, like proprietary medical schools, are looked upon with disfavor. Organized medicine has a financial reason to oppose proprietary institutions in both fields. Proprietary institutions are typically dominated by the owners' interest in maximizing profit. Non-profit institutions, on the other hand, frequently pursue other goals, many of which are consistent with the aims of organized medicine.

Non-profit medical schools, for example, tend to prefer longer, and more costly, periods of physician training than for-profit schools would prefer. This goal of non-profit medical schools is consistent with the desire of the American Medical Association (AMA) to make entry into the profession more difficult. In the case of the hospital sector, non-profit institutions are more likely to cooperate with another important AMA goal: that of restricting price competition among practicing physicians.

Non-profit hospitals, for example, are more likely to cooperate with the AMA policy of restricting the hospital medical staff to members of local medical societies. Expulsion from the medical society for "unethical" conduct, then, would mean that a physician would also lose his hospital privileges. The power to remove hospital privileges from physicians who commit what are essentially economic crimes (such as advertising and price-cutting) has been an important disciplinary weapon of organized medicine in the past.

Despite the fact that the lack of agressive competition in the hospital sector is in large part the result of government policy, rising hospital costs were the major excuse given for the wave of new regulations which occurred in the 1970's. A hospital in New York is now governed by 99 separate regulatory agencies. A hospital in New Jersey is governed by 119 regulatory bodies.[1] The evidence suggests that far from reducing hospital costs, the new regulations are becoming an important component of rising costs.

More Government Not the Answer

As the United States enters the decade of the 1980's the prospects for a free market for medical care seem especially bleak. Congress has been flooded with proposals to establish a full-blown system of national health insurance with controls on health care spending placed firmly in the hands of federal regulators.

What can patients and potential patients look forward to if such schemes are adopted? One thing they should not expect is a more efficient health care system. With all of its inefficiencies, distorted incentives, and regulatory burdens, our health care system is still more efficient than the systems of countries with comprehensive

---

[1]Council on Wage and Price Stability, *The Complex Puzzle of Rising Health Care Costs: Can the Private Sector Fit it Together?* (Washington, D.C.: U.S. Government Printing Office, 1976), p. 14.

national health insurance schemes. In fact, measured in terms of average length-of-stay statistics, the U.S. has the most efficient health care system in the industrialized world.[2]

The evidence, then, suggests that comprehensive regulation will raise, not lower, the true cost of medical care. It also suggests that patients can look forward to a lower quality of care in return for the health care dollars spent. I recently compared some indicators of the quality of health care received by patients in five countries: the United States, Canada, West Germany, Norway and Denmark.[3] In 1976, these countries were very similar in terms of per capita health care spending. Yet they had very different health care systems. The fraction of health care spending done by the government in the U.S. that year was approximately one-half what it was in the other four countries.

This difference in the role of government involvement in health care between the U.S. and the other four countries appears to have led to important differences in the quality of health care. Although the amount of health care spending was similar in all five countries, the four countries with national health care systems devoted fewer resources to those types of care which are known to actually improve the health care of patients: the other four countries had fewer CAT scanners per capita, fewer dialysis machines per capita and trained a much lower percentage of their physicians in specialized fields. Comparisons of mortality rates in these countries revealed that these differences in spending priorities affect the health of patients: for diseases for which medical intervention is known to make a real difference, and for which lifestyle and environment are inconsequential causes of disease, the U.S. had significantly lower mortality rates.

Space does not permit an analysis of why government health care systems produce greater inefficiency and a lower quality of care than Americans receive under our current system. I have elaborated on the reasons for these phenomena elsewhere.[4]

Suffice it to say that in the area of health care, as in so many other areas, the political marketplace operates very differently than the economic marketplace.

Perhaps the most disturbing trend in health care politics today is the attitude taken by so many of the providers of health care

---

[2]See The Organization for Economic Co-operation and Development, *Public Expenditures on Health* (Paris: OEDC, 1977), Table 5, p. 19.

[3]John C. Goodman, "The Politics of Medicine," *Policy Review*, forthcoming.

[4]John C. Goodman, *National Health Care in Great Britain: Lessons for the U.S.A.* (Dallas, Texas: The Fisher Institute, 1980), Ch. 10.

services. Although organized medicine and its allies in the health insurance, medical manufacturing and pharmaceutical industries have so far resisted the more extreme proposals for comprehensive national health insurance, there is no assurance that they will continue to do so in the future. Many within the health care industry are prone to work to shape and mold national health insurance proposals to fit their own economic interests rather than to oppose them outright. As they have done in so many other countries, the producers of health care may soon become the architects of national health insurance in this one.

The unfortunate result is that the burden of protecting our health care system from further government intrusions will likely fall squarely upon the shoulders of the general public. My prediction is that if socialized medicine is ultimately defeated in this country, it will be patients, not doctors, who will be primarily responsible.

When We Are Free

CHAPTER 53

Regulation — Political or Market?

by Dale M. Haywood

The free enterprise system is not perfect. So the question arises: What is the best way to deal with the imperfections in this system?

In an effort to provide at least a partial answer to this question, we shall begin by examining an alleged defect of free enterprise. Then, we shall look closely at the non-market, political regulation adopted to try to correct this defect. Both the defect and the regulation are representative of a number of alleged defects in free enterprise and a whole host of political "solutions" to these defects. But, it turns out, the particular regulation we examine has defects itself. These defects raise some question as to whether, in general and on balance, non-market, political solutions to the defects in free enterprise yield a net improvement in our economic well-being. But if political regulation is not "the way to go," what is? We shall conclude this chapter by suggesting an answer to this question.

An Alleged Defect — Improperly Installed Wiring

Every now and then we read about a family whose home is completely destroyed by fire. The family loses all of its personal possessions. In a few cases, one or more members of the family may even lose their lives. Certainly this is tragic.

Fire department and insurance investigators inquire into the causes of such fires. On occasion, they discover the cause is improperly installed wiring. But why would anyone install wiring improperly? To answer this question, let's turn to the electrical subcontractor who did the wiring in the house that was destroyed by fire.

Like most businessmen, and as a matter of fact like most human beings, this electrical subcontractor is profit-motivated. One way to make larger profits in the free enterprise system is to cut costs. And one way to cut costs is to use the least skilled labor one possibly can to do a given job. So some of us may be tempted to assume that the electrical subcontractor used less skilled labor than he should have for doing the wiring on this job.

At least this *seems* like a plausible explanation for some improperly installed wiring. Thus, at least on the surface, it appears that it may be unwise to leave profit-seeking electrical subcontractors entirely free to hire whomever they please to install wiring.

The "Cure" — Occupational Licensing

Sympathy for "doing something" arises. To many people, it seems obvious that electrical subcontractors should be regulated by some disinterested, nonprofit-oriented body. This means that electrical subcontractors should be forced to act differently from the way they act when left free. A widely approved specific form of regulation is occupational licensing by government.

The rationale for licensing electricians, to continue with our specific example, seems straightforward enough. To get a license, a person must pass a test. To pass the test, the person must demonstrate some minimum level of competence. If government then requires electrical subcontractors to hire only licensed electricians, it would seem that only individuals with some minimum level of competence would do all of the wiring done by electrical subcontractors. With only these individuals doing wiring, we assume we can be assured that all wiring will be properly installed. Then the tragedies stemming from improperly installed wiring should be largely eliminated. And thus to many people, it would appear that with a little judicious government regulation, we can correct some of the defects in the free market.

Good Intentions Aren't Enough

No doubt there are many different reasons why people support government regulation generally and occupational licensure specifically. Surely some of these people have excellent intentions. In the case at hand, probably most of the people who endorse occupational licensing intend all buildings to be safer from electrical hazards. But a little illustration may serve as a useful reminder that good intentions are not enough.

One day a little boy and his dog were walking on an ocean beach. The little boy succumbed to the temptation to venture into the ocean by himself. As he walked further and further out, the ocean floor suddenly dropped off. The little boy was startled. The water was over his head. He panicked. He was drowning. He shouted for help.

A man, also walking along the beach, heard the boy's cries for help. The man quickly went to the boy's rescue. To complete the rescue, the man came in physical contact with the little boy, of course. When the dog saw this, it construed that contact to be harm to his young master. So the dog vigorously attacked the man.

Now, because the water they were in was also over the man's head, the man had to devote all of his energy to fending off the dog in order to protect himself. It was while the man was defending himself against the dog's attack that the little boy drowned.

No doubt the dog had excellent intentions, viz., protecting his little master. But the dog apparently lacked the ability to discriminate between a person's contact with the boy that was harmful and a person's contact with the boy that was helpful. The dog apparently lacked the ability to appreciate all of the consequences of its actions. Yet, the overriding fact is that the little boy drowned.

Let's now see where the good intentions of those who advocate licensing electricians lead.

Political Regulation Has Unintended Consequences

Suppose that the wiring done by electrical subcontractors after the licensing is done correctly more often than before the licensing. (This, by the way, is by no means a certainty.) Then there are fewer tragedies due to improperly installed wiring *by electrical subcontractors*. But this is not the same thing as saying there will be fewer tragedies due to improperly installed wiring. Here's why.

Licensing tends to reduce the number of people practicing in the profession that is licensed. This is as true in the fields of medicine, plumbing, landscape architecture, law, cosmetology, real estate . . . as it is in electrical work. Reducing the number of people in any profession tends to raise the prices those people charge for their services.[1] After all, they *have* to ration their services somehow. And in most cases, it is simply advantageous to them to ration by price. But as the prices of their services go up, the number of people who can afford to pay those prices goes down.

In the case of electrical work, at least, fewer people who can afford to pay for higher priced licensed electricians means there will be more people who become do-it-yourselfers. No doubt these do-it-yourselfers have a wide range of abilities. Some of them may actually be more competent than the licensed electricians. Some of them, however, are likely to be less competent. Indeed, some of them are likely to be even less competent than the unskilled person who, we assumed, did the wiring in the home that burned. Thus

---

[1] Note that reducing the number of people in a particular profession may be a motive, perhaps even the *major* motive, of some advocates of occupational licensing, viz., the people being licensed. The higher prices that result from there being fewer people in the profession are the source of larger incomes for this particular group.

there may be *more* wiring done by people not qualified to do it properly after the licensing goes into effect than there was before the licensing went into effect. This may spawn *more* tragedies than there would have been in the free market. Of course this situation would be just the *opposite* of what some of the advocates of licensing electricians intended!

Let's carry our examination of occupational licensing one step further. Advocates of licensing may argue that if licensing is good, wouldn't stricter licensing be even better?

Two economists at the University of Tennessee, Knoxville, Robert J. Gaston and Sidney L. Carroll, investigated this very question. They found that "the seven states with the strictest licensing requirements have up to ten times more accidental electrocutions ... than the national average. Conversely, they found that New York and four other states with the lowest incidence of electrocutions have the most lenient licensing requirements."[2] So the harmful effects of licensing and of stricter licensing are not just theoretical. Empirical studies show that some harmful effects are real.

Market Regulation

It is a serious misunderstanding of free enterprise to suppose that if there is no political regulation of business, there is no regulation of business at all. One of the main features of free enterprise is the free market. In a free market, consumers may patronize or refuse to patronize whomever they please. In a free market, producers are free to enter the competition for consumers' patronage or to withdraw from that competition. These are two very powerful and effective regulators. Thus, where there is a free market, profit-seeking men and women (i.e., all of us) have considerable incentive to respond efficiently to consumer wishes.

Let's consider a specific example. If it is important to consumers that their homes be safe from fire hazards, they will be willing to demonstrate that importance by paying for it. Electrical subcontractors will be able to recover, through the selling prices of the houses they help build, money to pay skilled electricians who generally install wiring correctly. Any electrical contractor who succumbs to the temptation to cut costs by hiring insufficiently skilled people to do wiring work will quickly get a reputation for building homes with a feature, an above normal fire hazard, that people don't like. And homebuyers simply will not voluntarily buy homes with features they don't like, if they can afford to exercise their preferences.

---

[2] See "How Licensing Hurts Consumers," *Business Week*, November 28, 1977, pp. 127, 130, 132.

The "if they can afford" qualification is, of course, significant. Safety is an economic good. Like other economic goods, it has a price. The price of safety can get too high — too high as judged by the masses of consumers, although perhaps not too high as judged by a few utopians.

For example, let's suppose there are 50,000 people in the United States who install electrical wiring. Further suppose that of these 50,000 only 50 have never made any mistakes in their electrical work. (To suppose that even 1 out of 1,000 has never made any mistakes is probably to suppose the situation is better than it actually is.) Government decrees that *only* these 50 people can do electrical work. Everyone abides by the law. Now there will never be any losses due to fire caused by improperly installed wiring nor will there be any more accidental electrocutions due to unqualified people doing electrical wiring. But what would this cost?

The cost would be giving up 99.9 per cent of the electrical work done by 49,950 people in the United States who install electrical wiring but have made some mistakes. The cost would be not having the homes and other buildings for which this large group would have done the wiring. When taken to an extreme, as in this hypothetical example, it becomes clear that the price of perfect wiring is too high. Certainly it is too high as judged by the vast majority of consumers, if not by all of them. It is, in this imperfect world of ours, a rational trade-off to accept somewhat less than perfectly safe electrical wiring for a great many more wired homes and other buildings.

When men and women are free, they will strike a reasonable balance — reasonable as the men and women themselves judge it. They will give up some of one good (e.g., safety) so as to be able to get more of another good (e.g., houses). This is not ideal. Of course the ideal would be to have complete safety *and* all of the homes and other buildings we want. But the ideal, let us always remember, is not one of our choices.

In a free market, those businesses that produce goods and provide services with the combinations of features that free men and women want will survive and flourish. Businesses that do not produce goods and provide services with the combinations of qualities that consumers want will fail. This is market regulation.

Courts

It is easy to see how consumers (through their buying or not buying) and other producers (through their competing or not competing) effectively regulate a business if the business depends, as most do, on repeat patronage. But what about the business that does not depend on repeat patronage?

Many advocates of free enterprise believe that there is a need for limited government. Defense is the criterion that determines the limits. In other words, government is necessary and positively useful as long as it is confined to *defending* life, liberty, and property. To these advocates of free enterprise, government is out-of-bounds when it encroaches on life, liberty, and property.

A government limited to performing a defense function may have a court system. So in the small proportion of situations in which the market mechanism is an inadequate regulator, a person who suffers losses due to fraud or to the negligence of any businessman may seek redress through that court system.

Conclusion

In the free enterprise system there are tragedies. With political regulation, no matter how well-intended, there are still tragedies. So just where, on balance do these findings leave us?

For one thing, they suggest that Utopia is not one of our options. Perfection in such areas as installing electrical wiring may not be possible. Surely it is true generally that infallible work is not possible from fallible workers.

Secondly, our findings should cause us to have doubt about political regulation. The evidence indicates, in many cases, that the harm due to political regulation may be greater than the harm the political regulation was intended to correct.

Finally, in a free enterprise system, the courts may provide some regulation. However, *the free market will provide most of the regulation of business*. By a wide margin, market regulation will be the most powerful and efficacious regulator. Market regulation means consumers free to patronize or not patronize a given business. Market regulation means consumers free to decide for themselves what trade-offs to make. Lastly, market regulation means producers free to enter, expand, or withdraw from whatever undertakings their abilities and resources will support.

Since ideal situations are not possible, the best we can do is get closer to the ideal. It seems highly unlikely that political regulation, in the form of occupational licensing or in any other form, can force men and women closer to the ideal than they can come when left free.

Editors' note: For a further discussion of occupational licensure, see Milton Friedman's *Capitalism and Freedom*.

CHAPTER 54

A Free Market Foreign Policy

by Ron Paul

Can there be a foreign policy based on the same principles as a free-market economy?

Some would say that economic and foreign policies are unrelated, and that the latter must be "bipartisan," unlike the former. How else could we get a Henry Jackson and a Barry Goldwater agreeing on foreign policy? In reality, foreign and economic policies are intertwined.

Liberal and Conservative Interventionists

Economic interventionism allows some to support government action for the benefit of business, *e.g.*, tariffs and subsidies; and others to support labor with monopoly wage settlements and compulsory unionism.

Variations can also be found among those who endorse international interventionism.

Most liberal economic interventionists want to intervene overseas to help left-leaning countries.

Most conservatives want to do the same for right-leaning ones.

Is it inconsistent that "free-enterprise" Congressmen should support intervention overseas? Not really, because very few follow a free-market policy consistently. Generally, they endorse special assistance to business with loans, subsidies, and protectionism.

Our foreign policy is like our prevailing economic policy. We accept economic interventionism of liberal and conservative varieties, and we also accept, with little questioning, international interventionism of both varieties as well.

All sorts of liberal/conservative combinations can be seen in economic and foreign policy, but most Members of Congress are interventionists of some sort.

Editors' note: Dr. Paul, in our opinion, is the best example of a champion of liberty in the U.S. Congress today. A man of principle, he votes consistently to keep government in its proper place. This chapter is drawn from his speech before the third annual Freedom in Third Century America Seminar at Northwood Institute, August 1, 1980.

If our foreign policy reflects a general philosophy of economic interventionism and political pragmatism, could we assume that our foreign policy would change if our economic order were based on consistent free-market principles?

Freedom and Foreign Policy

The economic order of a nation reflects the prevailing attitude of its people towards individual liberty. If a strict definition of individual liberty, adequately protected by a Constitution, establishes the foundation on which a totally free economy operates, and we adhere to it, it would not be surprising to see a foreign policy quite different from that which we now suffer.

Generally, most people see foreign policy as being completely separate from economic policy. For instance, my concerns have always been much more oriented toward economic policy, and yet, as I spend more time in government, I have come to realize that the two are interwoven.

When the people of a country insist on maximum liberty, a free market will result and a non-interventionist foreign policy (armed neutrality) will follow. In our own history, when we had our freest economy and soundest currency, we did not fight on foreign soil. As our freedoms eroded and our government became dominated by special interests (labor and business), involvement in the internal affairs of other nations grew and foreign wars resulted. Although the Spanish-American War was late 19th century, the dramatic changes were in the 20th century, with World War I, World War II, Korea, Vietnam, and the pending conflict.

A free society is based on the fundamental premise of God-given, inalienable rights — rights that are individual, not collective, absolute, and not alterable by any state action. A nation so ordained will protect voluntary associations and free choices, demand that contracts be upheld, and insist that money be honest. Under these circumstances, no economic system other than a free-market economy can evolve.

Under these conditions, it follows that government is small with its power strictly limited, the very arrangement envisioned by the Founding Fathers.

The Responsibility of Government

If — for moral and constitutional reasons — we cannot interfere with our citizens' lives and property, to control the economy or individuals' preferences, we also cannot control the internal affairs of any other nation. The responsibility of the government is then limited to protection of life and property.

Robert Taft said, "The purpose of American foreign policy is to maintain the freedom of the people of *this* country, and insofar as it is consistent with that purpose, to keep this country at peace."

"No entangling alliances" was the foreign policy watchword for every administration from George Washington's to Grover Cleveland's.

Washington said, "It is our true policy to steer clear of permanent alliances with any portion of the foreign world.

"The great rule of conduct for us in regard to foreign nations in extending our commercial relations, is to have with them as little political connection as possible.

"Observe good faith and justice to all nations. Cultivate peace and harmony with all. In the execution of such a plan, nothing is more essential than that permanent, inveterate antipathies towards particular nations, and passionate attachments for others should be excluded; and that in place of them an amicable feeling toward all should be cultivated."

Cleveland reiterated by saying, "The genius of our institutions, the needs of our people in their home life, and the attention which is demanded for . . . our vast territory, dictate this scrupulous avoidance of any departure from that foreign policy commended by the history, the traditions and prosperity of our republic. It is the policy of independence favored by our position and defended by our known love of justice and by our power. It is the policy of peace suitable to our interest. It is the policy of neutrality, rejecting any share in foreign brawls, and ambitions upon other continents, and repelling their intrusion here. It is the policy of Monroe and of Washington and of Jefferson; peace, commerce, and honest friendship with all nations; entangling alliances with none."

When We Went Wrong

McKinley began the change in our foreign policy, leading us into the Spanish-American War. But it was Wilson who radically departed from the neutral, noninterventionist foreign policy which we had followed for more than 100 years.

Wilson's policy was "make the world safe for democracy." "America's duty," he said, "is to stand shoulder-to-shoulder, to lift the burdens of mankind in the future, and to show the path of freedom to all the world . . . The American flag is henceforth to stand for . . . the assertion of the right of one nation to serve other nations of the world . . . America is now rich enough and free enough to look abroad for great tasks to perform . . . Our duty is to serve the world."

The concept of individual rights requires that we reject, on a moral basis, any authority to use funds or lives to manipulate the affairs of other nations if we are not directly threatened. (But individuals should not be prohibited from volunteering for or contributing to any cause they support around the world. I would gladly contribute to buy arms for the Afghan rebels, for example, if the law allowed.)

Our Constitution follows this line of reasoning and gives no authority to the Congress to intervene illicitly around the world. We were not designated the policeman or savior of the world by the Founding Fathers. And all our attempts have failed. Our constitutional obligation is to protect our land and our people, and we cannot legally nor morally justify anything more.

Economically, intervention on the international level has turned out to be a disaster and it has not been endorsed by the people. The people have resisted more taxes, and have not been willing to loan the funds to the government to finance foreign aid. So it has been financed by inflation. The past 35 years of international intervention in particular have been a severe financial drain on us. Interventionism has destroyed the dollar, bankrupted our country, and has now caught up with us. Our policy has permitted Japan to spend essentially nothing on defense, and allowed them to subsidize the very industries that undersell competing American companies.

The Impracticality of Interventionism

Practical reasons alone mandate that we rethink our foreign policy. We are now militarily incapable of being the world's policeman. Our economy cannot stand further dollar weakness, and continual debt increase. Our foreign policy — financial aid to the entire world — is contributing significantly to the downfall of our economic system. We can show no good results from all this spending and intervention. We essentially have no friends in the world, we are seen as a paper tiger, and we continue to sign bad treaties. We are misled by administrations, both Republican and Democrat; by compromises; and by wishful thinking.

Leftists in our government have led us to subsidize our enemies. Arguing that we should only subsidize our "friends" is of no value, since the conservatives have argued this for 40 years, and it not only hasn't helped, it has made things worse. We have financed both sides of many major conflicts since 1945. It's time to look after ourselves.

What a Free-Market Foreign Policy Means

A free-market foreign policy would emphasize international free trade for both its economic benefits to our people, and its value in creating an atmosphere of friendly relations with all nations, and guiding us away from militant isolationism.

Free trade recognizes that the customer is sovereign, and that it is his right to buy any good or receive any service at the best price. Free trade also precludes favors to special interests. No foreign aid and no corporate welfare of any sort: no subsidies; no export assistance; no insurance help; no licensing restriction; and no tariffs.

When people and goods flow freely over borders, armies will not. Limitation of trade can only be justified for the direct security of the nation in an armed conflict. If there is any doubt about restraining trade, we should always lean towards permitting trade.

Under these conditions, businessmen would make better economic decisions. Without subsidies for his insurance, overseas investments, and exports, the businessman would anticipate world events, and would voluntarily curtail trade with nations unable to guarantee property protection and honest payment. Now we encourage bad investments and subsidies to the enemy at the innocent taxpayers' expense.

Instead of businessmen selling to Russia or China at American taxpayers' expense, they might demand gold rather than accept rubles or yuans. Public opinion would also restrain trade with perceived enemies.

The Third Choice

In our foreign policy debate, we have had only two choices: be weak, or be international policemen. A third choice is available to us: *neutrality, with a policy of nonintervention in the internal affairs of other nations, plus all the armed strength necessary to protect America.*

With such a foreign policy of strength and confidence, our system would prosper, our international respect would be heightened, and our example to the rest of the world would be much brighter. The complex messes, like the one involving Iran, would not occur, and we would not invite such anti-American resentment.

A liberal — known to follow the weak-America policy — said that he was delighted that our troops are in Europe, since they keep Western Europe from developing a stronger defense capability that might threaten the U.S.S.R.

European nations have never invited our nuclear missiles into their territory. The West Germans now are showing a great reluctance in setting themselves up as a target. They are delighted to let the U.S. be the potential target of Russia, if Russia chooses to wipe out the West's retaliatory capability.

Nations like West Germany must assume the responsibility of their own defense. We cannot afford it economically, nor is it militarily wise for us to continue to provide it for them. For instance, it certainly is in the best interests of the Germans and the French to develop the neutron bomb. The American taxpayer shouldn't do so. Encouraging dependency on the U.S. has neither helped the nations receiving aid, nor us who have provided it. Foreign assistance cannot create a "will to win." Vietnam proved that.

More than half our defense budget now goes to the defense of other nations. These funds would go a long way in providing adequate military pay and building the best weapons, with many dollars left over to use in budget-cutting.

A non-interventionist foreign policy would shift the lines of strategic confrontation. To do nothing about Soviet troops in Cuba and give away the Panama Canal, at taxpayers' expense, while allowing 50,000 men to die in a no-win war in Vietnam, is inconceivably inconsistent. Even though our opinions may vary on just when armed conflict is necessary, it's unforgivable to commit lives to a war with no intention of winning, without even a specific goal. This reflects a sick foreign policy. The Koreas and the Vietnams are preventable. Even our involvement in World War I and World War II can be seriously questioned. Overinvolvement, no matter how promoted by the government, will eventually fail if the will and the spirit of the people reject its intended goals. The draft, the lives, the bombs, and the dollars did not compensate for the bad policy that got us involved in Vietnam.

Non-intervention would also negate bad treaties. SALT I would be repealed, with due notice, and an anti-ballistic missile built, and SALT II would be scrapped. The Panama Canal would not have been handed over to the Marxists at the American taxpayers' expense. No twisted reasoning could trap us into trusting the communists by signing agreements with them, whether they be Russian, Chinese, Cuban, or Nicaraguan. Neither would we subsidize them.

No Isolationism

A free-market, non-interventionist foreign policy is frequently attacked as "isolationist." Nothing could be further from the truth. The image of a nation walling itself off from the rest of the world is impossible in a free society, and is instead exactly what happens under interventionism. With an "internationalist" foreign policy, which includes goals of government and international banking with a fiat currency, economic isolationism always results, with nations becoming more militarily nationalistic. Trade wars ensue, and protectionism runs rampant.

A society with a free-market foreign policy protects absolutely the rights of its citizens to travel and trade across the borders, without tariffs or licenses, and rejects all special-interest subsidies. Emigration is always permissible, and no attempts to curtail the movement of currency or people is made. The ultimate right of the free society is to be able to vote with your feet — to leave freely with your assets.

This freedom of movement, of people and goods, encourages the intermingling of people and a natural balance in trade, assuming nations do not participate in the fraud of inflation. Freedom would not create a Fortress America, or a country isolated. Only the opposite could result.

No Conscription

A crucial aspect of the free-market foreign policy is a volunteer military. The best vote on the advisability of war and the commitment needed to win comes from those who are forced to risk their lives. In America, a fight to defend our freedoms will bring out the volunteers by the millions. But another halfhearted fight to "contain" communism, or prop up a "Western-leaning" dictator, will not wash.

The best way to find out if a war is needed for our survival and security is to ask the people who are to risk their lives to volunteer.

Also, can the war be fought with open taxation or borrowing, and without resorting to the inflation machine? Remember, the American Revolution was fought without a draft, and it was won against great odds. With all our firepower, and with a conscripted army, we didn't even defeat North Vietnam.

As our children are forced to pay for the effects of borrowing on tomorrow through inflation, and suffer the erosion of the free market system, so too will they suffer the consequences of unwise treaty commitments. Why should a youngster born in 1960, pay with his life for a war fought to police the world, pursuant to a treaty signed in 1945? This is hardly fair. All of our international commitments need reassessment.

Some say we will need to fight for Middle Eastern oil. But these are the same economic interventionists who won't deregulate our energy industry,* who compel the use of coal, and who prohibit nuclear power. Economic policy and foreign policy cannot be separated. And, despite the scare talk, only 5% of total U.S. energy comes through the Straits of Hormuz.

The Need For Change

In spite of the dollars spent, the rhetoric heard, draft preparations, CIA activities, and troops around the world, we are weaker than ever before. Our policies need change, for even if it is still claimed that we need international commitments, it is precisely the policy of the past 40 years that has made us so weak. America now is desperately close to being undefended from Russian attack. This must be changed, but it won't be without a new policy. We can tolerate no more Koreas or Vietnams, economically, militarily, or psychologically.

The evidence is clear: the more intervention economically, the more intervention internationally, and the greater the chance of poverty and war. The less economic intervention, the less international intervention, and the greater the chance of prosperity and peace.

My vote is for non-intervention.

---

*Editors' Note: Most remaining energy price controls were finally abolished in early 1981 by President Reagan. A stronger domestic industry and less dependence on Middle Eastern oil should result in time.

Unit X: How To Advance Liberty

Liberty's friends must do more than complain about the erosion of liberty. We must *act*. It is imperative that we have a *forward strategy* and to that end we conclude our book with a unit on how to advance our cause.

In 1949, Dean Russell (then of the Foundation for Economic Education staff) wrote a letter in response to a question asked by a business executive. The letter was subsequently reprinted under the title, "A Thought Starter," and we further reprint its timely message here. The forward strategy we speak of begins with Russell's advice: "We as individuals must understand the philosophy of freedom so well that we can explain it convincingly and persuasively." We consider that advice so vital that we will end this unit with a chapter that repeats it.

Recognizing that "the battle for the perservation and advancement of liberty is a battle not against personalities but against opposing *ideas*," is important to the success of liberty's appeal. "Liberty and the Power of Ideas" is the text of a speech reprinted here because it neatly summarizes the ideas the freedom believer is up against. It also serves as a reminder of just what it means to be free.

Dr. Hans F. Sennholz of Grove City College is one of the most inspiring teachers of freedom this country has. He is well known for his emphasis on the role of morality in a free society. In "You Cannot Get Even," Dr. Sennholz offers a "new covenant of redemption" in which he implores Americans to withdraw from active participation in the redistribution of income.

"Isaiah's Job" by Albert J. Nock is an antidote for those occasional feelings of "Oh, what's the use!" Believers in liberty will find in this essay excellent counsel on how one may work most effectively for the cause.

"The Essence of a Free Society" by former Treasury Secretary

William Simon is a little dated in places (for instance, the national debt, at more than $1 trillion, is double the stated figure) but the principles and the inspiration are eternal. Simon appeals for "a return to the work ethic, family discipline, fiscal responsibility, belief in a strong and almighty God."

That great exponent of liberty, Leonard E. Read, concludes our book with "Voices in the Wilderness." What is his advice to those who would work for liberty? Read urges each individual to "advance his *own* enlightenment to such a brilliance that a few, at least, will turn away from the TV and other entertainment to an enlightenment effort of their own."

With that last chapter, our book is completed. Our mission, and that of other like-minded individuals, is not. Liberty, perhaps the noblest of earthly goals, is an eternal struggle against the forces of darkness. Its friends must remain true to its principles and committed to responsible action. We sincerely hope that after you have read this book of readings, we can count *you* among the friends of liberty.

CHAPTER 55

A Thought Starter

by Dean Russell

February 3, 1949

Mr. Norman F. Edwards
Holmes-Darst Coal Corporation
Hamilton Bank Building
Knoxville, Tennessee

Dear Mr. Edwards:

"What can I as an individual do to stop this mad rush toward compulsory collectivism in America today?" Few questions are as challenging as yours, and here's my attempt at an answer.

Fortunately for the cause of freedom, it is only as an individual that you or I can do anything at all. This is true because every good idea — as well as every bad idea — begins with one person. He in turn convinces another person. Soon there are several persons who have accepted this idea as advanced by one individual person.

This is the voluntary way of accomplishing a desired objective. This is the only method that is in accord with freedom. Unfortunately, it quite frequently happens that individual persons who have voluntarily accepted an idea then band themselves together to force — by vote or otherwise — their idea upon other persons. This, of course, is directly opposed to freedom. It is force and compulsion. This is the method used by those who desire to make other persons do as they think "best for them" or "for their own good." This concept is contained in the much used phrases, "There ought to be a law to make people do this" and "Every American should be forced to read this."

Force cannot be used in the interests of freedom — except for self-defense and rebellion against slavery. This holds true whether the force is applied by a majority or a minority. It holds true whether the force is applied by a robber with a pistol or by a representative of the majority of the people who have voted to force other persons to do what the majority considers "best for them." The theory now held in this country that the votes of the majority automatically insure freedom is incorrect. It is now leading us to our own destruction. *Might has never made right.* It never will.

This is not to deny that a republic or representative democracy is the most desirable form of government we have yet discovered. It is not to deny that freedom is safer in the hands of the many than in the hands of the few. But it is to deny that freedom is automatically safe just because the franchise has become widespread in America, just because we call ourselves "a democracy." It requires more than a vote to preserve liberty; it requires *understanding* on the part of the voters; it requires the knowledge that all governmental decrees and actions must be grounded on moral and natural law if they are to benefit the people.

And that is where *you as an individual* enter the picture. Without in any respect repudiating democracy and the right of universal franchise, all voters must understand that *what becomes law* is far more vital to freedom than the method used to secure its passage. Blinded by the erroneous belief that freedom is automatically guaranteed by the right to vote, we are now rapidly voting ourselves into abject dependence upon governmental control of our affairs. We are repudiating the responsibility that *is* freedom. We are adopting a "something for nothing" philosophy.

Serving the Cause of Freedom

If you would best serve the cause of freedom, you must explain this concept to all who will listen. If you as an individual neglect to do this, how else can it be done? I cannot do it because I do not know your family, your business associates, your fellow churchmen, your lodge brothers, your friends. They will listen to you — not to me.

Now you may say, "But all my associates and friends already agree with me. They are already on our side!"

It is true that most of your associates and friends may pay lip service to the principle of private ownership of the means of production. They may say that they are opposed to "special privileges" for anyone — but are they? How many of them are opposed to government's entry into the business of producing and selling electricity? How many of them understand the danger to personal freedom found in compulsory, government-guaranteed "security?" Who is the logical person to explain it to them — I or you?

Are all of your friends and associates opposed to government-decreed, compulsory unionism? How about our government's support of socialism in Europe? Do your associates understand that tariffs cause higher prices by protecting inefficient producers? What about the other violations of freedom such as rent control, progressive taxation, the decreasing of the value of our money by government decree and by deficit financing, price supports and a host of others? These are vital issues. Can you explain them convincingly to your friends and associates?

What can you as a lone individual do? First you can train yourself to *explain* instead of, like most of us, only to *sputter* on behalf of liberty. We here at The Foundation for Economic Education can be of help in that respect.* In many cases, we spend a thousand technically skilled hours to prepare a study that you or any other interested person can read and understand in less than an hour. Our sole purpose is to furnish this information to any person who will use it. Our work is ineffective unless individual persons read it, understand it and explain it to other individual persons.

Now it may be that you — like me — do not know the answers to all these questions. If that is true, I suggest that you and I learn them. Literally, we must *learn* freedom. We as individuals must understand the philosophy of freedom so well that we can explain it convincingly and persuasively.

Patience and Understanding

Above all, as individuals we must begin this job with other individuals. Don't expect to change the course of the nation overnight. Begin with just one person. Convince him or her that personal responsibility for one's own welfare is more desirable than government-guaranteed "security." Convince him that freedom will work if we will only trust in it. If this one person becomes convinced through understanding, he or she will in turn convince another person. And so on. In short, if you yourself understand and are able to explain the fallacies of compulsory, government collectivism — and the alternative advantages of voluntary cooperation — many persons will seek your opinion and advice. Only then will you become truly effective.

Slow? Yes! But it is the *only* way. Any short-cut must necessarily involve compulsion. That would defeat your own purpose! Education is indeed a slow process. That is because it must be voluntary. The person must want to know. He cannot learn until first he has a desire to learn. Thus your task as one individual person is indeed a hard one and a vital one. First you yourself must be able to explain your philosophy convincingly. Then you must be most tactful in approaching the other person. While it is not dangerous to be honest, one should not become cantankerous with his honesty. Don't argue; explain. Don't call names; you will only antagonize.

---

*Editors' note: We heartily commend the work of the Foundation for Economic Education to the reader. A subscription to the foundation's monthly publication, *The Freeman*, is available upon request by writing F.E.E., 30 South Broadway, Irvington-on-Hudson, New York 10533.

Since freedom is the world's finest product, there is no reason why a skilled salesman can't sell it to several of his friends and associates. Suppose that a million "individual persons" did that? The battle for freedom would soon be won. The voters would then automatically reject all socialistic candidates and proposals, by peaceful and voluntary means.

I hope that this purely personal answer may be of some aid or encouragement to you. And, finally, good luck!

Sincerely,
Dean Russell

CHAPTER 56

Liberty and the Power of Ideas

by Lawrence W. Reed

A belief which I stress again and again in my classes at Northwood Institute in Midland, Michigan is the belief that *we are at war* — not a physical, shooting war but nonetheless a war which is fully capable of becoming just as destructive and just as costly. It is a conflict whose outcome will be as decisive as any military engagement ever was, for on that outcome hinges the fate of the free society.

Let's understand at the outset that the battle for the preservation and advancement of liberty is a battle not against personalities but against opposing *ideas*. The French author Victor Hugo declared that "More powerful than armies is an idea whose time has come." Armies conquer bodies, but ideas capture minds. The English philosopher Carlyle put it this way many decades ago: "But the thing a man does practically believe (and this is often enough *without* asserting it to himself, much less to others): the thing a man does practically lay to heart, and know for certain, concerning his vital relations to this mysterious Universe, and his duty and destiny there, that is in all cases the primary thing for him, and creatively determines all the rest."

In the past, ideas have had earthshaking consequences. They have molded nothing less than the course of history.

After the fall of Rome and for the next thousand years, the system of feudalism prevailed in large part because scholars, teachers, intellectuals, educators, clergymen, and politicians propagated feudalistic ideas. The notion of "once a serf, always a serf" kept millions of people from ever questioning their station in life.

Then, under mercantilism, the widely-accepted concept that the world's wealth was fixed prompted men to take what they wanted from others in a long series of bloody wars from the War of Jenkins' Ear to the fall of Napoleon.

The publication of Adam Smith's *The Wealth of Nations* in 1776 is a landmark in the history of the power of ideas. As Smith's

---

*This is the text of a speech delivered before the fourth annual American Idea Seminar, Columbia Lakes, Texas, August 18, 1980.

message of free trade spread, political barriers to peaceful cooperation collapsed, the mercantilist era ended, and virtually the whole world decided to try free markets and political liberty for a change.

In arguing against freedom of the press in 1924, Lenin made the famous statement that "ideas are much more fatal than guns." To this day, ideas by themselves — just *believing* in something — can get you a prison sentence in communist lands.

Marx and the Marxists would have us believe that socialism is inevitable, that it will embrace the world as surely as the sun will rise in the east tomorrow. But as long as men have free will (the power to choose right from wrong), nothing that involves this human volition can ever be inevitable! Men do things because they are of the mind to do them; they are not robots programmed to carry out some preordained dictum. If socialism does come, it will come because men choose to embrace its principles!

Principles of Socialism

Winston Churchill once said that "Socialism is the philosophy of failure, the creed of ignorance, and the gospel of envy. Its inherent trait is the equal sharing of misery." Socialism is an age-old failure, yet the socialist idea constitutes the chief threat to liberty today. So it is that believers in liberty, to be effective, must first identify and isolate the socialist notions which are taking their toll on liberty. In doing that, and then refraining from advancing those ideas, we can at the same time advance liberty. As I see it, socialism can be broken down into five ideas:

1. *The Pass a Law Syndrome.* Passing laws has become a national pastime. When a problem in society is cited, the most frequent response seems to be, "Pass a law!" Business in trouble? Pass a law to give it public subsidies or restrict its freedom of action. Poverty? Pass a law to abolish it. Perhaps what America needs is a law against passing more laws.

Take a recent year, say, 1977. Congress enacted 223 new laws. It repealed hardly any. During that same year, the federal bureaucracy wrote 7,568 new regulations, all having the force of law.

James Madison in 1795 identified this syndrome as "the old trick of turning every difficulty into a reason for accumulating more force in government." His observation leads one to ask, "Just what happens when a new law goes on the books?" Almost invariably, a new law means: a) more taxes to finance its administration; b) additional government officials to regulate some heretofore unregulated aspect of life; and c) new penalties for violating the law. In brief, more laws mean more regimentation, more coercion! Let there be no doubt about what the word coercion means: force, plunder, compulsion, restraint. Synonyms for the verb form of the word are even more instructive: impel, exact, subject, conscript, extort, wring, pry, twist, dragoon, bludgeon, and squeeze!

When government begins to intervene in the free economy, bureaucrats and politicians spend most of their time undoing their own handiwork. To repair the damage of Provision A, they pass Provision B. Then they find that to repair Provision B, they need Provision C, and to undo C they need D, and so on until the alphabet and our freedoms are exhausted.

The Pass a Law Syndrome is evidence of a misplaced faith in the political process, a reliance on *force* which is anathema to the free society.

2. *The Get Something for Nothing Fantasy*. Government by definition has nothing to distribute except what it first takes from people. Taxes are not donations!

In the Welfare State, this basic fact gets lost in the rush for special favors and giveaways. People speak of "government money" as if it were truly "free."

One who is thinking of accepting something from government which he could not acquire voluntarily should ask, "From whose pocket is it coming? Am *I* being robbed myself to pay for this benefit or is government robbing someone else *on my behalf?*" Frequently, the answer will be *both*!

Today, what business group, what labor union, what city, what occupation or age group is not either receiving benefits through government or at least seeking them? The obvious answer is enough to render the message of Emerson's essay on "Self Reliance" almost a dead letter in America today.

The end result of this "fantasy" is that everyone in society has his hands in someone else's pockets. And this corrupting notion has given us a government which is consuming nearly one-half of national income today, compared to just one-tenth at the start of this century.

3. *The Pass the Buck Psychosis*. Recently a welfare recipient wrote her welfare office and demanded, "This is my sixth kid. What are *you* going to do about it?"

An individual is victim to the Pass the Buck Psychosis when he abandons himself as the solver of *his* problems. He might say, "My problems are really not mine at all. They are society's, and if society doesn't solve them and solve them quickly, there's going to be trouble!" I would submit to you that when individuals demand that solutions come from Washington, they are full speed ahead on a dangerous flight from responsibility.

Socialism thrives on the shirking of responsibility. When men lose their spirit of independence and initiative, their confidence in themselves, they become clay in the hands of tyrants and despots.

4. *The Know-It-All Affliction.* Leonard Read, in *The Free Market and Its Enemy,* identifies "know-it-allness" as a central feature of the socialist idea — that some men are capable of planning the lives of others.

The know-it-all is by nature a meddler in the affairs of others. His attitude may be expressed this way: "I know what's best for you, but I'm not content to merely *convince* you of my rightness; I'd rather *force* you to adopt my ways." The know-it-all evinces arrogance and a lack of tolerance for the great diversity among people.

In government, the know-it-all refrain sounds like this: "If I didn't think of it, then it can't be done, and since it can't be done, we must prevent anyone from trying."

A group of West Coast businessmen ran into this snag a few months back when their request to operate a barge service between the Pacific Northwest and Southern California was denied by the Interstate Commerce Commission because the agency felt the group could not operate such a service profitably!

The miracle of the marketplace is that when men are free to try, they can and do accomplish great things. Leonard Read's well-known admonition that there should be "no man-concocted restraints against the release of creative energy" is a powerful rejection of the Know-It-All Affliction.

5. *The Envy Obsession.* Coveting the wealth and income of others has given rise to a sizable chunk of today's socialist legislation. Envy is the fuel which runs the engine of income redistribution. Surely, the many soak-the-rich schemes are rooted in envy and covetousness.

What happens when people are obsessed with envy? They blame those who are better off than themselves for their troubles. Society is fractured into classes and faction preys upon faction. Children are taught to despise the successful and to lust after their wealth rather than to aspire to similar achievement. Civilizations have been known to crumble under the weight of envy and the disrespect for life and property which it entails.

A common thread runs through these five socialist ideas. They all appeal to the darker side of man: the primitive, noncreative, slothful, dependent, demoralizing, unproductive, and destructive side of human nature. No society can long endure if its people practice such suicidal notions on a grand scale!

Principles of Liberty

The ideal of liberty provides quite a stunning contrast. The very concept is uplifting, regenerative, motivating, creative, and dynamic! It rests, as I see it, upon these pillars of wisdom:

1. *Self-reliance* — A man's first duty after reverence to his Creator is to refrain from becoming a burden on others.

2. *Personal responsibility* — Every individual must recognize that he can choose between right and wrong and therefore is accountable and responsible for his actions.

3. *Respect for life and property* — Following the teachings of the "Golden Rule" and the commandments against murdering, coveting, and stealing, make possible a peaceful society in which liberty can flourish.

4. *Voluntary assistance to the needy* — Charity comes from the heart and material substance of a free people, not from government paternalism. When not burdened with excessive taxation and government interference, Americans have traditionally come to the aid of the needy. As de Tocqueville observed more than a century ago (paraphrasing): "America is great because America is good. When Americans cease to be good, America will cease to be great."

5. *Limited government* — The sole function of the State should be that of a "nightwatchman" — to provide for the common defense against those, at home or abroad, who would do violence to innocent citizens. It is not the duty of government to play Robin Hood or Santa Claus.

Don't take my words as the final description of liberty. Listen to what these individuals have said:

Epictetus: "No man is free who is not a master of himself."

Gandhi: "Freedom is not worth having if it does not mean the freedom to make mistakes."

Dwight Eisenhower: "Only our individual faith in freedom can keep us free."

William Allen White: "Liberty is the only thing you can't have unless you give it to others."

Robert Green Ingersoll: "What light is to our eyes, what air is to the lungs, what love is to the heart, liberty is to the soul of man."

W. Somerset Maugham: "If a nation values anything more than freedom, it will lose its freedom."

Abraham Lincoln: "Those who deny freedom to others deserve it not for themselves, and under a just God, cannot long retain it."

Edward Hiles: "Freedom is not free and it must not be taken for granted. It was won through sacrifice and will be maintained only through sacrifice. It can be lost — just as surely, just as completely, and just as permanently — tax by tax, subsidy by subsidy, and regulation by regulation, as it can be lost bullet by bullet, bomb by bomb, missile by missile."

It's cruel irony that even as we lose our liberties, we seem to take for granted those which we have left. Whether we realize it or not, the promise of America is still the promise of liberty, for there is hardly another place on earth which men and women can still come to in rags and pull themselves up to lofty heights of accomplishment.

A few weeks ago, a Cuban woman, one of thousands fleeing Castro's tyranny, arrived in Florida. She had nothing but the clothes on her back in a strange, new land. A reporter inquired, as she kissed the ground, "Are you happy?"

"Oh, yes!" she exclaimed.

"Why?" asked the reporter.

Tearfully, the woman replied, "I'm free! I'm free!"

Now there's a soul who understands better than most Americans what liberty really is. And my guess is that she will never forget as long as she lives what it means not to have it. To her, liberty was an idea whose time was long and painfully overdue.

Nobel Prize winner F. A. Hayek has called attention to the power of ideas in preserving liberty: "Unless we can make the philosophic foundations of a free society once more a living intellectual issue, and its implementation a task which challenges the ingenuity and imagination of our liveliest minds, the prospects of freedom are indeed dark."

The verdict of this epic struggle between liberty and serfdom depends entirely upon what percolates in the hearts and minds of men and women. At the present time, the jury is still deliberating.

CHAPTER 57

You Cannot Get Even

by Hans F. Sennholz

Government affects individual incomes by virtually every decision it makes. Agricultural programs, veterans' benefits, health and labor and welfare expenditures, housing and community development, federal expenditures on education, social insurance, medicare and medicaid programs, and last but not least, numerous regulations and controls affect the economic conditions of every citizen. In fact, modern government has become a universal transfer agency that utilizes the political process for distributing vast measures of economic income and wealth. It preys on millions of victims in order to allocate valuable goods and services to its beneficiaries. With the latter, transfer programs are so popular that few public officials and politicians dare oppose them.

The motive powers that drive the transfer order are as varied as human design itself. Surely, the true motives are often concealed, and a hollow pretext is pompously placed in the front for show. And yet, man is more accountable for his motives than for anything else. A good motive may exculpate a poor action, but a bad motive vitiates even the finest action. Conscience is merely our own judgment of the right and wrong of our action, and therefore can never be a safe guide unless it is enlightened by a thorough understanding of the implications and consequences of our actions. Without an enlightened conscience we may do evil thoroughly and heartily.

An important spring of action for the transfer society is the desire by most people to *get even* in the redistribution struggle. "I have been victimized in the past by taxation, inflation, regulation, or other devices," so the argument goes, "therefore I am entitled to partake in this particular benefit." Or the time sequence may be reversed: "I'll be victimized later in life," pleads the college student, "and therefore I want state aid and subsidy now."

This argument is probably the most powerful pacifier of conscience. It dulls our perception and discernment of what is evil and makes us slow to shun it. After all, we are merely getting back "what is rightfully our own." With a curious twist of specious de-

From *The Freeman*, June 1978

duction, the modern welfare state, which continually seizes and redistributes private property by force, is defended by the friends of individual liberty and private property. "Man is entitled to the fruits of his labor," they argue, "we are merely getting back that which is rightfully and morally our own." They borrow the arguments for the private property order to sustain the political transfer order.

Surely getting back that which is rightfully and morally our own is a principle that is rooted in our inalienable right to our lives. It is a property right that springs from our human rights and from the right to life itself. It is the right to restoration of the fruits of our efforts and labors of which we are deprived by deceit, force, or any other immoral practice. It is a specific right to recovery or compensation from those who are wronging us or have injured us in the past.

Don't Try To "Get Even"

This right to restoration does not beget the right to commit the very immoral act from which we seek restoration, to imitate others in acting immorally, or to seek revenge against the trespassers or innocent bystanders. But this is precisely what the "get-even" advisors urge us to do.

In an unfortunate automobile accident we are hurt or injured, or our vehicle may be damaged, because of the negligence of another driver. This gives us the right to demand restoration and compensation from the guilty party. But it does not give us the right to seize another car parked in the neighborhood, or return to the road and injure another driver. Or, our home is burglarized and we suffer deplorable losses in personal wealth and memorabilia. This does not bestow upon us the right to do likewise to others. But the "get even" advocates are drawing this very conclusion.

He who is desirous of "getting even" in the politics of redistribution longs to join the army of beneficiaries who are presently preying on their victims. They would like to get their "money back" from whomever they can find and victimize now. Like the victim of a burglary who becomes a burglar himself, they are searching for other victims. But in contrast to the new burglar who may be aware of the immorality of his actions, the "get-even" advocate openly defends his motives while he is pursuing his political craft.

We cannot get even with those individuals who deprived us of our property in the past. They may have long departed this life or may have fallen among the victims themselves. We cannot get even with them by enlisting in the standing army of redistributors. We merely perpetuate the evil by joining their forces. So we must stand immune to the temptations of evil, regardless of what others are doing to us. The redistribution must stop with us.

The redistributive society has victimized many millions of people through confiscatory taxation, inflation, and regulation. Government, acting as the political agency for coercive transfer, seized income and wealth from the more productive members and then redistributed the spoils to its beneficiaries. Although many millions of victims and beneficiaries were involved, which often obscures the morality of the issue, the forced transfer took place between certain individuals. It is true, the beneficiaries, who used political force to obtain the benefits, cannot easily be recognized in the mass process of transfer. But even if we could identify them, and establish a personal right to restoration, our property has been consumed long ago. A vast army of beneficiaries, together with their legions of government officials and civil servants, consumed or otherwise squandered our substance. There is nothing to retrieve from the beneficiaries who probably are poorer than ever before, having grown weak and dependent on the transfer process.

When seen in this light, the get-even argument is nothing more than a declaration of intention to join the redistribution forces. It may be born from the primitive urge for revenge against government, state or society. But it is individuals who form a government, make a state and constitute a society. By taking revenge against some of them for the injuries suffered from the hands of others, I am merely reinforcing the evil.

Revenge is a common passion that enslaves man's mind and clouds his vision. To the savage it is a noble aspiration that makes him even with his enemies. In a civilized society that is seeking peace and harmony it is a destructive force which law seeks to suppress. But when the law itself becomes an instrument of transfer, the primitive urge for revenge may burst forth as a demand for more redistribution. It becomes a primary force that gives rise to new demands or, at least, reinforces the popular demands for economic transfer. The common passion for revenge, no matter how well concealed, undoubtedly is an important motive power of social policy that leads a free society to its own destruction.

No wealth in the world and no political distribution of this wealth can purchase the peace and harmony so essential to human existence. Peace and harmony can be found only in moral elevation that reaches into every aspect of human life. A free society is the offspring of morality that guides the actions and policies of its members. To effect a rebirth of such a society is to revive the moral principles that gave it birth in the beginning. It is individual rebirth and rededication to the inexorable principles of morality that are the power and the might. The example of great individuals is useful to lead us on the way, for nothing is more contagious for greatness than the power of a great example.

A Covenant of Redemption

To spearhead a rebirth of our free society let us rededicate ourselves to a new covenant of redemption, which is a simple restatement of public morality. In the setting of our age of economic redistribution and social conflict it may be stated as follows:

- No matter how the transfer state may victimize me, I shall seek no transfer payments, or accept any.
- I shall seek no government grants, loans or other redistributive favors, or accept any.
- I shall seek no government orders on behalf of redistribution, or accept any.
- I shall seek no employment, or accept any, in the government apparatus of redistribution.
- I shall seek no favors, or accept any, from the regulatory agencies of government.
- I shall seek no protection from tariff barriers or any other institutional restrictions of trade and commerce.
- I shall seek no services from, or lend support to, collective institutions that are creatures of redistribution.
- I shall seek no support from, or give support to, associations that advocate or practice coercion and restraint.

We do not know whether our great republic will survive this century. If it can be saved, great men of conviction must lead the way — men who with religious fervor and unbounded courage resist all transfer temptations. The heroes of liberty are no less remarkable for what they suffer than for what they achieve.

CHAPTER 58

Isaiah's Job

by Albert J. Nock

One evening last autumn, I sat long hours with a European acquaintance while he expounded a politico-economic doctrine which seemed sound as a nut and in which I could find no defect. At the end, he said with great earnestness: "I have a mission to the masses. I feel that I am called to get the ear of the people. I shall devote the rest of my life to spreading my doctrine far and wide among the populace. What do you think?"

An embarrassing question in any case, and doubly so under the circumstances, because my acquaintance is a very learned man, one of the three or four really first-class minds that Europe produced in his generation; and naturally I, as one of the unlearned, was inclined to regard his lightest word with reverence amounting to awe....

I referred him to the story of the prophet Isaiah.... I shall paraphrase the story in our common speech since it has to be pieced out from various sources....

The prophet's career began at the end of King Uzziah's reign, say about 740 B.C. This reign was uncommonly long, almost half a century, and apparently prosperous. It was one of those prosperous reigns, however — like the reign of Marcus Aurelius at Rome, or the administration of Eubulus at Athens, or of Mr. Coolidge at Washington — where at the end the prosperity suddenly peters out and things go by the board with a resounding crash.

In the year of Uzziah's death, the Lord commissioned the prophet to go out and warn the people of the wrath to come. "Tell them what a worthless lot they are," He said. "Tell them what is wrong, and why, and what is going to happen unless they have a change of heart and straighten up. Don't mince matters. Make it clear that they are positively down to their last chance. Give it to them good and strong and keep on giving it to them. I suppose perhaps I ought to tell you," He added, "that it won't do any good. The official class and their intelligentsia will turn up their noses at

---

Extracted from Chapter 13 of Nock's 1937 book, *Free Speech and Plain Language*, and reprinted in *Notes from FEE*, July 1962.

you, and the masses will not even listen. They will all keep on in their own ways until they carry everything down to destruction, and you will probably be lucky if you get out with your life."

Isaiah had been very willing to take on the job — in fact, he had asked for it — but the prospect put a new face on the situation. It raised the obvious question: Why, if all that were so — if the enterprise were to be a failure from the start — was there any sense in starting it?

"Ah," the Lord said, "you do not get the point. There is a Remnant there that you know nothing about. They are obscure, unorganized, inarticulate, each one rubbing along as best he can. They need to be encouraged and braced up because when everything has gone completely to the dogs, they are the ones who will come back and build up a new society; and meanwhile, your preaching will reassure them and keep them hanging on. Your job is to take care of the Remnant, so be off now and set about it.". . .

Quality Distinguishes the Remnant

What do we mean by the masses, and what by the Remnant?

As the word *masses* is commonly used, it suggests agglomerations of poor and underprivileged people, laboring people, proletarians. But it means nothing like that; it means simply the majority. The mass-man is one who has neither the force of intellect to apprehend the principles issuing in what we know as the humane life, nor the force of character to adhere to those principles steadily and strictly as laws of conduct; and because such people make up the great, the overwhelming majority of mankind, they are called collectively *the masses*. The line of differentiation between the masses and the Remnant is set invariably by quality, not by circumstance. The Remnant are those who by force of intellect are able to apprehend these principles, and by force of character are able, at least measurably, to cleave to them. The masses are those who are unable to do either.

The picture which Isaiah presents of the Judean masses is most unfavorable. In his view, the mass-man — be he high or be he lowly, rich or poor, prince or pauper — gets off very badly. He appears as not only weak-minded and weak-willed, but as by consequence knavish, arrogant, grasping, dissipated, unprincipled, unscrupulous. . . .

As things now stand, Isaiah's job seems rather to go begging. Everyone with a message nowadays is, like my venerable European friend, eager to take it to the masses. His first, last, and only thought is of mass-acceptance and mass-approval. His great care is to put his doctrine in such shape as will capture the masses' attention and interest. . . .

The main trouble with this [mass-man approach] is its reaction upon the mission itself. It necessitates an opportunist sophistication of one's doctrine, which profoundly alters its character and reduces it to a mere placebo. If, say, you are a preacher, you wish to attract as large a congregation as you can, which means an appeal to the masses; and this, in turn, means adapting the terms of your message to the order of intellect and character that the masses exhibit. If you are an educator, say with a college on your hands, you wish to get as many students as possible, and you whittle down your requirements accordingly. If a writer, you aim at getting many readers; if a publisher, many purchasers; if a philosopher, many disciples; if a reformer, many converts; if a musician, many auditors; and so on. But as we see on all sides, in the realization of these several desires the prophetic message is so heavily adulterated with trivialities, in every instance, that its effect on the masses is merely to harden them in their sins. Meanwhile, the Remnant, aware of this adulteration and of the desires that prompt it, turn their backs on the prophet and will have nothing to do with him or his message.

Isaiah, on the other hand, worked under no such disabilities. He preached to the masses only in the sense that he preached publicly. Anyone who liked might listen; anyone who liked might pass by. He knew that the Remnant would listen. . . .

The Remnant want only the best you have, whatever that may be. Give them that, and they are satisfied; you have nothing more to worry about. . . .

In a sense, nevertheless, as I have said, it is not a rewarding job. . . . A prophet of the Remnant will not grow purse-proud on the financial returns from his work, nor is it likely that he will get any great renown out of it. Isaiah's case was exceptional to this second rule, and there are others — but not many.

It may be thought, then, that while taking care of the Remnant is no doubt a good job, it is not an especially interesting job because it is as a rule so poorly paid. I have my doubts about this. There are other compensations to be got out of a job besides money and notoriety, and some of them seem substantial enough to be attractive. Many jobs which do not pay well are yet profoundly interesting, as, for instance, the job of the research student in the sciences is said to be; and the job of looking after the Remnant seems to me, as I have surveyed it for many years from my seat in the grandstand, to be as interesting as any that can be found in the world.

What chiefly makes it so, I think, is that in any given society the Remnant are always so largely an unknown quantity. You do not know, and will never know, more than two things about them. You can be sure of those — dead sure, as our phrase is — but you will never be able to make even a respectable guess at anything else. You do not know, and will never know, who the Remnant are, nor where they are, nor how many of them there are, nor what they are doing or will do. Two things you know, and no more: first, that they exist; second, that they will find you. Except for these two certainties, working for the Remnant means working in impenetrable darkness; and this, I should say, is just the condition calculated most effectively to pique the interest of any prophet who is properly gifted with the imagination, insight, and intellectual curiosity necessary to a successful pursuit of his trade.

The Historian's Work

The fascination — as well as the despair — of the historian, as he looks back upon Isaiah's Jewry, upon Plato's Athens, or upon Rome of the Antonines, is the hope of discovering and laying bare the "substratum of right-thinking and well-doing" which he knows must have existed somewhere in those societies because no kind of collective life can possibly go on without it. He finds tantalizing intimations of it here and there in many places, as in the Greek Anthology, in the scrapbook of Aulus Gellius, in the poems of Ausonius, and in the brief and touching tribute, *Bene merenti*, bestowed upon the unknown occupants of Roman tombs. But these are vague and fragmentary; they lead him nowhere in his search for some kind of measure of this substratum, but merely testify to what he already knew *a priori* — that the substratum did somewhere exist. Where it was, how substantial it was, what its power of self-assertion and resistance was — of all this they tell him nothing.

Similarly, when the historian of two thousand years hence, or two hundred years, looks over the available testimony to the quality of our civilization and tries to get any kind of clear, competent evidence concerning the substratum of right-thinking and well-doing which he knows must have been here, he will have a devil of a time finding it. When he has assembled all he can get and has made even a minimum allowance for speciousness, vagueness, and confusion of motive, he will sadly acknowledge that his net result is simply nothing. A Remnant were here, building a substratum like coral insects; so much he knows, but he will find nothing to put him on the track of who and where and how many they were and what their work was like.

Concerning all this, too, the prophet of the present knows precisely as much and as little as the historian of the future; and that, I repeat, is what makes his job seem to me so profoundly interesting. One of the most suggestive episodes recounted in the Bible is that of a prophet's attempt — the only attempt of the kind on record, I believe — to count up the Remnant. Elijah had fled from persecution into the desert, where the Lord presently overhauled him and asked what he was doing so far away from his job. He said that he was running away, not because he was a coward, but because all the Remnant had been killed off except himself. He had got away only by the skin of his teeth, and, he being now all the Remnant there was, if he were killed the True Faith would go flat. The Lord replied that he need not worry about that, for even without him the True Faith could probably manage to squeeze along somehow if it had to; "and as for your figures on the Remnant," He said, "I don't mind telling you that there are seven thousand of them back there in Israel whom it seems you have not heard of, but you may take My word for it that there they are."

At that time, probably the population of Israel could not have run to much more than a million or so; and a Remnant of seven thousand out of a million is a highly encouraging percentage for any prophet. With seven thousand of the boys on his side, there was no great reason for Elijah to feel lonesome; and incidentally, that would be something for the modern prophet of the Remnant to think of when he has a touch of the blues. But the main point is that if Elijah the Prophet could not make a closer guess on the number of the Remnant than he made when he missed it by seven thousand, anyone else who tackled the problem would only waste his time.

The other certainty which the prophet of the Remnant may always have is that the Remnant will find him. He may rely on that with absolute assurance. They will find him without his doing anything about it; in fact, if he tries to do anything about it, he is pretty sure to put them off. He does not need to advertise for them nor resort to any schemes of publicity to get their attention. If he is a preacher or a public speaker, for example, he may be quite indifferent to going on show at receptions, getting his picture printed in the newspapers, or furnishing autobiographical material for publication on the side of "human interest." If a writer, he need not make a point of attending any pink teas, autographing books at wholesale, nor entering into any specious freemasonry with reviewers.

The Proper Technique

All this and much more of the same order lies in the regular and necessary routine laid down for the prophet of the masses. It is, and must be, part of the great general technique of getting the massman's ear — or as our vigorous and excellent publicist, Mr. H. L. Mencken, puts it, the technique of boob-bumping. The prophet of the Remnant is not bound to this technique. He may be quite sure that the Remnant will make their own way to him without any adventitious aids; and not only so, but if they find him employing such aids, as I said, it is ten to one that they will smell a rat in them and will sheer off.

The certainty that the Remnant will find him, however, leaves the prophet as much in the dark as ever, as helpless as ever in the matter of putting any estimate of any kind upon the Remnant; for, as appears in the case of Elijah, he remains ignorant of who they are that have found him or where they are or how many. They do not write in and tell him about it, after the manner of those who admire the vedettes of Hollywood, nor yet do they seek him out and attach themselves to his person. They are not that kind. They take his message much as drivers take the directions on a roadside signboard — that is, with very little thought about the signboard, beyond being gratefully glad that it happened to be there, but with very serious thought about the directions.

This impersonal attitude of the Remnant wonderfully enhances the interest of the imaginative prophet's job. Once in a while, just about often enough to keep his intellectual curiosity in good working order, he will quite accidentally come upon some distinct reflection of his own message in an unsuspected quarter. This enables him to entertain himself in his leisure moments with agreeable speculations about the course his message may have taken in reaching that particular quarter, and about what came of it after it got there. Most interesting of all are those instances, if one could only run them down (but one may always speculate about them), where the recipient himself no longer knows where nor when nor from whom he got the message — or even where, as sometimes happens, he has forgotten that he got it anywhere and imagines that it is all a self-sprung idea of his own.

Such instances as these are probably not infrequent, for, without presuming to enroll ourselves among the Remnant, we can all no doubt remember having found ourselves suddenly under the influence of an idea, the source of which we cannot possibly identify. "It came to us afterward," as we say; that is, we are aware of it only after it has shot up full-grown in our minds, leaving us quite ignorant of how and when and by what agency it was planted there and left to germinate. It seems highly probable that the prophet's message often takes some such course with the Remnant.

If, for example, you are a writer or a speaker or a preacher, you put forth an idea which lodges in the *Unbewusstsein* of a casual member of the Remnant and sticks fast there. For some time it is inert; then it begins to fret and fester until presently it invades the man's conscious mind and, as one might say, corrupts it. Meanwhile, he has quite forgotten how he came by the idea in the first instance, and even perhaps thinks he has invented it; and in those circumstances, the most interesting thing of all is that you never know what the pressure of that idea will make him do.

When We Are Free

CHAPTER 59

The Essence of a Free Society

by William Simon

What is Freedom?

Freedom is nothing more than the ability to discipline ourselves, rather than to be disciplined by others.

We Americans are indeed fortunate. We are free!

I am going to talk about one of our freedoms — the freedom we enjoy in our capitalist free enterprise system — because on its future rests the very future of our free society.

The American people, faced with many severe problems in recent years, tended to focus attention on the malaise of inflation, recession, unemployment, overtaxation and over-regulation. But I would subscribe that these severe maladies are the symptoms . . . yes, the results of an *over-governed* society. We Americans, and we are not unique, tend to focus on the short term. Not surprising, when you consider that we are led by politicians whose concept of the long term is the next election. By focusing on the symptoms, we are ignoring "the cancer" that is eating away at our society.

Yes, we Americans are indeed fortunate to be free.

But unfortunately . . . tragically, we take our freedom for granted — our guaranteed birthright. We fail to heed Webster's warning: *"God grants liberty to those who love it and are always willing to guard and defend it."* What I mean by "taking our freedom for granted" is that we are completely ignoring history and what it can teach us. Even a brief glance at history will show that freedom is not a common state. Indeed, it is just the opposite. But at the same time, the relationship of freedom and prosperity . . . yes, the two are related just as economic freedom, and personal and political freedom are inextricably related . . . "jumps out of the pages of history" as inviolable to even the casual observer.

Our Republic was founded on the basic principles of human dignity and individual liberty. Our founding fathers understood that our economic, political, religious, and social freedoms were

---

From *New Guard*, Winter 1978

inextricably bound together. Destroy one and the others will follow. They also knew the fragility of a democratic form of government, and its dismal historical record even up to that time. As Ben Franklin said to a Philadelphia woman who asked what the Constitution might bring to colonial America, *A Republic, ma'am, if you can keep it."* Franklin understood that democracy would be doomed when people first learned they could vote themselves the benefits of other people's money.

Today, there are less than two dozen countries in the world that can be defined as *free*. Let's look at three sad examples.

Chile, the Latin American country with the longest history of democratic government, is today authoritarian ... right or left, it makes no difference! Do you suppose that it's merely a coincidence that they were the first country in Latin America to institute a welfare state ... naturally, well-intentioned. The result? First government expansion, then domination, with the state ultimately controlling what people could or could not do. In the early 70's, government spending reached 40% of the national income. But being a poor country, no more taxes could be levied. So instead, government policies levied the cruel hidden tax — inflation ... 900% inflation, which led to economic and social chaos and brought on first a left-wing, then a right-wing dictator. In either case, Chile lost its freedom.

Now let's look at the United Kingdom. They have followed a course similar to Chile's, today demanding 60% of national income. Of course, Britain is wealthier, with a longer and stronger tradition of freedom, so it takes longer and stronger government to "strangle" its freedoms. It is illuminating to recall Winston Churchill's warning, spoken while he surveyed the wreckage of the British economy after the socialists took over the government after World War II: *"They have broken the mainspring, and until we get a new one, the watch will not go on. Set the people free, get out of the way, and let them make the best of themselves. I am sure that this policy of equalizing misery and organizing scarcity, instead of allowing diligence, self-interest and ingenuity to produce abundance, has only to be prolonged to kill this British Island 'stone dead'."* How prophetic and incredibly astute he was, in view of the massive deficits, high double-digit inflation, confiscatory taxation, nationalization and destruction of private industry today in the United Kingdom. And there is still enormous pressure for more. No one is satisfied, and society is being polarized. Can't we learn from this bitter experience?

The Essence of a Free Society

Erosion at Home

Closer to home, we have the situation in New York City. Just like every other economy that is doomed to stagnation by following a policy of ever-growing involvement in the affairs of its citizens, New York, with all its tragedies, unemployment, slums, social demoralization, flight of productive citizens, is also experiencing an inevitable loss of freedom. The city is no longer governed by its citizens or by those elected by its citizens, but by a committee of overseers appointed by the State of New York, with the power to overrule the elected officials.

The only real difference among New York City, Chile, and the United Kingdom is that New York City cannot print money to pay for its follies. But one thing we can be sure of — whether it's Chile, the United Kingdom, New York City, Italy, Sri Lanka, or ultimately, the United States of America — the results of these misguided policies are financial crisis, bankruptcy, social chaos, and most importantly, the loss of your freedom.

And this is exactly what is happening in America today. Our free enterprise system is being eroded and will ultimately be destroyed, "killing the goose" that is the source of our personal prosperity, our abundance, our hopes for the future, and incredibly, the source of the abundance for the government as well.

So when I speak of the ills of inflation, recession, etc., brought on by all-powerful government, I am not speaking of narrow economic issues, but fundamental issues of equity and social stability. It is a fact throughout history, that whenever government dominates the economic affairs of its citizens, a free society is eroded, then destroyed, and a minority government ensues. I think the most important point to be derived from my remarks tonight is this: *the free enterprise system and a free society are indivisible.* It is impossible to have a politically free society unless the major part of its economic resources are operating under the free enterprise system. Recognizing then that the future of the free enterprise system is also the future of a free society, the real issue here is human freedom. The question we must ask ourselves when we try to analyze our situation here in America is this: "Are we going to reverse this trend of the last 40 years toward a collectivist society, or will we choose to ignore history and suffer the inevitable fate of all those countries throughout history who chose not to, with all the tragic consequences?" Most people recognize a threat to their freedom, but may not realize that a threat may be *external* or *internal*.

We Americans have always mobilized and united to defeat attacks from external forces, but internal threats to freedom are so insidious that only one in a million realizes what is happening.

Let's look at what's happened here in America. Before the Great Depression, the government at all levels — Federal, state, and local — consumed 10% of the national income . . . two-thirds of this by the state and local levels. Today, government consumes 40% . . . two-thirds by the federal level. If this trend continues, by the year 2000 this figure will reach 60%. Anyone who doubts that a government that becomes all-powerful, demanding that you work through July of the year to pay for its munificence, has destroyed your freedoms, just isn't paying attention.

Today in America, we must work over four months of the year just to pay taxes before we can begin to keep the fruits of our labors.

Big Government's Excesses

And look at our federal regulations. They have become so pervasive, burdensome, and costly that they are threatening to strangle our free enterprise system. It costs small businessmen $40 billion just to do the paperwork . . . the American consumer, $150 billion. The policy in Washington seems to be that if it moves, regulate it; and if it doesn't, tax it. Last year alone, there were 60,000 pages of government regulations produced.

We have had deficits in 39 out of the last 48 years. Only once in the last 18 years did we have a balance . . . with all the inflationary and financial consequences. In the last 20 years alone, we have doubled our national debt, with $500 billion borrowed. Interest on the debt, now $45 billion, is the third largest item in the budget.* Have we forgotten Jefferson's warning?: *"To preserve our liberty we must not allow our leaders to load us with perpetual debts; we must make our choice between economy and liberty OR profusion and servitude."*

And finally, we are faced with the greatest enemy of them all — inflation legislated by irresponsible government policies. We have allowed inflation to dominate our economic affairs, with all the tragic consequences to our poor, those on fixed income, the disabled, and all those who cannot keep their income rising faster than the erosion of purchasing power.

Yes, this in brief is where we are as we start on our third century as the hope and inspiration of free people everywhere. We have indeed gone quite far down the road toward losing our freedom.

Free enterprise? Literally, it means the freedom to start an enterprise. It used to be that the first thing a fellow did when he

---

*Editors' note: The interest on the national debt is still the third largest item in the federal budget and has more than doubled since this essay was written. In 1981, it is expected to be in the neighborhood of $95 billion.

wanted to go into business for himself was to find customers. Now he goes out to look for a lawyer to find out if the government will let him do it, or how much they are going to regulate it.

Another one of our taken-for-granted birthrights is freedom of speech. How many businessmen will criticize government? Will a professor in a subsidized medical school criticize socialized medicine?

Looking back on our 200-year history, which has resulted in the greatest prosperity and highest standard of living ever known to man, one might well be tempted to ask, "How did this all happen?" Well, as I said earlier, the internal threat to our freedoms is an insidious one which has been happening for over four decades. In the last 15 years, though, this internal incursion has been accelerating. Actually, the closest we have come to free enterprise in this country occurred in the 19th century, described (and distortedly so) by so-called intellectuals who wish to destroy the free enterprise system as a disgraceful time, highlighted by robber barons pillaging the poor. In actuality, there is no period in history that compares with the development, growth, and ultimate prosperity achieved during that time. If one needs a dramatization of the attractiveness of this period, consider the millions of immigrants — your fathers and grandfathers ... and mine — who left their homelands and loved ones and streamed to the shores of America in the 1800's to participate in the American dream. Why did they come? *Freedom!* — economic, political, social, religious.

Reasons for the Drift Away from Freedom

Why have we drifted? In my judgment, due to a combination of factors: well-meaning people trying to do good ... always with other people's money; intellectuals who believe that they and only they know what is good for our society wishing to replace the decisions, and freedoms, of the millions of Americans with their own; and the special interest groups, which include you and me. How discouraging it was to me in Washington to see businessmen, these free enterprise champions from all over the country, coming to ask for quotas, tariffs, more regulation, a government handout ... begging for protection from the very competition that made our system so dynamic.

Where do we go from here? Well, we have a choice. We can see the dangers of our present course and begin to slow the growth of government, reduce taxation, remove regulations, and balance budgets. Or we can continue down this path of continued government growth and control, with the inevitable results of financial crisis and the loss of our freedoms.

Now there are some encouraging signs that we are starting to follow the first course. We hear a great deal about the country becoming more conservative, but in my judgment, this may be erroneous. The people saying this are the same ones who say, "Yes, we want balanced budgets, but let me tell you why you can't cut mine." We have a love-hate relationship with inflation: we hate inflation, but we love everything that causes it. Our basic challenge then, is to determine how much personal freedom, if any, we are willing to give up in seeking collectivist security. It is certainly not easy to live with the uncertainties that exist in a free society, but history has proven time and again that the real personal benefits for everyone are far superior to those of any other system. It is this great heritage of personal freedom that has made our nation so great, in both a material and a spiritual sense. What I am saying is that one must return to the fundamental principles and ideals. These principles will be every bit as true to us as we are true to them. A return to the work ethic, family discipline, fiscal responsibility; belief in a strong America and almighty God; putting our faith in people who are builders and creators, instead of an all-powerful federal government; a return to equality of opportunity, individual initiative, and individual responsibility . . . and all of this in the framework of the free marketplace that built this beautiful country.

But if we choose the destructive path we are now on, because it would require sacrifices to put us back on the road to lasting prosperity; if we are too selfish to think about our children and our children's children, and about turning over a country that is stronger and better morally, spiritually, and economically; and indeed choose to ignore the lessons of history — then the words of the great historian, Edith Hamilton, written of ancient Athens, will also be our epitaph: *"In the end,"* she wrote, *"more than they wanted freedom, they wanted security. They wanted a comfortable life and they lost all — security, comfort and freedom. When the Athenians finally wanted not to give to society, but for society to give to them; when the freedom they wished for most was freedom from responsibility, then Athens ceased to be free and was never free again."*

CHAPTER 60

Voices in the Wilderness

by Leonard E. Read

A man's humanity depends on how deeply he gains guidance through listening. — Karl Jaspers

Isaiah's phrase of some 27 centuries ago was applied to John the Baptist: "a voice crying in the wilderness." That phrasing persists as self-description in the minds of those whose devoted efforts go unheeded. For most of the present-day minority who oppose our plunge into socialism are saying, if not to others at least to themselves, "We are only voices crying in the wilderness."

Is the metaphor an apt one, as currently used? Cries are heard, yes, but they are cries of despair — which may, in no small measure, account for the fateful resignation so much observed around us.*

Further, the despair rests upon the dubious supposition that ours are voices of enlightenment within a wilderness, that is, among multitudes who do not or cannot hear our wise messages. "We are only talking to ourselves!" But this may be an occasion that calls for joyousness, not depression, for activity of mind, not resignation. At least the thought merits examination.

Voices? Let each of us examine his own voice for content and clarity and then render an honest, unbiased judgment. Simply put yourself in the position of those not of our turn of mind. How much ear would you or I give to our respective voices? Honest self-assessment results in a judgment that falls short of flattery — for me, at any rate.

It has been truly said, "a man will not be interested if you tell him that he can acquire by long and difficult work something which, in his opinion, he already has." Talking to myself, I muse:

From *Notes from FEE*, July 1972

*Editors' note: We believe that in the years since Mr. Read wrote this essay in 1972, much has been accomplished in the intellectual effort to restore the free society. The "movement" has blossomed from a tiny "remnant" to a vibrant network of publications, organizations, and activities. This revival of interest in and commitment to the free society has put hope and excitement in place of the despair and "fateful resignation" of not so long ago.

long and difficult work ahead for me after all of these years of effort, and rarely much in doubt about my own understanding? Yes, this is the answer I get upon careful self-examination.

There have been many capable thinkers over the centuries who have stressed the difficulty — the near impossibility — of standing off from oneself and having an unbiased look, seeing the self as others do. Robert Burns gave this problem a pretty phrasing:

*Oh wad some power the giftie gie us
To see oursels as others see us!*

Whatever be this power, the "giftie" it confers is an awakening from a slumber featured by dreams of self-satisfaction — a rather rude awakening!

With this feat accomplished, what do I find? First, an evaluation of self more realistic than it was, if not quite so satisfying. And, second, a relocated wilderness. Instead of regarding the wilderness as "out there," think of it as within me! How is it now? The wilderness is not comprised of countless others who supposedly cannot hear; it is a personal bewilderment reflected in a voice not skilled enough to attract many listeners. What a new face this puts on our problem! At the very least, it sets the stage for long and difficult work, the kind of undertaking that has the possibility of some accomplishment; whereas, the other way is doomed to failure. There is joy in headway, only frustration in fruitless effort.

Most People Don't Conceive Ideas

Before dealing further with my own bewilderment and such correction as is possible, let me clarify for myself one point about "out there," the wilderness where persons confront each other. True, it is the majority viewpoint or consensus that determines what goes on in society: the quality of men elected to public office, the kind of legislation passed, the degree of statism or freedom, the extent of coercive practices or violence that private groups can inflict, and so on. However, I am certain to be drawn off course unless I carefully assess what really constitutes a society's prevailing viewpoint or consensus. The appearance it gives of numerical strength is only the froth and not the brewing agent, the foam and not the starter. The brewing agent — the stuff itself — is thought, idea, be it true or false. *To say that the consensus rests on solid opinions by as much as one percent of the population is probably an exaggeration.*

The overwhelming majority of citizens have no well-grounded opinions, no thought-out ideas, on the subject of our concern. They merely lean toward or follow this or that ideological camp. For the most part, their allegiance follows impulsive acquiescence in clichés, attractive personalities, party labels, how the wind blows, and other forces lacking in idea content. Only lights of unprecedented brilliance can cause any of them to turn their eyes toward freedom. And, then, at best, only a few!

The few — The Remnant — are all who count. They are, as Albert Jay Nock observed, an odd lot: quiet, shy of show-offs; indeed, they will have nothing to do with them. These few — mostly unknowns — *are the ones who tip the scales*, and their search is always for those who, to some extent, make progress against their own bewilderment, who gain in understanding and clarity of expression, who evidence integrity and, above all, who try to enlighten themselves. Those of The Remnant "run a mile" from reformers; they resent all attempts at "ramming ideas down their necks." This attests to their realism for they know the futility of such an effort; it simply cannot be done.

A man's life is his own — and his Maker's — inalienable, nontransferable. It may be devoted or given to an ideal, or to an idea, but cannot be transplanted into another living being. This is to say that my ideas or yours cannot be implanted in another — except at that other's bidding or doing. If there is to be a transmission of ideas, the exchange occurs by the will and action of the receiver. And he draws into himself only that which he sees and values. I can perceive an idea, perhaps; but the idea itself is blind to me, can enter my mind only by my conscious effort and acceptance. The simplicity of this process is recognized by those rare individuals who comprise The Remnant. They are forever in search of light; and they are the ones who matter in the continuous upward struggle of man toward a better society.

These truisms bring into focus a problem that perplexes many devotees of freedom: the general apathy, the paralysis of thought in our time. Without question, the vast majority of Americans spend many of their leisure hours viewing TV. This tends to put their lives on a nonintellectual level, as does the energy they devote to idle conversation and the reading of frivolous material.

The Educational Problem

Such low forms of communication enormously influence participants to lean toward or to acquiesce in ways of life quite the opposite of freedom and self-responsibility. The winds of opinion blow in the wrong direction. And the reason for the wrong direction is usually ascribed to our failure to put the freedom message over the same channels or through the same media. The argument is that we should compete at this level. But I doubt that this gets at the educational problem we face.

TV and the like are, for the most part, entertainment media; and our objective is not entertainment. True, much nonsense can be blended with entertainment because the audience is not viewing, listening, reading for philosophical and ideological enlightenment. With no higher aim than merriment and diversion, the millions can indeed be blown in nonsensical directions. As Jacques Barzun phrases it, ". . . unless we *consciously* resist, the nonsense does not pass by us but into us." And I would add, unless we *consciously* try, the truth will not pass into us but will pass us by. Whenever *conscious* effort is lacking, people are easy and natural victims of the current winds that blow; they can be sold nonsense!

Ours, however, is not a selling problem, either, which is to say that no one has ever been "blown" into enlightenment. The gaining of understanding, knowledge, wisdom is, instead, a do-it-yourself, gathering-in project.

Let us now face up to the nature and enormity of our problem. A philosopher whose thoughts I admire asserted: "The known is what's no longer a problem." This appears to be true in one sense, yet false in another: the unknown has not yet been recognized as the problem. Our societal disarray, for instance, is no problem to an animal, to a person in slumber, or to the millions who are in a state of unawareness — the addicts of merriment and diversion. What does this mean to the thoughtful individual who is bent on the freedom way of life?

The Freedom-Lover's Strategy

It means that he must advance his own enlightenment to such a brilliance that a few, at least, will turn away from the TV and other entertainment to an enlightenment effort of their own. Never in the history of mankind have the distractions been more high-powered and glamorous than now. Nor, by the same token, has so much been required in the way of personal excellence to turn the trend toward freedom. *To succeed, we must excel those who have gone before us!* Personally, I would not have it any other way; this is a challenge worthy of any man who sees life's purpose as growth in consciousness.

Now to my own bewilderment and its correction. What shows forth as the obvious first step? What should my ambition be? To make of myself a prophet, a seer, one who is to enlighten mankind? Indeed, not! Any such aim is self-defeating. I must aspire to be a man, not a god. To concentrate on the latter would erase all chances of achieving the former. Further, no one who really counts in the upgrading struggle ever searches for light from those afflicted with egomania. I desire only what man's freedom opens up to him. "... *an opportunity to become that which he can authentically be.*"

What can I authentically be? A seeker bent on enlightenment! Where will that take me? Heaven only knows! But this I do know: no one who counts will ever look to me for light unless I have enlightenment to share.

The answer emerges in crystal clarity: try as best I can to qualify for membership in that odd lot, The Remnant — a seeker after light. A voice in the wilderness? No, quite the opposite — one listening for enlightened voices: the voice within, and from others, past and present, voices that may lead me, even if haltingly, out of my own bewilderment. Who knows! I may see the dawn and, if I do, a few others will see it with me.

When We Are Free

About The Editors

Lawrence W. Reed, Assistant Professor of Economics at Northwood Institute, is a native of Beaver Falls, Pennsylvania. He holds a B.A. degree with highest honors in economics from Grove City College, where he studied under the renowned "Austrian School" economist Dr. Hans F. Sennholz. From Grove City College, he went on to earn an M.A. degree in American history at Slippery Rock State College.

Professor Reed has been honored several times with awards from the Freedoms Foundation at Valley Forge recognizing his contributions to "the American way of life." He is the author of many articles, book reviews, columns, and radio commentaries. These have appeared in publications such as *The Freeman, Human Events, New Guard, Vital Speeches of the Day, Congressional Record, Enterprise, Conservative Digest,* and *Barron's.*

At Northwood Institute, Professor Reed teaches courses in Philosophy of American Life and Business, Principles of Economics, Economic History, International Trade, Securities, and Commodities. He is also founder and director of the college's annual, week-long Freedom in Third Century America Summer Seminar. He was awarded the Faculty Excellence Award by the sophomore classes of 1979, 1980, and 1981, and by the senior class of 1980.

Dale M. Haywood, Professor of Business and Finance at Northwood Institute, grew up in Arcadia, Nebraska. He began his collegiate education at the University of Nebraska in Lincoln.

However, it is not so much where he studied that is important to him. It is instead the thinking and influence of particular teachers that he values. Professor Haywood has studied under Campbell McConnell (University of Nebraska), Ludwig von Mises (New York University), Robert LeFevre and V. Orval Watts (Rampart College), and George A. Christy (North Texas State University). He received his Ph.D. degree in finance from North Texas State University in 1980.

Dr. Haywood began his teaching career at Northwood Institute. There, since 1965, he has found stimulating and fulfilling employment in teaching Philosophy of American Life and Business, Principles of Economics, Public Policy Toward Business, Financial Management, and Corporate Strategy and Policy. Of his accomplishments to date, he ranks most highly the Faculty Excellence Awards he received from the four senior classes at the college in 1977, 1978, 1979, and 1981.

Dr. Haywood is married and has two children.